MW00528414

BY MARGALIT FOX

The Talented Mrs. Mandelbaum:
The Rise and Fall of an American
Organized-Crime Boss

The Confidence Men:
How Two Prisoners of War Engineered
the Most Remarkable Escape in History

Conan Doyle for the Defense:
How Sherlock Holmes's Creator Turned
Real-Life Detective and Freed a Man
Wrongly Imprisoned for Murder

The Riddle of the Labyrinth:
The Quest to Crack an Ancient Code

Talking Hands:
What Sign Language Reveals About the Mind

Death Becomes Her:
Selected Obituaries by Margalit Fox
(a *New York Times* ebook)

THE TALENTED
MRS. MANDELBAUM

The Talented Mrs. Mandelbaum

The Rise and Fall of an American Organized-Crime Boss

Margalit Fox

RANDOM HOUSE

NEW YORK

Published in the United States by Random House,
an imprint and division of Penguin Random House LLC, New York.

RANDOM HOUSE and the HOUSE colophon are
registered trademarks of Penguin Random House LLC.

Illustration credits are located on pages 285–286.

LIBRARY OF CONGRESS CATALOGING-IN-PUBLICATION DATA
NAMES: Fox, Margalit, author.
TITLE: The talented Mrs. Mandelbaum : the rise and fall of
an American organized-crime boss / by Margalit Fox.
DESCRIPTION: First edition. | New York : Random House, [2024] |
Includes bibliographical references and index.
IDENTIFIERS: LCCN 2023044598 | ISBN 9780593243855
(hardcover ; alk. paper) | ISBN 9780593243862 (ebook)
SUBJECTS: LCSH: Mandelbaum, Fredericka, 1825–1894. |
Thieves—New York (State)—New York—Biography. |
Criminals—New York (State) —New York—Biography. |
Receiving stolen goods—New York (State)—New York—
History—19th century. | Organized crime—New York (State) —
New York—History—19th century.
CLASSIFICATION: LCC HV6653.M288 F69 2023 |
DDC 364.109747092 [B] —dc23/eng/20231219
LC record available at https://lccn.loc.gov/2023044598

Printed in the United States of America on acid-free paper

randomhousebooks.com

2 4 6 8 9 7 5 3 1

FIRST EDITION

Maps by Jonathan Corum. Used by permission.

For two remarkable Elizabeths:

Rogers and Lorris Ritter—my New York homegirls.

And for Teresa Elizabeth Williams.

RYAN: Who runs things?

HAMMETT: The same people who run things everywhere.

RYAN: The cops, the crooks and the big rich, huh?

HAMMETT: Who else? . . .

—*Hammett*, dir. Wim Wenders, 1982

Contents

Book Three: Nemesis

Prologue:
A Glittering Hoard

New York, July 22, 1884

THEY WERE DETECTIVES, ACCUSTOMED TO PLUNDER, BUT THEY'D NEVER seen anything like this.

It had taken some doing to open the safe. After bursting into the modest haberdashery shop on Manhattan's Lower East Side, they'd demanded the keys from the shopkeeper, Fredericka Mandelbaum. But Mrs. Mandelbaum, a towering woman of fifty-nine, tastefully attired in diamond cluster earrings and a lace-trimmed gown of dotted blue, held firm. "No," she declared, in her heavy Germanic English. "Just to think of such a thing!"

Her refusal forced the detectives, employees of the storied Pinkerton Agency, to become safecrackers themselves. They summoned a blacksmith, who arrived at the shop with hammer and chisel. He attacked the safe; amid the din, a pretty teenage girl ran in from the next room—Mrs. Mandelbaum's daughter Annie.

"Stop!" Annie cried. She handed over the keys and the safe was unlocked. An Aladdin's Cave spilled out.

There were gems and jewelry of every description: rings, chains, scarf pins, bracelets, glittering cufflinks and collar buttons—"almost every ornament you could mention," one detective recalled. Beside them were "heaps of gold watches" and, wrapped carefully in tissue paper, watch movements and cases. There was a clutch of fine silverware. There were loose diamonds the size of peas.

Elsewhere in the shop's clandestine back rooms—protected by a metal grille and linked to the outdoors by a set of secret passages—the detectives came upon priceless antique furniture, a trunk brimming with shawls of the finest cashmere and curtains of exquisite lace, and bolts of silk worth thousands of dollars alone. Concealed under newspapers were bars of gold, fashioned from melted-down jewelry. Upstairs, in Mrs. Mandelbaum's gracious bedroom, they found melting pots and scales for weighing gold and diamonds. She and an employee were promptly arrested.

With that, the Pinkerton detectives, who had staged the raid at the behest of the city's district attorney, accomplished in a single outing what New York's police force[*] had not managed to do in more than twenty years. "You are caught this time, and the best thing that you can do is to make a clean breast of it," one of the Pinkertons, Gustave Frank, advised Mrs. Mandelbaum as she was led away.

In reply, Fredericka Mandelbaum—upright widow, philanthropic synagogue-goer, doting mother of four and boss of the country's most notorious crime syndicate—whirled and punched him in the face.

FOR TWENTY-FIVE YEARS, Fredericka Mandelbaum reigned as one of the most infamous underworld figures in America. Working from her humble Manhattan storefront, she presided over a multi-million-dollar criminal operation that centered on stolen luxury goods and later diversified into bank robbery. Conceived in the mid-1800s—long before the accepted starting date for organized

---

[*]   The force, which bore various names over time, would not be known as the New York City Police Department until 1898, when the five boroughs that constitute present-day New York were consolidated into a single city.

Montage depicting Mrs. Mandelbaum's ill-gotten gains, the raid on her shop and the courtroom drama that followed, from an 1884 issue of the *National Police Gazette*, a nineteenth- and early-twentieth-century scandal sheet

crime in the United States—her empire extended across the country and beyond. In 1884, the *New-York Times* called her "the nucleus and centre of the whole organization of crime in New-York."*

---

* Until the late nineteenth century, "New-York" was often hyphenated, in the manner of compound adjectives. The *New-York Times* was among several of the city's newspapers to employ this form; then, on December 1, 1896, "without a word of explanation to readers," the *Times* jettisoned the hyphen forever.

Revered in some quarters, reviled in others, Marm Mandelbaum, as she was known, towered over the city as an earthy, expansive, diamond-encrusted presence: self-made entrepreneur, generous philanthropist, thieves' mentor and gracious society hostess who plied her illicit trade largely in the open. A swath of the public admired her. Many criminals adored her. Over the course of her long, lucrative career, she would spend scarcely a day behind bars. "Without question," a twentieth-century criminologist has written, "the fullest attribution of energy, presence, and personal magnetism in the literature of criminology belongs to 'Ma' Mandelbaum."

For Mrs. Mandelbaum, trafficking in other people's property was staggeringly good business: Her network of thieves and resale agents was reported to extend throughout the United States, into Mexico and, it was said, as far away as Europe. At her death, in 1894, she had amassed a personal fortune of at least half a million dollars (in some accounts as much as a million), the equivalent of more than $14 million to $28 million today.* As the New York police chief George Washington Walling,† who knew her well, recalled, "The ramifications of her business net were so widespread, her ingenuity as an assistant to criminals so nearly approached genius, that if a silk robbery occurred in St. Louis, and the criminals were known as 'belonging to "Marm Baum,"' she always had the first choice of the 'swag.'"

In her heyday and for some years afterward, Marm was a storied figure, the subject of news articles, editorial cartoons and more than one stage play.‡ The world press covered her criminal prowess with

---

*   Here and throughout, contemporary dollar figures reflect the historical inflation rate of late 2023, when this book went into production.

†   Walling (1823–91) served as superintendent of police, as the chief's post was then known, from 1874 to 1885.

‡   The plays include *The Two Orphans* (*Les Deux Orphelines*), an 1874 French melodrama featuring the nefarious matriarch of an underworld family, produced in New York in English translation that year, and *The Great Diamond Robbery*, an American melodrama by Edward M. Alfriend and A. C. Wheeler, which premiered on Broadway in 1895, the year after Mrs. Mandelbaum's death. That production starred the Prague-born actress Fanny Janauschek as "Mother Rosenbaum," a successful receiver of stolen goods indisputably modeled on Marm.

PROLOGUE *xvii*

a kind of grudging admiration; it covered her downfall with post-hoc smugness.* But despite her renown in her own time, she is far less well known today, an all-too-common fate for history's women. Though there are passing references to Mrs. Mandelbaum in a spate of books on New York City history, there are few in-depth studies of her life and work.

Marm kept no written records: No fool, she clearly knew it would have been professional suicide to do so. As Chief Walling observed: "She was shrewd, careful, methodical in character and to the point in speech. . . . Wary in the extreme." But her career turns out to have been amply chronicled, not only in the news accounts of her day, but also in the reminiscences of her contemporaries on both sides of the law. As a result, she can be conjured whole from the glittering nineteenth-century city in which she operated—the redoubtable star of an urban picaresque awash in pickpockets and sneak thieves, bank burglars and high-toned shysters. And from her glittering presence it is possible in turn to conjure the city: a wide-open town careering its way through "the Flash Age," a time when the mantra of one suspiciously well-heeled pol, "I seen my opportunities and I took 'em," was a guiding principle for many New Yorkers.

WHEN TWENTY-FIRST-CENTURY AMERICANS hear the phrase "organized crime," it almost always evokes the Prohibition-era, "guns-and-garlic" gangsterism of *Scarface* and *The Untouchables*.† But the term was first attested in the United States in the 1890s, and, as Mrs. Mandelbaum's career makes plain, the practice was a going concern here well before that—in Europe, earlier still.‡

---

* Mrs. Mandelbaum's death, for instance, was reported in newspapers throughout the United States and as far away as London.

† In keeping with common usage, this book employs the phrases "organized crime" and "syndicated crime" interchangeably.

‡ These days, one analyst notes, "organized crime" is "a fuzzy and contested umbrella concept": It has been applied variously—at times promiscuously—to entities as distinct as the Sicilian Mafia, the Yakuza of Japan and the drug cartels of Colombia

Unlike the organized crime of the tommy-gun age, Fredericka Mandelbaum's profession entailed little violence. She was, from the first, a specialist in property crime, buying, camouflaging and reselling a welter of stolen luxury items. Beginning her ascent in the late 1850s, she quickly established her reputation as a criminal receiver—a "fence," in popular parlance. There had been legions of fences before Marm Mandelbaum, and there have been legions after. But what she accomplished had by all accounts not been done before in America on so broad a scale, in so sustained and methodical a fashion: Fredericka Mandelbaum transformed herself, almost singlehandedly, into "a mogul of illegitimate capitalism," running her operation as a well-oiled, for-profit corporate machine. Strikingly, she did so more than half a century before the Prohibition-era syndicates celebrated in popular culture, a milieu in which women, if they featured at all, were little more than gangsters' molls.

"Crime cannot be carried on by individuals," a longtime member of the Mandelbaum syndicate wrote in 1913. "It requires an elaborate permanent organization. While the individual operators, from pickpockets to bank burglars, come and go, working from coast to coast, they must be affiliated with some permanent substantial person.... Such a permanent head was 'Mother' Mandelbaum."

Late-nineteenth-century newspapers reveled in Marm's doings, and liked to say she could "unload" anything, including, in one account, a flock of stolen sheep. But it is beyond doubt that by the mid-1880s as much as $10 million[*] had passed through her little haberdashery shop on the Lower East Side. The full story of her rise to underworld stardom as "the undisputed financier, guide, counsellor, and friend of crime in New York"—and her ultimate fall at the hands of the city's increasingly powerful bourgeois elite—is a window onto a little-explored side of Gilded Age America: the world of

---

and Mexico. In short, about the only thing on which scholars of the field can agree is that when it comes to a precise definition, there is no agreement. It seems fitting, somehow, that the term is slippery and elusive.

[*]   Equivalent to nearly $300 million today.

Herbert Asbury's *Gangs of New York* from the perspective of a sharp-witted, fiercely determined woman.[*]

Some modern observers have called Mrs. Mandelbaum a proto-feminist. Perhaps she was, though she appeared as committed to wifely and maternal duties as any woman of her era. What can be said with certainty is that she was among the first—quite possibly the very first—to systematize the formerly scattershot enterprise of property crime, working out logistics, organizing chains of supply and demand, and constructing the entire venture first and foremost as a *business*. And in so doing, she simultaneously embodied and upended the cherished rags-to-riches narrative of Victorian America, starring, on entirely her own terms, in a Horatio Alger story of a very different kind.

ARRIVING IN NEW YORK in 1850 with little more than the clothes on her back, Fredericka Mandelbaum began her working life as a peddler on the streets of Lower Manhattan. Professional advancement, to say nothing of great wealth, seemed beyond contemplation for someone who, like her, was marginalized three times over: immigrant, woman and Jew. (Organized crime, as a twentieth-century writer has sagely noted, "is not an equal-opportunity employer.") Yet before the decade was out, she had established herself as one of the city's premier receivers of stolen goods; by the end of the 1860s she had become, in the words of a modern-day headline, "New York's First Female Crime Boss."

Though she stole little to nothing herself, Mrs. Mandelbaum trained a cadre of acolytes to help themselves—and thereby help *her*—to the choicest spoils that Gilded Age America had to offer. She orchestrated decades' worth of high-end thefts, selecting the foremost men and women for each job, underwriting their expenses and advising them on "best practices" peculiar to their trade: why it's especially prudent for a thief to specialize in diamonds and silk;

[*] Mrs. Mandelbaum makes several cameo appearances in Asbury's book.

why, when entering an establishment like Tiffany & Company, it is supremely helpful to be chewing a piece of gum; how to dress for success—success, that is, in pilfering luxury goods from department stores; and, ultimately, how to relieve a bank of its contents.

"What plannings of great robberies took place there, in Madame Mandelbaum's store!" one old-time crook recalled fondly. "She would buy any kind of stolen property, from an ostrich feather to hundreds and thousands of dollars' worth of gems. The common shop-lifter and the great cracksman* alike did business at this famous place."

Mrs. Mandelbaum bailed out her disciples whenever they were arrested, wined and dined them at her groaning table, supplied fistfuls of cash when they were down and out, and furnished getaway horses and carriages as the need arose. For her maternal devotion to her handpicked phalanx of foot soldiers—her "chicks," she called them—criminals and the press alike referred to her as "Marm," "Mother," "Ma" or "Mother Baum."

"There is still standing, I believe, a little . . . house at the corner of Clinton and Rivington Streets, which was for many years the headquarters of some of the greatest criminals in the country and in which many of the most daring robberies of the period were planned," an American newspaperman wrote in 1921:

> The front part of the ground floor was devoted to the sale of cheap dry-goods but the parlor in the rear contained many articles of furniture and silver of a sort seldom seen in that quarter of town. It was in this room that "Mother Mandelbaum," as she was affectionately termed by more than one generation of crooks, transacted business. . . .
>
> Her place of business [was] a market in which jewelry, rolls of silk, silverware and other spoils could be disposed of for about half their real value, the old lady assuming all the risks of the transaction. . . . She looked as if she might have

---

*   A housebreaker or bank burglar.

stepped out of the pages of a Viennese comic paper, yet she was a sort of female Moriarty who could plan a robbery, furnish the necessary funds for carrying it out and even choose the man best fitted to accomplish it.

If that isn't the textbook definition of an organized-crime boss, then I don't know what is.

Fredericka Mandelbaum, characteristically hatted, in a period illustration

IN ANY ERA, MOTHER MANDELBAUM would have cut an imposing figure, but in her own time she fairly loomed over New York. About six feet tall and of Falstaffian girth (she was said to have weighed between 250 and 300 pounds), pouchy-faced, apple-cheeked and beetle-browed, she resembled the product of a congenial liaison between a dumpling and a mountain. She dressed soberly but expensively in vast gowns of black, brown or dark blue silk, topped by a sealskin cape, with a plumed fascinator or bonnet. She dripped diamonds—earrings, necklaces, brooches, bracelets, rings—but then, in her line of work, diamonds were as easy to come by as the ostrich feathers that waved gaily from her hats. "Her attire was at once gorgeous and vulgar," the *Cincinnati Enquirer* observed in 1894. "She often wore $40,000* worth of jewels at once."

Mrs. Mandelbaum lived above the shop, but the ground floor of her clapboard building, with its unremarkable public salesroom, did little to hint at the New World Versailles above. A look in on one of her famous dinner parties—sought-after affairs as opulent as anything Mrs. Astor might give uptown—starts to convey the full effect:

Inside Mrs. Mandelbaum's apartment, her guests, attended by her large staff of servants, are dining on lamb, accompanied by fine wines from her extensive cellars. Here, at the head of the mahogany dining table, Marm, swathed in silk and weighted down with diamonds, sits on a wide embroidered ottoman, making animated conversation. Down one side of the table, in full evening dress, are some of the most distinguished members of uptown society, leading lights of New York commerce and industry. Down the other, also in evening dress, are the crème de la crème of criminality: Adam Worth, a master thief who learned his craft at Mrs. Mandelbaum's side; the bank-burgling virtuoso George Leonidas Leslie; pretty, light-fingered Sophie Lyons, a shoplifter who under Marm's tutelage became "perhaps the most notorious confidence woman America has ever produced"; and Sophie's husband, the bank burglar Ned Lyons, who was said to have fallen in love with Sophie at one of Marm's parties, after she presented him with a gold watch and handsome stickpin she'd just lifted from another guest. In a corner, playing Beethoven on Marm's white baby grand, is "Piano Charley" Bullard, a trained musician who regularly turned his nimble fingers to safecracking.

---

*   About $1.3 million today.

Sophie and Ned Lyons, from a nineteenth-century rogues' gallery

Marm's table, adorned along its length with gold candelabra, is laid with the finest china and crystal, and set with silver that "would have been rated as 'A+ swag' had a 'client' of the old woman called on her to dispose of it," a knowledgeable visitor recalled. The windows are hung with rich silk draperies; the furniture is of ornate Victorian mahogany that "would have attracted the cupidity of an antiquarian"; the floors are cushioned with thick carpets of red and gold; the walls are a profusion of rare old paintings; and the coffered ceiling is hung with crystal chandeliers. "Scattered about the room," a newspaper recounted, are "many pieces of bronze and bric-a-brac, the retail price of which is beyond the reach of ordinary mortals." If some of Marm's furnishings look remarkably like items once owned by her blue-blood uptown guests . . . well, in an age of mass production, who can truly be certain?* In any case, as one guest recalled, the entire evening would have been "conducted with as much attention to the proprieties of society as though Mrs. Mandelbaum's establishment was in Fifth Avenue instead of in a suspicious corner of the East Side."

---

* As a member of Marm's organization would write, "Servants of wealthy New York families learned that 'Mother' Mandelbaum paid well for tips and plans of houses."

Mrs. Mandelbaum, at far right, with fan, presides over one of her famous dinner parties. The woman in the foreground, second from left, is almost certainly Marm's protégée Sophie Lyons.

THE MOST REMARKABLE THING about Marm's calling was that she pursued it for decades with almost complete impunity: Until her downfall, in 1884, she hadn't spent so much as a day in jail. "The police of New York were never able to catch Mother Mandelbaum," the *Brooklyn Daily Eagle* reported that year. "Any citizen could go to her place and see her in the act of carrying on her trade, and yet 2,500 policemen, the expensive detective bureau and the vast machinery of the force was utterly unable to arrest her."

There were two primary reasons she was able to skirt the law for so long. The first was that she kept on permanent retainer two of the most satisfyingly crooked lawyers American jurisprudence has ever known. The second, even more vital, can be gleaned from a renewed look round her table. Here, seated in Marm's carved mahogany chairs, wining, dining and laughing alongside the tycoons, the swindlers and the shoplifters, are—

But, no. We are getting ahead of ourselves.

BOOK ONE

Ascent

Chapter One

"The Mere Privilege of Breath"

S HE CAME HERE WITH NOTHING.

One of seven children of Samuel Abraham Weisner and the former Rahel Lea Solling, Fredericka Henriette Auguste Weisner was born on March 28, 1825, in Kassel, in what is now central Germany.* Her family, which appears to have included itinerant peddlers, had been part of the region's Jewish community—numbering fourteen to fifteen thousand in a population of just over half a million—for several generations.

Jewish life there was far from easy. Restrictive laws in many German states of the period governed what trades Jews could ply and where they could live, which by extension restricted whom they could marry. Physical violence against Jews by their Gentile neighbors was not unknown: Jews sometimes paid protection money to keep themselves and their families safe.

"Jews occupied a distinct and inferior status," a twentieth-century history has noted. "Except for a tiny, wealthy elite who had gained the special favor of Christian rulers or aristocrats, the Jewish

---

* A unified German Empire did not come into being until 1871, with the establishment of the Second Reich under the Kaiser. Before then, as a modern history notes, "a variety of local rulers, nobles, and town councils ruled a patchwork of duchies, counties, principalities, free cities, and other small entities. Residents of these states and statelets lived under the laws established and enforced by their particular lords or legislators."

people of Central Europe remained what their ancestors had been for centuries past: traditional, pious, generally poor *Dorfjuden*—village Jews.... With agriculture, most guild-based crafts, and other more secure and lucrative occupations traditionally forbidden to them, Central European Jews overwhelmingly earned their often meagre livelihoods as minor traders, small-scale moneylenders, or petty artisans in such crafts as tailoring."

As a girl, Fredericka would have had a basic education in reading, writing and arithmetic, taught either at home or at a local Jewish elementary school. She would also have received training, standard for Jewish girls of the day, in childcare and domestic arts, which typically included sewing, spinning, knitting, lacemaking, laundering and cooking. "Whatever the precise circumstances," the historian Rona L. Holub has written, "she developed a keen intellect, a strong work ethic, and confidence in her own abilities."

In 1848, Fredericka married Wolf Israel Mandelbaum, an itinerant peddler a few years her senior. Wolf, possibly with Fredericka helping him, spent days on the road each week, peddling in the countryside before returning home in time for the start of the Sabbath on Friday nights. Whether gained from direct experience or simply from knowledge of her husband's trade, Mrs. Mandelbaum's understanding of the mechanics of salesmanship would greatly abet her career in the criminal underworld.

The birth, in 1849, of the Mandelbaums' first child, Breine (also known as Bertha or Bessy), would have further strained their precarious finances: The region was in the midst of an economic depression and was affected by a potato blight. In 1850, the Mandelbaums joined the thousands of European Jews who had emigrated to America in search of economic opportunity:* "Das Dollarland," some Germans called the United States. Wolf left first, traveling overland to

* As the historian Hasia R. Diner and the journalist Beryl Lieff Benderly write: "In 1820 the Jewish population of the United States stood at two to three thousand. Sixty years later, it numbered more than 250,000. During those six decades, at least 150,000 Jewish men, women, and children left their homes, journeyed to a European port, booked passage to an American destination, and endured a dangerous and uncomfortable voyage."

Amsterdam, where he embarked on the *Baltimore*, arriving in New York in July 1850. After traveling to Bremen with baby Bertha, Fredericka boarded the bark *Erie*.

THE ATLANTIC CROSSING, A voyage of six weeks or longer under sail, was rigorous enough for the first-class passengers, who paid roughly $140 U.S.* for cabin accommodations. Mrs. Mandelbaum traveled in steerage, paying twenty dollars† to live below deck, crammed together in a low-ceilinged, badly ventilated space with scores of other immigrants, an arrangement that made spectacularly good business for owners of the shipping lines. Steerage passengers would have been supplied with only meager food and narrow wooden bunks in which to sleep—structures that Herman Melville, writing in 1849, described as comprising "three tiers, one above another . . . rapidly knocked together with coarse planks." He added: "They looked more like dog-kennels than any thing else."

In September 1850, Fredericka disembarked in the Port of New York. At the time, "New York City" denoted a far more modest entity than it would even half a century later: It comprised only Manhattan, with a population of just over half a million.‡ The city, which had been expanding slowly northward since colonial times, had by 1850 advanced only about three miles from Manhattan's southern tip. Most of the population lived below Fourteenth Street; above, the island remained partly pastoral.

From Fourteenth Street down to the Battery, the city teemed. The sidewalks teemed with pedestrians; the streets teemed with pushcarts and a tangle of horse-drawn vehicles—wagons, carriages, streetcars, omnibuses, hearses—the harbor teemed with ships and barges. On the Lower East Side, where the Mandelbaums settled,

* The equivalent of more than $5,000 in today's money.

† More than $700 today.

‡ Portions of what is now the Bronx were annexed by the city in 1874 and 1895. The five boroughs that constitute present-day New York City were not consolidated into a single political entity until January 1, 1898.

congestion was especially fierce, with slum tenements crammed alongside industrial buildings like factories, foundries and slaughterhouses. And while few immigrants, if any, believed the folk saying that New World streets were paved with gold, they were almost certainly unprepared for streets filled with ordure: garbage and manure lying uncollected, snapped at by bands of roaming pigs; sewage overflowing; horses, dead of overwork, lying where they fell, their rotting carcasses swarming with flies. As Charles Dickens observed dryly after an 1842 visit to America, New York was "by no means so clean a city as Boston."

Let Dickens recount his tour of Five Points,* the Lower East Side quarter that a modern history calls "the world's most notorious slum." Touring the neighborhood (an excursion he felt it necessary to make in the company of two policemen), he recoiled in bourgeois Victorian horror. In modern parlance, he was slumming, his visit of a piece with the voyeuristic tours of the district that well-off New Yorkers had begun making in the 1830s, and which became even more popular after Dickens's account of his outing appeared in print. But while Dickens was clearly discomforted by the neighborhood's myriad houses of prostitution—and by the lively social mixing of its white and African American residents—the poverty he described was real enough:

> This is the place: these narrow ways, diverging to the right and left, and reeking everywhere with dirt and filth.... Debauchery has made the very houses prematurely old. See how the rotten beams are tumbling down, and how the patched and broken windows seem to scowl dimly, like eyes that have been hurt in drunken frays....

* So named because the neighborhood, in the city's Sixth Ward, encompassed five streets—Mulberry, Anthony, Cross, Orange and Little Water—that together formed the sides of an irregular pentagon. The area is now part of Manhattan's Chinatown: Anthony Street is now Worth Street; Cross Street is now Mosco Street; Orange Street is now Baxter Street; Mulberry Street is status quo; Little Water Street no longer exists.

What place is this, to which the squalid street conducts us?
A kind of square of leprous houses, some of which are attainable only by crazy wooden stairs without. What lies beyond
this tottering flight of steps, that creak beneath our tread?—
a miserable room, lighted by one dim candle, and destitute of
all comfort, save that which may be hidden in a wretched
bed. . . .

Here too are lanes and alleys, paved with mud knee-deep,
underground chambers, where they dance and game . . . ru-
ined houses, open to the street, whence, through wide gaps in
the walls, other ruins loom upon the eye, as though the world
of vice and misery had nothing else to show: hideous tenements which take their name from robbery and murder: all
that is loathsome, drooping, and decayed is here.

The Mandelbaums found lodgings in Kleindeutschland ("Little
Germany"), an immigrant enclave on the Lower East Side covering about a square mile and eventually spanning the city's Tenth,
Eleventh, Thirteenth and Seventeenth wards.* The couple lived at
various addresses during their first decade and a half in the city—
including 383 East Eighth Street, on a tenement block between
Avenues C and D in the Eleventh Ward, and 141 East Sixth Street,
near the Bowery in the Seventeenth†—before settling permanently
in the Thirteenth Ward in the mid-1860s.

In the tenements—dark, flimsy, badly ventilated structures—
twenty families or more might occupy a single small apartment house.

---

* The ward was for more than 250 years the smallest official administrative unit of
New York City. Typically comprising a slice of a neighborhood, it was a seat of local
political power and was responsible for electing certain municipal officials, which over
the years included aldermen, tax collectors and constables. The city's ward system was
established in 1686 with six wards; by 1898, when the five boroughs were consolidated,
Manhattan boasted twenty-two wards, and Brooklyn, which before consolidation had
been a separate city, had thirty-two. The ward system was formally abandoned city-
wide only in 1938.

† In present-day Manhattan, the Eighth and Sixth Street addresses are part of the
East Village.

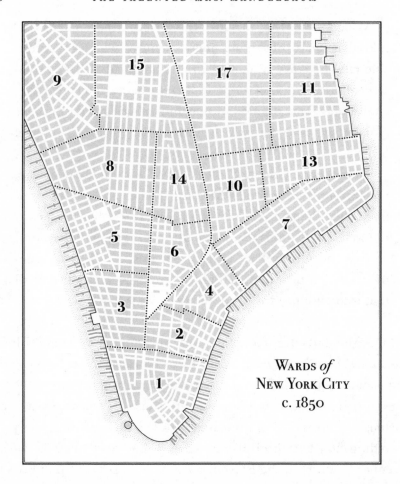

WARDS *of*
NEW YORK CITY
c. 1850

There was no running water: Residents hauled water up the stairs from pumps in the streets and relieved themselves in shabby, back-alley wooden privies. "The most modern and sophisticated" of the city's plumbing facilities, a historian explains, "connected the outdoor toilets directly to sewer lines, flushing sewage directly and immediately away from the tenement yard. But . . . in 1857, only one-quarter of the city had sewer lines. . . . Raw sewage thus often sat festering in the backyards of the tenements for weeks or months at a time."

Amid the crowded, unsanitary conditions, diseases like consumption, typhoid, dysentery, diphtheria and scarlet fever were rampant. Among immigrant families, infant and childhood mortality rates were especially high.* And indeed, in haunting absence, little Bertha Mandelbaum's name is missing from census records of the period: It is likely that she succumbed to one such disease.†

FOR ALL ITS PRIVATIONS, Kleindeutschland—the first of the country's large foreign-language settlements—offered much succor. "German New York was the third capital of the German-speaking world," a historian has written. "Only Vienna and Berlin had larger German populations than New York City between 1855 and 1880. When the German Empire was created in 1871, the single New York city neighborhood of Kleindeutschland . . . would have been the empire's fifth-largest city."

There, the Mandelbaums could work, shop and socialize alongside their countrymen—Jews and Gentiles alike—attending German-language theater performances, watching traditional German folk parades, singing and dancing at the neighborhood's beer gardens. They could pass their days speaking nothing but German, though Fredericka, at least, did master English.‡ "Unser Haus" ("Our house"), one resident called Kleindeutschland. The neighborhood would be Fredericka Mandelbaum's home for the rest of

* In New York City in 1865, sixty-five children of immigrants died for every eight native-born white children.

† It is even possible, the historian Rona L. Holub writes, that Bertha died on the voyage to America: In the cramped, unhygienic conditions of steerage, communicable diseases were also rampant.

‡ The Jews of Eastern Europe, whose large-scale emigration to the United States did not begin until the 1880s, spoke Yiddish, a language closely related to German. As the historian Hasia R. Diner points out, it is likely that Fredericka, like many village Jews of her era from German-speaking regions, grew up speaking a dialect "that has been denoted as Western Yiddish—more German than East European Yiddish but still with Hebrew words, and [like Eastern Yiddish] written in Hebrew characters." The mid-1800s, when Fredericka came to America, was "a moment in time when Jews in the German-speaking lands were becoming German speakers," Diner explains. "A few memoirs of Jews who came to America in those years remarked that they . . . learned real German once [they were] in America and living in German neighborhoods like Kleindeutschland."

her life in America. She forsook it only three decades later, with deep reluctance, when fallout from her criminal career gave her no alternative.

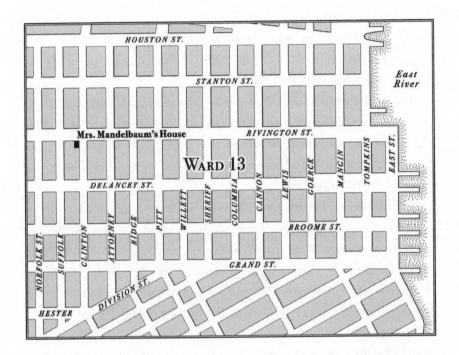

FOR IMMIGRANTS IN NINETEENTH-CENTURY New York, employment opportunities were severely limited, with the available work often menial, exploitative, irregular and dangerous. A man might be hired to dig ditches, haul bricks and mortar on his shoulders, or load and unload masses of cargo on the city's waterfront docks. Safety was anything but assured: Workers might fall from construction sites or be crushed by wayward cargo. They were paid hourly, or by the day, and when cold or wet weather precluded work, there was no pay.

Some German men continued the trades they had practiced in the old country, working as butchers, bakers, brewers, grocers, cobblers, tailors and cigarmakers. But even for those with steady work, there were abundant rags and few riches, with many tradesmen forced to operate out of dank, unsanitary tenement basements. In 1845, for instance, as part of a series on labor conditions in the city, the *New-York Daily Tribune* reported on the lives of immigrant shoemakers:

> There is no class of mechanics in New York who average so great an amount of work for so little money as the Journeymen Shoe-Makers. The number of Journeymen out of employment is also large, and out of all just proportion. There are hundreds of them in the City constantly wandering from shop to shop in search of work, while many of them have families in a state of absolute want. One by one the articles of their furniture have been sold to supply bread which the disheartened workman could not earn, and at last the family are turned out of their miserable garret or cellar because they cannot pay their rent. Even those who work fare badly enough, and many of them live in such a way as to deprive life of everything save the mere privilege of breath. . . .
>
> We have been in more than fifty cellars in different parts of the City, each inhabited by a Shoe-Maker and his family. This floor is made of rough plank laid loosely down, the ceiling is not quite so high as a tall man. The walls are dark and damp. . . . There is no outlet [in] back and of course no yard privileges [i.e., outhouses] of any kind. . . . In this apartment often live the man with his workbench, his wife and five or six children of all ages and perhaps a palsied grandfather or grandmother and often both. In one corner is a squalid bed, and the room elsewhere is occupied by the workbench, a cradle made from a dry-goods box, two or three broken and seatless chairs, a stewpan and a kettle.

In New York, Wolf Mandelbaum resumed his work as a peddler, a trade plied by many of the city's German Jews. German Jewish women, whose work in the Old Country had let them contribute meaningfully to the family economy, expected to do likewise in America, but they quickly discovered that women's job prospects were even more circumscribed than the men's.* Some German women found employment as household servants, a profession entailing backbreaking labor of up to sixteen hours a day for little more than room, board and a dollar a week.† Others worked as laundresses, took in boarders or did hand sewing at home, where hour after hour they sat hunched over their work, making thousands of tiny stitches by candlelight.

"The Sewing-Girl's Home," from a Victorian account of New York's demimonde

For these "tailoresses," whose profession stamped itself indelibly on their bodies in the form of stooped posture and impaired eyesight, the average yearly income in the mid-1800s was just ninety-one dol-

* So, too, was a woman's ability to obtain credit from lending institutions.

† A dollar in 1850 is equivalent to about thirty-seven dollars today.

lars.* A historian relates the fate of two of them, contemporaries of Fredericka Mandelbaum:

> The condition of women who depended on sewing for a liv-
> ing was ... very precarious. The extreme poverty of these
> women is exemplified by two German sisters who migrated
> to New York in 1852. Cecelia and Wanda Stein were both un-
> married when they arrived in Kleindeutschland with Wan-
> da's young illegitimate child. The two women took up
> embroidery for a living, but it wasn't much of a living. Even
> with the two sisters putting in long hours at their craft, life
> was very hard and they sometimes had to borrow money from
> friends to survive. After two years in New York, they confided
> to a friend that "if things grew much worse," they would
> send the boy to his father and take poison. In the fall of 1855
> things grew worse. Their employer went out of business and
> the two sisters were unable to find work. Soon the rent was
> due and the larder was empty. They had already borrowed all
> that they could, their money was almost gone, and they were
> unwilling to become prostitutes. On September 4 they reached
> the end of their rope. They got their landlady to give them
> another day to pay the rent and used their last few pennies to
> buy some flowers. Setting out the flowers to cheer up the bare
> room, they got into their one bed with six-year-old Edward.
> Settled in bed, each of the three took a drink from a bottle of
> prussic acid—and their troubles were soon over.

With so many routes to economic advancement closed, what options remained? Some immigrants turned to criminal activity—the
so-called "crooked ladder"—as a means of upward mobility. For
men of the period, these activities might include illegal gambling
operations, numbers running, protection rackets, muscle for hire,

---

* About $3,400 today.

criminal fencing and New York City ward politics in the avaricious heyday of Tammany Hall. But for women, there were even fewer career options in the underworld than there were in the "upper world"—the realm of legal enterprise. Throughout the nineteenth century, shoplifting and prostitution were very nearly the only callings open to the woman who, whether in bold economic self-determination or desperate last resort, sought a criminal livelihood.

Among immigrant German women, prostitution was the commonest form of criminality. It was dangerous work, in harsh conditions: An 1858 study found that roughly a quarter of the thousands of prostitutes in the city died each year. For a young woman entering the trade, the average life expectancy was about four years.

FOR A PROPER MARRIED WOMAN like Fredericka Mandelbaum, prostitution was clearly out of the question. But it's also clear that she was not content to remain in poverty. Crucially, she recognized very early that the jobs open to immigrant women would never offer the security, or the chance of upward mobility, that entrepreneurship could. "While lower-class women have always worked, their occupations generally hewed much more closely to the domestic sphere as maids, nurses, laundresses, seamstresses or boardinghouse landladies," a historian remarked to me recently. "Mandelbaum grasped the difference between wage work and *the accrual of capital* as the means of becoming wealthy well before Marx published his magnum opus."*

During her first years in New York, Fredericka, too, worked as a peddler, selling lace door to door in streets already massed with men, women and children proffering their wares. From pushcarts, baskets and buckets, they hawked cheap jewelry, combs and second-hand clothing; buttons and ribbon and thread and straw; suspenders, shoelaces and gloves; detachable collars and cuffs; matches and

---

* Karl Marx's masterwork, *Das Kapital: A Critique of Political Economy,* was published in three volumes, beginning in 1867 and continuing, posthumously, in 1885 and 1894.

kindling; pots and pans; brooms, newspapers and fiddle strings; fruit and vegetables; oysters and clams; gingerbread and roast peanuts; hot corn, baked potatoes and baked beans; buttermilk, ice cream and apple pie. Knife sharpeners, tinkers, and chimney sweeps; bootblacks, glaziers, ragpickers and umbrella menders further swelled the throng.*

The streets were a polyphonic chorus: "Rags—rags—any rags?" . . . "Fresh sha-a-d!" . . . "Oysters, here's your brave, good oysters!" . . . "Pots and pans. Mend your pots and pans." . . . "Here's clams, here's clams, here's clams today / They late came from Rockaway; / They're good to roast, they're good to fry, / They're good to make a clam pot pie." . . . "Glass put'een! Glass put'een!" . . . "Hot corn! Hot corn! / Here's your lily white corn. / All you that's got money / Poor me that's got none / Come buy my lily white corn / And let me go home." . . . "Sweepho! Sweepho!" . . . "Strawberries, any straw be-e-erees!" . . . "Umbrellas to mend!"

But Mrs. Mandelbaum soon saw that there was little future in peddling.† Sometime during the 1850s, she appears to have become a protégée of "General Abe" Greenthal, a master fence. Greenthal, as the *New-York Times* would observe in 1889, was "one of the oldest and shrewdest criminals in this country," the head of a band of Jewish criminals known—even, proudly, among themselves—as the Sheeny Mob.‡ (The mob, as the *Times* genteelly put it, was "a gang of clever pickpockets and shoplifters," and Greenthal, "when he was not actually engaged in thefts . . . was instrumental in dis-

---

* The particular goods and services a vendor hawked often cleaved along demographic lines. African American New Yorkers, for instance, tended to sell the straw and buttermilk. The Irish sold seafood. Jews often dealt in old clothing. Young Black boys worked as itinerant chimney sweeps. And a ragged cohort of small girls, many of them Irish American and among the most perennially destitute of the city's street peddlers, sold hot corn.

† Street peddling, in the words of a modern observer, was "the bottom level of business activity."

‡ Then as now, "sheeny" (a word of obscure origin, sometimes spelled "sheeney") was a deeply offensive anti-Semitic slur. In the nineteenth century, however, some Jewish underworld figures embraced the term as a badge of honor.

posing of plunder.") Under his tutelage, and that of Mose Ehrich, also a noted fence, Mrs. Mandelbaum became expert in appraising the value of the lace, silk, cashmere, sealskin and other luxury goods that passed, fleetingly, through their hands. The skills she acquired laid the foundation for her criminal career.

"General Abe" Greenthal,
a noted New York fence of
the mid-nineteenth century.
Under his tutelage,
Marm Mandelbaum
learned the business.

By all accounts, Wolf Mandelbaum was largely uninvolved in his wife's early foray into fencing, just as he would be largely uninvolved in the long, lucrative criminal enterprise that followed. As the police chief George Washington Walling would recall: "The woman took the lead in these nefarious transactions. . . . She was a thorough business woman; her husband was a nonentity."

With her intelligence and drive, Fredericka would not have wanted to spend her life as a peddler, subordinate to a series of bosses. She could maximize her income, she knew, by striking out on her own and diversifying the range of merchandise she handled. But without capital, how could she acquire that merchandise in the first place? For the answer, she looked to the streets.

Chapter Two

No Questions Asked

IT IS AN ENDURING TENET OF THIEVERY THAT A SCROUNGER BEARING coal or copper or cotton—to say nothing of a burglar laden with silk or silver or sapphires—must be in want of a fence. If theft has existed since the advent of personal property, then criminal receiving has existed since very nearly the advent of theft, because the thief rarely has the patience, the contacts or the finesse to unload the goods himself for worthwhile profit. That is where the fence comes in.

In Britain, fencing has been attested for more than half a millennium. In his magnum opus, *A History of Crime in England,* the Victorian barrister Luke Owen Pike describes cases of criminal receiving as far back as the fourteenth century. "The Common Receiver is by no means a creation of our great modern cities," he writes, "but has descended to us from the days when Europe was in a state of brigandage.... Men and women are thus described in numerous cases recorded in the rolls, and were the fitting associates of the classes described as . . . common thieves or robbers."

Though fences take great pains to outmaneuver the police, few consider themselves criminals: They are businesspeople pure and simple, serving as the vital Point B's in a supply chain designed to usher goods efficiently from Point A (the thief) to Point C (the consumer). As the middleman, the receiver serves as a double layer of insulation, first between thief and police, then between consumer and thief.* It is an occupational irritant—at times a hazard—that the brand of commercial logistics at which the fence is so adept happens to be against the law.

Part of the insulation the fence provides takes the form of a "front"—a quasi-legitimate business like a pawnshop, junk shop ... or haberdashery shop—through which ill-gotten goods can be sold publicly. Yet fencing and pawnbroking are two very different things. A client who takes a diamond brooch to a pawnbroker, and collects a ticket for it, has (at least in principle) the expectation of getting it back. A thief taking the same brooch to a criminal receiver has no such expectation, and that is precisely the point: Once the item is in the fence's possession, the thief can exit the equation altogether, in relative safety.

BY THE TIME MRS. MANDELBAUM arrived in the New World, several factors had converged to made reselling stolen goods an attractive business proposition. Among them were America's continuing shift from its agrarian past to an economy propelled by commerce and industry, the corresponding growth of its cities, and the rise of New York as a world center of manufacturing and trade. In addition, the ill-defined status of criminal receiving in American law of the day, combined with the disorganized character of New York City's fledgling police force, made the successful prosecution of fences rare. Throughout her first decade in America, Fredericka learned to capitalize on all of these things.

During this period, New York was subject to cycles of unchecked economic activity followed by financial panics that swept over the city like flash floods.† Fredericka recognized that both ends of the

---

* "Fence" in this sense is a truncation of "defence," in its British spelling.

† The city experienced major financial panics, as such downturns were generally known at the time, in 1837, 1857 and 1873, for instance. The more euphemistic term "depression" was widely applied to such situations only in the early 1930s, when President Herbert Hoover invoked it in an attempt to dampen the terrifying overtones of "panic."

cycle could be exploited for profit. "Her success, in part, depended on what happened during economic downturns," Rona Holub explained. "When businesses failed, banks closed, and tens of thousands of people lost their jobs, poor and working class people took to the streets."

Boom periods ensured that more and more fungible goods poured into the city, including the luxury items that the emerging middle class was being taught to crave. Bust times meant that the city teemed with scavengers—the destitute, the dispossessed, the abruptly unemployed—who snagged whatever they could from streets, waterfront docks, delivery wagons and warehouses.

Many of these scavengers were women, and Mrs. Mandelbaum would have encountered them daily in and around Kleindeutschland: Had she not been shrewd enough to parlay the city's downturns into cash, she could easily have been one of them. While some of their haul—bits of coal and wood, spilled flour, sugar and coffee—was for home use, the rest, including rags, rope and scrap metal, was destined for resale to junk dealers, tradesmen and fences in the underground economic system then flourishing among New York's poor.*

Throughout Marm's years as a New York peddler, at least some of her wares came from scavengers, as well as from pickpockets and small-time thieves. It was a beneficial arrangement for all concerned: The scavenger was spared the onus of finding a buyer; Mrs. Mandelbaum was spared the onus of overhead. Proceeds from the resale would be split between Marm and the scavenger, with Marm getting the lion's share. By the end of the 1850s, she had amassed

---

* In the 1860s, a scavenger of rags or paper might realize two cents a pound (about twenty cents a pound in today's money), selling forty pounds on an exceptionally good day. At the heart of this "street economy" were an estimated three thousand children, real-life Dickensian urchins who scoured the city for whatever could be scrounged or stolen. "By midcentury, New York was the capital of American crime, and there was a place for children, small and adept as they were, on its margins," a historian has noted. "Its full-blown economy of contraband, with the junk shops at the center, allowed children to exchange pilfered and stolen goods quickly and easily. Anything, from scavenged bottles to nicked top hats, could be sold immediately."

enough capital to forsake peddling entirely and go to work as a solo entrepreneur—continuing to receive goods of dubious provenance from scavengers and petty thieves, asking no questions, and selling the swag onward at a profit. Fredericka Mandelbaum had become a fence.

But as she knew, rags and rope would scarcely bring her riches. Uptown, far better quarry beguiled.

AT THE TIME MARM was setting up shop, the era that would soon be called America's Gilded Age*—a period of rapacious greed, unregulated speculation, rampant corruption and a widening chasm of income inequality—was just beginning. Not coincidentally, those years also heralded the start of what has been called the country's first Golden Age of robbery, which would reach full flower after the Civil War. By midcentury, the opportunities for picking pockets were already so numerous and varied that New York's "dips," as pickpockets were colloquially known, had begun to specialize. A corresponding vocabulary identified their "beats"—the particular arenas in which they might snag "leather" (a pocketbook) or a "roll" (paper money). "Carbuzzers" worked streetcars and horse-drawn omnibuses. "Kirkbuzzers" put the "touch" on church congregants. "Reader merchants" targeted bank customers.† "Groaners" sat through charity sermons in order to bag some charity of their own. "Mollbuzzers" focused on women. "Files" used small knives to slice open pockets and discreetly "nick" their contents.

This explosion of thievery was rooted in pure pragmatic calculus: Upper- and middle-class Americans now owned much better personal property, and far more of it, than ever before. Uptown, titans of industry—Vanderbilts, Rockefellers, Astors and their ilk—

---

* Though the phrase would not be popularized until 1873, with the publication of *The Gilded Age: A Tale of Today*, the satirical novel by Mark Twain and Charles Dudley Warner, historians locate the start of the era as far back as the 1850s.

† Per the *Oxford English Dictionary*, "reader" was eighteenth- and nineteenth-century criminals' slang for a pocketbook or wallet.

who had forged empires from railroads and oil and furs, were erecting vast mansions, rococo riots of gold, silk and Old Master paintings. Amid an economic downturn, one branch of the Vanderbilt family erected a seventy-room summer home, staffed with thirty-three servants and thirteen grooms, at a cost of $5 million. Not to be outdone, a rival branch built a home that, while costing a mere $2 million, boasted $9 million worth of interior decoration.

But for the first time in the country's history, the chance to amass personal property wasn't confined to the upper class. By the mid-1800s, an American middle class had begun to emerge, a product of industrialization, urbanization and the growth of professional work. Its members soon began to crave more, and better, things of their own. Once mere purchasers, they were now *consumers*.

IN AMERICA'S AGRICULTURAL PAST, as in Europe's, wealth was typically measured in land and livestock. Articles needed for the home were generally made *in* the home: timber fashioned into furniture, fleece spun into yarn and woven into textiles. A rich man might own a few elegant, artisan pieces—a gold watch, an engraved snuff box, a signet ring—but there was nothing like the tide of mass-produced consumer goods that would start to inundate the West in the wake of the Industrial Revolution. By the mid-nineteenth century, however, the production of goods like furniture, jewelry and textiles had begun to move out of artisans' workshops and into centralized "manufactories"—i.e., *factories*—making such items less costly and more widely available. And so, during the second half of that century, America's newly emerged bourgeois class started clamoring for those things, tangible incarnations of the American Dream.*

* The phrase "American Dream" would be coined in 1931, with the publication of *The Epic of America*, by the journalist James Truslow Adams. But it is clear that the vision Adams describes—"a better, deeper, richer life for every individual, regardless of the position in society which he or she may occupy by the accident of birth"—had been instilled in the American mind, along with its attendant materialism, long before.

For criminal receivers, it was a halcyon time, as they found themselves at the center of an epidemic of longing—a mass acquisitive
drive instilled by newspaper and magazine advertisements, and by
the ubiquitous manuals of domestic advice aimed at middle-class
women. Inflamed by this rhetoric, the bourgeois American house-
wife was under pressure to transform her home into a showplace of
contemporary material culture. Her parlor, above all, was to be ag-
gressively force-fed: glutted with settees, sofas and end tables; knick-
knacks and bric-a-brac; mantel clocks, crystal and ornate lamps;
fussily framed oils and watercolors; oceans of cushions; pianos draped
in piano scarves; flocked wallpaper, decorative screens and vases of
artificial flowers; velvets and plush and doilies and fringe; draperies,
carpets and chintz. As a Victorian tastemaker would write, without
irony, "Provided there is space to move about, without knocking over
the furniture, there is hardly likely to be too much in the room."

With so much to acquire, the new middle-class woman was eager
for discounts. So was the small businessman—the tailor, the dressmaker, the bric-a-brac salesman—who was anxious to stock merchandise or acquire raw materials he could not normally afford. And it was
here, at the intersection of thrift, stuff, class and desire, that Fredericka Mandelbaum found her calling. It would center on a singular
kind of recycling: availing herself of choice items from one bourgeois
home so that they might adorn another, or lifting bolts of silk from
large textile concerns for sale to neighborhood tailors. "Everything is
elaborately arranged," a nineteenth-century observer would note of
her business model. "Two days after [the stolen goods] are gone, the
chances are that the owner is probably rubbing elbows in a [street]car
with the girl whose shirtwaist is made of the stolen material."

Mrs. Mandelbaum was disinclined to steal things firsthand, an
aversion born not of scruple but of self-protection: She had learned
from experience that shoplifting was risky business. Reporting one
of her rare early arrests, the *National Police Gazette*,[*] a popular

---

[*]   Published from 1845 until 1932, and again from 1933 to 1977, the *National Police
Gazette* prefigured twentieth-century men's magazines, offering crime news, sports
and celebrity gossip, along with images—first engravings, later photographs—of

magazine that makes modern supermarket tabloids look like church circulars, offered a characteristically lurid, unabashedly anti-Semitic account:

> Mike Weaver* unquestionably has his hands full; he has more business than he can legitimately attend to in work of a peculiar character. In the first place, he has to see to the interests of his own true "moll" Mary, who was "pinched" with the "sheeny," Mrs. Mendelbaum [sic], and a "sheeny" apprentice to shoplifting. They were all three caught "dead foul" in a store on Broadway, and by this time they would have had their deserts by "doing" time, had it not been for the interference and interest that the greatest receiver of stolen goods of modern times has taken in them.
>
> Mose Ehrick [sic], who was bound in honor to see the "sheeny" woman [Mrs. Mandelbaum] get out of the difficulty, rather than there should be a "squeal," put up $2,000, and got a merchant in Chambers Street to go bail for Mary Hyman. Mose boasts that he has got all the controlling power everywhere, and that this "sheeny" shoplifter will never be tried.†

THE MID- TO LATE nineteenth century was a time of widespread professionalization, with fields like medicine and law establishing rigorous protocols for education, certification and conduct. The American Medical Association was founded in 1847 to combat the

---

scantily clad women. The *Gazette* was one of the most enduring entrants in an urban American field now known as the "Flash Press": heavily illustrated, often sensationalistic nineteenth-century tabloids that could be enjoyed even by illiterate consumers.

* According to Thomas Byrnes, New York City's chief of detectives from 1880 to 1895, Michael Weaver, alias Edward Collins, was "an old New York safe burglar, shoplifter, and scuttle thief"—i.e., a burglar who enters premises through an exterior coal scuttle or trapdoor.

† Indeed, Mrs. Mandelbaum was not brought to trial in any known case of shoplifting.

"rampant quackery" embodied by hawkers of patent medicines and other professed miracle cures. The American Bar Association was established in 1878, for analogous reasons: Earlier in the century, an aspiring attorney could simply read for the law, and then attempt to pass the bar exam, without going to law school.* Abraham Lincoln, whose formal education had been threadbare, had done precisely this. So had Mrs. Mandelbaum's longtime attorneys, William Howe and Abraham Hummel, among the country's best-known, best-compensated and most breathtakingly corrupt members of the bar. So, too, had William M. Tweed,† the longtime, even more breathtakingly corrupt boss of the Tammany Hall machine. "In the course of the century," a scholar has noted, "the term 'amateur' had for the first time acquired pejorative connotations. A 'professional,' by way of contrast, was dependable, skillful and committed."

As America's upper-world professions were becoming streamlined, organized and hierarchical, so was the American underworld. While there had been some professional theft in America from colonial days onward, it was only with the rise of large urban centers— teeming with the propertied classes and offering malefactors a welcome measure of anonymity—that stealing became a viable full-time occupation.

By the 1840s, the Five Points in Lower Manhattan had begun to seethe with ethnic gangs, chiefly Irish immigrants who had banded together to defend themselves against violence from nativist Anglo-Saxon Americans. Among these early groups were those memorialized by Herbert Asbury in his 1927 book, *The Gangs of New York:*‡ the Plug Uglies, the Shirt Tails, the Roach Guards. Barred by their ethnicity from most jobs in polite society, gang members grew

---

*   In 1870, only 25 percent of American lawyers admitted to the bar had attended law school. Today, several U.S. states still allow aspirants to sit the bar exam without having gone to law school.

†   Although Tweed's middle name is given in myriad sources as Marcy, it was actually Magear.

‡   As the historian Tyler Anbinder writes, Asbury is now regarded as "a usually careful if somewhat overly dramatic chronicler of old New York."

skilled at pilfering a vast range of goods from the city's warehouses and docks.* But their kind of crime, though widespread, remained largely "disorganized": ad hoc, unprofessional, often violent, not especially remunerative.† ("Eye-gougers and mayhem artists," Asbury called them.) The gangs also supplied hired muscle to ward heelers eager to get out the vote on Election Day—the vote, that is, for members of the Tammany Hall Democratic machine.‡

In decades that followed, women began to enter gang life, but most, like their male counterparts, were bruisers and not businesspeople. "Among the ladies, Gallus Mag, Sadie the Goat, Hell-Cat Maggie, Battle Annie . . . and Euchre Kate Burns, whom a newspaper called the 'champion heavyweight female brick hurler' of Hell's Kitchen, were all specialists in election day mayhem," a historian has written:

> Gallus Mag, who supported her skirt with suspenders,§ was a mean six-foot female who, armed with a pistol and a club, was employed as a bouncer at a dive called the Hole-in-the-Wall. Sadie the Goat, a prostitute and all around rough-and-tumble fighter, ran with the Charlton Street Gang, a group of river pirates. She won her nickname by the way she would lower her head and butt like a goat in a fight. . . . Hell-Cat Maggie looked like an enraged tiger. Her teeth were filed to

---

* By 1860, as a modern historian notes, New York had become "both the nation's premier port and its largest manufacturing city," so there was no shortage of things to steal.

† The Whyos, considered the city's most violent gang and the first to pursue crime as an organized business enterprise, did not come to power until the early 1880s.

‡ As a historian of Kleindeutschland writes, the early Irish gangs "had few German counterparts. . . . Kleindeutschland did have its own gang for about a dozen years after the Civil War, but the 'Dutch Mob' (led by 'Sheeny' Mike Kurtz, Little Freddy, and Johnny Irving) never made it into the leading ranks of New York's underworld. In the end, it was easily dispersed by a police terror campaign in 1877. . . . Which is not to say that there was no criminal element [in the German community], only that it took other forms."

§ "Galluses" was a U.S. dialect term for suspenders. The word "gallus" derives from "gallows"—i.e., that from which something is suspended.

points and over her fingers she wore sharp brass spikes. Even the bravest of men lost their poise when she charged scream- ing into a polling place. (In a celebrated fight, she bit off the ear of Sadie the Goat.) The huge and violent Battle Annie, "the sweetheart of Hell's Kitchen," was a terrifying bully. She commanded a gang of ferocious Amazons called the Bat- tle Row Ladies Social and Athletic Club.

Truly professional crime emerged only in the 1860s, side by side with upper-world professionalism—and as upper-world and under- world men strove simultaneously for wealth and power, the bound- ary between their worlds could grow indistinct. The robber barons had won their uptown fortunes through tactics that included brib- ery, perjury, embezzlement and intimidation. They "bought" pub- lic officials, solicited kickbacks, manipulated prices of stocks and currency, forced mergers and takeovers, and put down strikes, often violently. ("I can hire one half the working class"—i.e., the Pinkertons—"to kill the other half," the financier and railroad magnate Jay Gould bragged.)* They cornered markets, which could trigger financial panics. In wartime, they sold defective goods to the military at extortionate prices. ("Law! What do I care about law?" Cornelius Vanderbilt scoffed in 1865, after supplying the Union with decaying ships. "Hain't I got the power?") They turned perennial blind eyes to their employees' safety and solvency.

"While workers starved or died on the job ... the rich of the Gilded Age ... enjoyed their wealth as never before," a modern his- tory recounts. "Diamonds were set into teeth. Black pearls were placed into the oysters of dinner guests. At one function, after- dinner cigars were wrapped in $100 bills. ... The collars on dogs were made of gold or diamonds, worth as much as $15,000.† One

---

* Gould, who as a young man received a seminary education, wrote his senior thesis on the theme "Honesty Is the Best Policy."

† Fifteen thousand dollars in 1865, for instance, is equivalent to nearly $280,000 today.

plutocrat kept a private carriage and personal valet for a pet monkey who was driven about town every afternoon."

Yet it was only the tactics of underworld figures that were widely viewed as criminal. "The larger society . . . overwhelmingly condemned those engaged in *ethnic* crime," a scholar observes. "The nation has remained remarkably unconcerned with white-collar crime that, by definition, excludes most lower-class minority newcomers."

IN THE POPULAR IMAGINATION, American organized crime is largely synonymous with the Mafia, whose roots lie in thirteenth-century Sicily. That organization arrived in the United States at the end of the nineteenth century,* with the first great wave of Italian immigration; it took firm hold across the country in the early twentieth, amid Prohibition. A generation of Jewish gangsters—men like Arnold Rothstein, Meyer Lansky and Abraham "Kid Twist" Reles— would also come to dominate the urban underworld, though their heyday did not take place until the 1920s and '30s.

But in reality, organized criminal activity could be discerned at least as far back as the mid-1800s, if one knew where to look. In an 1866 report, the Prison Association of New York, an independent watchdog group, observed:

> A survey of the State this year shows that there is a strong and increasing tendency of crime to crystallize into aggregates and masses. Men, more rarely now than formerly, commit robberies and burglaries alone. They operate extensively in groups. . . . This tendency to aggregation is apparent in our larger cities as well as in the rural districts. Through the agency of these affiliated societies of thieves, property once stolen is passed rap-

---

* The killing that is often described as the first recorded Mafia murder in America took place in New Orleans in 1889, when a man named Vincenzo Ottumvo had his throat cut during a card game.

Mrs. Mandelbaum's home and shop, at the southwest corner of Clinton and Rivington streets. The building no longer exists.

idly from hand to hand, until it becomes almost impossible to trace it, or, if it is discovered, the original depredators cannot be ascertained, and therefore go unwhipped of justice.

At the center of this crystallization was Fredericka Mandelbaum, who by the mid-1860s had a growing family to support. A son, Julius, was born in 1860, followed by Sarah in 1862 and Gustav in 1864. (Anna, familiarly known as Annie, would be born in 1867.) It was imperative that she expand her business. In 1864, she rented the street-level shop and cellar at 163 Rivington Street, on the southwest corner of Clinton and Rivington, in the Thirteenth Ward. The rent was $375 for the first year,* rising to $400 the next. The premises, which over time would grow to sprawling dimensions, would serve as Marm's headquarters for the next twenty years. Gathering her handpicked acolytes around her, she began the criminal ascent that would soon make her "the most celebrated fence in the history of this nation."

THOUGH SHE WAS DOUBTLESS unaware of the fact, the business model Fredericka would adopt harked back to eighteenth-century England. There, it had been perfected by a pickpocket, prostitute's "bully,"† criminal receiver, extortionist and unreconstructed rogue named Jonathan Wild.

Wild, who ruled the London underworld in the 1710s and '20s, is considered one of the most dominant criminals in Western history—and the father of modern professional fencing. In his own day he was a celebrity: Feared and revered in equal measure, he was the subject of imaginatively embellished works of "biographical" fiction, including a satirical novel by Henry Fielding and a pamphlet attributed to Daniel Defoe.

Wild was born in Wolverhampton, about 115 miles northwest of London, circa 1682, the eldest of five children in a family of modest means: His father was a joiner, his mother a fruit seller. At fifteen, Jonathan was apprenticed to a buckle maker; while still in his teens, he married and became the father of a son. But a life spent turning out buckles was unambiguously not for him, and in his early twenties he abandoned his wife and child and struck out for London. There, his résumé included stints as a lawyer's manservant, a debt collector and, in hairpin reversal, an inmate in debtor's prison, a

*   Just under $7,000 a year in today's money.

†   Attested from the early seventeenth to the early eighteenth centuries, "bully" in this sense denotes a man who protects prostitutes and lives off their earnings.

sojourn that put him in close contact with some of the choicest spec-imens of the London underworld.

On leaving prison, Wild moved into a brothel with his mistress, a "buttock and file"* named Mary Milliner. Together, in back alleys, they proceeded to relieve a string of London gentlemen of their valuables. The system, as described by an early-eighteenth-century chronicler, worked this way:

> The *Buttock and Twang* by Night, . . . picking up a *Cull, Cully,* or *Spark*,† . . . takes him into some dark Alley, so whilst the decoy'd Fool is groping her with his Breeches down, she picks his Fob or Pocket, of his Watch or Money, and giving a sort of "Hem" as a signal she hath succeeded in her Design, then the Fellow with whom she keeps Company, blundering up in the Dark, he knocks down the Gallant, and carries off the Prize.

For Wild, a pressing concern was what to do with the prize once he had it. Money could be spent outright, but there remained the question of the valuables. In preindustrial days, personal property was artisan-made and thus readily identifiable: bespoke jewelry, or objects bearing inscriptions or makers' marks. The system of theft and resale that Marm would exploit in the age of mass production was far too risky for an early-eighteenth-century fence. Instead, Wild did what criminal receivers had been doing for generations, only he did it better: He transformed himself into the country's preeminent tracer of lost objects.

London in those years was a thieves' paradise. There was no city-wide police force: The London Metropolitan Police Department would be established only in 1829. The patchwork of local watch-men, marshals and constables that patrolled the city in Wild's day proved eminently bribable: Thieves often sold their plunder directly to them, at an attractive discount, which kept them safe from the

---

*   A prostitute and pickpocket. Also called "buttock and twang."

†   Seventeenth- and eighteenth-century underworld slang terms for a dupe.

hangman's noose. Capitalizing on prevailing conditions, Wild began to gather London's foremost thieves around him. He set up shop in the parlor of a London tavern, where he presided over the boldly named "Office for the Recovery of Lost and Stolen Property."

Suppose an English gentleman awoke one morning to find his gold watch and silver snuff box missing. Calling on Wild in his "office," he would be informed that Wild "had an idea where the goods might be found, or at least who it was that had possession of them," and that they could soon be returned to their rightful owner—for a fee. "If the person questioned Wild's integrity, or asked how he should know so much about the theft, Wild answered 'that it was meerly Providential; being, by meer Accident, at a Tavern, or at a Friend's House in the Neighbourhood, [he] heard that such a Gentleman had his House broken open, and such and such Goods Stolen, and the like.'"

Needless to say, Wild knew exactly where the goods were, because they'd been stolen by one of his own employees. What he'd done, in short, was to perfect a kind of property-kidnapping for ransom. The system proved so effective that he did not hesitate to target some of the country's wealthiest men and women. A biographer recounts a remunerative gambit:

> Lady Henrietta Godolphin[*] paid a visit to ... St. James's Street, Piccadilly. Her chairmen left her sedan chair, which had crimson velvet cushions and damask curtains, outside the house and went to a neighbouring alehouse to await her return. While they were drinking, the chair "was carried entirely off." The chairmen immediately applied to Wild.... After taking their crown deposit, he told them to come back in a day or two. When they presented themselves accordingly, he insisted on a considerable reward (some accounts say it was ten guineas). As soon as they had paid it, he told them to be sure to attend prayers at Lincoln's Inn Chapel next morn-

---

[*]   Lady Henrietta Godolphin (1681–1733) was the Duchess of Marlborough.

ing. They did so, and on coming out of the chapel were surprised and pleased to find the chair waiting under the piazza of the chapel, its cushions and curtains undamaged.

In the unlikely event that an object had been stolen by someone outside Wild's organization, he could often recover it anyhow. Taking out an advertisement in a local newspaper, he would describe the missing item, assuring readers that it was "of no use to anyone but the Owner"—in other words, warning the thief that it had no resale value. "Whoever will bring [it] to Mr. Jonathan Wild," the ad continued, "shall have a Guinea reward." It concluded, crucially, "No Questions asked." Thus Wild could induce the thief to deliver the goods without fear of reprisal, and quite possibly recruit him into his employ.

Over time, Wild built an immense fortune, and an immense organization, spanning the country and encompassing not only "highwaymen, pick-pockets, housebreakers, shop-lifters, and other thieves" but also "several artists to make alterations, and transform watches, seals, snuff-boxes, rings, and other valuable things, that they might not be known." He also owned a constellation of warehouses in which to store stolen goods, and a ship in which to carry them off for resale on the Continent.

THERE WAS A SECOND COMPONENT of Wild's business model, and it was this, more than anything else, that kept him immune from prosecution for years: Jonathan Wild was a rat. Until the late seventeenth century, English law had paid little attention to criminal receivers, and they operated more or less in the open.* Fencing was then a

---

*   As Wild's biographer Gerald Howson notes: "From about 1605 until the [English] Civil War [of 1642–51], Mary Frith, nicknamed 'Moll Cutpurse' . . . ran a shop in Fleet Street which was nothing less than a reception centre for stolen goods of all kinds. . . . She only ceased business when, being a fanatical Royalist, she followed the King's Party out of London. By the 1680s, there were hundreds of warehouses and repositories where thieves could sell their booty, within minutes of stealing it, at a price not far below its full value."

Jonathan Wild, in a
period caricature, at
work in his "office"

misdemeanor, carrying only the prospect of a fine, or at worst a
whipping, on the rare occasions that a fence was brought to justice.
Then, in 1692, Parliament passed "An Act for Encourageing the Apprehending of Highway Men," which criminalized fencing in England and Wales: It was now, like robbery, punishable by hanging.
What was more, in an effort to break up the gangs of thieves that
roamed the country, the Highwaymen Act offered a reward of £40
to anyone who turned in a robber, provided a conviction was obtained.

Forty pounds* was a princely sum, enough to buy seven horses or
nine head of cattle. The public responded accordingly, avidly informing on their fellow citizens, truthfully or otherwise. So, too, did
professional thief-takers, and none so masterfully as Jonathan Wild.

In 1718, Wild placed an advertisement in a weekly journal pro-
claiming himself "THIEF-TAKER GENERAL OF GREAT BRITAIN AND IRE-

---

* About £4,800, or $6,000, in today's money.

LAND." It was a public-relations masterstroke, positioning him as a highly visible defender of law and order. In the years that followed, Wild appeared to be a tireless, if unofficial, agent of criminal justice, throwing the authorities sacrificial small fish from his organizational pool, or bigger fish who'd displeased him. "He . . . was oblig'd every now and then to give up one or two of his Clients to the Gallows, to support his . . . Reputation," the pamphlet attributed to Defoe recounts. "He never fail'd to publish *how useful* a Man he was to the Publick . . . [and] he got a general Applause for it, as a proper Man to bring Rogues to Justice and detect their Villainies."

The arrangement, while it lasted, benefited almost everyone: The owner got his property back; Wild got the "ransom" money, plus the £40 government reward; the public got a renewed feeling

A ticket to Jonathan Wild's hanging— at "ye Tripple Tree, where he's to make his last Exit . . . and his Corps to be Carry'd from thence to be decently Interr'd amongst his Ancestors"—topped by his own official seal

of security; and the hangman got a highwayman. As for the high-wayman, well, he was expendable: Writing in 1724, Defoe estimated that Wild employed some seven thousand thieves.

Little by little, though, public sentiment turned against Wild. In February 1725, he was arrested and jailed on a fairly minor charge: having accepted a £10 reward for returning a length of stolen lace to its owner. (It went without saying that one of Wild's underlings had carried out the theft.) "Further disclosures revealed," Wild's biographer Gerald Howson writes, "that far from combating the crime wave, Wild had been the principal driving force behind it . . . and that the hundreds of criminals he had 'brought to Justice' were [in fact] 'fall guys.'"

Wild was tried and convicted in May 1725. On May 24, he was hanged in London before a large, enthusiastic crowd.

With minor variations, Jonathan Wild's two-part modus operandi—receiving stolen goods and sacrificing lesser thieves—has been the professional template for fences ever since. The method would assure Fredericka Mandelbaum's rise and prolonged success. It would also help bring about her downfall.

Chapter Three

Breakfast at Tiffany's

Now that she had headquarters, Mrs. Mandelbaum could start to assemble the components of a first-rate criminal-receiving concern. Her approach—centering on skilled personnel, productivity and clearly defined best practices—anticipated by two decades the work of the high-profile efficiency experts who in the 1880s would start do likewise for corporate America.* "In the public imagination, . . . crime is a departure from the norm *brought* to the United States by 'others,'" Rona Holub observes. "In reality, the efforts of Mandelbaum . . . to organize crime more efficiently [were] motivated by the same atmosphere that motivated the great capitalists and robber barons of the nineteenth century."

As Jonathan Wild had done a century and a half before, Marm began to amass her troops. Street scavengers would not do this time; nor would petty thieves or Five Points brawlers. Instead, she turned her eye to the cohort of skilled shoplifters already circulating in 1860s New York.

---

* The best known of these was Frederick Winslow Taylor (1856–1915), whose theory of "scientific management"—it became known as Taylorism—was widely influential among business leaders of the late nineteenth and early twentieth centuries. Its goal, of a piece with Mrs. Mandelbaum's, was increased profitability through increased efficiency.

By long-standing criminal tradition, shoplifting was "women's work," and New York department stores like Lord & Taylor; Arnold, Constable & Company; and the opulent A. T. Stewart* were at mid-century aswarm with larcenous females.† Marm, who would become renowned as a mentor to underworld women, could offer them steady employment at minimal risk, with the promise of bail should they ever be arrested. Many joined her earliest broods of "chicks"— each woman equal parts employee and disciple. Besides Sophie Lyons, they included "Black Lena" Kleinschmidt, a German-born jewel thief nicknamed for her olive complexion; "Old Mother Hubbard," a grandmotherly Irishwoman who specialized in "satchel work" (the dexterous opening of ladies' handbags and the imperceptible removal of the purses inside); and Kid Glove Rosey, a deft German-born shoplifter who, at four feet eleven inches tall, could easily disappear into crowds.

"Black Lena" Kleinschmidt (left) and Margaret Brown, aka "Old Mother Hubbard," two early employees of the Mandelbaum organization

* Opened, respectively, in 1824, 1825 and 1846.

† As a historian points out, "Unlike other retail businesses,... department stores catered to women almost exclusively, becoming locations where unaccompanied women would not draw any undue attention." They also made natural havens for female shoplifters.

"Mother Mandelbaum," the *Boston Daily Globe* would relate, "is described as . . . true as steel to her 'chickens.' It had been her custom for years to start two or three new 'chicks' on the road yearly and their standing in her favor was dependent on their success as burglars or thieves. . . . Her customary greeting on meeting a pal has always been 'Come Jack, Billy [whatever the name may be], let us have a drink' or 'Let us have a bite to eat.'"

Marm became so well known as a thieves' mentor that an urban legend sprang up in her own lifetime—it persists to this day—that she ran a brick-and-mortar educational academy in which she taught aspiring young criminals the arts of pickpocketing, house-breaking and safecracking.* (She was forced to close the school, the legend continues, when the son of a prominent New York police official applied for admission.)

Though the legend is no more than that, a tantalizing newspaper article from 1884 suggests its origin—and attests to Marm's authentic talent for self-protection. HE WANTED TO BE A KNUCK,† the headline crows:

A bright, intelligent lad, neatly dressed and plausible in speech, yesterday visited the store of Frederica [*sic*] Mandelbaum, No. 79 Clinton Street—the well-known "Mother Mandelbaum" of the East Side. He handed her a letter, neatly written, the burden of which was that he . . . wished to be introduced to a professional pickpocket, as he, the open-eyed,

---

* Pedagogy of this kind actually took place in Europe for generations. As an American criminologist has written, "During the fifteenth and sixteenth centuries master thieves entrusted with the education of novices were well known in England, France, and Italy, and were archrogues in the various associations of beggars and vagabonds." In his monumental work *London Labour and the London Poor*, the Victorian journalist Henry Mayhew describes how such education worked: "Many . . . ragged urchins are taught to steal by their companions, others are taught by trainers of thieves, young men and women, and some middle-aged convicted thieves. They are learned to be expert in this way. A coat is suspended on the wall with a bell attached to it, and the boy attempts to take the handkerchief from the pocket without the bell ringing. Until he is able to do this with proficiency he is not considered well trained."

† A pickpocket. The term is a truncation of "knuckle."

chipper youngster, wanted to learn the trade. The lady, who is alleged to be the greatest "fence" in the city, eyed the lad for a moment. Having decided what action to take, she told the applicant to call again in the afternoon and she would see what she could do for him. . . .

In the mean time Mother Mandelbaum sent word to Captain Leary at the Thirteenth Precinct Station-house. . . . The Captain . . . called in person at Mrs. Mandelbaum's. The lad was there already, but no sooner did he espy the police officer than he rushed out of the store and fled down Rivington Street.

The Captain followed in hot pursuit. . . . The boy was caught. . . . He took the youth with the strange desire before Judge Patterson at the Essex Market Court. . . .

"Now, what is your real name?" asked the Court.

"Louis Gabriel," the youth answered. . . .

[The] Court Clerk . . . got up from his desk and, peering over his eye-glasses, took a good look at the young fellow. . . .

"I know him," said the Clerk. "That boy is the son of Patrolman Charles Gabriel, who is attached to the Steamboat Squad." . . .

The boy [on being discharged from court] went at once.

"There will be a warm meeting between him and the old man when they meet," said Leary. . . .

No reports are attainable in regard to the matinee between the patrolman and his young hopeful.

IN 1864, WHEN MARM opened her shop, the climate for criminal receivers was more hospitable than it had ever been. Three things made it so: First, as she was well aware, the status of fencing in American criminal law was refreshingly ill defined. At the time, fencing had scant legal status independent of the theft itself. In order to prosecute a fence, a district attorney would have to prove not only that the fence had received stolen goods, but also that he had *known* those goods to be stolen. "Since the parties to such a transaction are usually only thief and the fence," a modern criminologist observes, "it is hard to get testimony against the fence which would convict him; merely receiving the property without guilty knowledge is not sufficient." It would be no small trick, Fredericka knew, for the authorities to prove that a well-dressed, convivial, synagogue-going mother of four had possessed such knowledge, even once.

Second, the city's police force was in a state of sustained chaos. Barely five years old when Mrs. Mandelbaum landed in America, it had continued to operate in a maelstrom of lassitude, befuddlement and corruption. It was also roiled by power struggles within the department—or, more precisely, between the two separate police departments that battled for control of the city in the mid-1800s.

In colonial times and for years afterward, Americans had resisted the idea of official police forces: Anything even vaguely resembling a professional militia was inimical to the republican ideals of the emerging nation. But by the mid-nineteenth century, with urban crime on the rise, the new bourgeoisie began to accept the prospect of a police force as a necessary evil. In 1844, the New York State legislature passed a law authorizing the creation of such a force in New York City; that body, the Municipal Police Force, was established the next year.

Much as in London, the new force replaced a haphazard array of constables, marshals and night watchmen that had existed for generations. Those early enforcers had been unsalaried, and were barely committed to their work. "These men were objects of ridicule," a historian writes, "seen as drunken, lazy, good-for-nothings, who would sooner run away than deal with any real problems." Like their London counterparts, they were readily corruptible, often working in concert with thieves to extract rewards from the owners of stolen property in exchange for its safe return—a fleet of American Jonathan Wilds.

The city's new Municipal force wasn't much better. There were few actual requirements for the job: Policemen were appointed for one-year terms, with the appointments controlled by machine politicians in each ward. Nor did the early recruits get any training. In 1848, when the police department issued its first full rulebook, "it was received with amazement and alarm by the men," a scholar writes. "Reading about regulations might cause consternation; actually obeying orders could occasion outright resistance, even in trivial matters." When a formal training program finally was instituted, in 1853, it consisted of little more than military drills and instruction in riot control. There was also the requirement—new that year—that a recruit be able to read, but the official test demanded only that the applicant read the name of a newspaper off its front page.

In establishing the force, the state legislature had abolished some eighteen hundred civil-service posts in the city, including "inspectors of hacks and stages, inspectors of pawnbrokers, and health wardens." Their duties were transferred to the new policemen, who "were also used . . . as ringers of the fire alarm bells." These tasks aside, policemen had little idea of what their responsibilities actually were. To make matters worse, there were neither physical nor age requirements for the job at first, allowing elderly and feeble men to join the force.

In terms of sheer numbers, the police force—comprising eight hundred men in 1845 and just under twelve hundred ten years later—was ill equipped to deal with New York's rapid growth. The city's population, about 300,000 in 1844, nearly tripled over the next two decades, reaching almost 900,000 in 1865.* As a result, a de facto triage, shaped largely by the dictates of the city's bourgeoisie, determined the types of offenses the police chose to pursue. The vast majority of arrests at midcentury were for what would today be called "quality of life" crimes, chiefly vagrancy and public drunkenness. " 'Assault, Battery,' 'Petit Larceny,' 'Violating Corporation Ordinances,' 'Exposure of Person,' 'Keeping Disorderly Houses,' and 'Malicious Mischief' accounted for smaller numbers of arrests."

---

* At midcentury, London had more than twice as many policemen per capita than New York did.

The ethnic gangs were left largely to police themselves through internecine violence, provided they confined their activities to their own neighborhoods and did not venture onto middle-class turf. They also enjoyed the tacit protection of city politicians in exchange for their help in corralling the vote—and, by extension, of the police, who were effectively an arm of Tammany Hall. As for the thieves, the Municipal Police continued the tradition of their corruptible forebears, colluding with robbers—sometimes even before a robbery was committed—to split the owner's reward.

Things took a bizarre turn in 1857, when the city suddenly found itself in possession of two police departments. That year, a Republican-dominated state legislature was seated in Albany, and it took aim at the city's powerful mayor, Fernando Wood, a Democrat and Tammany Hall stalwart: "The Republicans believed that the Wood machine was based on the mayor's control over the Municipal police and decided to break that power," a historian writes. In April 1857, Albany abolished the Municipal force and created in its place a new, state-controlled Metropolitan Police, which would oversee New York City, Brooklyn, Staten Island and Westchester County.

Mayor Wood refused to acknowledge the new force, and for the next several months, the Municipals and the Metropolitans waged a "battle of the bulls," duking it out over control of city station houses: At times, suspects arrested by the Municipals would be let go by the Metropolitans, and vice versa. The Metropolitan Police took full control of the city in July 1857, a position they would hold for the next thirteen years.* But as Mrs. Mandelbaum well knew, the Metropolitans wielded little influence in Kleindeutschland and the city's other ethnic neighborhoods, all loyal Tammany strongholds.

There was a third factor that made 1864 a heady time to be a fence: The nation was in the midst of a civil war, and "a state of war is a school of violence and crime," as a Metropolitan Police report observed that year. It was a rapacious era, spawning profiteers of every kind in both the upper world and underworld. As the coun-

---

* In 1870, the legislature returned control of the city to the Municipal Police.

The Municipals and the Metropolitans duke it out amid the "Battle of the Bulls" of 1857.

try's premier center of manufacturing and commerce, New York was well positioned to meet the Union Army's unremitting need for clothing, boots, arms, horses, ships and more. The federal money that poured into the city to assist this effort "triggered a wild scramble for wealth and a pandemic of corruption."*

Upper-world profiteers included a class of merchants that came to be known as the "shoddy aristocracy" for the substandard goods they palmed off on the troops. Among the most egregious offenders was Brooks Brothers, the high-toned haberdasher founded in the city in 1818. In the spring of 1861, the assistant quartermaster of the New York State Militia, Chester Alan Arthur,† awarded Brooks Brothers a contract to make uniforms for the Union Army.‡ To turn out the new

---

* During a single week in 1861 alone, the federal government channeled nearly $3 million—the equivalent of nearly $99 million today—into New York City.

† Arthur, who became quartermaster general of the state militia in 1862, would be elected vice president of the United States in 1880. He became the nation's twenty-first president on the assassination of James A. Garfield the next year.

‡ The Brooks Brothers contract was additionally approved by a New York State clothing inspector named George Opdyke. A clothing manufacturer himself, Opdyke

uniforms quickly and cheaply, the company eschewed fine fabric in favor of cloth woven from "shoddy"—a recycled yarn that is little more than a loose amalgam of shredded rags. The uniforms soon fell apart, ushering "shoddy" into common parlance as an adjective.

There was profit to be made in the underworld, too, with ample opportunities for thieves to plunder the newly rich, and for fences to deal in black-market goods, otherwise needed for the war effort, that the general public longed to buy. "Robbery, burglary and larceny are pursued by a large class of remarkably acute persons," the 1864 Metropolitan Police report declared. "It is vain to expect to wholly suppress or seriously diminish the extent of these offences so long as these operations are safe and profitable. . . . *Robberies and larcenies would be hazardous and unprofitable if there did not exist safe facilities for converting plundered property into money. They are furnished by pawnbrokers and receivers of stolen goods.*" It was in this exceptionally lucrative environment that Fredericka continued to build her empire.

TO THE END OF HER CAREER, Mrs. Mandelbaum would continue to fence almost anything, "from silks to securities": A nineteenth-century newspaper article describes her as once having resold fifty thousand stolen cigars. But one of her earliest tasks as an entrepreneur was to select a product line in which to specialize, and she chose diamonds. It was an inspired decision—or, far more likely, a carefully considered one. Diamonds are spectacularly good business for a fence: They're highly portable and have immense value in proportion to their weight. Once parted from their settings, they can rarely be identified by anyone except the man who cut them.

---

would profit handsomely later in 1861, after winning a contract to supply 4,884 blankets to the military. In 1862, he became New York City's seventy-sixth mayor, succeeding Fernando Wood. As mayor, Opdyke, who also owned a gun factory, produced more than a thousand carbines for the army at twenty-five dollars apiece, "a price that by one estimate was $10"—nearly $300 in today's money—"above the cost of manufacturing each weapon."

Even in the favorable climate of the 1860s, Marm was prudent enough to start small: She exhorted her early thieves to go after little things, in particular diamond stickpins. The pins were in fashion and thus widely accessible; they could be tenderly extracted from a cravat or lapel with the wearer none the wiser. Once the thieves brought the swag to her shop, it passed through the next link in the supply chain: effacement. In one of her grille-protected back rooms, stones were divorced from their original settings and engravings eradicated. Now unidentifiable, the items were sold on to waiting customers.

Mrs. Mandelbaum's customers came in two varieties: witting and un-. Some, who wandered into her haberdashery shop from the street, bought the fabric, ribbons, lace and trinkets on offer there in all innocence, though they must surely have marveled at the deep discounts. Others, including the middle-class housewives and small merchants who furtively sought her out, knew exactly what they were getting. The economics of a transaction worked as follows: On receiving stolen merchandise, Marm typically paid the thief 10 to 25 percent of its wholesale price. She then charged the buyer half to two-thirds of wholesale, allowing both her and the client to exit the deal satisfied.

But over time, Marm realized that there was no great fortune in small stuff. Petty shoplifting was proving inadequate to her needs, and stickpins turned out to have their drawbacks: What glitters alluringly in a lapel may on later inspection prove no more than glass. "While pickpockets are 'pickers,' they cannot always be choosers," her protégée Sophie Lyons explained. "The percentage of diamonds remained disappointingly low." Fredericka responded accordingly, resolving to expand her trade from picking pockets to planning robberies.

SOON AFTERWARD, FREDERICKA MANDELBAUM paid several visits to Tiffany & Company, then at 550 Broadway, between Spring and Prince streets.* She asked to be shown their arrays of loose diamonds, though each time she bought nothing. She was window shopping, although it was a far different kind of window shopping from what you or I would do: She was getting a sense of the inventory, and the lay of the land inside the store. A customer as expensively dressed as she would have aroused no suspicion; nor was she yet so notorious a figure that clerks would have recognized her.

Once she'd conceived a plan, Mrs. Mandelbaum assembled her team, meeting quietly with them in the secret back rooms of her shop. For his dapper, gentlemanly appearance, she'd selected a confidence man known as "Swell" Robinson; for her fleet fingers, she chose a shoplifter named Mary Wallenstein.

On the appointed day, Robinson entered Tiffany's alone. Approaching the diamond counter, he asked to see one large stone after another. After some time, he declared that he couldn't decide which one to buy. He'd give the matter some thought, he said, and would return later. As the clerk returned the diamonds to their case, he noticed one was missing. Robinson was asked if he would consent to being searched. Incensed at the implication, he nonetheless agreed. No stone materialized, and he was allowed to leave.

Moments later, Mary Wallenstein entered and walked to the diamond counter. She asked to see a series of small stones but, like Robinson, couldn't settle on one. She, too, told the clerk that she would return, and promptly left the store. "There was no objection made, for there was nothing missing this time," a chronicler recounted. An hour later, Wallenstein presented Mrs. Mandelbaum with a single large diamond, worth $8,000.†

Marm's scheme had worked brilliantly. Robinson had entered Tiffany's with a discreet wad of chewing gum concealed in his mouth. At the diamond counter, he deftly secreted the gum beneath

---

* Founded in 1837, the store occupied various addresses in Manhattan over the years—from Lower Broadway to Union Square to Fifth Avenue and Thirty-seventh Street—before moving to its present location, Fifth Avenue and Fifty-seventh Street, in 1940.

† About $150,000 in today's money.

the countertop. Then, when the clerk's back was turned, he palmed a large diamond and pressed it into the gum. Later, Wallenstein, standing precisely where he'd stood, felt beneath the counter, plucked out the stone and spirited it from the store. That first robbery "was so delightfully successful that the pickpocket industry seemed slow by comparison," Sophie Lyons said.

The gum trick proved to be short lived, however, for the otherwise adroit Wallenstein had made a single mistake: When removing the diamond from underneath the counter, she did not also take the chewing gum. The next morning, a Tiffany's employee, polishing that counter, came upon the gum. It bore the clear imprint of the facets of a large diamond. The store alerted the jewelers' association, which apprised its members of the scheme. But never mind: There were many other strategies for high-end larceny, and they would one day be set out in a remarkable instruction manual.

THOUGH THE MANUAL WOULD NOT be formally published until 1886, the advice it contained had been circulating in underworld oral tradition for generations: From very early on, Marm's disciples used many of the techniques it described. Entitled *Danger!** the book ostensibly warned visitors to New York about the perils of the city.

"The revelations of the newspapers, from week to week, but too plainly indicate an undercurrent of vice and iniquity, whose depth and foulness defy all computation," the preface gallantly declares. "By hoisting the Danger signal at the mast-head, as it were, we have attempted to warn young men and young women—the future fathers and mothers of America—against the snares and pitfalls of the crime and the vice that await the unwary in New York. . . . In the earnest hope that, by its influence, some few may be saved from prison, penitentiary, lunatic asylum, or suicides' purgatory, [this book] is now submitted to the intelligent readers of America."

* Titled *In Danger!* in some editions.

On its face, *Danger!* was simply the newest of the spate of late-nineteenth-century guidebooks that alerted visitors to the city's myriad traps. (At once "moralistic and titillating," they bore titles like *The Nether Side of New York* and *Lights and Shadows of New York Life.*) The volume's actual function was to serve as a how-to manual for crooks who wanted to improve their paydays—"a kind of Real Estate Board brochure apprising out-of-town criminals of the superior facilities offered by New York," as a later commentator observed. A seductive passage near the start makes this plain:

> New York, from being the largest city [in] the western hemi-sphere; in almost hourly communication with every part of the known world; the vast wealth of its merchants; elegant storehouses crowded with the choicest and most costly goods, manufactured fabrics, and every kind of valuable represent-ing money; with its great banks, whose vaults and safes con-tain more bullion than could be transported by the largest ship afloat; its colossal establishments teeming with dia-monds, jewelry and precious stones gathered from all parts of the known and uncivilized portions of the globe; with all this countless wealth, these boundless riches, in some cases inse-curely guarded, in all temptingly displayed, is it any wonder, then, that this city should always have proved the paradise of thieves?

Danger! goes on to furnish two hundred pages' worth of "warnings"—in reality thinly veiled, step-by-step instructions on topics of pressing interest to the underworld: Chapters include "Shop-Lifters—Who They Are and How They Are Made," "Black-Mail," "Quacks and Quackery" and "Gambling Made Easy." A chapter called "Street Arabs of Both Sexes" was a primer for Amer-ican Oliver Twists who aspired to work New York's waterfront:

> Ships are unloading cargoes of assorted merchandise, which is being placed upon the dock. Bags of coffee are in one place,

chests of tea in another, hogsheads of molasses and sugar, and various other kinds of goods are distributed all over the place. Some boys are playing "tag," and they run around and over the bags of coffee, behind the hogsheads of sugar, ostensibly in play, but all the while keeping a sharp eye on the watch-men, police and people employed there. A favorable chance occurring, a boy drops behind one of the bags of coffee and quickly and expeditiously rips it open with a sharp knife and bounds away.... The bung of a molasses barrel is burst in, a stick inserted, which, when pulled out, has some of the con-tents thickly adhering to it. Thus much accomplished, every boy provides himself with an old tomato or other can, and it would surprise anyone not familiar with these things, to see how rapidly and ingeniously these dock rats will fill those cans to overflowing with all kinds of goods.

The book's crown jewel is the chapter on shoplifting, whose ad-vice (explaining how to pull off large, premeditated hauls from the city's upscale shops) was already being used profitably by Marm's acolytes. What had made these techniques possible was the birth of the mercantile pleasure palaces that would later be called depart-ment stores.* Though the stores would not come into their full glory until the 1880s and '90s, they had begun to blossom in major Amer-ican cities at midcentury: In New York alone, R. H. Macy & Com-pany was founded in 1858, Bloomingdale's in 1861, and B. Altman & Company in 1865. Brooklyn, then a separate city, was home to Abra-ham & Straus, also established in 1865.

---

* Though such stores were already fixtures of large American cities at midcentury, the term "department store" would not be coined until 1876, when it was used by John Wanamaker to describe the Philadelphia emporium, opened that year, that bore his name. "A converted Pennsylvania Railroad station, occupying a full city block at Thirteenth and Market Streets at the center of the city, it dazzled with color and bustle," a twenty-first-century chronicler has written. "Lit by the stained glass ceiling in daylight and by hundreds of gas lights at night, the counters were arranged in con-centric circles, as much as two-thirds of a mile long, with 1,100 counter stools, so a lady could sit and discuss her purchase. And, indeed, the seventy thousand people who showed up on opening day were mostly women, as Wanamaker intended."

The grandest of the New York stores was indisputably A. T.
Stewart, a sprawling Italianate "marble palace" at 280 Broadway, in
Lower Manhattan. Opened in 1846 and spanning four stories, it had
grown within its first five years to fill five stories and an entire city
block. Inside was a profusion of ornate columns, frescoes, a great
domed rotunda and balconies that let shoppers gaze acquisitively
down on the bounty below.

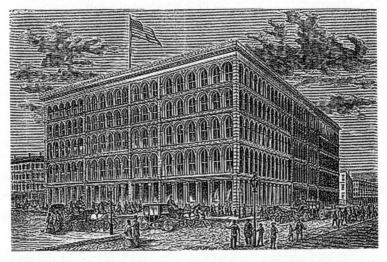

A. T. Stewart's vast, seductive department store opened on Broadway in 1846.

Emporiums like these were gradually replacing the unassuming
dry-goods stores and street vendors' pushcarts that had served shoppers for generations. "Traditional dry-goods store interiors had been
less than inviting," a historian of consumer culture notes. "Descriptions refer to them as uniformly small, gloomy, dusty, and cramped;
many stores appeared rather dilapidated. Counters were of solid wood
with enclosed shelving. Notions and the few ready-made goods remained hidden in boxes. . . . A customer had to know what she wanted
and ask for it. Other than some stiffly draped fabric, very little was
openly displayed, and there was almost no attempt to create demand."
    The aim of the department store, by contrast, was to foment de-
sire. The new stores were open, airy and well lighted. Interiors were

a voluptuous celebration of consumer culture, with a profusion of luxury goods on view. Significantly, though, the move toward light, bright display did not yet include the countertops: Department stores would not begin the transition to glass counters and display cases until the late 1880s. While these new fixtures would allow expensive items to be prominently displayed yet safely inaccessible, at midcentury the old wooden counters remained the status quo.

As a result, the welter of fine goods that had been strategically arranged to seduce consumers—kid gloves, silk scarves, cashmere shawls, perfume in elegant bottles—lay fanned out *atop* the counters. And if this exquisite combination of desirability and accessibility enticed the consumer, it also greatly abetted the work of the shoplifter. *Danger!* told her precisely how that work should be accomplished.

A larcenous woman's first order of business, the book explains, was to dress for the part. Women's apparel of the period already furnished voluminous hiding places in the form of long, wide skirts, but as *Danger!* discloses, there was more sartorial preparation to be done. Before she left for a job, the text continues, the shoplifter should attire herself in this manner: She starts by donning a specially constructed corset, "with broad, strong bands which pass over the shoulders." Suspended from the corset is a sturdy cloth bag, which hangs between the wearer's legs and is entirely concealed by her skirt. In that skirt, hidden among its folds, is a long vertical slit that gives discreet access to the bag. "Upon selecting a store that suits her, she walks boldly in, going at once, and without noticeable hesitation, to the lace or other department, before the counter of which she seats herself, adroitly arranging her dress and the slit," the instructions advise:

Asking the saleswoman to be shown some [kind] of lace, she examines it critically, and, laying it down upon the counter, asks to see another kind, or some feathers, or something else, and so contrives to have several articles just before her, one covering the other, if possible. Having accumulated a number of articles upon the counter in an eligible position, she points to some things high up on a shelf behind the counter, thus getting the saleswoman's back turned towards her for an instant, when, with soft dexterity, she conveys anything that happens to be handily in the way through the slit in her dress into the bag between her legs. The goods examined and priced, "not suiting" her, and other customers coming up, she takes the opportunity of moving to another counter, where the same tactics are repeated, and so on, till she is satisfied with her haul or [has] exhausted her stowage capacity.

For the small, tantalizing items arrayed on the countertop, the well-dressed shoplifter had another weapon at her disposal: the retrofitted muff. Outwardly, it resembled any other muff of the period: compact, cylindrical and covered in elegant fur. But its inner architecture had been carefully contrived. Surrounding the space where the woman's hands went was a sturdy cylinder of wire mesh. Between this cylinder and the outer fur covering, there would normally have been cotton wadding, which helped the muff hold its shape. In a shoplifter's muff, as *Danger!* explained, that wadding was removed, leaving only empty space. "In the bottom of the muff there is a small slide, on the inside, worked by the hand of the wearer, who, after introducing the stolen article into the muff, presses back this slide and drops the plunder into the cavity between the frame and the fur."

A visitor unacquainted with Gotham's depravity would be *shocked*, the book continued, by the volume of purloined goods that a muff or bag could accommodate:

> At police headquarters, once, in examining the contents of one of these bags, it was found to actually hold a piece of satin, several cards of lace, a camel's-hair shawl, two large china ornaments, a number of spools of silk, several elegant fans, expensive ostrich plumes, and numberless smaller articles, feathers, artificial flowers and some minor trinkets.

Shop-lifters are the terror of the shop-keepers, for the thefts embrace everything of convenient character lying about. With one dexterous sweep they will frequently put out of sight a dozen small articles.

A shoplifter takes full advantage of her capacious skirt.

Danger! also took care to outfit the male shoplifter: Among his chief weapons was an impeccable leather valise with a built-in secret panel that opened silently. Nor did the book neglect the jewel thief. Working with a confederate—and a discreet piece of string— the thief was to enter a jewelry store holding one end of the string. His partner, "window shopping" on the sidewalk outside, held the other. Inside, the first man would ask the clerk to show him a selection of diamond rings. "While pretending to examine them with severe criticism, and keeping the salesman engaged, he cleverly attached one end of the string . . . to several of the most valuable, and quietly dropped them at his feet. His 'pal' then quietly pulled them along the floor, out through the door, into the street and decamped. A search of the thief who remained behind disclosed nothing and, as proof was thus wanting, he had to be discharged."

But for all the astounding advice in the pages of *Danger!*, the most astounding thing about the volume is its authorship. It was written by William Howe and Abraham Hummel, Mrs. Mandelbaum's longtime attorneys and criminal lawyers in every sense of the phrase. For decades, Howe & Hummel would go to lavish extremes in defense of Marm and her foot soldiers. And afterward, when even they could do no more for her, the firm would help stage the most vital caper of her career: an eleventh-hour act of self-preservation, coordinated with military precision. But all this lay far in the future in the mid-1860s, as Fredericka Mandelbaum continued her rise, transforming herself into a large-scale receiver of stolen luxury goods, an orchestrator of theft-to-order and, before long, an impresario of bank robberies.

BOOK TWO

Hubris

Chapter Four

Home Improvements

THE FRUITS OF MARM'S SHOPLIFTING ENTERPRISE WERE STREAMING
in: kid gloves and lace scarves; handkerchiefs of silk and fine linen;
cashmere shawls and sealskin bags; stickpins and brooches and diamonds and pearls. "She would buy the whole 'swag' of a burglar,"
Robert Pinkerton, a son of the detective agency's founder, told the
New York Times. "She sold to dealers and dressmakers in Trenton,
Albany, Buffalo, Cincinnati—she had agents everywhere."

Fredericka knew the wholesale value of every article brought
into the shop, and she held a firm line on the prices she offered her
thieves. This encouraged crooks to do business with her, as they
knew what to expect. "She was scheming . . . as the day is long,"
recalled "Banjo Pete" Emerson, an actor and musician turned robber. "But she could be like an angel to the worst devil so long as he
played square with her." For a sealskin bag that wholesaled for $300,
for instance, she would give a thief $70; for a cashmere shawl, she
paid $100. (The shawls, among the most coveted luxury items of the
era, could wholesale for $1,000 each.)*

---

* Some $20,000 in today's money. Authentic cashmere shawls, imported from India
and woven from the soft, fine-spun undercoat of the cashmere goat, were then retailing for astronomical sums in American stores. An 1865 article in the *New-York Times*
about Christmas shopping reported that "at Messrs. A.T. Stewart & Co.'s up-town
marble palace, Broadway and Tenth-street, we find . . . a $2,500 cashmere shawl"—
a price equivalent to nearly $45,000 today.

"Mandelbaum gained respect as someone who drove a hard bargain, generally considered okay for men and unfeminine for women in legitimate business," Rona Holub has observed. "[She] gained accolades both for her 'motherliness' and her business skills and, ironically, her honesty in a crooked business, a combination of praise that women in legitimate business could never expect or receive."

With so much merchandise coming in, Fredericka needed storage space. When she first rented the shop at the corner of Clinton and Rivington in 1864, she and her family lived next door, on the Clinton Street side. She would eventually buy the whole building and would also own warehouses in Manhattan; Brooklyn; Hoboken; Passaic, New Jersey; and elsewhere.* But until she could afford all that real estate, Mother Mandelbaum served as an enterprising angel of Kleindeutschland: She paid the monthly rental on a string of local apartments, allowing the families who lived there to remain, rent free, in exchange for the use of a room or two.

Many of those apartments were occupied by women whose husbands were doing a stretch behind bars, so the rent relief was especially welcome. Strikingly, though, Fredericka, who had worked all her life, offered them no further means of support. As the *New-York Times* reported: "Mrs. Mandelbaum invariably refused to give money to wives of thieves unluckily caught and sent to prison, telling them to go to work if they wanted money."

Fredericka would purchase her entire building (actually conjoined buildings encompassing 79 Clinton and 163 Rivington streets) in 1873. At the time, her declared net worth was $5,000;† over the next twenty years, her personal fortune would increase at least a hundredfold. But she had clearly begun renovating the property long before she bought it—for very particular professional reasons.

---

* Holub writes: "She also held property in Albany, New York . . . that she acquired when a thief for whom she provided bail did not show up for trial."

† Roughly $120,000 today.

"Mrs. Mandelbaum was very suspicious," the *New-York Times* would report in 1884. "No one could stand on the street near her home without being spotted and followed until his personality was determined. At her front door a watch was always kept. Thieves walked by this to a side door which was opened without a knock being required—if the thieves were known. Another entrance was through a saloon on Rivington-street to a yard, from which access was gained to the yard in the rear of Mrs. Mandelbaum's house. . . . Through the rear way the cautious ones entered with plunder, which was never taken openly into the house from the front."

The interior was even more carefully conceived. As soon as she took occupancy, Marm began making alterations unlike any a conventional shopkeeper would undertake, transforming the space into what the *Times* would call "the most notorious depot for the reception of stolen goods on this continent."

Security was paramount. With so many fine goods on hand, she was vulnerable not only to police raids but also to pillage by other criminals, even those in her own organization. If she had ever believed there was honor among thieves, she was shrewd enough to hedge her bet. "Every member of the underworld knew that stolen goods of great value were constantly coming into her resort," her protégée Sophie Lyons recalled. "From time to time schemes were devised to plunder the famous old 'fence.' "

Walled off from the public haberdashery shop was a warren of private back rooms, which could be entered from the salesroom only via a heavy oak door, kept securely bolted on the far side. Also set into the dividing wall was a small arched window, overlaid with heavy steel bars. On the other side of the window was a clandestine parlor, and there Mrs. Mandelbaum sat, day in and day out, zealously watching the goings-on in the shop. " 'Mother' Mandelbaum was never seen in the front room . . . where a clerk was always kept on guard," Lyons wrote. "But, realizing that thieves might at any moment raid her establishment and finally force their way into her den, she provided still another safeguard."

That safeguard—the pièce de résistance of Marm's bespoke security system—was a trick chimney in the parlor fireplace. To all appearances an ordinary chimney, it had been equipped with a false back. Inside the back was a dumbwaiter that communicated with the floor above. If Marm, peering through the bars, saw a suspicious character enter the shop, she could make whatever swag she had on hand vanish in an instant. With the pull of a hidden lever, she would lower the dumbwaiter, stow her cache and hoist it safely out of sight.

A vigilant Marm Mandelbaum monitors the shop from her clandestine parlor. Her trick chimney, with concealed dumbwaiter, is at right.

Opening off the parlor were more secret chambers. As converted by Marm, they formed the infrastructure of an efficient mail-order fulfillment house. One room was a bulk storage area, where stolen merchandise could repose in safety until "the heat was off." Another housed the shipping department, where employees packed crates and barrels with luxury goods destined for customers around the country. A third room, furnished with beds, was a dormitory for out-of-town thieves. "At the end of the passageway leading to one of the rooms was a secret trap door," Lyons recalled. "In case of a raid by the police, and if her front and back doors were guarded by detectives, she could use the trap door to let thieves escape down through a hole in the basement wall which led up into the house next door, which 'Mother' Mandelbaum also owned under another name."

Another back room served as a combination boardroom, in which Fredericka and her employees plotted increasingly lucrative thefts, and hiring hall, where hopeful burglars gathered to await assignments. "Many able and successful burglars are unimaginative, and, left to their own devices, would never discover anything to rob," Lyons said. "These earnest but unimaginative souls hung about the premises as if it were an employment agency waiting for the 'boss' to find a job suited to their particular talents."

The most vital of Marm's secret spaces was the chamber in which a handpicked team of immigrant German artisans worked to efface identifying marks from jewelry and silver. "Suppose you are a burglar and last-night's labors resulted mostly in jewelry and silverware, you would have neither the time nor the plant to melt down the silver and disguise or unset the stones," Lyons explained. " 'Mother' Mandelbaum would attend to all that for you on about a 75 per cent commission.... What would you do with a stolen watch which bore, deeply engraved on the back, the name and address of its rightful owner? You might melt down the case and get a little something for the works, but 'Mother' would do better. She would turn it over to one of her engravers who would rapidly and not inartistically engrave a little scene or decoration on the watch case, completely masking the name and address."*

With her interior renovations complete, Marm could handle much bigger swag than scarves and stickpins. She turned an acquisitive eye toward silk—silk in immense, expensive bolts.

---

* Such practices serve fences well to this day. Two twenty-first-century scholars quote a longtime professional receiver: "Some merchandise I would alter.... Take antiques that come out of private homes or from a dealer whose shop has been clipped. If I was leery, I would 'doctor' them. Maybe break off a leg, or upholster part of a chair. Take the stain off and refinish it. On the wicker, I would usually repaint it. Put doubt in the person's mind that this piece was theirs, and it had been stolen from them."

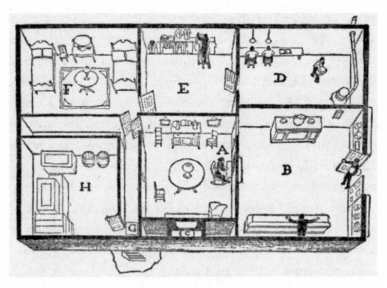

Bird's-eye view of Mrs. Mandelbaum's shop, with its warren of secret rooms. **A:** Marm's hidden parlor, protected by metal bars and a heavy oak door; **B:** The public salesroom; **C:** Trick chimney; **D:** Effacement chamber; **E:** Bulk-storage room; **F:** Thieves' dormitory; **G:** Trap door to basement; **H:** Shipping department.

By the 1860s, 80 percent of U.S. textile imports were entering the country through New York, and the city had become the nation's garment-making center. In this congenial climate, thieves and receivers of luxury fabrics could thrive. Silk was excellent business, Marm knew: Like diamonds, it had great value relative to weight. In an era when women either made their own clothes or had them made by a dressmaker, fine-quality silk at bargain prices was in wide demand.* And since one bolt of fabric looks exactly like another bolt of the same fabric, stolen silk was largely untraceable.

But to go after serious silk—not mere department-store handkerchiefs, but big bolts in quantity—Marm could not enlist her cadre of women: A bolt (comprising 40 or more yards of fabric wrapped around a stiff cardboard core) was generally too unwieldy

---

* Ready-to-wear skirts and shirtwaists would not become widely available in American shops until the last decade of the nineteenth century; ready-to-wear dresses only after World War I.

to sweep off a countertop and stash beneath a skirt. What she had to do now was expand her business from genteel daytime shoplifting to large-scale, after-hours burglary. And for that, she would need a cadre of men.

JUST AS UPPER-WORLD PROFESSIONS have long been stratified along lines of class and gender—a financier is said to trump a doctor, who trumps a longshoreman, and all three trump a laundress—so, too, were those of the underworld. Among American crooks, it was a given that the lowest rung of their profession was inhabited by pickpockets, whose quarry was considered trifling and whose ranks included many women. Just above the pickpockets were the shoplifters—almost all women. Above the shoplifters came "shake-down workers" and hotel burglars; above them were muggers, stickup men and petty store burglars. Above this group were the house burglars, or "sneak thieves," and high-end store burglars; above them, forgers and counterfeiters.*

The topmost echelon—"the aristocrats of the underworld," Sophie Lyons called them—were the bank burglars. A nineteenth-century British newspaper would laud them as "the High Mob, the Gentlemen Joes of the trade, who scorn small affairs, and who are regarded in the highest reverence by the smaller practitioners in private plunder. They keep step with science, and they have every new invention at their command. . . . With what contemptuous amusement must the masters of this great mystery watch the ordinary [man] fastening up for the night! His bolts of iron, his rusty

---

* Similar class distinctions had existed for centuries among British criminals. "Already within the Elizabethan underworld, status levels among thieves were apparent," two modern-day criminologists write. "Rogues and sharpers, followed by curbers or housebreakers, were ranked the highest. Pickpockets and shoplifters were ranked somewhat lower, and extortion by prostitutes ranked at the bottom of status level. Status levels also existed within criminal specialties. Among pickpockets, for example, the 'foist' commanded greater prestige than the 'nip,' and city nips were considered more skilled than country nips." (A sharper was a swindler; a curber extracted booty through a window by means of a long-handled hook known as a "curb." A foist picked pockets skillfully by hand; a nip was a crude cutpurse.)

chain, and his cumbrous slip lock for the front door, in their experienced eyes, belong to the very infancy of precaution."

It was to these upper-level masters of covert entry—already
hard at work plundering the stately homes and fancy shops of
America—that Fredericka turned. Foremost among them were
George Leonidas Leslie; "Banjo Pete" Emerson; "Piano Charley"
Bullard; Sophie's husband, Ned Lyons; Adam Worth; and Mark
Shinburn, once a safe-company employee and now a safecracker.
Others she conscripted, as the police chief George Washington
Walling noted, included "the champion burglar of America, Mi-
chael Kurtz, alias 'Sheeney Mike'; 'Shang' Draper, 'Red' Leary,
'Jimmy' Hope, 'Ed' Goodie . . . and a host of smaller fry."

Mark Shinburn   "Banjo Pete" Emerson

With this phalanx at her command, Marm could start to plot
complex burglaries in advance. All around her, docks and warehouses and textile emporiums brimming with silk were beckoning.
Training her sights on their glistening hoard, she worked out a
modus operandi for stealing large bolts in relative safety. " 'Marm'
Mandelbaum's methods grew bolder as her reputation increased,"
Walling explained. "The majority of her transactions were conducted by correspondence, or through messengers. . . . Suppose, for

instance, there had been a robbery of silk in the city. The 'swag' would be first 'planted' (stored). A messenger would call on her, and she would send a trusted agent to examine the goods thoroughly and report to her. She would estimate their value, . . . make an offer, . . . pay cash for the 'stuff,' take the risk of shipping it or secreting it elsewhere, and afterwards make arrangements for its disposal at a profit."

Mrs. Mandelbaum took great care not to have stolen goods dispatched directly to her shop. Once she'd agreed to purchase them, they'd be transported to one or more of the properties she leased covertly in and around the city. "Her custom to rent an obscure flat or a small house out of town," a *New York Star* article explained, "caused the goods to pass through several hands before they reached her store and made it almost impossible to trace them."

In 1876, for instance, two of Marm's foot soldiers, Johnny Irving and Billy Valte, robbed the Manhattan dry-goods firm H. B. Claflin & Company of $30,000* worth of silk on her orders. The loot was first secreted in a Lower Manhattan stable. After Marm concluded the deal, it was ferried across the Hudson, where it was stored in a house in the Hackensack Meadowlands. From there, it "was carted piecemeal to a dozen places before it arrived in Clinton street."

Before Fredericka would accept cloth of any kind, all identifying marks had to be sought and removed. Because one length of fabric is normally indistinguishable from another, manufacturers and retailers wanting to prove ownership had to resort to careful subterfuge to mark their wares. Labels could be attached, of course, but they were easy to spot. More subtle methods might include stamping tiny letters or numbers at regular intervals along the fabric edge, or weaving a barely discernible pattern into the edge itself. It was up to the thief to find all such marks and cut them away, an operation that entailed unwinding the entire bolt and examining every inch. "With silk," Robert Pinkerton said, "she was very particular that all marks be removed before it was offered to her. She warned

---

*   More than $800,000 in today's money.

a thief if the marks were left. If left a second time she never dealt with him again."

Mrs. Mandelbaum typically paid a thief sixty-five cents a yard for silk that wholesaled for three dollars a yard; that the system served her well is attested by the thousands of dollars' worth of silk uncovered in the 1884 raid on her shop. Her practice of careful effacement came to her aid many times, as in 1875, when, in a rare raid on her premises, the Municipal Police confiscated a large quantity of silks and shawls. "None of the merchandise could be identified because she had removed all product marks," Rona Holub wrote. "She received the property back."

She would not always be so lucky. In the 1880s, when Mrs. Mandelbaum's fortunes had begun to turn, a single strip of silk was all it would take to bring her down.

IF THE SHIFT FROM AN AGRARIAN to a mercantile economy had been a boon to American criminals, then the Civil War–era transition from a mercantile to a financial economy was an unqualified bonanza. "The bulls toss stocks higher than ever, and the most inveterate bears have borrowed two horns and a tail, and outbully the bulls," the *New York Herald* declared in 1862. "Wall Street is an El Dorado where every man can pocket all the money he pleases." One of the primary things that had brought this El Dorado about was the wild torrent of "fiat money"—paper tender, backed not by gold or silver but simply by the government's word—that began flooding the country at the start of the Civil War.

Paper money had been used in America since colonial times, but until the 1860s its issue had been sporadic and local. In 1690, the Massachusetts Bay Colony printed notes, intended to finance a military expedition to Canada, that are believed to be the first issue of paper tender by a Western governmental body. Other American colonies began printing notes of their own; by the time of the Revolutionary War, all thirteen colonies were issuing paper money of some kind. Like those of Massachusetts, however, the notes were crude and thus easily counterfeited. So, too, was the "Continental Currency"—the first national paper money—issued by the Continental Congress during the war. As a result, all paper money was widely distrusted by the public, and before long was devalued nearly to the point of worthlessness.[*]

Mindful of this history, the framers of the Constitution empowered Congress to coin money but made no provision for printing it, and for the nation's first seven decades, gold and silver were coin of the realm. Then came the Civil War, and the Union's urgent need to raise the funds to wage it. In 1861, President Lincoln empowered the federal government to issue "Demand Notes," non-interest-bearing bills that could be exchanged on demand for gold or silver at any of seven designated banks around the country. Because of the dense geometric pattern of deep green printed on the reverse side, the notes soon came to be known as greenbacks. In 1862, needing still more money, the government made Demand Notes less readily redeemable, replacing them with "United States Notes," a new paper currency that was entirely divorced from gold and silver.[†] These notes, also called greenbacks, were legal tender for most business transactions.[‡]

"The dollar had been America's official currency for decades, but it had always been chained to precious metal," a historian has written. "By creating fiat money, backed only by the credit—and credibility—of the federal government, Lincoln made possible innovations in finance unimagined by previous generations. Some of these innovations would be felt at once, as the greenback underwrote the Union victory in the Civil War and accelerated America's industrial revolution."

But despite the government's assurance—or, more likely, because of it—the new notes were a hard sell. Many Americans bris-

---

[*]   The derisive expression "not worth a Continental" became current as a result.

[†]   Meanwhile, "the Confederate government printed reams of money that rapidly grew worthless."

[‡]   The new notes could not be used to pay import duties or interest on federal bonds.

tled at the idea that stuff as insubstantial as paper could, with a wave of the governmental wand, be endowed with the dependable materiality of gold and silver. Nevertheless, the Legal Tender Act, which created the first national paper currency, was passed by Congress on February 25, 1862, and signed into law by Lincoln.* The next year, at the urging of the treasury secretary, Salmon P. Chase, the administration authorized the creation of a constellation of national banks, spread across the Union, intended to make the new money a ubiquitous presence.

THE LEGAL TENDER ACT had authorized the government to issue $150 million in United States Notes; by the time the war was over, it had issued nearly $500 million of this paper.† The underworld snapped to attention: Counterfeiters, safecrackers and bank robbers understood immediately that from all this money, there was money to be made. "Fully recognizable professional crime came into its own after the large-scale issuance of greenbacks ... during the 1860s," a legal historian has written. "With a sizeable volume of negotiable paper in circulation, property criminals began investing time and money in sophisticated counterfeiting operations and in the robbery of banks and express companies."

Before the Civil War, safecracking and bank burglary had been relatively rare: It was impractical, unwieldy and conspicuously loud for a man to plunder a mess of gold and then go clanking down the street—to say nothing of the strain on the poor horse that had to haul the getaway carriage. Paper, by contrast, was discreet, quiet and portable, and by its very nature had huge value proportional to weight. And thanks to Chase's innovation, there were more banks in existence than ever. For Mother Mandelbaum, the way forward was clear. Daytime shoplifting and nighttime silk hauls would continue as mainstays of her business. But now the fair economic winds, to-

---

*   The United States abandoned the gold standard permanently only in 1933.

†   Equivalent to almost $9 billion today.

gether with her crew of nimble men, would let her diversify her enterprise even further: The time had come to heist a bank.

As it had with the stickpins, Fredericka's constitutional caution induced her to start small. She would make an early foray into bank burglary in the summer of 1869, serving before the fact as an angel, and after the fact—in a singular twist on a time-honored job for immigrant women—as a laundress.

Chapter Five

Ocean's Four

Early in the morning on Monday, June 28, 1869, Edward Dunn, the porter of the Ocean National Bank in Lower Manhattan, smelled smoke. It seemed to emanate from the bank president's private office, and, making his rounds before opening time, Dunn followed his nose to the source. Before long it wasn't only smoke he was smelling: It was gunpowder.

Directly off the president's office was the bank's triple-locked vault, built of immense granite blocks and lined with iron. As Dunn approached, he saw that the vault's outer door was standing open. The floor around it was a chaos of books, papers, discarded clothing, a bounty of nickels in still-smoldering cloth bags, a dark lantern,* half-eaten sandwiches, and tin safe-deposit boxes, pulled from their moorings and smashed open.

The lock on the vault's outer door appeared not to have been tampered with; likewise, that of the middle door. The inner door, a slab of solid iron an inch and a quarter thick, had been laboriously pried open by means of a hydraulic jack, "the force exerted being sufficient to depress the floor under the door perceptibly," the *New York Herald* reported the next day.

---

* A lantern with a movable panel that lets its light be hidden from view.

Behind that door was the vault's inner sanctum, and here the smell of powder was intense. The floor was another riot: tins of gunpower, fuses, bits of chipped iron, cigar stubs, more papers and coins, all dumped pell-mell together with sheaves of checks, bonds and securities. Inside the sanctum stood two massive safes, vaunted as burglarproof. One had been painstakingly drilled open. The door of the other was on the floor, blasted clean off its hinges. It was clear, as the *Herald* declared in breathless capitals, that "a MOST AUDACIOUS burglary had been committed."

Dunn alerted the authorities. Members of the Metropolitan Police arrived, and the press soon after. Outside, a crowd of panicked depositors was already forming in the street; they tried to rush the front door before police officers restrained them.* The mob's concern proved well founded: The thieves had gotten away with nearly $800,000—in some estimates, well over $1 million.† Working in secret over the weekend, they had pulled off what was then the largest bank burglary in American history. "There is no clue to the burglars," an early newspaper report announced.

As striking as what the thieves took was what they left behind. Besides the smoldering bags of small change, the checks and the securities, they had littered the vault floor with expensive jewelry, pulled from depositors' boxes and flung away, along with some $30,000 in gold coins—a sure sign that the new breed of bank burglar favored the whisper of paper over the clangor of gold and jewels.

Just as noteworthy was the welter of tools and equipment also left in the vault: "Every thing that could suggest itself to a burglar's mind as likely to be of use—even to the small detail of a bottle of machine oil—was found in the place," a newspaper report said. "The burglars were also evidently prepared for a desperate resistance in case they were surprised at their work, as among the effects left behind were two pair of steel handcuffs, several bowie knives, a

* Bank deposits were not federally insured until 1933, when, as part of the New Deal, President Franklin Delano Roosevelt signed into law the Glass-Steagall Act, familiarly known as the Banking Act.

† About $17 million to $20 million in today's money.

coil of rope to tie the person or persons entering, and a box of cartridges, showing that they also carried revolvers."

The burglars also left behind their hydraulic jack—all 125 pounds of it—plus a range of smaller jacks, as well as saws, jimmies, chisels, wedges, blowpipes, sledgehammers, drills with drill bits in more than a hundred different sizes, "six or seven overcoats," men's caps, machinists' overalls, "three pairs of elegant rubber shoes," oilcloths and "various kinds of liquor." There were also augers "of the finest steel and most beautiful finish," together with crowbars, braces, files, skeleton keys, pulleys, wrenches and spikes. "The entire kit comprises 400 pieces, which, experts say, is one of the finest collections they have ever seen, and must have cost in manufacture fully $2,000,"* the *Herald* reported.

Such an impressive compilation, the newspapers agreed, was a resounding sign that professional bank burglary had come into its own. "It is more than a business—it is a fine art, requiring time, labor and capital," one report proclaimed. "Witness the costly character of the tools . . . left behind by the Ocean Bank burglars after the consummation of their recent feat." The New York *Journal of Commerce* declared: "Most of the articles were specially made for the business, it would seem, by skilled manufacturers in this country or abroad—another evidence of the recognized status of burglary as a means of livelihood. . . . Nothing was omitted necessary to the object sought, and that is the very essence of art."

One of the patrons of that art, whose contribution of more than $3,000† had helped make the Ocean Bank venture possible, was Fredericka Mandelbaum. She was clearly using this heist as an economic trial balloon: It behooved her as an entrepreneur to gauge whether bank burglary was an enterprise whose rewards were worth the risks. It is obvious from the outcome, and from her continued, deepening involvement in bank burglaries, that the answer was a resounding yes.

---

*   Nearly $43,000 in today's money.

†   The equivalent of some $64,000 today.

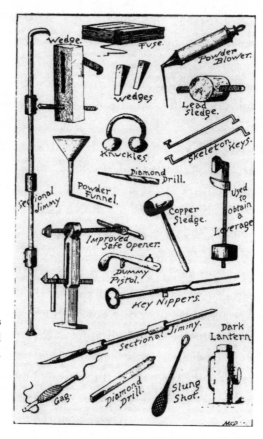

Bank burglars' tools
of the period
included these.

IN COMMON PARLANCE, "bank robbery" and "bank burglary" are used interchangeably, but they describe two radically different ways of separating a bank from its contents. Bank robbery is the armed, daylight, stick-'em-up affair conducted during business hours. It is often remunerative, but in the canon of nineteenth-century crooks it was considered thuggish and déclassé. Bank burglary, by contrast, is a covert, painstaking, nighttime operation. It entails subtlety and supreme skill, encompassing the delicate working of tumblers, the discreet picking of locks and a life-or-death knowledge of explosives. It requires wit and enterprise: In the post–Civil War period, burglars needed to stay one step ahead of safe makers in a constant battle between those paid to keep men out of safes and those paid to get them in.

"Cracksmen of this class head the list of mechanical thieves," Thomas Byrnes, New York's chief of detectives, observed:

> It requires rare qualities in a criminal to become an expert bank-safe robber. Thieves of this high grade stand unrivaled among their kind. The professional bank burglar must have patience, intelligence, mechanical knowledge, industry, determination, fertility of resources, and courage—all in high degree. But, even if he possess all these, they cannot be utilized unless he can find suitable associates or gain admission to one of the already organized gangs. Sometimes the arrest of a single man out of a gang will put a stop to the operations of the remainder for a long time, simply because they need another man, and can find nobody they can trust. Bank burglars have been known to spend years in preparation—gleaning necessary information of the habits of bank officials, forming advantageous acquaintances, and making approaches to the coveted treasure all the time, but with the patience to wait until the iron is fully hot before striking a blow.

The Ocean National Bank caper was a canonical example of the bank burglar's art. It took many months of planning and involved some of the foremost cracksmen of the day. While accounts over the years have differed as to precisely who was involved, it is well established that the job featured four principals:[*] George White (alias George Bliss), a Massachusetts hotelkeeper who in 1864 became accidentally embroiled in a bank heist and afterward deliberately em-

---

[*]   Myriad modern-day sources credit the master bank burglar George Leonidas Leslie with having taken part in the Ocean National Bank heist; the story of his participation has become something of an urban legend, accepted on faith and widely recapitulated. In nineteenth- and early-twentieth-century accounts, however—including those of New York's chief of detectives, Thomas Byrnes, and George White, whose 1905 memoir discloses his own deep involvement in the caper—Leslie is entirely absent. As a comprehensive 2021 study of crime in Gilded Age New York concludes, Leslie "probably had nothing to do" with the Ocean Bank burglary. (The erroneous conflation of George Leslie with George White may account for the wide misattribution.) We will meet Leslie, at the height of his larcenous prowess, later on.

broiled himself in many more; Mark Shinburn (né Maximilian Schenbein), a dandified, Prussian-born burglar with aristocratic yearnings; Jimmy Hope, "a daring and skillful" bank burglar from Philadelphia; and Ned Lyons, Sophie's English-born husband and a former protégé of Hope's; along with sundry supporting players. Shinburn, Hope and Lyons were all close associates of Fredericka Mandelbaum.

THE FIRST RECORDED BANK BURGLARY in New York City took place in 1831, when two men used homemade duplicate keys to let themselves into the City Bank of New York,* at 52 Wall Street, and help themselves to some \$245,000†—including "138,911 dollars in notes of various Banks" and "200 doubloons." Their task was remarkably easy. Once they'd used their keys (cut from surreptitious wax impressions of the locks) to pass through the street door and into the vault, the safe would have posed no trouble: Bank safes in those years were simply metal-plated wooden chests—little more than glorified strongboxes. Small safes could be picked up, carried off and opened at leisure. Even larger ones could normally be disassembled in situ with ordinary tools. "The essential design," a historian of safecracking has written, "was exactly what a blacksmith would make if asked to provide a strong cupboard or closet."‡

Partly in response to the City Bank burglary, safe makers began using stronger metals, better bolts, tighter joints and much less wood. Safecrackers responded enthusiastically with more powerful, purpose-built tools and, eventually, explosives. The escalating war between the two sides continued through the nineteenth century and on into the twentieth.

* Now Citibank. The first recorded bank burglary in the United States had taken place in Philadelphia in 1798, when two men heisted \$162,821 (more than \$3 million in today's money) from the Bank of Pennsylvania.

† About \$8 million today.

‡ The City Bank burglars, James Honeyman and William J. Murray, were apprehended soon after the heist. Each was convicted and sentenced to five years in Sing Sing.

There was also the matter of the locks themselves. At the time of the City Bank burglary, bank safes were typically secured by means of a padlock, opened with a key. Combination locks were not widely adopted by American safe makers until the 1860s and '70s. But even these were child's play at first: The earliest, introduced by the Lillie Safe Company of Troy, New York, in 1860, had only three numbers on its dial. If a sequence of three digits was required to spring the lock, then the number of possible combinations (assuming no repetitions within the sequence) was just six. If a burglar needed ten seconds to try each combination, he could whirl through all of them in a minute.

Then Lillie put out a dial numbered from 0 to 100, and things got interesting. On such a dial, a three-digit sequence with no repeated numbers offers nearly a million possible combinations. A four-digit sequence offers nearly 100 million. A very skilled safecracker might put his ear to the safe and listen profitably for telltale clicks as he worked the dial, but that MO belongs more to Hollywood screenwriting than to practical safecracking. It would scarcely have aided nineteenth-century safecrackers in any case: Electronic stethoscopes, which make the method more viable, were not developed until the mid-twentieth century.

To foil a complex lock, a bank burglar could always resort to blasting: During the nineteenth century, gunpowder, dynamite and eventually nitroglycerine were the safecracker's explosives of choice. But the method entailed great risk—to plunderer and plunder— and produced an awful lot of noise. "Gunpowder first appeared in the burglar's equipment in 1848, but the early history of the underworld's use of explosives was punctuated by a series of loud failures and quiet fizzles," a historian writes. "An unsuccessful assault on a strongbox in 1857 provides an illustration of the problem. Some thieves poured the powder into the safe's keyhole and ignited it. The subsequent blast shattered the front and back walls of the store, nearly causing the whole building to collapse."

George White and Mark Shinburn employed an ingenious device to induce combination locks to yield their secrets. Nicknamed the Little Joker, it was a thin, flexible piece of wire, designed to be inserted covertly beneath the dial of a safe.* When a bank employee next worked the dial, the points at which it stopped would be scribed onto the wire. The device had its drawbacks: It required burglars to break into the bank twice before the actual heist—once to install the Joker, and again to take it out. It had no way to record the order in which the scribed points were dialed, though this was a small impediment: The Joker effectively re-created Lillie's old three-number setup. Retrieving it by night, the burglar had only to note the positions of the three scribe marks, and the numbers on the dial to which they corresponded. On the day of the burglary, he would have just six combinations to try.

White and Shinburn, who were longtime partners, used the Joker to great effect during the 1860s, pulling bank heists in Connecticut, Vermont and Maryland. They planned to deploy it in the Ocean Bank job, but they never got the chance: Earlier that year, as the two men were preparing the ground for a bank burglary in New Jersey, bank employees came upon the device before the burglars could retrieve it. "After that," a chronicler recounts, "Lillie altered its locks to make them joker-proof." But no matter. White had another way in.

FOUNDED AFTER THE CIVIL WAR as a result of Salmon P. Chase's national banking scheme, the Ocean National Bank occupied the ground floor of a brownstone building at the southeast corner of Fulton and Greenwich streets. George White began toying with the idea of a heist late in 1868, after he befriended a young clerk there, a man he calls John Taylor. With the Little Joker out of commission, White would need a man on the inside to furnish him with the combination to the safe. Happily, Taylor had a gambling problem.

---

* Although it is well documented that White and Shinburn used the device, sources differ as to who actually invented it. White himself takes credit in his memoir of 1905. Other accounts, which possibly conflate George Leslie with George White, name Leslie (who also used the device, or one like it) as its creator.

Over the coming months, Taylor supplied White with descriptions of the layout of the bank, the construction of the vault, and the make and model of the lock on the vault's outer door. White's first problem lay in finding a way to defeat that door. "The lock on the vault," he wrote long afterward, "was a three-tumbler combination made by Briggs and Huntington of Rochester, New York, and was at that time one of the most secure of its kind, and was practically, if not absolutely, non-pickable." In addition, he said, "I had seen from the first that it would be next to impossible to force the outer vault doors by means of explosives without bringing detection upon us before we could accomplish more; and that, therefore, our only hope for success lay in obtaining the combination to the lock."

But how to get it? Taylor, who had no authority to open the vault, didn't know the combination. He could see fellow employees when they worked the dial, but couldn't get close enough to read the numbers they were dialing. And thus, in the guise of an out-of-town banker needing to beef up security, White visited Briggs & Huntington and requested a similar model. The company was only too happy to sell him one. Back in the city, with Taylor watching him from a distance, he schooled the young clerk in how to extrapolate the combination by observing the hand positions of the man operating the dial.

"We kept at it night after night," White recalled, "while, in the daytime, Taylor, having made it a point to be always on hand before the vault was opened, would watch the process of unlocking its doors. He had a quick eye and was very apt, and, after some weeks of practice and watching, he felt sure that he had the combination."

White's next order of business was to put the bank and surrounding area under constant surveillance, so that the comings and goings of employees, customers and neighborhood policemen could be monitored. In January 1869, he rented a room on the second floor of a building on Fulton Street, directly opposite the bank, and installed two associates—quite possibly Hope and Lyons—as tenants. These confederates would keep watch on the premises for the next six months.

Then came the problem of gaining entry to the bank itself. The corner of Fulton and Greenwich got too much foot traffic to make covert admission through the front door possible, even at night. Consulting with Shinburn, White concluded that the only way in was to tunnel, either through the ceiling from the floor above, or through the vault floor from the basement. "We discussed the advisability of having a room directly over the vault," White recalled, "but decided that, by reason of the massive masonry which we would have to cut through, it would be much more practicable to go through the floor."

The basement of the building, which had a row of windows just above sidewalk level, contained rental offices. In March, a man called Kohler, posing as an insurance broker, rented office space there.* Kohler was Mark Shinburn's brother-in-law, and the space he rented was directly under the office of the bank president.† With Marm's backing, White and Shinburn had a set of bespoke burglar's tools made; in May, they installed them in their basement office, together with explosives and the massive hydraulic jack. Working by night, with blankets hung over the windows to conceal lantern light and muffle sound, they began, laboriously, to chip away at the ceiling.

But after making it partway through, they got a nasty surprise. "When the plastering of the ceiling was removed, we expected to find an open space between the girders of the floor above," White said. "But, instead, we found the space filled with rubble set in cement—a solid mass fourteen inches thick." Their tools had been designed to cut through wood and steel, but neither they nor Marm could have foreseen that they would need something that could cope with cement. The burglars would have to suspend the operation until new tools could be made.

---

* In one later account, it was Marm Mandelbaum herself who supplied the rent money for the office.

† The burglars' modus operandi anticipates the plot of "The Red-Headed League," a Sherlock Holmes story of 1891 in which burglars commandeer a London office with the aim of tunneling across to the bank next door and up through the bank floor to the vault.

They were left, meanwhile, with a conspicuous hole in the ceiling of the "insurance office"—something that a janitor or watchman would be sure to spot. "We used up all the mucilage in the office in plastering paper over it, but still it was only too apparent," White wrote. "We could do no more that night, so we watched our opportunity and got away unobserved." From a secondhand shop on Canal Street, the burglars bought a tall wardrobe, which they placed beneath the hole; piled high with books and boxes, it hid the hole completely. It also gave them a handy place to store their tools.

Just after eleven o'clock on the night of Saturday, June 26, White and Shinburn began a renewed attack on the ceiling. Stripped to their underclothes in the summer heat and wielding their new tools, they hacked away at the cement. Three hours later, they found themselves on the underside of the wooden floor of the president's office. Gingerly, they cut through the floor, taking care not to damage the carpet above: They would need it to conceal the hole later on.

Pushing the carpet aside, White and Shinburn pulled themselves through the hole and into the president's office. The vault beckoned, but they didn't dare use a lantern to see the dial: The shutters on the windows had gaps at the top that would let its light be seen from the street. By the almost imperceptible light of a cigar, White dialed the combination Taylor had given him, and the vault door swung open. Happily, the keys to the second door were in their usual place—hanging up just inside the first. Returning to the basement, White began passing their hundreds of tools, wrapped in cloth to dampen clanging, up to Shinburn. The hydraulic jack, hauled painstakingly through the hole, made short work of the third door.

Once inside the windowless inner sanctum, the burglars could strike a light. They set to work first on the safe-deposit boxes, pulling them out and smashing them open. Taking only cash and negotiable securities, they left all jewelry behind. "That was not our graft," White explained, "and, besides, we felt that we would have a full load with the money and bonds."

Vault of the Ocean
National Bank

Turning next to the safes, they attacked the first of the two with their drills. "The cutting, or drilling, of steel by hand is very slow and hard work," White said, "and it was not until eleven o'clock in the morning that the bolts were sprung and the doors of the safe opened. The contents of this safe were gone over and all that were negotiable were put in the satchel containing the other valuables, and the satchel let down into Kohler's office, so that we might be sure of that much were we disturbed in our further work."

The second safe proved to be made of much sterner stuff, and the burglars drilled and drilled to no avail. (The space inside the vault was too narrow for them to wield the hydraulic jack.) Finally, exhausted, and with the safe still tightly shut, they withdrew from the vault, closing and locking all three doors, and dropped down to the basement. Pulling the rug back over the hole, they replaced the cut-out flooring from below, bracing it underneath in case someone walked across that spot. Then they retired to a hotel for a well-earned sleep.

The next afternoon, Sunday, June 27, White and Shinburn entered the insurance office, reopened the hole, admitted themselves to the vault by cigar light, and renewed their attack on the second safe. They realized they would never be able to crack it before the bank opened on Monday morning, so they decided to summon the fire department to their aid. Slipping out of the building and across Fulton Street, White gave instructions to his co-conspirators there. Reentering the bank, he shimmied up through the hole. "Shinburn and I at once set to work with wedges and copper hammers to make a seam between the jamb and the door of the safe so that we could insert explosive. Finally everything was ready, the charge was connected with a battery which Shinburn held outside the vault, and the vault doors closed."

Then, as arranged, White signaled to his confederates across the street, and they did not fail him. The burglars took cover, and soon afterward heard the unmistakable "rumble and gongs of the fire carts." As the brigade swept past the bank, "Shinburn turned the switch, the charge went off, and as we returned to the vault, we found the safe door lying on the floor."* They bundled as much of its contents as they could into a small trunk, about two feet long and a foot high, that they'd found in the vault. Lowering the trunk and themselves into the basement, they slipped out of the building and boarded a waiting carriage. Back in White's rooms, they began to count their prodigious haul.

It went without saying that the proceeds would have to be laundered, and a time-honored way to launder ill-gotten money is through a criminal receiver. The fence can use dirty money to buy real estate, for instance, which is quickly flipped and resold. Or she can purchase a mass of wholesale goods to retail to the public in her "legitimate" shop. The cash from these sales—now clean, untraceable money—is divided among receiver and thieves. "Nearly all of the $800,000 taken in the Ocean National Bank robbery was turned over to Marm Mandelbaum to launder through her various and

---

* Employing a similar strategy in the late nineteenth century, as a modern criminologist notes, "a division of the Hell's Kitchen gangs from New York City's West Side coordinated their explosions with community-organized Fourth of July fireworks and pyrotechnic displays."

sundry channels," a modern-day chronicler has written. Marm's cut for the transaction is reported to have been as much as 50 percent.

On Wednesday, June 30, two days after the Ocean Bank burglary was discovered, the *New York Herald* carried an advertisement from one of the bank's depositors. As if taking a leaf from the Jonathan Wild playbook, he offered a $500 reward for the return of $3,500 in bonds stolen in the heist . . . "NO QUESTIONS ASKED."

THOUGH WHITE, SHINBURN AND THEIR ASSOCIATES were widely suspected of the Ocean Bank job, they were never apprehended; in the end, no one was charged with the crime. But the affair had a curious coda: On the afternoon of June 30, two young men, "known to the police as honest, hard-working mechanics,"* happened upon a small trunk, abandoned on the sidewalk of Elizabeth Street in Lower Manhattan. The trunk, about two feet long and a foot high, was bound with cord, and attached to the cord was a note:

FOR CAPT. JOURDAN

OF THE SIXTH WARD

The young men summoned a passing policeman, who carried the trunk to the Franklin Street station house. Officers there regarded it with apprehension: Did the trunk contain a dead infant? Or perhaps some "infernal machine intended for the destruction of Captain Jourdan"? Captain John Jourdan was summoned, and he bravely opened the lid. Inside were more than $268,000† in railroad bonds and other non-negotiable securities from the Ocean Bank burglary: In their haste to make off with the contents of the second

---

* "Mechanic" in this sense denotes a manual laborer: Think of Shakespeare's "rude mechanicals" in *A Midsummer Night's Dream*. In the nineteenth century, "Mechanics' Institutes" were established in many American cities; they offered free lectures and lending libraries for workingmen in an effort to provide "an alternative to the barroom."

† More than $5 million today.

safe, the burglars had accidentally taken those things along with the good stuff. Now they were returning them—in the same trunk they'd lifted from the vault. News of the discovery filled the next day's papers. It also, the *New-York Times* remarked, "filled the hearts of unhappy depositors with hopeful anticipations."

"The police seemed to have no idea from whom the securities came," the *New-York Tribune* reported, "or by what means the trunk so mysteriously made its appearance on the walk. The young men who called the officer's attention to it . . . did not see anything of the persons who brought it there. Capt. Jourdan, one of the best detective officers in the country, will undoubtedly put forth every exertion to capture the impudent rascals, who have so coolly ventured into his precinct for the purpose of presenting him with a token of their regard."

What seems not to have occurred to the newspapers was the possibility that the appearance of the trunk, with its lavish contents, was the product of a negotiated settlement. Marm would have been able to launder the negotiable bonds, "having a safe outlet for such things among a certain class of brokers, who for a large percentage would deal in securities whose ownership was doubtful." But since even she couldn't unload non-negotiable securities, the burglars' best option was to return them to the bank via the police—and pocket a "finder's fee" from the bank in exchange. "The policy of the bank," police chief Walling wrote years later, "was to get possession, not of the thieves, but of the stolen property."

There could be no clearer evidence than that little trunk, sitting all alone on Elizabeth Street, that the extortion tactics Jonathan Wild used so profitably in the eighteenth century were alive, well and just as profitable among property criminals of the nineteenth. What would not be known publicly until the early twentieth century, however, was the reason Captain John Jourdan had been so utterly unafraid to open it.

Chapter Six

Bureau for the Prevention
of Conviction

THE LATE 1860S THROUGH THE MID-1870S WERE THE APEX OF MARM'S career. She was now a woman of means, though her most ambitious bank burglary lay ahead. But by 1873, when she bought the entire building at Clinton and Rivington and installed her family in splendor upstairs, she was already one of the best known—and richest—criminal receivers in New York. The robberies of high-end stores, textile houses and rich men's homes were a going concern, with Fredericka taking an active role in planning the crimes and underwriting the associated expenses.

"It takes money for a first-class thief to go through a store properly; and to frustrate watchfulness the criminal must spend money freely," police chief George Washington Walling explained:

A building must be watched for days prior to a robbery, and its ins and outs located. If fellowship is to be cultivated with the watchman of the building, sometimes months elapse before the thief and the guardian are on intimate terms. Invitations to drink are continuous. I have even known women in the employ of burglars becoming acquainted with the wives of the watchmen of large stores, and in time the men were introduced. Not infrequently a horse and wagon must be provided. If there is money in the job, money is required to launch it, and in all this it is the receiver who is the financial backer of the robber. Affiliations between the receivers and the criminal classes are constant. If there were no markets for stolen goods, there would be no robberies.

There was no shortage of markets for the goods that passed through Fredericka's hands. She was said, for instance, to have received—and resold at great profit—much of the merchandise looted amid the Chicago fire of 1871. She also continued to handle huge quantities of cash and securities, including a haul of at least $150,000* (in some estimates as much as $1 million)† from the burglary of the Boylston National Bank in Boston.

The Boylston heist, in November 1869, was impeccably carried out by her foot soldiers Adam Worth, "Piano Charley" Bullard and Ike Marsh. Worth and Bullard had first joined forces the previous spring, after a boss—"almost certainly Marm Mandelbaum"— enlisted Worth to help break Bullard out of the White Plains, New York, jail, where he was doing time for train robbery. Renting headquarters in an empty office building next door to the prison, Worth and a partner, Mark Shinburn, managed to tunnel covertly through the prison wall from the outside. They sprang Bullard handily.‡

Now, in November, posing as makers of patent medicine, Worth, Bullard and Marsh rented a shop abutting the Boylston Bank. Inside, they erected a partition across the back of the shop and filled the front window with row upon row of bottles labeled "Gray's Oriental Tonic," an elixir they'd had specially brewed for the occasion. "Quite what was in Gray's Oriental Tonic has never been revealed," Worth's biographer writes, "since not a single bottle was ever sold."§

---

*   More than $3 million in today's money.

†   More than $20 million today.

‡   That endeavor, Worth's biographer notes, "was the first and only time" Worth and Shinburn would work together.

§   As Sophie Lyons, who knew all three crooks well, would explain, "The partition was to hide the piles of debris which would accumulate as the robbers burrowed into the bank next door; the bottles in the window to prevent passersby seeing too much of the interior."

Their plunder, gained after a week of nocturnal tunneling, was packed into trunks and shipped by train to New York to be laundered by Marm.

Adam Worth in 1905   "Piano Charley" Bullard

Thefts like these had let Fredericka attain a glittering, antithetical version of the American Dream, the mass yearning popularized in *Ragged Dick*, Horatio Alger's sentimental novel of 1868. That book, together with five sequels, championed hard work and virtuous living as the route from poverty to bourgeois respectability. The written invitations to Marm's fabulous dinner parties, issued by "The Honorable and Mrs. William Mandelbaum,"* were black-and-white testaments to social ground gained. For the recipients' part, "thieves knew that they had joined the elite of crime upon receiving those coveted invitations."

Intensely conscious of her hard-won standing, Mrs. Mandelbaum was determined that it not be usurped. When her former protégée "Black Lena" Kleinschmidt made a fortune as a jewel thief and blackmailer and began holding opulent dinner parties of her own in a Hackensack, New Jersey, mansion, Marm would have none

---

* Wolf sometimes used the name William in the New World; Fredericka was sometimes called Frances or Fanny.

The Boylston Bank burglary. Note the partition (center right) and the bottles of "tonic" on display in the window.

of it. And sure enough, when Lena eventually got her comeuppance, Fredericka had the last word. At one of Lena's grand parties, a guest noticed his hostess flaunting an emerald ring that had belonged to his wife; even worse, the guest was a judge. Black Lena was promptly arrested. "It just goes to prove," Marm opined from her side of the river, "that it takes brains to be a real lady."*

She was a public figure now, known far beyond her circle of thieves: A bevy of newspaper articles described Marm's shop, expounded on her wealth and at least hinted at her illicit trade. In an era when social standing was as prized a commodity as cash (even, or perhaps especially, for high-class crooks), Fredericka Mandelbaum, amid her glimmer of jewels and rustle of fine silk, was resolute that nothing appear in public to tarnish hers. A nineteenth-century thief recounted this story:

---

* In one account, Marm herself deliberately compromised Black Lena by arranging to have the ring stolen from one of Lena's regular guests and then sending it to her in the guise of a present from an admirer.

Once a bright reporter wrote a play, in which the central character was [based on] Madame Mandelbaum.* She read about it in the newspapers and went, with her two daughters, to see it. They occupied a private box, and were gorgeously dressed. The old lady was very indignant when she saw the woman who was supposed to be herself appear on the stage. The actress, badly dressed, and made up with a hooked nose, was jeered by the audience. After the play, Madame Mandelbaum insisted on seeing the manager of the theatre. She showed him her silks and her costly diamonds and then said: "Look at me. I am Madame Mandelbaum. Does that huzzy look anything like me?" Pointing to her daughters she continued: "What must my children think of such an impersonation? Both of them are better dressed and have more money and education than that strut, who is only a moment's plaything for bankers and brokers!"

These demonstrations show Marm at her righteous, indomitable best, but they have a self-serving aspect, too. She carried herself in public as an upstanding member of the community, an attentive wife and mother and a generous member of her synagogue, Congregation Temple Rodeph Sholom, then on Clinton Street.† Her neighbors adored her. As someone who created jobs, offered dis-

---

* The play was *The Two Orphans* (*Les Deux Orphelines*), an 1874 melodrama written not by "a bright reporter" but by the well-known French playwrights Adolphe d'Ennery and Eugène Cormon. The English translation, by N. Hart Jackson, premiered on December 21, 1874, at the Union Square Theatre in New York to much acclaim. Set amid the French Revolution, the play features a character, La Frochard, a hard-drinking, hovel-dwelling "old hag," who is the matriarch of a family of murderous grifters; in the New York production she was played by the actress Marie Wilkins. An article in the *New York Evening World* describes Mrs. Mandelbaum, in attendance at that production, as having "sat in a box one night to see her double." The play was filmed in 1921 as *Orphans of the Storm*, directed by D. W. Griffith and starring Lillian and Dorothy Gish as the orphans and Lucille La Verne as "Mother Frochard."

† Rodeph Sholom, established in Lower Manhattan in 1842, is still active; it is now a Reform synagogue on Manhattan's Upper West Side.

Kate Claxton (left) as the imperiled orphan Louise and Marie Wilkins as the "old hag" La Frochard in the English-language production of *The Two Orphans* (*Les Deux Orphelines*), which opened in New York at the Union Square Theatre in 1874. La Frochard, the head of a Parisian crime family, was said to have been modeled on Fredericka Mandelbaum. Mrs. Mandelbaum saw the production and was incensed at the character's frowsy appearance.

counts and dispensed charity when needed, she was seen as a local benefactor. She was also adored by her own extended family—kids and crooks alike. "All of her children were devoted and loyal to their doting mother," Holub says. "Not only was Mandelbaum a devoted mother to her own children, she was considered 'motherly' in her dealings with her cohort." Even Chief Walling acknowledged that "as a woman and a mother she is spoken of with respect."

There was pleasure, solidarity and security in being a thief in the Mandelbaum syndicate. Besides the dinner parties, Fredericka hosted elegant dances, as well as "company picnics" for her larcenous crew, held in the countryside of Brooklyn or Upper Manhattan. For a time, at least, she kept her foremost thieves on a regular salary, reported in 1884 to have been $25 a week.* " 'Marm' Mandelbaum was . . . as adept in her business as the best stock-broker in Wall Street in his," Walling recalled:

> She attained a reputation as a business woman whose honesty in criminal matters was absolute, by her adherence to criminal ethics so far as they regarded men who had been graduates in the school of housebreaking and shop-lifting, and the promptness with which she settled her accounts with them. And not only this, she never left a criminal her creditor. When he was in need—caught *flagrante delicto,* red-handed, under circumstances which she could not control—she became his banker, and he could draw on her for sums which, in her estimation of the capabilities of a first-class criminal, he could not hope to repay within many years. . . . Not only has she sent money for the defence of criminals, but . . . on receipt of information that their operations were delayed by want of funds, she has promptly sent out generous letters of credit.

But while this tender care of her "chicks" may have sprung from genuine maternal impulse, it had a second function: to keep her foot soldiers happy—and loyal. Throughout her working life, a fence confronts two threats: First is the threat of arrest. Second is the prospect of betrayal to law enforcement by other criminals—even those in her own organization—an occupational hazard that has existed since fencing first began.

---

* More than $750 a week in today's money.

What was more, because "criminals lack the institutional supports available to respectable people," Fredericka had to work much
harder than the average bourgeois woman to preserve her reputation. Though some members of the public esteemed her as a rogue,
the fact remained that she was a career criminal—one who engaged
a cohort of underlings to commit crimes for her benefit. And while
her associates cleaned up nicely for parties, some of them were truly
unsavory. Among them were William Mosher and Joe Douglas, who
in 1874 committed what was then the most notorious kidnapping in
American history, grabbing four-year-old Charley Ross from his
home in Germantown, Pennsylvania. The child was never found.[*]
Others would be involved in a bank heist, underwritten by Marm,
that went badly wrong and resulted in a death.

Strikingly, though, despite her growing notoriety as a "captain
of crime," Marm herself was rarely arrested and almost never
brought to trial. "There are thieves and receivers of stolen goods
everywhere," the *New-York Times* would lament. "The peculiarity
and the disgrace of [Mrs. Mandelbaum's] case is that . . . the receiving and sale of stolen goods been carried on for years as openly if it
were a legitimate industry."

Besides her innate savvy, impeccable organization and well-honed
self-preservation instinct ("She changed character like a chameleon,"
Walling observed), there was a reason Fredericka Mandelbaum was
able to slip the net time after time. It can be gleaned from a renewed
look round her table: We are back in the lush dining room, with its
crystal chandeliers, tinkling piano and clinking glasses. And here,
seated in Fredericka's carved mahogany chairs, wining, dining and
laughing alongside the tycoons, the shoplifters and the swindlers, is
a pack of Tammany Hall judges, aldermen, ward captains and other
officials—some of the most powerful fixtures on the political landscape of late-nineteenth-century New York.

---

[*]   Mosher and Douglas were shot later in 1874 while attempting a robbery in Brooklyn. Mosher was killed instantly; Douglas, gravely wounded, confessed to the Ross
kidnapping but died before making the child's fate or whereabouts known.

FOUNDED IN 1788 as a fraternal organization of craftsmen, Tammany Hall was by the mid-1860s the dominant force in New York City Democratic politics. "By the end of the Civil War, [the] paths to political power had been systematized into a relatively well-defined hierarchy," a historian explains. "At the top sat the city's party 'boss.' His lieutenants each controlled one of the city's assembly districts, and they in turn relied upon the ward leaders. Every ward was divided into election districts, headed by a single leader or a committee of ward captains or 'heelers.' In the postbellum years, the subdivisions continued until every block (and sometimes even single buildings within a block) had its designated party leader."

Tammany reached its avaricious zenith in the 1860s and early '70s under William M. Tweed, its king-size, diamond-decked, mansion-dwelling, kickback-grubbing Grand Sachem.* During his years in power, he and his associates were said to have pocketed between $30 million and $200 million† earmarked for public works projects in the city: If you wanted to get anything done in New York—from erecting a building to running a railroad to beating a criminal charge—it was an extremely good idea to grease the palm of Tweed or one of his cronies, who collectively formed what one historian has called "an empire of patronage."

Nearly every vendor who supplied the city with goods or services, for instance, was quietly ordered to pad his bills. (The traditional overcharge, an 1878 investigation found, was 15 percent.) This surplus was split among a ring of corrupt members of the city's Board of Supervisors; the vendor received the city's assurance of continuing contracts.

It is not known whether Boss Tweed himself was ever among Marm's guests, but for her purposes that particular contact wouldn't

---

*   Tweed, who served as Grand Sachem from 1863 to 1871, also held a range of elective offices over the years, including city alderman, state senator and United States congressman.

†   More than $600 million to more than $4 billion today.

have mattered. "Whether or not Mandelbaum and Tweed had any *direct* association," Rona Holub points out, "Mandelbaum benefited from the connections that existed between the municipal government run by Tammany Hall and immigrant and other lower class individuals. She made friends over the years with judges . . . [and] at least one alderman."

From Marm's vantage point, it was the neighborhood officials—aldermen, district leaders, ward captains—who were the most useful in any case. These were the men who, year in and year out, saw to it that constituents got turkeys at Thanksgiving, buckets of coal in winter and fistfuls of dollars when they were down and out, in return for which they could expect a resounding Democratic vote on Election Day.

In an era before government-backed safety nets like welfare, Social Security and unemployment insurance, the Tammany system, corrupt though it was, had a welcome reciprocity, benefiting threadbare city dwellers as well as prosperous pols. "The ward captain was to Tammany what the sergeant was to the army—the backbone of the organization," a historian writes. "He cultivated a following by dispensing favors, by catering to local interests and problems. He found jobs for needy families, or loaned them money, honored them with his presence at weddings and wakes. . . . For gamblers, prostitutes, and gangsters in trouble, he found bail."

Even at this micro-local level, Tammany politics could be staggeringly profitable. There are few more colorful exemplars of ward capitalism in action than George Washington Plunkitt, an alderman, state senator and Tammany district leader during the 1860s, '70s and '80s. It was he who famously said, "I seen my opportunities and I took 'em," and indeed he did, raking in more than $1 million through what he called "honest graft." In a voice that could have sprung from the lips of one of Mark Twain's confidence men, Plunkitt explained how honest graft worked:

> Everybody is talkin' these days about Tammany men growin'
> rich on graft, but nobody thinks of drawin' the distinction

between honest graft and dishonest graft. There's all the difference in the world between the two. Yes, many of our men have grown rich in politics. I have myself. I've made a big fortune out of the game, and I'm gettin' richer every day, but I've not gone in for dishonest graft—blackmailin' gamblers, saloonkeepers, disorderly people, etc. . . .

Just let me explain by examples. My party's in power in the city, and it's goin' to undertake a lot of public improvements. Well, I'm tipped off, say, that they're going to lay out a new park at a certain place. I see my opportunity and I take it. I go to that place and I buy up all the land I can in the neighborhood. Then the board of this or that makes its plan public, and there is a rush to get my land, which nobody cared particular for before.

Ain't it perfectly honest to charge a good price and make a profit on my investment and foresight? Of course, it is. Well, that's honest graft. Or supposin' it's a new bridge they're goin' to build. I get tipped off and I buy as much property as I can that has to be taken for approaches. I sell at my own price later on and drop some more money in the bank.

Wouldn't you? It's just like lookin' ahead in Wall Street or in the coffee or cotton market. . . . Now, let me tell you that most politicians who are accused of robbin' the city get rich the same way. . . . They just seen their opportunities and took them.

For immigrant men, New York City ward politics was yet another rung on the "crooked ladder"—a chance to climb from poverty to a level of wealth and power they could not otherwise attain. But for women, this avenue was closed. Effectively barred from electoral politics, they would not even win the right to vote until 1920, a quarter century after Fredericka Mandelbaum's death. Nor did they have access to the fertile culture of the saloon, where the backroom horse-trading that is the lifeblood of local politics had long been transacted: For a respectable nineteenth-century woman, setting foot in a barroom was utterly out of the question.

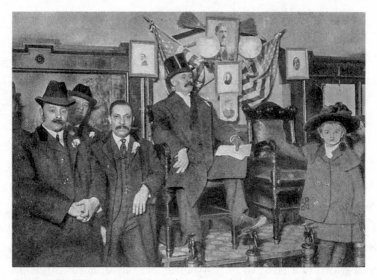

George Washington Plunkitt (1842–1924), photographed in 1905, holding forth from his favorite rostrum, the bootblack stand of the New York County Courthouse

Yet in forming her organization, Marm managed to create a de facto Tammany-in-miniature: an efficient syndicate, dedicated to the pursuit of profit by illegal means, that she could run however she saw fit. "In this way," Holub writes, "she became a center of power." And because "crime organizes successfully only if relationships between the 'underworld' and 'upper world' are established," Mother Mandelbaum wisely saw fit to keep filling the chronically outstretched hands of the boys of Tammany Hall.

THERE WAS ANOTHER REASON Fredericka was able to evade the law for so long, and it can be gleaned from a last look around her table. There, having a grand time alongside the crooks and the capitalists and the pols, was a passel of policemen, from the cop on the beat to high-ranking department officials. Graft to the politicians, she knew, entailed corresponding graft to the police, for at the height of the Tammany era those two bodies, and their attendant corruption, were inextricably intertwined.

"Machine rule in American municipalities has been made pos-sible only through control of the police," a historian has written. "From the days of Fernando Wood, down well into the twentieth century, it was exemplified by a long line of predatory police cap-tains whose motto, *'Hear, see and say nothin'. Eat, drink and pay nothin','* seemed to characterize New York's 'finest' at their worst."

That ethos had infused the department from its very start in the 300-pound form of George Washington Matsell, the city's first chief of police and, in the words of a modern history, "probably the most corrupt policeman in New York." A loyal Tammany soldier who was a bookseller and publisher by trade (he would one day own the *National Police Gazette*), Matsell was named chief of the newly cre-ated Municipal Police in 1845; he held the post until 1857, when the department was supplanted by the Metropolitans. Before his tenure was out, Matsell—a "Beastly Bloated Booby," one journalist called him—had built, ostensibly on civil servant's pay, a twenty-room sum-mer home, complete with a cellarful of fine wines, on a 3,000-acre estate in Viola, Iowa, where he entertained visitors in lordly style.

George Washington Matsell, a "Beastly Bloated Booby" and New York's first chief of police

Only in the mid-1890s, amid mounting pressure from reformers, would a New York State Senate committee be convened to investi-

gate the city's long tradition of "politically protected vice."* Taking
testimony from nearly seven hundred witnesses, the committee
learned of decades of extortion of the city's underworld figures—
and of its legitimate businesspeople—by the police.† "A veritable
parade of brothel keepers, prostitutes, counterfeiters, and burglars
told how regular payments to police captains were just another cost
of doing business," a historian recounts. "More respectable entrepreneurs described the payoffs required to run a steamship line or
put up a new building."

Newspapers of the day brimmed with revelations about "the unholy wolf police of this city," as one crusading minister called them.
The *New York Morning Journal* enumerated the disclosures this
way: "Tribute from harlots, tribute from dive-keepers, tribute from
saloonkeepers, tribute from gamblers, tribute from bunco men, tribute from green goods men,‡ tribute from sidewalk obstructers, tribute from steamship operators, tribute from peddlers—blackmail
and licensing of crime and law-breaking everywhere."

For Mrs. Mandelbaum, paying tribute was an article of faith
throughout her years in New York. The happy result, which took
physical form around her dining table, was what Chief George
Washington Walling astringently called the "Bureau for the Prevention of Conviction." For years, the bureau worked wonders for
Marm and her subordinates.

"With the capital she had amassed, she was in a position to . . .
'protect' those with whom she worked through bribes, bail money,

---

* Fredericka Mandelbaum died, far from New York, the month the committee was
convened.

† Known as the Lexow Committee for its chairman, State Senator Clarence Lexow,
it convened in February 1894 and issued its final report in early 1885. The hearings,
which had been brought about chiefly through the agitation of the Reverend
Charles H. Parkhurst, a reformist minster in the city, were widely covered in the press.
The committee's work resulted in a dramatic defeat of city and state Tammany candidates in elections of November 1894 and gave rise, as a historian writes, "to a powerful
national movement for urban reform."

‡ The "green-goods game" was a swindle in which an unscrupulous victim was
prevailed upon to buy a satchel full of impeccably printed counterfeit money at a good
price—only to find himself with a satchel full of sand, or cut-up newspaper, instead.

Police chief George
Washington Walling
decried Marm's
"Bureau for the
Prevention of
Conviction."

and legal representation," Holub has written. "She also bribed or saw to it that the appropriate officials were bribed in order to get her proteges off on whatever charges had been brought against them. If these attempts failed, witnesses were found to testify to whatever it took to get the charges dropped. Mandelbaum saw to it that a good number of cases were fixed. All of this activity in the service of criminals made her 'as well known around the Tombs and police courts as any well-known lawyer.' "

Marm's program of police gratification had three time-honored components. First, there was the offering of discounts. New York City cops freely patronized her shop, and doubtless relished the "bargains" there as much any consumer did. Policemen's wives, like other women of the period, made their own clothes, and would have welcomed Marm's below-wholesale prices on fine silks, lace and other fabrics.

Second, there was outright graft in the form of cash payments, which could include shares of the proceeds from bank heists. We can get a sense of the scale involved from George White, ringleader of the Ocean National Bank burglary, whose 1905 memoir contains a precise accounting of the division of spoils from that job. Line items include these:

> To James Irving, head of Detective Bureau 17,000
> To John McCord, detective 17,000
> To George Radford, detective 17,000
> To one other police detective 1,000
> To Inspector Johnson 1,800
> To Frank Houghtaling, Clerk Jefferson Market
>   Police Court 10,000.

White called his trusted circle of police officers, whom he apprised of heists in advance, his "Bank Ring." And also on his accounts list is a payment to one of the Ring's most valuable members: $17,000 "to John Jourdan, Captain Sixth Precinct"—the man conspicuously unafraid to open the strange little trunk abandoned on Elizabeth Street.*

John Jourdan,
high-ranking police
official and
accomplice of
bank robbers

---

* In April 1870, the year after the Ocean Bank job, Jourdan was named to the department's top post, superintendent of police. On his death six months later, after an illness, an official resolution from the city's Board of Aldermen praised his "inflexible integrity, stern devotion, untiring energy, [and] indomitable perseverance, guided and controlled by a conscientiousness and Christian purity of motive and intention that endeared him to all."

The third way a fence can assuage the police is to throw them periodic small fish: rivals or associates, deemed expendable, whose arrest and conviction will bolster law enforcement's public image. The method had worked splendidly for Jonathan Wild, as it did for every fence before him, and every fence after, Mrs. Mandelbaum included. "Like Fagin, she was the custodian of secrets which she could use to threaten her proteges when it became necessary," a newspaper article would declare. "Prominent among her friends were two New York police detectives who have, through their dangerous knowledge of her business, compelled her to aid in the betrayal of many a thief."

Marm herself had a few brushes with the law in the early to mid-1870s, but each time her luck held. There was the 1875 raid on her shop, in which the police seized a quantity of fine silk and "some costly shawls." "There was not the slightest doubt that every dollar's worth was stolen property, but none of it could be identified," the *New-York Times* reported. "The Police were compelled to surrender all this property to Mrs. Mandelbaum and set the burglar at liberty." On another occasion, she was arraigned at the Essex Market Courthouse in Lower Manhattan on a charge of having received silk, stolen from a New York textile firm, that was later recovered in Ohio. There is no indication that the case ever went to trial—a clear sign that the Bureau for the Prevention of Conviction was doing its job. And so the parties and the picnics and the thieving and the fencing went merrily on.

IN THE SECOND HALF OF THE 1870s, Marm's glimmering life began to darken. In March 1875, Wolf Mandelbaum died, at fifty-one, from a "wasting away disease," most likely tuberculosis; he and Fredricka had been married for twenty-seven years. Wolf was buried in the family plot Fredericka purchased at Rodeph Sholom's burial ground, Union Field Cemetery in Queens. To whatever extent Wolf's peddling had augmented the family income, that revenue stream was now gone. Fredericka was left as the sole support of four children, ranging in age from eight to fifteen; she also had to contend with the ever-present financial demands of police and politicians. It was time to contemplate another bank heist.

The Ocean National Bank trial balloon had been a proven success. Now, with her favorite thief, George Leonidas Leslie, Marm set her sights on the Manhattan Savings Institution, at Broadway and Bleecker streets. That operation would take three years of planning. But before her men undertook it, there would be a disastrous dry run.

Chapter Seven

Where the Money Was

GEORGE LESLIE WAS THE KIND OF PERSON MARM MANDELBAUM liked best: cultured, erudite, from a bourgeois background and almost preternaturally good at stealing large sums of money. Leslie, who for two decades of his short life was known nationwide as "King of the Bank Robbers," was in point of fact a bank *burglar*—so skilled at nocturnal withdrawals that he and his gang were said to have made off with some $7 million* over the years. Their plunder was regularly laundered by Marm.

George Leonidas Leslie, "alias Western George, George Howard, J. G. Allison, George K. Leslie, C. G. Greene, etc., *ad Infinitum*," was born in the early 1840s in Upstate New York, where his father, an immigrant from England, had settled. When George was a child, the family moved to Cincinnati, where his father prospered as a brewer. "His parents were well to do and highly respectable people," the *New-York Times* reported in 1878. "He received a good education, and was destined for one of the learned professions. His mother died while he was quite a youth, and his father married again soon after her death. His stepmother treated him so unkindly

---

* Seven million dollars in 1870, for example, is the equivalent of nearly $160 million today.

that he ran away from home and fell in with unsavory companions, and he soon made his debut as a burglar."

Leslie may have attended college for a time, though he did not, as he widely claimed,* earn a degree in architecture from the University of Cincinnati: There is no record of his having been enrolled there, nor did the university grant architecture degrees in those years in any case. But peddling falsehoods about his education would be the least of George Leslie's transgressions. Entranced throughout his life by the exploits of outlaws like Jesse James (hence the nickname Western George, bestowed fondly by Marm), he shunned "the learned professions" and turned his talents to crime.

Though Leslie valorized the bandits of the American West, he disdained their shoot-'em-up methods. His preferred weapon was an impeccably tailored dinner jacket, which, with his upper-class diction and manners, was the sheep's clothing that let him move undetected in the country's most rarefied social circles. And while he had no degree in architecture, he did possess a vast knowledge of the subject—in particular of the interior organization of bank buildings. Passing himself off as an architect with a bank-design commission in the works, he could often obtain bank blueprints straight from the bank presidents in his elegant orbit. Otherwise, he could draw on his superb visual memory to re-create blueprints accurately after a series of watchful daytime visits as a customer of the bank in question.

The result, starting in the 1860s, was a series of meticulously calculated, thrillingly remunerative bank burglaries in towns around the country. Leslie grew so adept at planning heists that he would eventually be engaged as a "consulting" burglar, called upon to fine-tune the plans of other crooks—for a share of the profits. "George Leslie's special gift was as a big-picture man," a modern commentator observes:

Like a film director who visualizes the screenplay and controls the actors, set design, and technical crew to fulfill that

* The claim is reprised by many later writers on Leslie.

vision, Leslie was the creative force behind many of the biggest bank robberies of his time. At the peak of his career, he acted as a "putter-up," planning the jobs that other men executed. He'd target a bank or store, select the burglar team, and assign them their roles. A telegram might summon him ... to Baltimore, or Kalamazoo, Michigan, or Macon, Georgia, to look over a scheme for a burglary to be carried out by others. Or he might be sought out to arrange with criminal fences for the disposal of what had already been stolen.

His larcenous reputation preceding him, Leslie moved to New York in 1869. He knew he had truly "arrived" on the city's criminal scene when he was able to wangle an invitation to one of Marm's high-toned parties. She was quickly taken with him, for both his personal charm and his thieving prowess. Before long, as Walling would write, Leslie had become "the chief of her clique of silk-stealing and bank-breaking friends, a man who had brought to her coffers many thousands of dollars."

With all that postwar New York had to offer, Leslie did not want for work. "Outside of bank robberies, according to the New York Police authorities, he had been engaged in 60 affairs in that city alone, footing up $418,339,* and had never been under arrest," an 1870s newspaper article reported. "The bulk of the proceeds had been handled by a woman named Frances Mandelbaum."

In her relationship with Leslie, Mrs. Mandelbaum's singular combination of nice-Jewish-motherdom and keen criminal savvy appears to have reached its most exquisite distillation: By the early 1870s, she was urging him to settle down and get married. For Marm, there were two considerations: First, old-fashioned solicitude, and second, avoiding a storm of notoriety just then swirling in the press. The newspapers were busily dissecting the love affair between a New York showgirl, Josie Mansfield, and "Jubilee Jim" Fisk, a Wall Street financier who was one of the foremost robber

* The equivalent, in the 1870s, of $10 million or more today.

barons of the Gilded Age.* The trouble was that Mansfield's impressive list of lovers also included George Leonidas Leslie. Though Leslie had not been named in the newspaper accounts thus far, Marm would have known that it was only a matter of time before his connection to Mansfield surfaced—and that such coverage would focus unwanted attention on his bank-burgling career and, by extension, her syndicate.

Happily, a solution presented itself: Leslie, who had decamped to Philadelphia in an apparent attempt to steer clear of Mansfield, had fallen in love there and was eager to marry. The object of his affections was Mary Henrietta Coath, known as Mollie, the daughter of his landlady. (The Coath boardinghouse was a "resort for thieves and ballet dancers," the *Brooklyn Daily Eagle* reported censoriously some years later. "There is not a pickpocket all over the country that does not know 'Old Mammy Coath' and her daughter.") Less happily, there was an impediment to the union. It wasn't Mollie's age, though she was just fifteen: It was the existence of a rival suitor, a fellow boarder and small-time crook named "Pretty Tom" Parnell.

Fredericka swooped in to play Cupid as only a crime boss could. Through her contacts in the Philadelphia underworld, she hired Parnell for a job, the nighttime burglary of a jewelry store in Norristown, Pennsylvania. Following her instructions to the letter, Parnell smashed a window of the store to gain entry—an indiscretion Marm knew would alert the neighbors, who, she also knew, would summon the police. Parnell was arrested and jailed, and the happy couple were married.

Returning to New York with his bride, Leslie settled in Brooklyn, where he was soon availing himself of Marm's capacious warehouses to erect full-scale interior models of the banks he planned to plunder. "Leslie was given free rein to use those warehouses as a

---

* With the financier Jay Gould, Fisk was responsible for having brought about Black Friday, the financial panic of September 24, 1869, by conspiring to corner the gold market. Fisk met an abrupt, unrelated and highly public end in 1872, when he was shot and killed by another of Mansfield's lovers, the oilman Edward Stokes.

kind of architectural training ground for future burglaries," an architectural historian has written:

> Here Leslie's spatial skills truly flourished.... [He] set the
> template for this technique way back in the 1870s, construct-
> ing life-size, 1:1 mock-ups of bank vaults, buying black-
> market copies of private safes, and installing them all like a
> burglar's showroom in an archipelago of gaslit warehouses
> scattered around the cobblestone streets of old Brooklyn. Les-
> lie's obsession with specifics extended even down to pieces of
> furniture that might get in the way during his gangs' im-
> pending assaults. He would arrange chairs and sofas, work
> desks and cabinets, in their proper places, then coach his team
> in the darkness with a stopwatch to make sure they got the
> sequence exactly right, without bumping a single table.

The resulting burglaries were a kind of covert theater, each per-
formance playing one night only, with the actors its sole audience.
And, like any producer mounting a play, Leslie would need an
"angel" to underwrite his expenses each time.

Together, he and Marm looked hungrily toward the Manhattan
Savings Institution. Founded in 1851,* with deposits of $397,000† in
its first year, it became home not only to large sums of cash but also
to jewels, securities and other valuables. Leslie and his crew—now
"composed of men bound by the strongest of ties to 'Marm'
Mandelbaum"—considered the bank a "pudding": a rich repository from which they would be only too happy to pull out the plums.
"The bank was wealthy, and always kept a large amount of cash
and negotiable security on hand," Walling explained. "The vault,
although apparently impregnable, was easy to enter, and enough
police protection from subordinates in the department was assured

---

*   The bank is today HSBC.

†   More than $15 million in today's money.

to render surprise in the commission of the burglary difficult. The bank premises were as accurately surveyed by Leslie as they would have been had a professional architect been employed. Every nook and corner was perfectly well known to the members of the gang."

By the start of 1878, Leslie was nearly ready to set the caper in motion. But first came a debacle.

The Manhattan
Savings Institution

IN FEBRUARY 1878, George Leslie and a small band of men arrived separately in Dexter, Maine, thirty miles northwest of Bangor. The town, home to thriving grain and textile mills, was the site of an especially tantalizing pudding: the Dexter Savings Bank, reported to be flush with deposits totaling nearly $800,000.* Leslie had recruited the bank's cashier, James W. Barron, as his "inside man"; he had also recruited an enormous investment, reported to be many thousands of dollars, from Marm. Besides first-rate tools, the job would entail the purchase of a half dozen round-trip train fares, local room and

---

* Some $23 million today.

board for Leslie and his gang, a getaway horse and sleigh to let them flee over the Maine snows, assorted bribes, and a set of stout railway trunks in which to ship their plunder back to New York.

Leslie had planned and rehearsed the Dexter burglary with his usual precision, gathering intelligence about the bank building, the vault and the safe. Coveted for its own sake, this job was also intended as an out-of-town tryout for the Manhattan Savings heist, a means of testing whether his chosen crew—including the New York crooks Johnny Irving, Billy Porter, "Red" Leary, "Shang" Draper and Gilbert Yost—could work smoothly together.

Billy Porter

In Dexter, the crew took lodgings at separate boardinghouses. On the evening of Friday, February 22, they donned the disguises on which Leslie insisted: an assortment of wigs, bald caps, false beards, mustaches and hats that he'd stolen from New York's Grand Opera House.* James Barron, working alone in the bank after hours,† had agreed to let them into the building, and from there into the vault, in exchange for a cut of the proceeds. Leslie, who was skilled at defeating locks, planned to open the safe himself.

---

* The Opera House, at Eighth Avenue and Twenty-third Street, had been acquired by Jay Gould and Jim Fisk in 1868. Fisk staged elaborate theatrical productions there, some featuring his mistress, Josie Mansfield. Leslie was a regular visitor to the place throughout his own affair with Mansfield.

† The bank would have been open during regular business hours that day. February 22, Washington's birthday, did not become a federal holiday until the next year.

But that night, when Leslie and his gang knocked on the bank door as arranged, they got no answer. They broke it down. Inside, they confronted Barron, who had reconsidered his involvement and now refused to turn over the keys to the vault. Incensed, Leslie's men pistol-whipped and beat Barron, and, in one account, "slashed him with knives, assaulted him with all sorts of indignities, and in short tried to murder him by slow torture." Leslie tried to intervene, but his men would not yield. Neither would Barron, steadfast in his refusal to give up the keys. Seizing the keys from him, the gang locked Barron—gagged, handcuffed and badly wounded—in the vault before fleeing the scene.

Marm Mandelbaum lost her investment: The gang made off with a grand total of $600—$100 nabbed from one of the bank's cash drawers and a $500 United States bond taken from Barron. Barron lost his life: Discovered late that night, he died the next morning.* On reading of Barron's death in the newspapers,† Leslie was said to have been so shaken that he swore off bank burglary—

Heist of the Dexter Savings Bank: The cashier, James Barron, tries to resist the burglars.

---

*   None of Leslie's gang would ever stand trial for his murder.

†   Accounts of the Dexter Bank heist over the years have an unmistakable *Rashomon* quality: Much of the initial press coverage casts Barron as a hero rather than a co-conspirator—a brave innocent victim who happened to be working in the bank after it had closed for the day. Even stranger, a year after the crime, several newspaper

though not until he pulled off what was to be his magnum opus, the heist of the Manhattan Savings Institution.

ON THE MORNING OF SUNDAY, October 27, 1878, a half-crazed man came tearing into the barbershop that occupied the basement level of the Manhattan Savings Institution building. With his hands cuffed and a gag in his mouth, "he danced up and down and made growling sounds like a mad dog." It took the barber some moments to recognize his friend Louis Werkle, the bank's janitor. The barber removed the gag, and Werkle cried, "The bank's been robbed!"

Just after six o'clock that morning, a small band of men wearing black muslin masks and brandishing pistols had crept into Werkle's apartment, on the second floor of the building. They bound and gagged Werkle, "a little old man, of no physical strength," along with his wife and elderly mother-in-law. Descending to the main floor, they breached the vault and then the safe, emerging less than three hours later with nearly $3 million* in cash and securities. The heist—"one of the most daring and successful burglaries ever perpetrated," the *New-York Times* declared—was the culmination of George Leslie's three years of planning.

The job was so ambitious that two "angels" had been required: Marm and "Traveling Mike" Grady, "the number-two fence in New York City after Mandelbaum." Besides providing financial backing, Fredericka also gave Leslie the use of one of her Brooklyn warehouses, where he erected a stage set of the bank's interior and

---

articles propounded the theory that Barron, whom they now described as having embezzled funds from the bank, had somehow managed to commit handcuffed suicide in the vault after staging a violent break-in. Stranger still, two men who apparently had nothing to do with the heist, the infelicitously named David L. Stain and the even more infelicitously named Oliver Cromwell, were convicted in 1888 of Barron's murder and sentenced to life imprisonment. Their conviction, based on testimony from Stain's son, was overturned in 1900, after the son recanted: "He explained that he was angry with his father because he had refused to give him $25.00 which was necessary to keep him out of jail for a minor offense."

* Equivalent to nearly $90 million today.

began rehearsals. He obtained a lock of the same make as that of the safe and began practicing on it at home. As Sophie Lyons, who knew him well, observed, Leslie "undoubtedly was the greatest inventive genius in locks that ever lived [excepting], perhaps, Mark Shinburn, a burglar of a similar mechanical turn of mind. He could have made no end of money designing burglar-proof devices, but preferred demonstrating the weakness of the existing ones in a practical way.... Within a few days George [found] he could open the lock by the simple procedure of drilling a small hole just below it and inserting a wire."

Through his social contacts with the bank's president, Leslie installed a confederate, Patrick Shevlin, as his inside man, securing him the post of daytime watchman—and substitute night watchman. During the nights he was on duty, Shevlin let Leslie into the bank at least twice, first to plant the wire behind the dial of the safe and afterward to remove it. Before long, Leslie had worked out the combination, though in the end his calculations would be unnecessary.

The precise makeup of the group that pulled the robbery varies with the telling, but it's generally agreed that the principal actors, drawn from Leslie's cohort, included Jimmy Hope, a veteran of the Ocean National Bank burglary; his son, Johnny Hope; Billy Kelly, an

A father and son who plied the same trade: Jimmy (left) and Johnny Hope

experienced bank burglar; and a new man, John Nugent. "Banjo Pete" Emerson, "Shang" Draper and Ned Lyons are reported to have been among the supporting players. Late at night on Saturday, October 26, Shevlin admitted the burglars to the bank, concealing them in a storeroom on an upper floor. At dawn, wearing rubber-soled shoes, they stole into Werkle's quarters and overpowered him as he was dressing.

Shevlin had learned shortly before that the bank had entrusted Werkle, an employee of twenty years, with the keys to the vault and the combination of the safe. Pressing a gun to Werkle's head, the burglars seized the keys and demanded the combination. Werkle demurred at first, but the gun was a powerful persuader. The gang bound and gagged him and his family, leaving Johnny Hope and John Nugent, pistols cocked, to guard them. They left "Banjo Pete," armed with a feather duster and made up with false whiskers to look like Werkle, tidying the bank's front room, in full view of the street. Passing the bank on his rounds, the cop on the beat bade him a cheery good morning.

The rest of the gang entered the vault, carrying "the finest kit of tools ever used in a bank burglary," Chief Walling said. "Every article composing it was of the best workmanship and material, and the cost of getting up such a collection could not have been less than $2500 or $3000."[*] Those tools had been paid for by Marm Mandelbaum.

Inside the safe were several smaller compartments. Using Marm's tools, the thieves forced them open one by one, cramming their contents into bags. "The gang [was] growing richer at the rate of about a hundred thousand dollars a minute," Sophie Lyons noted. As the hour neared for the barber to arrive and open his shop, they quickly stopped work, fleeing the bank before they could open the last compartment. Had they had time to do so, Lyons writes, "ten extra minutes would have doubled the value of the 'haul.'" But as it was, they left with $2,758,700—$11,000 of it in cash and the rest in securities. The new man, Nugent, helped carry the bags to the street.

---

[*]   About $74,000 to $89,000 in today's money.

The Manhattan Savings Institution burglary. **1**: Nugent, pistol drawn, covers the janitor, Louis Werkle; **2**: Johnny Hope covers Mrs. Werkle; **3**: A third burglar covers Werkle's mother-in-law; **4**: A confederate watches Broadway; **5**: Another watches Bleecker Street; **6**: A third, just inside, protects the line of retreat; **7**: "Banjo Pete" Emerson, made up to look like Werkle, dusts the front office in full view of the street.

The heist was front-page news throughout the country, and the Municipal Police were under immense pressure to solve it. "Though any number of clues had been worked out by the detectives," the *Times* reported on November 1, 1878, "they had not led to any satisfactory result." But Shevlin, the inside man, proved to be the weak link. Alcoholic, garrulous and bitter at having been awarded a vastly smaller share than he'd been led to believe—initially promised $250,000, he ultimately got just $600—he began airing his discontent in some of the city's well-trafficked watering holes.

Before long, Thomas Byrnes, then an ambitious police captain, broke Shevlin down and obtained a confession.* (The case made Byrnes's career: He went on to serve as the department's chief of

---

* Small wonder. Byrnes, the author of *Professional Criminals of America*, was an enthusiastic early adopter of the aggressive method of interrogation that would soon be known as the third degree. "Perhaps he was a tyrant because he was set over crooks, and crooks are cowards in the presence of authority," the reformer Jacob Riis wrote of Byrnes in 1901. "His famous 'third degree' was chiefly what he no doubt considered a little wholesome 'slugging.' He would beat a thief into telling him what he wanted to know."

detectives and was later named superintendent of police.) Shevlin's confession led to the arrests of several members of Leslie's gang: Some, including Johnny Hope and Billy Kelly, were convicted and sentenced to long prison terms.* Defending other members of the gang, William Howe and Abraham Hummel furnished their customary assistance, to the tune of $90,000—a fee doubtless provided, at least in part, by Marm.

The bagman of the heist, John Nugent, was acquitted after standing trial in 1880. Perhaps that verdict was to be expected: In his daytime life, he had been, until his trial, Police Officer John Nugent of the city's Eighteenth Precinct.

CONSPICUOUSLY ABSENT FROM THE BURGLARY that was to have been his masterwork was George Leonidas Leslie. On June 4, 1878, nearly five months before the heist, the body of an unknown man was found at Tramp's Rock, an isolated spot in the countryside near Yonkers, just north of New York City. The dead man, elegantly dressed, with an expensive diamond pin and pearl studs in his shirt, had been shot in the chest; the presence of a pearl-handled pistol near the body suggested suicide. That impression was quickly dispelled by the discovery of a second bullet hole through the victim's head.

Reading a description of the man in the newspapers, Marm grew deeply worried: She was aware that Leslie had been missing for several days. But traveling to Yonkers to view the body was out of the question—it would make her long, clandestine business association with Leslie far too public. She quietly sent one of her underlings, Hermann Stoude, in her place; he identified the dead man as George Leslie. Curiously, as detectives discovered, though Leslie would have bled heavily from his wounds, the clothes on his body were completely unstained, suggesting that he had been shot while naked and dressed post-mortem. That finding all but eliminated robbery as the motive.

---

* Johnny Hope's conviction was overturned in 1890.

In fact, the *New-York Times* concluded in its coverage of the case, it was lust rather than avarice that had caused Leslie's death. "[Leslie] had a wife, who lives in Philadelphia, and [he] had supplanted another 'professional' in the love of a New-York woman. . . . His wife was cognizant of this *liaison,* knows the name of the woman, and, on account of her husband's criminal intimacy with her, left him and went to her home in the Quaker City. The New-York woman, it appears . . . was aware that her former lover or husband cherished a feeling of revenge toward [Leslie] and she was on that account very much alarmed about his welfare."

She was right to be. The woman in question appears to have been Babe Draper, the wife of Leslie's fellow "professional" "Shang" Draper. Though no one was ever charged in Leslie's murder, it appears that he had been killed at Draper's home in Brooklyn (where he was quite possibly caught *in flagrante* with Babe) before his body was transported north to Tramp's Rock.

Mrs. Mandelbaum notified Mollie Leslie of her husband's death, paid her fare to New York and supplied her with money to tide her over. Marm also paid the funeral expenses for the man she esteemed as "her one pet and star"; Leslie was buried in Cypress Hills Cemetery, a sprawling necropolis that today straddles Brooklyn and Queens.* After the funeral, Fredericka brought the young widow back to her home on Clinton Street. There, a later chronicler wrote, "this hard-faced, crime-laden old woman, sat rocking herself to and fro."

"Poor George," she murmured over and over as she rocked. "He was such a nice man."

AS THINGS TRANSPIRED THAT October, the heist George Leslie had engineered augmented neither his legacy nor Marm's fortune. In their haste to flee the vault, the Manhattan Savings Institution bur-

---

* Other notable people buried in Cypress Hills over the years include Piet Mondrian, Mae West, the Collyer Brothers, Eubie Blake, Nella Larsen and Jackie Robinson.

glars committed a blunder that Leslie almost certainly wouldn't have made: They pulled from the safe a huge number of securities that couldn't be resold. Of the $2,747,700 in securities they took, fully $2,506,700 worth were registered in the bank's name and therefore non-negotiable. They could be ransomed back to the bank, of course, but any reward would be vastly less than their face value and would be hugely outweighed by the risks involved. Of the negotiable bonds that remained, most were recovered by the police.

In the end, the entire cohort got away with little more than the $11,000 in cash. The fiasco, together with Leslie's murder, seems in hindsight like a dark augury of the coming decade, which would bring Fredericka great trouble, great sorrow and the irreversible decline of her career. Yet it is in these years that she rises to her full glory—cunning, resourceful, defiant—even as the edifice she built so painstakingly starts to be dismantled around her.

BOOK THREE

Nemesis

Chapter Eight

Thieves Fall Out

DESPITE THE FAILINGS OF THE DEXTER BANK AND MANHATTAN SAVINGS jobs, despite the loss of her beloved "Western George," Fredericka's life in the late 1870s had assumed a largely satisfying routine. The burglaries of elegant homes and exclusive shops continued apace, with Marm intimately involved in their orchestration. One, of a New York dry-goods store, netted "eight or nine pieces of silk" collectively worth $10,000.* Another, by her regular foot soldiers Billy Porter and Michael Kurtz, known in the underworld as "Sheeny Mike," relieved a Lower Manhattan jewelry shop of $30,000 worth of gems.†

Life was also satisfying on a personal level, for Mrs. Mandelbaum had the sustained pleasure of working daily with those closest to her. Her eldest son, Julius, who would turn twenty in 1880, had been helping out in the shop and running errands for her since he was in his early teens. And her trusted assistant Hermann Stoude—a burly blond widower and "the only person . . . Mandelbaum kept in her complete confidence"—had become her life partner as well. Marm being Marm, however, "he was . . . always seen as a lackey to Mandelbaum and [was] in no way in control of any of her operations."

---

* More than $200,000 in today's money.

† More than $800,000 worth today.

Then, in 1881, fallout from a crime committed four years earlier would bring about Fredericka's first significant public defeat.

ON THE NIGHT OF January 15, 1877, thieves armed with a duplicate key had entered the outer door of a building on Washington Street in Boston.* Inside, they bored a hole in the wall that separated them from James Scott & Co., a prosperous dry-goods shop. Among the burglars was Michael Kurtz, who packed the swag—twenty-six shawls, with a combined value of $780,† and 2,000 yards of fine black silk, valued at $4,000‡—into several trunks and walked coolly out the front door.

Michael Kurtz

Taking a waiting carriage to the station, Kurtz boarded the night train to New York. There, he brought the trunks to the Lower East Side home of his sister, Sarah Fox. Joining him at Mrs. Fox's house

---

* This burglary took place a year and a half before the death of George Leslie, and according to an account in the *New-York Times*, Leslie himself (alias George Howard) was one of the burglars.

† About $22,000 in today's money.

‡ Nearly $113,000 today.

to look the goods over was his longtime fence, Fredericka Mandelbaum, accompanied by Hermann Stoude. She paid Kurtz about
$1,600 for the lot, on which she expected to make many thousands
when she sold it onward.

Though the robbery was a sensation in Boston, the police there
had no leads. Only some months later, after the store owner, James
Scott, engaged a Boston private detective agency, Wiggin & Wood,
was Kurtz apprehended and arrested in Washington, D.C.* " 'Sheeny
Mike' is one of the cleverest store robbers in the country, making a
specialty of stealing silks," the *Boston Globe* would declare. "There
is hardly a large city in the country that has not at times received a
visit from this well-known crook, and many a large establishment . . .
has had cause to mourn his advent to the place."

Whenever a member of the Mandelbaum organization was arrested, there was a Plan B. As Kurtz rode the train back to Boston in
the custody of Detectives Wiggin and Wood, he asked to be permitted to cable Marm; he appears to have told the detectives that he
would prevail upon her to return Scott's stolen merchandise. On
reaching Philadelphia, Kurtz was allowed to send his telegram,
which asked her to meet the train in Jersey City, New Jersey. But on
receiving it, Marm recognized immediately that a rendezvous there
would give her insufficient time for what she had to do. And thus it
was not until the train pulled into the Harlem station, a dozen miles
north of Jersey City, that Fredericka Mandelbaum, all towering,
silk-clad six feet of her, was spied waiting on the platform, armed
with a writ of habeas corpus.

Marm demanded that Kurtz be released, as the writ required.
But in their haste to draw it up, Howe & Hummel had made a costly,
uncharacteristic mistake: The writ was served only on Detective
Wiggin. Providentially for his captors, Kurtz was just then out of
sight in a compartment of the train, handcuffed to Detective Wood.
Stepping onto the platform alone, Wiggin declared, in all literal

---

* In that era, some private investigators, including those of the Pinkerton National
Detective Agency, had the power of arrest.

honesty, that he had no prisoner. The train left the station with Michael Kurtz, both detectives and Mrs. Mandelbaum aboard.

As they rode, Kurtz exhorted Marm to return the goods to James Scott.

"What goods?" she asked innocently.

The goods he'd brought her, Kurtz replied.

The exchange left Fredericka incensed: Kurtz's request was a sign of capitulation—and a deep breach of underworld etiquette. ("Now what do you think of that sucker talking that way to me?" she asked a criminal associate when she recounted the incident soon afterward.) Mrs. Mandelbaum then held a hurried conversation with Kurtz in German before she got off the train at New Rochelle: She had a Plan C, though it seemed designed more to protect herself than to help Kurtz. As her contingency plans so often did, it involved a considerable sum of money.

Returning to the city, Marm convened a meeting at her Clinton Street home. Present were Kurtz's sister, Sarah Fox, along with several foot soldiers, including the "notorious" burglar Jimmy Hoey, and Hoey's wife, Mollie, an equally notorious, and equally accomplished, thief. Marm gave Jimmy Hoey $500,* together with a $1,000 government bond contributed by another attendee, and dispatched him to Boston to persuade James Scott to drop the charges against Kurtz.

Fredericka's gambit, the kind of thing that had worked splendidly in the days of Jonathan Wild, might have served her well early in her career. By the 1870s, however, attitudes toward property crime (especially property crime committed by people who weren't male, native born and of Anglo-Saxon Protestant stock) were changing. Through his attorney, Scott declared that he would accept only the return of the stolen goods or their full value. Marm replied that she had long since sold the goods onward, and held firm on the monetary offer. There was no deal.

---

*   About $14,000 today.

Mollie Hoey

Marm's obstinacy left Kurtz languishing unredeemed in a Boston jail. He pleaded guilty to the Scott burglary and was sentenced to twelve years in the state prison at Concord, Massachusetts. But less than four years later, when he was abruptly released, Mrs. Mandelbaum's troubles began in earnest.

THROUGHOUT THE 1850s AND '60s, American law enforcement had left operators like Marm Mandelbaum largely alone. In New York City, for instance, the focus of the police on "quality of life" issues meant that property criminals could work more or less unimpeded. But by the 1870s, the public's definition of criminality had altered. The nation's increasingly powerful bourgeois elite were now urging the law to take a harder line, especially when crime interfered with commerce. A reform campaign was sweeping American cities, and it boded ill for underworld entrepreneurs.

From America's colonial beginnings through the mid-nineteenth century, a cohort of moneyed Protestant men had governed the nation's cities and states, viewing leadership as equal parts ennobling civic duty and God-given moral right. "Politics as a vocation was never truly 'legitimate work,' " a historian notes. "Most successful politicians continued to designate themselves lawyers or businessmen or generals, as if they were temporarily on leave from their real occupations."

But by the mid-1800s, professional politics in American cities had increasingly become the domain of working-class immigrants—"saloonkeepers, grocers, policemen, and firemen rather than manufacturers and wealthy merchants." In response to this new proletarian power, the elites began walling themselves off from the masses in certain spheres. Earlier in the century, Gotham's gentry had sometimes frequented attractions like music halls and boxing matches side by side with their immigrant brethren. Now, at midcentury, they got busy founding rarefied institutions like the New York Philharmonic, established in 1842;* the American Museum of Natural History (1869); and the Metropolitan Museum of Art (1870).

New York's bourgeois elite next turned their attention to the conspicuously corrupt, now largely working-class, movers and shakers of Tammany Hall. "While corruption was no stranger to New York City and State governments when the elites held power," Rona Holub explains, "the access of the proletariat to this means of enhancing their self-interest seemed far more dangerous than anything that more privileged citizens might have done."

Bit by bit, these self-appointed reformers sought to kick the crooked ladder out from under the city's politicians and police. Undergirding their efforts were the class bigotry and xenophobia that had increasingly polarized New York. To further those aims, a spate of "good government" groups sprang up, their agendas largely reactionary. Among them was the New York Society for the Suppression of Vice, founded in 1873 by Anthony Comstock, a devout Congregationalist and an ardent campaigner against much that was related to sex, including obscenity, prostitution and birth control.[†]

---

* The ensemble, originally known as the Philharmonic Society of New York, presented its first concert on December 7, 1842. Tickets were by subscription only.

[†] One of Comstock's most notorious crusades was a sting operation in 1878 against the New York City birth-control provider and abortionist Ann Lohman, known profes-

The Women's Christian Temperance Union, founded the next year, aimed to stamp out immoderate drinking. The Society for the Prevention of Crime, established in 1877 by the Presbyterian minister Howard Crosby, was devoted to curbing gambling, prostitution and the violation of Sunday closing laws by saloons.

Reformers had already brought down Tammany Hall's most rapaciously visible representative, Boss William M. Tweed. In the wake of crusading political cartoons by Thomas Nast in *Harper's Weekly* in 1870–71 and, in July 1871, a multipart exposé in the *New-York Times* on the Tweed Ring's history of graft and extortion, Tweed was arrested late that year. Indicted on 220 counts of corruption, he was convicted of 204 of them in 1873. Tweed was sentenced to twelve years in prison, but in the picaresque arc that described his life, he wound up being released after only a year—before being rearrested, fleeing the country, living on the lam in Florida and Cuba, being captured in Spain and being reincarcerated in New York. He died in the city's Ludlow Street Jail in 1878, at fifty-five.

For Fredericka, this new climate was anything but favorable. "It could not have been lost on some reformers from the business community," Holub notes, "that Mandelbaum . . . cut into the profits of capitalists who . . . ran large and growing businesses in the garment, jewelry, and banking industries." One of those capitalists was James Scott of Boston, and he wanted his money.

WHILE IN PRISON FOR THE SCOTT ROBBERY, Michael Kurtz made a remarkable discovery: "that soap, taken internally, produced effects on the eater which would reduce him to a skeleton and induce those in authority to pardon him," the *New-York Daily Tribune* commented

---

sionally as Madame Restell; arrested and jailed, she committed suicide in prison. The coinage "comstockery," a byword for American neo-Puritanism, is attested in American newspapers as far back as 1889. The term was widely popularized by George Bernard Shaw, a frequent Comstock target, in a front-page open letter in the *New York Times* in 1905; in it, Shaw declared, "Comstockery is the world's standing joke at the expense of the United States."

afterward. And indeed, in 1881, the governor of Massachusetts, John Davis Long, granted Kurtz an official pardon "on his plea that he . . . would probably die were he to remain in prison."

On his release, Kurtz made a remarkable recovery.* Then, to pre-empt any return trips to prison and the renewed acquaintance with soapsuds they would entail, he began to sing. Meeting with Scott's attorney, he swore out an affidavit attesting to his part in the robbery. He further swore that Mrs. Mandelbaum had paid him seventy-five to eighty-five cents a yard for the silk and five dollars apiece for the shawls, and that she had helped him remove identifying marks from some of the stolen articles. Marm's underlings Jimmy and Mollie Hoey, who had been present at the meeting at which she proposed buying Kurtz's freedom, also gave sworn statements implicating her, as did Kurtz's sister, Sarah Fox.

"The most peculiar thing about the case," the *Boston Globe* would note, "is that 'Sheeny Mike,' Jimmy Hoey and his wife, Molly [*sic*], three notoriously solid thieves, should peach† and testify against Marm Mendelbaum [*sic*] in a suit of this sort." But given the law's hardening stance toward property crime, it was clearly in their interest to do so. And given that Marm, through fiscal obstinacy, had more or less sacrificed Kurtz, he would have felt he owed her nothing.

Armed with these affidavits, James Scott filed a civil suit against Mrs. Mandelbaum in early 1881: It sought $6,666,‡ plus court costs. "Mrs. Mandelbaum is a very sharp woman . . . and is not often caught napping," New York's police chief, George Washington Walling, would tell the *Boston Globe*. "I am glad that for once the old lady had been outwitted, and made to suffer for her violation of the law."

---

*   Kurtz (born c.1850) would live until 1904.

†   To inform on someone; from the obsolete verb *appeach*, "to accuse, inform on" (cf. *impeach*).

‡   Scott's suit demanded $4,000 for the stolen silk, $600 for the shawls and $2,066 in interest.

But Marm's day in court did not come quickly. The moment Scott's suit was filed, her attorneys, Howe & Hummel, swung into action, putting their guiding ethos—"Delay, delay, delay"—into glorious practice. First, they denied all allegations against their client and demanded that the suit be dismissed. There followed a flurry of pretrial court dates, and here the defense team was staggeringly lucky—or staggeringly canny—in the choice of pretrial judge: The Hon. Charles Donohue, of the New York State Supreme Court,* was a Mandelbaum crony.

Next, a small epidemic overtook the defense: "The case was again passed for the day . . . upon the ground that Mr. Howe, the defendant's counsel, was ill and could not try the case, and that the defendant herself was sick in bed and could not attend," court papers noted in January 1882. After that came a series of procedural snarls, including the dismissal of Scott's suit, though it was later reinstated. In 1883—the case still hadn't come to trial—Judge Donohue abruptly ordered that Scott's lawyers be replaced by attorneys from another firm, a move that would have delayed the proceedings further. There is no recorded rationale for his order, but for Donohue, hindrance was a time-honored modus operandi: He would later be investigated by the city's bar association[†] on the grounds that he had "grossly abused his powers . . . and been guilty of numerous wrongful and corrupt acts in his said office."[‡]

---

* Despite its august name, the New York State Supreme Court is a trial court and not the highest court in the state. That distinction has belonged, then as now, to the New York State Court of Appeals.

[†] Then known as the Association of the Bar of the City of New York, it is today the New York City Bar Association.

[‡] The bar association charged that Justice Donohue had "granted to corrupt and powerful classes, and to favored individuals of such classes, sometimes for months, a virtual exemption from the laws . . . and . . . brought the administration of justice into contempt by making it apparent that influence and not justice controls his action." In 1886, the bar association requested a further investigation into Donohue's judicial conduct by the judiciary committee of the New York State Assembly; after investigating, the committee held that the charges were unsupported. Donohue left the bench in 1889 and joined the New York attorneys Richard Newcombe and Albert Cardozo, Jr. (brother of the future United States Supreme Court justice Benjamin N. Cardozo), in the firm that would be known as Cardozo, Newcombe & Donohue.

——

ON JANUARY 23, 1884, in the State Supreme Court in Manhattan, *James Scott vs. Fredericka Mandelbaum* opened at last; presiding was Judge Hooper C. Van Vorst. Marm entered the courtroom clad in "somber though rich" attire: a black silk dress, trimmed with lace;* an "immense sealskin sacque"—a long, loose-fitting cloak that cascaded behind her; a beaded black velvet hat "with a beautiful bird's wing across the front"; brown kid gloves; a collar pin "set thick with pearls"; and diamond earrings. In the gallery were "a score of New York and Boston detectives," along with a Burke's Peerage of New York property criminals: " 'Bill' Smith, 'Big Bill,' 'Sheeny Rosy,' 'Big French Louis,' 'Whitey Bob,' 'Red Leary,' George Williams, and 'Tommy' King," all of whom looked, the *New-York Times* observed, "as honest as anybody else."

Taking the stand, James Scott described the robbery and listed the value of the stolen articles. Detective Wood recounted the apprehension of Michael Kurtz in Washington and the alerting of Mrs. Mandelbaum by telegram. The burglar Jimmy Hoey testified about the clandestine meeting at Mrs. Mandelbaum's home—"She wanted me to go to Boston and secure Mike's release"—and his unsuccessful attempt to buy Scott off. Hoey's wife, Mollie, was not available to testify: She was just then in jail. Her affidavit was read to the court. There would be far worse to come from Mollie Hoey before the year was out.

The star witness for Scott's side, Michael Kurtz, was also absent— and nowhere to be found. Nor was his sister, Sarah Fox, in the courtroom. (Covering the trial, the *Buffalo Evening News* commented dryly on the siblings' "sudden resumption of friendship for Mrs. Mandelbaum and the presumption that they kept out of the way in order not to testify against her.") Their affidavits, too, were read aloud.

---

* One cannot help wondering whether that black silk had once been the property of James Scott—a delicious way for Marm to thumb her nose at the proceedings.

As stage-managed by Howe & Hummel, the defense strategy was to show that Mrs. Mandelbaum "had been made the victim of a wicked conspiracy, hatched by Hoey and his wife and Kurtz, to obtain money." Taking the stand, Detective Sergeant Thomas Dusenbury, a twenty-five-year veteran of New York's police force, sought to impeach the Hoeys' affidavits. He had known the couple for years, he said, and "would not believe them under oath." Other police officers testified along similar lines.

After the last policeman stepped down, a visible stir ran through the courtroom: Fredericka Mandelbaum was called as the next witness.* Her sober, measured testimony was clearly designed to establish her respectability. "I am fifty-one years of age,"† she said. "I have four children. I live at 79 Clinton Street. I have lived there twenty years next September. I was once arrested but was immediately discharged. My husband has been dead nine years."

Mrs. Mandelbaum went on to deny all charges against her, testifying that Kurtz had telegraphed her only to ask her to inform his mother of his arrest. "She had *heard* that Sheeny Mike was a burglar," the *Times* recounted her saying. "She knew nothing about the writ of habeas corpus." And so it went. "The counsel for the defense declined to sum up," a news account said, "except to say that the prosecution was a cruel and wicked thing, and that there was no trustworthy evidence that Mrs. Mandelbaum ever had the goods in her possession."

In his summary, Scott's lawyer "referred to the array of policemen summoned to defend Mrs. Mandelbaum, and said there was not a policeman in the city who could not put his hand on receivers of stolen goods and gamblers and keepers of disreputable houses, if he saw fit." This case plainly showed, he argued, the extent to which

---

*   The account of her appearance that day by the *New-York Times* fully embodies the cavalier anti-Semitism and misogyny of the era: "She is a gross woman, a German Jewess, with heavy, almost masculine features, restless black eyes and a dark, unhealthy looking complexion."

†   Testifying under oath, Mrs. Mandelbaum, born March 28, 1825, shaved almost eight years off her actual age.

the police of New York City were beholden to Marm. Then, after a trial of a single day, the case went to the jury.

The jury deliberated only a short time. It returned a verdict for James Scott, awarding him the full $6,666, plus court costs, for a total of $7,267.75.* On January 25, two days after the trial, Mrs. Mandelbaum received the formal order to pay Scott that sum.

She could well afford it, but that was scarcely the point: The verdict, born of the reformist ardor now enveloping the country, was a public shaming, trumpeted far and wide in the press. Even worse, it emboldened the New York City district attorney, Peter B. Olney, to embark on a crusade that none of his predecessors had been inclined to take on: to mount a watertight criminal case against Fredericka Mandelbaum. But given the number of city policemen who were Mrs. Mandelbaum's lapdogs, Olney couldn't entrust the legwork to them. Auspiciously for him, there was another option at hand.

---

*   Nearly $220,000 in today's money.

Chapter Nine

The Thief-Taker General
of the United States of America

ONE DAY IN 1847, AN IMMIGRANT COOPER WAS SCOUTING AN ISLAND in the Fox River, northwest of Chicago, looking for timber with which to ply his trade. But what he came upon there would cause him to forsake barrel-making altogether: a covert encampment being used as a hideout by a band of counterfeiters, all wanted men. The cooper summoned the county sheriff, pocketed the reward for the counterfeiters' capture, and a going concern was born. Before long, other local businessmen were hiring him to apprehend the spate of counterfeiters who were crippling the region's commerce. And thus the cooper, Allan Pinkerton, became one of the first exemplars of a new breed of American entrepreneur, the private detective.

Pinkerton had been born in Glasgow, Scotland, on August 25, 1819, the son of a weaver who also served as a local police sergeant. When Allan was nine, his father died after being injured by a prisoner in his custody, leaving the family in poverty. As a youth, Allan apprenticed first to a printer, then to a cooper. He became an impassioned Chartist—a follower of the working-class reform movement that took root in Britain in the late 1830s to address widespread social inequities, including the lack of universal male suffrage.* (Pinkerton's position on workers' rights would change markedly

---

* At the time, British law granted the right to vote only to men who owned property.

after he became a detective.) In 1842, fleeing an arrest warrant resulting from his political activities, Pinkerton emigrated to the United States; after surviving a shipwreck, he fetched up in Chicago. The following year he settled in Dundee, Illinois, a Scottish enclave in the Fox River Valley. There, he continued his work as a cooper until the fateful encounter on the island four years later.

At the time, with the growth of American cities and the corresponding growth of American crime, there was a need for law enforcement that the country's fledgling police departments could not reliably fill. Spying this void, Pinkerton and his competitors rushed avidly in. "Private policing grew into a thriving enterprise," a historian writes. "Allan Pinkerton . . . was the most successful and probably the most efficient of this new type—although he had a penchant for publicity and a talent for self-glorification."

After discovering the counterfeiters, Pinkerton was made a sheriff's deputy, first in Kane County, Illinois, which includes Dundee, and then in Cook County, whose seat is Chicago. He was later named a special agent of the United States Postal Service, charged with investigating mail fraud and counterfeiting. In 1855, he was widely lauded in the press for making "the most important arrest in the annals of post office depredations ever brought to light in this country": the apprehension of Theodore Denniston, a Chicago postal clerk who had stolen thousands of dollars from the mails.

Pinkerton had opened his own office, on Washington Street in Chicago, in the early 1850s, devoted to "the transaction of a general Detective Police Business in Illinois, Wisconsin, Michigan and Indiana." A committed abolitionist, he also let his headquarters be used an Underground Railroad station for fugitive slaves traveling north to freedom. The agency would bear various names in its early years, including the North West Police Agency and Pinkerton's National Police Agency, before becoming Pinkerton's National Detective Agency in the late 1860s. By then the company, with its familiar logo of an all-seeing eye and the motto "We Never Sleep," had become a nationwide business "without jurisdictional limits," with branch offices in New York, Philadelphia and elsewhere.

Pinkerton agents, who had full power of arrest, pursued and captured miscreants throughout the country, including counterfeiters, forgers and bank burglars, along with myriad lawbreakers amid the lawless free-for-all of the frontier. By the end of the 1860s, Allan Pinkerton was, as the *Brooklyn Eagle* rapturously proclaimed, "the best known and most successful detective, not only of this country but of the world." He had enjoyed conspicuous success during the Civil War, when the Union general George B. McClellan recruited him to supply intelligence to the Army of the Potomac: His duties included monitoring Washington for subversives and overseeing Union spies working undercover in the Confederacy. He also furnished private security for President Lincoln.*

Allan Pinkerton (left), with President Lincoln and Maj. Gen. John A. McClernand at Antietam in 1862

*   While Pinkerton's presidential security work is a matter of historical fact, he also claimed that he thwarted an assassination plot against Lincoln, to have been carried out in February 1861. Some later chroniclers have posited that Pinkerton's habitual self-aggrandizement led him to overstate his own importance in foiling the plot; still others suggest that he made up the assassination threat out of whole cloth to curry favor with the newly elected president.

The agency's successes were widely disseminated in Allan Pinkerton's triumphalist memoirs: seventeen volumes, published between 1875 and 1884, that were a vital part of his company's public self-mythologizing.* Its failures, including the inability to capture Jesse James and his gang in Missouri in the 1870s, after a sustained pursuit that left two Pinkerton agents dead, were less loudly trumpeted.

While Pinkerton's memoirs served up his men as modern-day knights errant—sterling champions of law and order—the reality was far darker. Increasingly, the agency was hired by railroad tycoons, coal barons and other powerful industrialists to frame labor activists and break strikes, often violently, in the effort to quash working-class power that had begun to define the era. Once "a quasi-official arm of the state [for] chasing criminals and bandits," Pinkerton's National Detective Agency had become, by the last quarter of the nineteenth century, "capital's muscle."

Between 1877 and 1892, a historian notes, the Pinkertons played aggressive roles in at least seventy strikes around the country—on more than one occasion firing into the crowd and killing a striker or bystander. By the 1880s, "Pinkertonism" had become a bitter byword for the ethos of such hired mercenaries. "Capital is marshaling its forces under the black banner of Pinkertonism," the American labor newspaper *John Swinton's Paper* warned in 1887. "Prepare to meet it!"†

ON JULY 1, 1884, Allan Pinkerton died at his home in Chicago, at sixty-four, after a long illness. Even in death, he had fabulous press:

---

* A twenty-first-century historian of the agency calls the books "novelizations" of Pinkerton's case files.

† As a modern-day historian observes: "Perhaps the most infamous of these enterprises, and certainly the one that has drawn the most direct comparisons to the Pinkertons, is Blackwater USA. . . . Blackwater and the dozens of similar companies that have emerged since 2001 reconfirm the lessons learned about the Gilded Age Pinkertons; it is problematic for the state to privatize the authority to kill."

"[His] name has been a terror to all the great thieves and other rascals in this country for the past thirty years," the *Boston Globe* declared. "His whole record in ferreting out crime is probably without
parallel in modern history," the *Kansas City Daily Times* proclaimed. From the *New-York Times:* "Very few great crimes have
occurred in this country in the last 20 years in the detection of
which Pinkerton's agency has not had a hand."

There was no question that the agency he built would endure:*
Pinkerton's son William had already taken over the Chicago office,
which handled the company's Western cases; his son Robert, based
in New York, had charge of operations in the East. In late 1883,
when New York City's new district attorney, Peter Olney, took office,
he began to contemplate a criminal case against Fredericka Mandelbaum. He recognized immediately that a police force for hire—
especially one that was "for all intents and purposes . . . capital's
private army"—was exactly what he needed.

The agency's next
generation: Robert (left)
and William Pinkerton,
on the trail of outlaws
in the American West

* It endures to this day, now known simply as Pinkerton.

THE SON OF A BANKER and textile manufacturer, Peter Butler Olney was born in Oxford, Massachusetts, in 1843, to an old and distinguished New England family: His elder brother, Richard, would serve as United States attorney general, and later secretary of state, under President Grover Cleveland.

Peter was educated at Phillips Andover Academy and earned bachelor's and law degrees from Harvard. He spent two years with the New York firm Evarts, Southmayd & Choate before going into partnership with Francis C. Barlow, a lawyer and retired Union Army general, in 1869. After Barlow, a Republican, became New York State attorney general in 1872, Olney, a reformist Democrat, helped him investigate and prosecute members of the Tweed Ring.

In 1875, Peter Olney ran for New York County district attorney as a post-Tweed Tammany candidate; he lost to the Republican incumbent, Benjamin K. Phelps, and returned to his law practice. In December 1883, New York's sitting D.A., the Democrat Wheeler H. Peckham, resigned after little more than a week in office, citing ill health. Grover Cleveland, then governor of New York,* appointed Olney to fill the post. "This office was not sought by me, and I have accepted it at considerable personal sacrifice," Olney told the *New-York Times* immediately afterward. "I enter upon the discharge of my duties untrammeled and without prejudices. I intend to faithfully perform every duty of the office to the satisfaction of the public as far as I can, and to the satisfaction of my own sense of what is right."

To bourgeois New Yorkers of the day, the sense of what was right included apprehending and prosecuting underworld property criminals—and one underworld property criminal in particular. By all accounts Peter Olney shared this view. "If [Olney's] private utterances are to be believed, and there has never been, among re-

---

* Cleveland served as governor of New York from January 1883 to January 1885. He began the first of his two nonconsecutive terms as president of the United States on March 4, 1885. (Inauguration Day for U.S. presidents was moved from March 4 to January 20 upon ratification of the Twentieth Amendment in 1933.)

Peter B. Olney
in 1883

spectable persons, a doubt in this regard," police chief Walling would write, "he thought that the existence of a woman who by various means had been enabled to control the most dangerous and wealthy criminal interests of America was a burning shame."

The Municipal Police, Olney knew, would be of no avail: "Her intimacy with the detectives of the police force was only less close and confidential than her intimacy with the thieves," the *Times* observed. "It was not imbecility but interest that prevented the making of a [police] case against the woman." But as Olney also knew, the Pinkertons could handily meet his needs: They had already helped apprehend Marm's associate "Shang" Draper for an 1876 bank burglary in Massachusetts.* And so, in early 1884, D.A. Olney engaged one private entrepreneur, Robert Pinkerton, to bring down another, Fredericka Mandelbaum.

DESCENDING ON KLEINDEUTSCHLAND, Pinkerton agents spent weeks covertly watching the outside of Mrs. Mandelbaum's shop from

* Mrs. Mandelbaum appears to have had no involvement in this burglary, of the Northampton National Bank, on January 26, 1876. Robert Pinkerton would arrest Draper for the crime in 1878.

rented rooms nearby. "They say that among the visitors were pick-pockets and shoplifters, and that some of the latter came direct from large dry goods stores loaded with merchandise," the *New York Sun* reported afterward. "There were also many apparently respectable persons, who made purchases, which were invariably delivered by Stoude. These persons, they say, were shopkeepers of this city, who bought good stock cheap from Mother Mandelbaum."

But nothing the Pinkertons saw would let them arrest Marm herself: It was impossible to demonstrate purely from these comings and goings that she was knowingly buying stolen goods. In addition, her neighbors, who revered her, would alert her whenever close scrutiny, much less a raid, appeared imminent.*

"We shadowed the place night and day," Robert Pinkerton would recall:

It was difficult work. All [Mrs. Mandelbaum's] neighbors knew what her business was, and when they saw anybody watching, they ran and told her. Down the . . . window shades would come, and they remained down for days. After six weeks' spying, the family dropped on[†] us. They must have noticed that whenever anybody left the store with a bundle we followed to see where he went. One day . . . Stoude sallied forth with his arms filled with packages. He got on a horse car and our men sat behind him. He turned around and pre-sented them each with a bundle.

"Take them now," he said; "it will save you the trouble of following me." They were bundles of paper.

---

* This kind of thing also happened on the frontier, where townspeople, who often venerated Western bandits as Robin Hood figures, might thwart the Pinkertons' efforts to apprehend them.

† Per the *Oxford English Dictionary*, "drop on," in late-nineteenth-century usage, meant "to come casually or accidentally to knowledge of (something); to understand, become aware of, recognize."

Faced with these obstacles, Pinkerton and Olney determined that only a single course of action remained: entrapment.

To lead the operation, Pinkerton chose Agent Gustave Frank. Frank, who had worked for the Pinkertons since 1865, had emigrated to America from Cologne and spoke German fluently. Now, in the spring of 1884, as he prepared to go after Mrs. Mandelbaum, Frank shaved his conspicuous black beard, memorized the latest silk prices and slipped quietly into Kleindeutschland.

Olney had already written to the city's leading silk merchants, asking them to mark their wares: The plan was for Frank to catch Fredericka in the act of knowingly handling stolen silk, and then to prove as much in court by means of the dealers' covert markings. Armed with $1,000 from Robert Pinkerton, Frank presented himself at Marm's shop as a shady silk jobber named Stein. He asked to buy a large quantity of silk that he might profitably resell elsewhere. Always wary, Marm had grown even more so in the wake of her civil-court defeat. She turned Frank down. "Burned children," she confided to Stoude, "are shy of the fire."

But Frank returned amiably to the shop again and again and slowly won her confidence. At last, she let him become one of her resale agents—though not before she tested his bona fides by making him judge various grades of silk and quizzing him on current prices. Thanks to his diligent study, Frank passed handily, and Marm sold "Stein" his first lot, with strict orders not to resell it in New York, where it might be recognized. "As fast as the silks were bought by Frank, they went into the hands of other detectives," the *Times* reported. "Those marked were taken to dealers until the right owner was found."

But this alone was not enough to make Frank's case: Not every silk merchant had responded to Olney's request, which meant that much of what Frank bought couldn't be traced. Even when it could, a merchant would first need to identify his own silk beyond doubt, and then be able to show, as the *Times* genteelly put it, that it had "disappeared in other than the usual business style." And even if a merchant could demonstrate that a piece of silk had been stolen, Frank still had the onus of proving that Marm had *known* it was stolen when she bought it. What was more, Marm's son Julius diligently examined all silk that came into the shop for private marks.*

Throughout that spring, Frank bought silk from Mrs. Mandelbaum—in such quantity, Robert Pinkerton would note, "that he shut out other customers." At last, early in the summer, there was a break in the case. On June 22, Frank was in Marm's shop, where she and Julius were pricing a newly arrived lot of silk. As Marm was tallying the yardage, Julius paused over a speckled gray piece. "Hold on, Mother," he exclaimed. "This piece is marked." The letters LL were faintly discernible on the edge of the cloth.

Frank withdrew his pocket knife and offered to cut off the marked strip, though the knife proved too dull. But his charade had worked as intended: It left him holding the silk by the marked edge, so that when Fredericka sheared through it with a pair of scissors, Frank retained possession of the edge. She ordered him to destroy it, and he carried the strip into the backyard.

Returning to the shop, Frank announced that he had thrown the marked piece into the privy. "You mustn't be so careless," Fredericka admonished him. "You'll get us caught." Next time, she said, he should burn it. In fact, Frank had pocketed the strip as evidence: The telltale "LL" was the private mark of Simpson, Crawford & Simpson, the New York textile firm from which the silk had been stolen.

Of the 12,000 yards of silk that Frank would buy from Mrs. Mandelbaum during the spring and summer of 1884, only 160 yielded identifiable markings—"a bit," a modern chronicler observes, "like nabbing a multimillion-dollar tax cheat for having falsified a few business lunches." But for Olney, those 160 yards were enough. On July 18, 1884, he obtained a search warrant for Mrs.

---

* The few marked pieces that Frank did manage to secure had evidently escaped the watchful eyes of Marm and her staff.

Mandelbaum's building, along with arrest warrants for her, Julius and Stoude.

On the morning of Tuesday, July 22, 1884, Frank and three fellow agents burst into Fredericka's shop. The safe was opened, the jewels spilled out, Frank urged her to come clean and Fredericka socked him in the face. "So you are the one who is at the bottom of this, you wretch, you!" she cried, adding: "I can't believe you have tricked me. We both have families. Don't give us away." But Frank led her away, together with Stoude. Julius, who was not in the shop at the time, was arrested later that day.

NEWS OF FREDERICKA'S ARREST made front pages around the country and was reported as far away as Ireland. "Got Mother Mandelbaum," the *New York Sun* crowed; "A Clever Capture," said the *St. Louis Post-Dispatch*. "She will doubtless go to the penitentiary and her business [be] broken up," the *Philadelphia Times* prophesied.

In years past, Fredericka could have preempted that outcome with a few well-timed contributions to her powerful cronies. Back then, many Americans had looked upon the robber barons as the real crooks: "These were the perpetrators of rampant frauds; these were the *professional* criminals of the day, not a woman who may have bought and sold some stolen property," Rona Holub observed. But by the 1880s, the bourgeoisie were eager "to deflect attention from crime that could be connected to businessmen of their own class." Their social platform, which aimed to retrain the spotlight onto working-class criminals, now included a stout plank labeled "Crime Does Not Pay."*

* One of the most visible standard-bearers for the new "Crime Does Not Pay" agenda was Marm's former protégée Sophie Lyons. With the waning of crime's post–Civil War Golden Age, in which Lyons had flourished handsomely, and the arrival of the late-nineteenth- and early-twentieth-century neo-Puritan era, in which she knew she wouldn't, she published a breathless, seemingly repentant memoir. First issued in 1913, it was released over the years under various titles, including *Why Crime Does Not Pay*. In it, Lyons repudiates her life as a shoplifter and swindler and denounces

Sophie Lyons, author
and investor, in her
publicly repentant
years

Where Marm's street savvy had guided her nimbly through the era of "I seen my opportunities and I took 'em," she was now confronting a New York in flux, a city both more and less corrupt than it had been in her heyday. For one thing, she could no longer depend on the sustained protection of the police—not because policemen had grown more honest, but because they had grown more extortionate. What had once been a manageable level of genteel graft had over the years become the perennial, no-holds-barred blackmail of Marm by numerous members of the department. "She claimed that if she had greased the right palms, she could have

---

Mrs. Mandelbaum. "Alas! I knew her well—too well," she writes. "A hundred, yes, perhaps near five hundred transactions I have had with her, little and big." In later years, Lyons, who had retained enough of her ill-gotten gains to grow wealthy from real-estate investments, wrote for the newspapers as a society gossip columnist. She died in 1924, at seventy-six.

evaded prosecution and continued her life and her business as in the past," Holub wrote. "But by the fall of 1884, she resented the idea that she could spend the rest of her life and a good deal of her fortune keeping 'unethical' and 'dishonest' authorities at bay."

Nor could Marm depend on the judicial system anymore for kid-glove treatment. Amid the new Puritanism that underlay the city's reformist fervor, Fredericka Mandelbaum, a brazen immigrant Jewish woman who unabashedly did not know her place, stood little chance: Olney had vowed that he would prosecute her "to the end, if it is the last act of his life." For the first time in her career, despite her grit, acumen and great wealth, Fredericka Mandelbaum found herself in a spot she might not be able to pay her way out of. Two options remained: to trust Howe and Hummel to work their underhanded magic, or to become a fugitive from the law.

Chapter Ten

The Maypole and the Egg

THE "FLASH AGE," WHEN FREDERICKA MADE HER FORTUNE, WAS AN ERA of "crime, reckless extravagance [and] political corruption," a journalist has noted. "Its annals are punctuated with murders, bank robberies, spectacular Wall Street gambling and the doings of many bizarre characters." Few New Yorkers took more dazzling advantage of this urban free-for-all, or were more bizarre characters themselves, than William Howe and Abraham Hummel. For had Howe and Hummel not already existed, Damon Runyon would have had to invent them.

If the partners' instruction manual, *Danger!*, had been conceived to get thieves into trouble, then the partnership was in business to get them out again: From start to finish, the book was intended as professional advertising for the firm that was, in the immodest words of its introduction, "what we may be pardoned for designating the best-known criminal law offices in America."

Established in 1869, Howe & Hummel was "the unofficial bar of the New York underworld." It represented a rogues' gallery of the era's foremost criminals: arsonists, murderers, robbers, forgers, con men, dope peddlers, safecrackers, bucket-shop owners,* Five Points gangsters, Tammany pols. Its offices, at 89 Centre Street, were con-

---

*   A bucket shop was an illicit office for betting on the stock market.

veniently across the street from the Tombs,* the venerable Lower
Manhattan house of detention that in that wide-open era boasted
an on-site saloon. Though professional advertising by lawyers was
then deeply discouraged, the partners gleefully flouted convention
by erecting, on the façade of their building, an immense sign, some
25 feet long and illuminated at night, trumpeting the firm's name
in great capital letters.

Even in an age when ethical elasticity among lawyers was far
from unknown, Howe & Hummel's methods stood out: They bribed,
they blackmailed, they swindled, they slandered, they suborned
perjury, they fabricated evidence, they fixed judges,† they staged
elaborate courtroom spectaculars that, in Howe's bejeweled, corpu-
lent case, were costumed within an inch of their lives. Even a temporary disbarment (for Hummel, in 1872)‡ and a declaration of
personal bankruptcy (by Howe, in 1875) could not derail them for
long. So famous were they in their own time that a standard drinking man's toast—to hoist a glass and declare "Here's how!"—was
almost invariably met with "Here's Hummel!"

Writing in 1903, the year after Howe died, *The Law Student's
Helper*, a monthly magazine, recalled a characteristic courtroom
ploy:

* The prison's nickname stems from an earlier incarnation, an Egyptian Revival
building designed by the architect John Haviland, erected in the Five Points area in
1838 and said to resemble an Egyptian tomb. The building occupied a lot bounded by
Centre, Franklin, Elm (now Lafayette) and Leonard streets. Today known formally as
the Manhattan Detention Complex, the Tombs is located just north of that site, at 125
White Street.

† As the journalist Richard H. Rovere writes in his history of the firm: "There are
no recorded instances of Howe fixing or even attempting to fix, a juryman. He and
Hummel had bribed judges, suborned perjury, and engaged in every other malprac-
tice, but the record is clean on juries. Yet in spite of the record, and in spite of the low
esteem in which virtue generally was held in the Howe & Hummel office, there was
never so much as a single charge of jury-fixing on Howe's part." He adds: "More likely
than not the record is clean because the attempts that were made were successful."

‡ The disbarment was "for a bit of careless bribery upstate," another historian of
the firm recounts. Hummel was later reinstated, though he would be disbarred permanently, for conspiracy, in 1906. He spent a year in the city penitentiary on Blackwell's Island (now Roosevelt Island) before decamping for England in 1908.

Another story is told of Mr. Howe's tears while pleading for a client's life or liberty. . . . During the trial of [a] homicide case the alleged wife of the prisoner sat with a baby on her lap. While Mr. Howe was pleading for his client's acquittal, he was seen to scowl at the mother. She gazed at him in blank amazement. Mr. Howe stopped and moved close up to the mother and the baby. Suddenly the baby began to cry. Mr. Howe also wept. The baby's cries almost immediately subsided. Recorder Hackett* looked up with a smile and remarked:

"Mr. Howe, you had better give the baby another jab with a pin."

The Howe & Hummel modus operandi produced one acquittal after another. Marm Mandelbaum valued their work so much—on her own behalf and that of the cadre of shoplifters, housebreakers and bank burglars in her employ—that she was said to have kept them on an annual retainer of $5,000.† The firm had no shortage of clients. "The timing was simply right for their kind of law," the firm's chronicler Richard H. Rovere has noted. "It certainly helped that after the Civil War, crime in New York got more organized and more ambitious—and there was more of it. By the early 1870s, there were 30,000 thieves, 2,000 gambling dens, thousands of prostitutes, and a critical mass of highly skilled bank robbers and con artists." Howe & Hummel represented an awful lot of them.

Besides Marm and her syndicate, clients over the years included Marm's old mentor "General Abe" Greenthal and his pocket-picking "Sheeny Mob"; the McLaughlin-Valentine gang, a group of expert forgers; the Pool Sellers Association, a consortium of book-

---

* John Keteltas Hackett was the recorder of New York City from 1866 to 1879. The post of recorder, which existed from 1683 to 1907, entailed various duties over time, including the holding of judgeships and serving as deputy mayor.

† Five thousand dollars in the 1870s was the equivalent of well over $100,000 today.

makers and policy-shop* owners; the Whyos, "an organization of thugs and killers that was perhaps the toughest of all the nineteenth-century gangs"; and the den mothers of the city's premier houses of prostitution ("When seventy-four madams were rounded up during a purity drive in 1884, every one of them named Howe & Hummel as counsel"). Because of the quantity and quality of forgers it represented, the firm would not take personal checks, accepting payment—which could run to many tens of thousands of dollars per case—only in cash.

HOWE, A CONTEMPORARY OF FREDERICKA'S, was born circa 1828, possibly in England.† As a young man, he appears to have been a clerk in the office of a London lawyer. In 1854, Howe was convicted of conspiracy at the Old Bailey, London's chief criminal court: The case involved the submission of a false affidavit designed to secure a convict's release from prison. He was sentenced to eighteen months behind bars, though whether he actually served any time is unknown. By the late 1850s, Howe had "washed up in New York to make his fortune"; within a few years he had hung out a shingle as a practicing attorney.

"The evolution from criminal into criminal lawyer was a natural enough one in a period when . . . the criminal bar consisted mainly of unfrocked priests, drunkards, ex-police magistrates, and political riffraff of all sorts," Rovere writes. "At any rate, by 1861, Howe was

---

* An illegal betting parlor in which patrons could wager on the numbers to be drawn in a lottery.

† In an autobiographical note in *Danger!*, Howe states that he was born in Boston on July 7, 1828, the son of the Reverend Samuel Howe, "a rather well-known and popular Episcopal clergyman." This, however, like nearly everything else in the note, is a textbook example of the art of imaginative fiction. (The fictitious impulse extends to the dimensions of the note itself, which despite Howe's assertion—"However much the inclination and, I might add, temptation may run in the direction of fluency and diffuseness in this case, my utterance shall be as brief as possible"—spans six fluent, diffuse pages.)

William Howe

practicing in the local criminal courts. . . . There is no record of how or when he got his education in American law, but that in itself presents no mystery. The courts in those days were full of lawyers with no academic training . . . and a year or two in the office of any member of the bar would have sufficed."

By the postwar period, he had clearly made the fortune he sought, for if there was anyone in the city who could outdo Fredericka Mandelbaum for sheer volume of personal jewelry, and sheer expanse of surface area available for its display, it was William Frederick Howe. A commanding, spherical presence, he was a sight never beheld before—or since—in the sober confines of New York's courtrooms. His oratory before the bar was a vibrant purple and so, quite often, was his suit coat. In 1884, when he was representing Mrs. Mandelbaum after her arrest, the *New-York Times* recounted his courtroom entrance with a kind of awestruck horror:

When Mr. Howe made his appearance upon the scene . . . a titter was heard at the back of the room which was gradually extended until it reached the judicial bench, where it could go no further. The cause of this slight ripple of mirth was Mr. Howe's personal appearance, or, in other words, his "get up." The gentleman's suit was of the brightest bottle green slashed with indigo blue. . . . His shirt was of a pink and green draught-board pattern, though this was nearly hidden by diamonds of all sizes. Mr. Howe looked like a Maypole of more than ordinary circumference. He was unconscious of the amusement his appearance caused, or if he did notice any demonstration, he doubtless attributed it to his excessive popularity.

Then there was the jewelry: rings, collar buttons, cuff buttons, shirt buttons, watches, watch fobs, chains, lockets, lapel pins—all pendulous with diamonds and most worn simultaneously. "When the notorious Mother Mandelbaum appeared in a New York court the other day . . . she was attired in a gorgeous silk and ablaze with diamonds," the *Atlanta Constitution* wrote, reporting on the same proceedings:

> She was able to afford her fine rig, as a quarter of a century in the business of receiving stolen goods had netted her over a million dollars. This woman's counsel, Mr. Howe, of the firm of Howe & Hummel, also made quite a show of himself. He wore a diamond collar button, a diamond cravat ring, a diamond shirt stud, a diamond-studded chain fob, and his fingers glittered with a Masonic ring set in diamonds. . . . Lawyer and client seemed well mated, and they made a dazzling pair. Mother Mandelbaum has made her fortune through thieves, and so has Mr. Howe, but the calling of the one is under the ban of the law, while that of the other is a learned and honorable profession.

Howe's courtroom performances were as operatic as his wardrobe: "He had the voice of a pre-Stanislavsky tragedian and the personality of an accomplished carnival grifter," Rovere said.

"Howe's defenses were such good theatre that very often . . . the old Bowery Playhouse would contrive an evening's entertainment by acting them out straight from the court records."*

Howe was once called upon to defend an arsonist-for-hire named Owen Reilly. Reilly was prepared to stand trial for the crime, but Howe enjoined him to plead guilty to *attempted* arson instead. The district attorney accepted the plea. When Reilly appeared in court to be sentenced, Howe turned to the judge. By law, he reminded the court, the sentence for an attempted crime was half the maximum penalty for the actual commission of that crime. The maximum penalty for arson was life in prison. "Scripture tells us that we knoweth not the day nor the hour of our departure," Howe intoned. "Can this court sentence the prisoner at the bar to half of his natural life? Will it, then, sentence him to half a minute or to half the days of Methuselah?"

"The court agreed that the problem was beyond its earthbound wisdom," Rovere wrote. "Reilly walked out, presumably to arm himself with a new supply of matches and tinder, and the legislature revised the arson statutes soon thereafter."

ABRAHAM HUMMEL WAS HOWE'S INVERSE in nearly all respects: So thin that he was barely perceptible, he resembled a little Dickensian clerk from Central Casting—even in youth the very model of a fastidious, wizened old man. "I guess that most of what they say about me is true," Hummel once told a journalist. "I'm a crook and I'm a black-mailer. But there's one thing about me—I'm a neat son-of-a-bitch."

Habitually clad all in black ("probably to highlight his partner's gorgeous outfits," Rovere conjectures), Hummel wore elevator shoes with strange, long, pointy toes, "called 'toothpick shoes' by most of the reporters who described them." His head resembled a hard-

---

* The two "honest, hard-working mechanics" who in 1869 found the trunk containing proceeds from the Ocean National Bank burglary, were employees of that playhouse, located nearby. It is deeply satisfying to imagine them on their way to a staged reading of Howe & Hummel trial transcripts.

Abraham Hummel

boiled egg—but an egg turned laterally, longer front to back than top to bottom. Contemplating Howe and Hummel jointly in 1884, the *New-York Times* imagined them bookending a newspaper advertisement for a weight-loss tonic: " 'Before I took anti-fat' and 'After I took anti-fat.' "

Hummel had been born in Boston, circa 1850, to German Jewish parents. As a small child, he moved with his family to New York and was brought up in Kleindeutschland. As a youth, he said long afterward, he earned his first dollar one summer day by going out, armed with a pail and dipper, and selling "cold, clear water, fresh from Croton" to a regiment of Union soldiers that was massed, hot and thirsty, in Tompkins Square nearby. The water in his pail was ordinary tap water—"fresh from Croton" by way of a city street pump accessible to anyone.* Young Abe joined Howe's practice in 1863 as

---

* In 1832, a cholera epidemic caused by the city's polluted well water had killed more than 3,500 New Yorkers—one resident in 60. In response, the Croton Aqueduct was opened in 1842 in Westchester County, some 40 miles north, to supply the city with fresh water. "'Croton,'" a historian writes, "became a byword for good water." A newer incarnation of the aqueduct supplies as much as 30 percent of the city's water today.

a thirteen-year-old office boy; he would remain there to the end of his career.

As law partners, Howe and Hummel "evolved a division of labor and responsibility that satisfied both men and made it possible for them to handle anything the underworld had to offer," Rovere writes. "Howe handled the trials. All the murderers, bank robbers, and brothel keepers were his charges. Hummel took on the more complex criminal matters, such as gambling [and] fraud.... While Howe was down the block dazzling jurors with his diamonds and fouling their thought processes with his sonorous oratory, Little Abe holed up in his office and put his brains at the service of bookmakers, bucket-shop proprietors, and all the fancier elements of the firm's criminal clientele."

Hummel also oversaw the firm's large stable of theatrical clients, which included luminaries like P. T. Barnum, Edwin Booth, Sir Henry Irving, Fay Templeton, Lillie Langtry and Fahreda Mahzar, the hootchy-kootchy dancer known professionally as Little Egypt, who "scandalized Victorian New York."

"The firm's theatrical practice was the only respectable part of its [business]"—though in the Howe & Hummel universe, "respectable" was a profoundly relative term. Work for their thespian clients did include routine matters like divorces and contracts:* Hummel, for instance, oversaw the merger of circuses that produced Barnum & Bailey. But Howe & Hummel also ran a kind of judicial casting office, giving some of those clients roles in its staged courtroom dramas. If a defendant lacked a tearful bride, a frail white-haired mother or a passel of angelic children—all vital supporting players in a Howe & Hummel trial—they could be readily supplied from the firm's fount of theatrical talent. As a result, "repulsive and ape-like killers often turned up in court with lamblike children and wives of fragile beauty."

---

* Perhaps not exclusively routine. Rovere writes: "When Barnum, a prohibitionist of strong conviction, wanted contracts that would effectively enjoin the midgets and the dog-faced boys from ever using alcohol, Howe & Hummel, who had nothing against virtue when it paid, drew them for him."

Hummel's particular specialty was the form of genteel black-mail known as the breach-of-promise action. This, too, was abetted by the firm's theatrical clientele, in particular by its flock of comely young actresses, many of whom—providentially—had been wooed by prominent, wealthy men. At Hummel's direction, one of those women would swear out an affidavit that Mr. So-and-So had seduced her, promised marriage and then reneged. In an age when respectability was de rigueur, Mr. So-and-So (who was almost certainly already married) would do anything rather than have the affair exposed at trial. It generally cost him between $5,000 and $10,000* to ransom the affidavit, which would be burned, in his presence, in the iron brazier kept in Hummel's office for that purpose. The ransom money was split fifty-fifty between the firm and the actress. This breach-of-promise racket was so successful that it "was said to have enriched the partners by well over a million dollars in the course of its operations."†

Howe & Hummel's penchant for drama was on especially vivid display whenever a subpoena had to be served. It once served papers, theatrically, in an actual theater. In the late 1890s, the firm was suing the producer David Belasco: It charged that he was then staging an unauthorized Broadway adaptation of *Zaza*, a drama about a young prostitute by the French playwrights Pierre Berton and Charles Simon. Among those to be served was the play's star, Mrs. Leslie Carter, a celebrated actress‡ known as "the American Sarah

---

*   Five thousand dollars in the 1870s, for instance, was the equivalent of more than $100,000 today.

†   Occasionally the racket had unintended consequences. After being stung twice by Hummel for breach of promise, the distinguished architect Stanford White concluded that it would be more cost-effective simply to keep the firm on permanent retainer. And while Hummel's attempts to extort John Barrymore in this manner proved unsuccessful, Barrymore was so charmed by Hummel's craftiness that he retained him as his civil attorney.

‡   Mrs. Leslie Carter (c.1862–1937), born Caroline Louise Dudley, was a leading light of the Broadway stage. She starred in many of Belasco's productions, including *The Heart of Maryland* (1895), *Du Barry* (1901) and *Adrea* (1905). She later appeared in several silent films and in the talkie *Rocky Mountain Mystery* (1935), starring Randolph Scott.

Bernhardt." Hummel purchased a front-row seat for an especially nimble process server. As soon as the actress, decked out as the beauteous Zaza, made her entrance, the server sprang from his seat and leaped onto the stage. "Mrs. Carter met the applause of the audience and the outstretched hand of the process server at the same moment. The incident upset the temperamental Mrs. Carter so much that she had to retire for several minutes, summons in hand, and begin all over again."

After Howe's death in 1902, Hummel kept the firm going until his disbarment four years later. (He had been convicted, in 1905, of conspiracy to deceive the courts.) In 1907, following a lavish going-away party at his townhouse, he entered the city prison on Blackwell's Island to serve his one-year term. On his release, he settled in London, where he spent his last two decades in self-imposed exile; he died in his flat there in 1926. (Fittingly for one so long allied with the criminal world, the flat was in Baker Street.)

Despite having been out of work for twenty years, Hummel was said to have left an estate of more than $1 million;* his death was reported in newspapers around the world. His passing, the Associated Press wrote, "also marks the passing of a former school of criminal barristers who went to any extreme to gain their cases." Now, in the summer of 1884, two of those barristers would deploy every weapon in their arsenal as they tried to keep Fredericka Mandelbaum out of jail.

---

* The equivalent of some $17 million today.

Chapter Eleven

A Strip of Silk

THE COURTHOUSES OF LOWER MANHATTAN WERE JUST A MILE FROM Fredericka's shop, but the Pinkertons ushered her and Stoude onto the elevated train and conveyed them to the Harlem Police Court, more than six miles away. The reason, it was conjectured afterward, was that Marm's sway over the court system was weaker uptown than downtown. In addition, the presiding judge at the Harlem court, Justice Henry Murray, had a reputation as an honest jurist— someone unallied with the Bureau for the Prevention of Conviction. It was he who had issued the arrest warrants for Marm, Julius and Stoude.

Appearing before Judge Murray, Mandelbaum and Stoude were arraigned on five counts of grand larceny each; Julius, who joined them in court after his arrest, was also arraigned on five counts. All three pleaded not guilty. Because it would take time to vet Marm's associates for those the court deemed trustworthy enough to post bail ("I am going to be very particular about accepting bail in this case," Judge Murray declared), the defendants were held for the night in the cells beneath the courtroom.* "It is all unjust," Freder-

---

* This appears be the first time in her career that Fredericka was imprisoned overnight.

icka raged as she paced the prison corridor. "There were no stolen goods at all. And just to think that my Julius is arrested too!"

The bail hearing took place before Murray the next morning, Wednesday, July 23. Accompanied by Howe, the three defendants entered the courtroom, Marm "looking as meek as her heavy jewelry would allow." In the gallery, her twenty-year-old son, Gustav, sat at the end of a row of young women—unquestionably some of his mother's fleet-fingered employees—who fluttered their fans against the summer heat and looked daggers at a group of Pinkerton agents in the back of the room.

D.A. Olney was away on vacation, but his office, represented in court by Assistant District Attorney Leroy Gove, had a nearly unassailable case: "The chances looked more blue for her than they ever did before," Robert Pinkerton would say of Marm. As a result, Howe would spend the coming months working every delaying trick in his playbook. Now, starting off at a simmer that was the prelude to his full rolling boil, he decried the choice of venue, accusing the district attorney of having moved the proceedings to Harlem "because the Justice of his choice was sitting here." Judge Murray rejected the argument, saying that the location had been chosen simply "because it was cool up here." Next, Howe demanded a pretrial hearing to examine the charges and determine whether there was enough evidence to support them. Murray consented, and the hearing was set for Friday, two days hence.

Justice Murray next proceeded to interrogate the small parade of hopefuls who had applied to post Mrs. Mandelbaum's bail, most of them Kleindeutschland neighbors. He rejected one, Manassah Goldman, a dry-goods merchant, because Goldman had already pledged thousands of dollars' bond for two other members of the community. He turned down another, a retired wine importer named Shatler, because he was saddled with a sizable mortgage. At last, the judge accepted Susan Chambetta, a wine importer's wife, who stated that she was worth \$100,000[*] and was a friend of Mrs.

---

[*]   The equivalent of more than \$3 million today.

Mandelbaum's. "I consider her a very nice person," Mrs. Chambetta told the court. "I have sold her a great deal of property, and in her dealings with me she has always acted fairly, squarely and honestly."

When the proceedings reconvened after lunch, A.D.A. Gove, accompanied by Robert Pinkerton, approached the bench: A second textile merchant had come forward and identified some of the silk seized in the raid as having been stolen from his shop, James A. Hearn & Son. As a result, two more charges were brought against Mrs. Mandelbaum, for a total of seven. There could easily have been further charges, but the Pinkertons had confiscated only specific, marked pieces of silk from Marm's premises: Their search warrant didn't cover anything else. "Silks worth thousands of dollars were left undisturbed, because the law gives the authority to take only what is described in the warrant," Pinkerton told the press. "It would have taken us two weeks to handle all the articles in the store." At $2,000 per count, the rate set by Judge Murray, Marm's bail now stood at $14,000—more than $400,000 in today's money.

Turning to Murray, Howe made a handsome speech—one that hinted darkly at subterfuge to come. "A good deal has been said against this woman," he intoned:

> She has never been indicted. Her arrest was accomplished by conspiracy. She is not imprisoned upon the word of the police, but upon the word of a detective about whom there are rumors that he was her accomplice. It is a violation of the Constitution to demand that such excessive bail shall be given for the release of this woman, who I think we will show has done nothing wrong. A magistrate who violates the law is worse than the criminal. I don't wish to believe that you had the ear of the District Attorney before you came into the court room any more than you have mine now.

Howe then moved that Mrs. Mandelbaum's bail be reduced by half.

"I don't believe that I have done anything wrong," Justice Murray replied, "or that I have put on a cent too much. I shall not change the bail."

"Yes," A.D.A. Gove concurred. "We want bail sufficient to insure Mrs. Mandelbaum's presence in court."

Susan Chambetta posted the bail, and Fredericka stepped forward and kissed her. Marm signed the bail bond, indemnifying Chambetta by executing a mortgage on her Clinton Street property in Chambetta's name.* "Just to think, poor Julius is downstairs yet," Marm lamented, drawing her arm around young Gustav. "Hermann, too. It is on Friday morning that we will show them it is all wrong." And with that, Mother Mandelbaum sailed from the courtroom. The young women from the gallery flocked round and showered her with kisses.

THE PRETRIAL HEARING SOUGHT by Howe opened on the morning of Friday, July 25, 1884; as he'd requested, it would be devoted to examining the charges against the three defendants—seven for Mrs. Mandelbaum, five each for Julius and Stoude. The courtroom, the *New York Herald* said, "was a picture worthy of a Hogarth or a Cruikshank—such a grouping of quaint faces and remarkable characters as one sees only in the criminal courts of a great metropolis."

Fredericka entered, attired in a gown of glossy black satin, ornamented with beaded stars and much lace, a gold brooch fastening its wide lace collar. The ensemble was complemented by diamond earrings, long black gloves, and a black-veiled hat crowned with ostrich feathers "which stood up erect," the *New-York Times* reported, " 'like quills upon the fretful porcupine.' "† The case against her was

---

* According to some sources, Judge Murray also accepted a bail contribution for Marm from George Speckhardt, a Lower East Side baker.

† The *Times* is quoting *Hamlet*, Act I, Scene 5, in which the ghost of Hamlet's father says: "But that I am forbid / To tell the secrets of my prison house, / I could a tale unfold whose lightest word / Would harrow up thy soul, freeze thy young blood, / Make thy two eyes, like stars, start from their spheres, / Thy knotted and combined

already a sensation in the press, and on her arrival she was mobbed by sketch artists attempting to draw her portrait. Taking her seat on a bench next to Julius, she turned her back to the artists, buried her face in a newspaper, and sat "sulking like a caged tigress." A police officer who caught her eye and tried to stare her down was met with a glower that reduced him, the *New York Star* reported, to "a placid heap of invertebrate limpness—a protoplasm in brass buttons and uniform." Seated behind his mother in the gallery, Gustav Mandelbaum was joined by his younger sister, Annie.

Howe blazed into court with Hummel in tow. "[Howe] wore a big white vest and a rolling collar," the *Herald* reported. "In his collar button was a large diamond and another diamond was set in a massive cravat ring, below which was a diamond stud as big as a hazel nut. From a ponderous gold chain depended a huge gold locket set with diamonds. The third finger of his right hand was encircled by a ring in which were set nine very large diamonds.... From his cuffs hung two enormous solid gold handcuffs.... The lawyer blazed and twinkled and sparkled from head to foot with jewelled splendor."

Assistant District Attorney Gove, "whose countenance wore an expression in which real interest struggled with becoming sadness," called the first witness, Henry B. Porter, a silk buyer for Simpson, Crawford & Simpson. As Porter was shown a piece of speckled gray silk, Howe approached the witness stand.

"Did you ever see this piece before?" Howe asked him.

"Yes, Sir," Porter replied. "I bought 100 pieces."

"Did you have 100 pieces of the silk marked?" Howe inquired.

"I can't say every one," Porter replied, "but nearly every one."

"Where," Howe countered, "is the mark on the piece you hold in your hand?"

"Cut off," Porter ventured.

"Will you swear that you saw a mark upon this particular piece of silk?"

---

locks to part, / And each particular hair to stand on end / Like quills upon the fretful porcupine."

"I can't," Porter admitted.

Howe might well be forgiven for thinking he had scored a point, but A.D.A. Gove immediately stepped forward. "Is there any part of this piece missing?" Gove inquired.

"Yes, Sir," Porter said.

Gove reached into his pocket and withdrew a blue envelope. From the envelope he took a strip of speckled gray silk—the strip Gustave Frank had pocketed in June. Gove handed it to Porter. "Have you ever seen the piece corresponding to that?" he asked.

"Yes, Sir," Porter replied. "Our private mark is upon it—'LL.'"

Howe interrupted: "Are you able to swear that this particular piece of silk was never sold by any of your salesmen?"

"I can swear," Porter replied, "that no piece of this size was sold." The implication resounded: A piece of that size could only have left Porter's shop "in other than the usual business style." Porter stepped down.

After this disheartening opening, Howe laid vigorously into the next witness, Detective Frank. His questions prefigured the defense strategy to come.

"What's your name and business?" Howe barked.

"Gustav[e] Frank, a Pinkerton detective."

"Now tell us what your real name is," Howe ordered.

"That is the name I was born under," Frank said.

"How many names have you gone under?" Howe asked.

"Always my real name in my real life," Frank said.

"Aren't you alive now?" Howe shot back.

"I was when I arrested Mother Baum," Frank replied, to laughter in the court.

Frank went on to testify about the sting operation, his undercover role as "Stein," and Marm's cutting of the telltale strip of silk while he and Julius looked on.

"Upon all this evidence," Howe told the court, "I ask for the discharge of the prisoner Julius, who has simply been shown to be an employee. There is no evidence to show that he had possession of the property." He likewise moved to dismiss the charges against Stoude.

"It is refreshing to see the extraordinary position which the learned gentleman takes," A.D.A. Gove retorted. "The man [Julius] has been proved to have called attention to the distinguishing mark on the goods and to have advised his mother to burn the marked portions. It is an insult on Your Honor to ask for his discharge."

"As long as I live and have my faculties," Howe proclaimed, "I shall never deem it an insult to an intelligent man to submit a proposition of law which my mind tells me is correct. There is not a judge on the Supreme Bench who would not think as I do."

Judge Murray didn't. Both motions to dismiss were denied.

The day's last order of business was Julius's bail, which Murray had set at $5,000. Howe proposed that Marm herself bail him out—after all, he reminded the court, she owned real estate worth $30,000.* Murray declined. "I don't think it is proper to take one of the codefendants as bail for the other," he said. "There is an indecent look about it."

"Your Honor will be committing a glaring, wicked and shameful act if you refuse the bail of a mother for her son," Howe railed. "The question is whether the security is sufficient. It is immaterial by whom it is offered. If Mr. Jay Gould or some of those Wall Street magnates—some of those at least who have been committing frauds which have hurt the community more than a thousand Fredericka Mandelbaums . . . I say if they can go bail for anybody, on what grounds can you refuse [Mrs.] Mandelbaum?"

Murray was unmoved. Just then, an elderly man stepped forward from the gallery. Identifying himself as John Briggs, a retired merchant, he volunteered to post bail for Julius as a matter of principle. "I do it from impulse," Briggs told the court. "I bailed a man in an assault and battery case the other day because I thought he was in the right. I don't know Mrs. Mandelbaum from Adam." Bail was accepted,† and court adjourned for the weekend.

* About $900,000 today.

† Briggs was evidently an underworld character whom Howe & Hummel had recruited for the purpose.

———

THE PRETRIAL HEARING RESUMED on Monday, July 28. "A purple ostrich feather nodded on Mother Mandelbaum's hat," the *New York
Sun* reported. "Her face was partly veiled. Black lisle thread gloves
encased her hands, and gold bracelets shone on her wrists." A reporter for the *Herald* observed that "she grasped her green silk umbrella as if she had the District Attorney by the neck." Stoude joined
her in the courtroom; Julius, who had waived examination, was absent. Pinkerton entered, followed by dry-goods dealers carrying
bolts of silk. In the gallery, the row of young women was again in
attendance, together with Annie, who looked, the *Sun* wrote, "like a
rosebud."

As Detective Frank retook the stand, the defendants "turned
their faces away from 'Mr. Stein.'" Howe approached, "the glare of
diamonds from his shirt bosom, watch chain and hands . . . distress-
ing in the strong sunlight."

"I'm going to test this paid witness from his cradle to the present
time," Howe declared. He proceeded to grill Frank about Stoude's
work in Marm's shop, then moved again that the charges against
Stoude be dropped. Judge Murray denied the motion.

Stoude himself was next to take the stand, though not before
Howe had moved for his discharge one more time. The motion was
denied. Stoude kissed the Bible and said: "I have been in Mrs. Mandelbaum's employ sixteen years, at a salary of nine dollars a week.*
My duties were to open the store in the morning and close it at
night and to sell goods and deliver them. I never knew that a single
thing was stolen." After Gove queried him about the shop's lavish
inventory, Howe again moved for dismissal, this time of the charges
against Mrs. Mandelbaum. (It could not be proved, he argued, that
the gray silk hadn't been her own property all along.) "You're making too many motions," Murray admonished him.

---

* Even in 1884, nine dollars a week—about $270 in today's money—was a paltry
salary. It is possible that Stoude deliberately reduced the figure in court to make himself appear more peripheral to the crime syndicate than he actually was.

Stoude stepped down, and a series of dry-goods men took the stand. One after another, they identified pieces of the confiscated silk as having been stolen from their respective shops. When the day's testimony ended, Howe, whether from duty or delusion, moved for the dismissal of all seventeen charges against all three defendants. Judge Murray declined, though he did reduce the charges against Stoude from five to three. The proceedings would continue in two days' time.

THE THIRD AND LAST day of the hearing opened on the afternoon of Wednesday, July 30. To the defense, it was painfully apparent that witness-badgering and repeated requests for dismissal would not work. The next step was full-scale thespianism.

At three o'clock, Howe made his grand entrance, attired in his Maypole getup of pink, green and indigo, along with a treasure chest's worth of diamonds. When the laughter had died down, he addressed the court, reading aloud a statement from Marm. "My name is Fredericka Mandelbaum," he began:

> I am fifty-two years old* and a widow. I live at No. 79 Clinton-street, New-York City. I have resided there with my children for twenty years. I keep a dry-goods store, and have done so for twenty years past. I buy and sell dry goods as other dry-goods people do. I have never knowingly bought stolen goods; neither did my son Julius. I have never, never stolen in my life. *["There was a world of pathos in Mr. Howe's voice,"* the Times *reported, "as he duplicated his adverb of time.]*
>
> I feel that these charges are brought out against me for spite. I have never bribed the police, nor had their protection. I never needed their protection. I never gave money to any

---

* Marm, born March 28, 1825, was in fact fifty-nine. She apparently possessed enough vanity to lie about her age even in a sworn statement, much as she had done on the stand in her civil trial.

person whatsoever, to bribe or influence any officials, so help me God! *["There were tears in Mr. Howe's voice at this point."]*

I and my son are innocent of these charges preferred against us. I never knew that any one piece of silk was stolen, nor do I believe it was. I got the property now produced—the subjects of these charges—in an honest and business-like way. I insist on being discharged. *[Here the lawyer paused for effect.]*

Hermann Stoude was my employee and was in no way responsible for the buying or selling of anything in my store. He was simply a clerk to open and close the store, arrange the goods, wait on the customers and obey my orders. My arrest and detention on these charges is an outrage. I claim that the war on the police is the cause of my arrest, and has created a prejudice against me, of which I am the victim.

I say that in many respects the testimony of the witness Frank is false, and he knows it to be so. I say that I will not be the cat's-paw to suffer because there is a feud and a fight against the police and other officers. I am innocent of the crimes charged against me, and say that they are preferred simply to attack the police. There are, I believe, very many retail dry-goods dealers who innocently purchase goods which may have been stolen.

The statement's barely veiled allegations of police corruption appeared to bewilder Justice Murray.* "Well," he said, after Howe had wound down, "what have the police to do with the lady's statement?"

"She shall make her defense according to the statute if she has to bring in the president of the United States," Howe harrumphed. "She has a right to do it in her own defense."

---

* The Lexow Committee report, which illuminated the extensive ties between the police and the underworld, would not be released for another decade.

"I don't think it was ever meant that a person could make a slanderous statement in her defense," the judge replied.

"Bring in the criminal code," Howe roared. "I make this motion, and I desire that the stenographer take it down. I move that the defendant, pursuant to Section 198 of the Code of Criminal Procedure, be permitted to make to each charge against her the explanation she thinks proper."

Motion denied. "I refuse to let her make a stump speech," Judge Murray said.

"You must not speak like that to me," Howe cried. (His face, now bright crimson, furnished "the only missing color about his person," the *Times* observed.) He added, bellowing: "It is very disgusting, very indecent, very injudicious." He threatened to have Murray impeached.

Howe then demanded that the court stenographer, who had been sitting idle, pencil behind his ear, take down Marm's statement: This would let him declaim the entire speech a second time. Murray allowed it, with the proviso that "she must confine herself to the evidence given in court."

The stenographer took up his pencil, and Howe swung into his encore. "Strike it out," the judge ordered the stenographer repeatedly as the monologue unfolded again. "Strike it out. . . . Strike it out."

In the end, Howe's histrionics were for nothing. After Stoude posted his bail of $3,000, Judge Murray ruled that the evidence was sufficient to remand the defendants for trial. In mid-August, a grand jury returned formal indictments on multiple counts against all three.

The case was placed on the docket of the Court of General Sessions,* to begin on September 22, 1884. Recorder Frederick Smyth, a widely respected New York jurist with a reputation as "the

---

* New York City's Court of General Sessions, in existence from 1683 to 1962, oversaw cases of felonies not punishable by death or life imprisonment.

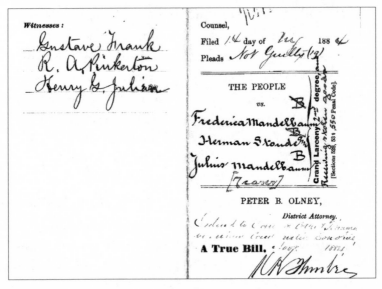

First page of the indictment, on multiple counts of grand larceny, of Fredericka Mandelbaum, Julius Mandelbaum and Hermann Stoude

terror of evildoers," would preside. "Should justice fail this time," a newspaper editorial opined that summer, "it would be a public calamity."

WITH LESS THAN TWO MONTHS before the trial, the defense strategy called for desperate measures. Temperate oratory had failed. So had roseate shouting. It was now time for unreconstructed slander.

On Monday, September 8, when the case came up for a pretrial review in the Court of General Sessions, Howe asked Recorder Smyth for an adjournment of a day or more, in order to gather evidence of Detective Frank's past: He declared that Frank had been guilty of forgery and fraudulent bankruptcy in Cologne and was now a fugitive from justice.* Howe then moved that a commission be formed to investigate Frank. As he envisioned it, members would travel to Germany to question officials there in person—an effort

---

*   In an affidavit submitted to the court, Frank denied Howe's allegations.

that would greatly delay the start of the proceedings against his clients.

"Is Detective Frank on Trial?" a *New-York Times* headline asked. In the end, Frank got a reprieve: On September 15, after considering Howe's motion, Recorder Smyth turned it down. There would be no commission. The trial was to start, as scheduled, on September 22.

FOR D.A. OLNEY, THERE WAS an incentive to press the case that trumped even the chance to put Fredericka in jail. As was widely discussed in the newspapers that summer, he was hoping to use the Mandelbaum trial as a pry bar that would open the door to future prosecutions of corrupt cops. (In this respect, Marm's contention that "the war on the police is the cause of my arrest" was at least partly correct.) "The detective force is in a terrible stew over the bold charges of District Attorney Olney," the *Detroit Free Press* reported, "and to-day the Police Board sent him an order requesting copies of the affidavits which he claims make blackmailers and thieves of half the leading detective officers in the city." The article continued:

> The greatest scandal in the history of the [New York City] Police Force is on the eve of ventilation. District Attorney Olney possesses every affidavit he claims, and they number almost one hundred, gathered rapidly and quietly in anticipation of the Mandelbaum case. They cover the ground for fifteen years and are very explicit, with names, dates and circumstances. . . . It is believed that as soon as "Marm" gets her property in shape she will make a general confession criminating officials of the police force.

Olney's affidavits threw into stark relief the double-edged nature of Fredericka's relationship with the law. "She was protected *and* blackmailed by the police," an unnamed law-enforcement official told the *New-York World*. "They not only blackmailed her, but they made her thieves and shoplifters contribute money and goods":

In the affidavits ... names, places and dates are mentioned, the details of the blackmailing operations set forth so ... as not to be gainsaid, and the close connection of the woman with the police and the protection extended to her by them established beyond the possibility of a doubt. As an illustration, when a wagon-load of stolen silks was removed from a house in Fourth street to another place of concealment, a central office detective followed the wagon to see that it was not interfered with en route. The same detective used to get drunk in Mme. Mandelbaum's house, and every stitch of clothes that his wife and family has worn for years has been supplied by her.

When the police were asked to try and induce Sheeny Mike to testify against Mme. Mandelbaum in the civil suit, the answer given was: "We will do nothing to injure the old woman. We would like to help her." The next day five of Inspector Byrnes's men appeared to testify in favor of Mme. Mandelbaum.

In late July, amid what had become a highly public feud between the district attorney's office and the police, Inspector Byrnes publicly disavowed Olney's charges. But to Marm and her lawyers, the strength of the D.A.'s case was plain. As they also knew, one of the most damning accusations against Fredericka had been made by a former employee, the shoplifter Mollie Hoey, who had furnished Olney's office with "a complete history of 'Marm' Mandelbaum and her police intrigues." Hoey was just then in prison, and, as the *Times* strongly implied, it was Mrs. Mandelbaum who had put her there, in retribution for her affidavit in the civil trial. "Mollie ... came under a threat from the famous fence that if she appeared against her she would have her sent up for five years," the newspaper reported, adding: "Mollie is now serving a five years' sentence on Blackwell's Island."

As every fence in history has been aware, there is risk involved in throwing the authorities a fish, however small. Now, in the summer

AN OLD SAYING TWISTED.

In the summer of 1884, the American satirical magazine *Puck* devoted its cover to the public feud between D.A. Olney, depicted at left, and police inspector Byrnes. In the middle, drawn in blatantly anti-Semitic caricature, is a bejeweled Mrs. Mandelbaum.

of 1884, it was Hoey's turn to settle the score. For her efforts, she was rewarded, at Olney's request, with an official pardon from Governor Cleveland, an ardent anti-Tammany Democrat. It seemed inevitable that the case against Fredericka Mandelbaum would go forward.

ON FRIDAY, SEPTEMBER 19, three days before the trial was to open, Howe and Hummel, ever mindful of their professional mantra, "Delay, delay, delay," applied for a change of venue. Their application was made in State Supreme Court, and as luck—or design—would have it, they made it before Marm's old pal Judge Charles Donohue. Arguing that "intricate, novel, and perplexing questions of law will arise in the course of [the] trial," defense counsel moved that the case be transferred to the city's Court of Oyer and Terminer.*

D.A. Olney opposed the motion, condemning it as dilatory. But two months later, on November 19—for Justice Donohue had delayed, delayed, delayed—the change of venue was granted. The case was placed on the docket of Oyer and Terminer for December 2, 1884.

ON THE MORNING OF TUESDAY, December 2, *The People vs. Fredericka Mandelbaum, Hermann Stoude [and] Julius Mandelbaum* opened downtown in the Court of Oyer and Terminer before Justice George C. Barrett. The gallery was packed: Spectators, some wielding opera glasses, were "all anxious to see the woman who had made such a peculiar reputation for herself," the *Chicago Tribune* reported. "Detective Pinkerton leaned against the court railing, and a dozen of his detectives stood round like pickets."

Olney entered, accompanied by three assistant district attorneys and fourteen witnesses. Howe and Hummel arrived unaccompanied; Howe immediately asked that the proceedings be adjourned. Then, in a last bid to have the case dismissed altogether, he argued "that the indictments charged both grand larceny *and* the receiving of stolen goods, while the Code expressly provided that an indictment must charge but *one* crime unless they were committed by different means."

Olney protested vehemently, pointing out that it would be difficult to keep all fourteen witnesses; Howe shot back that he should keep them on ice. Judge Barrett ruled against Howe, but he did

---

*   New York City's Court of Oyer and Terminer existed from 1788 to 1895; its bench comprised a State Supreme Court justice and two or more judges from the city's Court of Common Pleas. Oyer and Terminer was empowered to hear "all felony cases including those punishable by life imprisonment or death." (Per the *Oxford English Dictionary*, the name derives from the Anglo-Norman phrase *oyer et terminer*, "to hear and determine.")

grant an adjournment, until Thursday, December 4. Howe's gambit had served its real purpose: The extra two days would buy his clients time to set a critical plan in motion, for Fredericka had reached a wrenching decision.

ON THE MORNING OF DECEMBER 4, District Attorney Olney sat, "sternly imposing," with his three assistants at the front of the courtroom. Howe, "plumply serene and ponderously gracious," was also present.

The clock struck eleven—time for the principal defendant to take the stand.

"Hear ye! Hear ye!" the court clerk cried. "Fredericka Mandelbaum!"

No answer.

"Fredericka Mandelbaum!" he called again.

No answer.

"Hermann Stoude!" the clerk called. "Julius Mandelbaum!"

As before, there was only silence.

Chapter Twelve

North by Northwest

THE COURT WAITED AN HOUR BEFORE JUDGE BARRETT DECLARED the defendants' bonds forfeit. It was clear to everyone present, as the *Brooklyn Daily Eagle* would say, that Mrs. Mandelbaum "had, in the parlance of the street, 'jumped her bail.' "

"The defendants are not here, Your Honor," Howe intoned, stating the unmistakable. "In the words of Shakespeare, the District Attorney must have the due and forfeit of his bond." (Howe, the *Times* noted, "seemed proud of his quotation even under the trying circumstances of the case.")* Barrett then issued bench warrants for the arrest of Fredericka Mandelbaum, Julius Mandelbaum and Hermann Stoude.

"I suspected it," D.A. Olney said afterward. "I thought all along that she could never face the trial." He vowed to "scour the United States" for the three fugitives. But by then, they were nearly out of the country.

---

* Howe was quoting *The Merchant of Venice*, Act IV, Scene 1, in which Shylock declares: "I have possessed your Grace of what I purpose, / And by our holy Sabbath have I sworn / To have the due and forfeit of my bond. / If you deny it, let the danger light / Upon your charter and your city's freedom!"

———

THE FORTY-EIGHT HOURS before the trial had seen a blizzard of activity in the defense camp. One real estate transfer after another was concluded: First, the defendants' bondsmen transferred to third parties the property they'd put up as collateral. Then, in mirror image, the defendants transferred to third parties the property *they'd* put up to indemnify the bondsmen. Fredericka alone transferred several pieces of real estate, worth some $30,000,* to a criminal associate. As a result, if the defendants were to forfeit their bond, neither they nor their bondsmen stood to lose anything, at least in principle.

"Of course the claim of bail renders the transfer null and void," Howe, in a state of "profound tranquillity," explained to the *Times* later that day. "But it will cause a trial, and it may be two years before the thing is settled."

Howe was also profoundly tranquil about securing his own pound of flesh, despite his client's precipitate departure. "In the course of being interviewed by the *Herald* on Mother Mandelbaum's bail-hopping, Howe and Hummel were asked if she had left town without settling her account with them," a twentieth-century chronicler has written:

> Howe replied, according to the story, by looking "toward the ceiling and jingling some silver in his pocket. Lawyer Hummel, also looking heavenward, softly hummed a tune." The reporter, one of the more impertinent men in the history of his impertinent profession, wrote that he had seen a scratch-pad on Howe's desk bearing such notations as "fair divvy ... my share ... whack up the real estate." "Real estate" meant, presumably, the hot property which Mother Mandelbaum ... had left behind. Neither Howe nor Hummel would say what

---

*   More than $900,000 today.

arrangements they had made with their vanished client, but Howe, in discussing the general question of retainers, said: "We always look ahead. When we take a case, we secure fees covering even an appeal to the Court of Appeals. If our client dies before the appeal is granted, he will never need the money and we might as well have it. If it does go to the higher court, we are secured for our trouble. We look far ahead. We look much further ahead, I may say, than the District Attorney."

The two-day adjournment also bought Fredericka time to lay her escape plans, which would require her to evade the Pinkerton detectives who were watching her house round the clock. One morning a day or two before the trial, Marm Mandelbaum, clad in a capacious black shawl, emerged from her home and took a carriage to the Howe & Hummel offices on Centre Street, about a mile away. The Pinkertons, in their own carriage, followed close behind. A short time later, she emerged from the lawyers' office, still swathed in her shawl, and boarded her carriage once more. The Pinkertons tailed it as it meandered aimlessly through Lower Manhattan before returning to her home on Clinton Street.

The trouble was, the person they were tailing wasn't Mother Mandelbaum. After Fredericka entered her lawyers' office, a carefully chosen double, selected for height and breadth and costumed just alike, emerged.* Once her carriage and the Pinkertons' had pulled away, the real Mrs. Mandelbaum exited covertly and stepped into another waiting horse cab. She was driven to the railway station,† where she boarded a train for Chatham, New York, some 120 miles north of the city. At Chatham, she transferred to a train to Canada. At some point along the journey Julius and Stoude joined

---

* In most accounts, the double was one of Marm Mandelbaum's maids. Rona Holub speculates that because of the need to mirror Mrs. Mandelbaum's size, the duplicate Marm may actually have been a man. It bears wondering whether Howe himself might have risen to the task.

† In some accounts Grand Central Depot, in others New Rochelle.

her; on or about December 5, 1884, the three fugitives arrived together in Toronto, carrying with them a ten-pound package.

In New York, the press grilled Robert Pinkerton as to how the escape could have happened. "How did we let her get away?" he replied. "The fact of the matter is you can't watch a person who doesn't want to be watched." He added elsewhere: "I had no right to touch Mrs. Mandelbaum. She was on bail. She could go wherever she pleased, and it had nothing to do with me. Until she had forfeited her bonds not a soul had a right to touch her. . . . But it is victory enough to have got rid of her, and we ought to be thankful for the redemption."

One thing that may have made that "redemption" possible was help from law enforcement: It behooved many of the city's police officers to preempt a trial. On the one hand, now that Marm was refusing to grease their palms any longer, they had no incentive to keep quiet about her business dealings. "I'm sick and tired of putting up money to 'square' things, and I don't intend to do it anymore," she would tell a reporter. "The more money you produce, the more they want. If I hadn't been so free with my money, I wouldn't have got in this scrape."

But on the other, as the police were uncomfortably aware, courtroom testimony could cut both ways: Ultimately, the safest thing they could do would be to help spirit her out of the jurisdiction. "The police have been too powerful for the District Attorney and his private detectives," an editorial in the *New-York Times* said:

> That, at least, will be the explanation generally accepted of the escape of "Mother" Mandelbaum. It is a pity that Mr. Olney should not have been able to complete his excellent work in this case by securing a conviction and imprisonment of the woman who for so many years has been at the centre of the organization of crime in New-York. . . . The rumor [has] got about that some members of the police force were quite as warmly interested as the woman herself in her es-

cape from justice. If she had been tried and convicted her indignation at the failure of her allies to protect her might have found expression in . . . explanations of the methods by which she had kept the police from interfering with her criminal business.

IN TORONTO, THE THREE FUGITIVES registered at Rossin House, one of the city's most opulent hotels, as "C. Newman and mother," of Boston, and "J. Pink," of that city. But their reputation preceded them—news of their flight had made the Toronto papers—and, growing nervous, they left the hotel after only a day. Taking furnished rooms in an elegant part of town, they attempted to live discreetly. But descriptions of Marm's singular appearance had also been published, and a few days later they took the evening train for Hamilton, Ontario, about thirty miles away.

In Hamilton, they registered at Allerton House, a seedy tavern near the railway depot with rooms for rent on an upper floor. Stoude, Julius and Fredericka signed in, to all appearances, as father, son and aunt: "H. and L. Harris and sister, Detroit," artfully smearing the ink to make the names almost illegible. Marm, especially fearful of discovery, took her meals in her room; Stoude and Julius ate in the dining room, at separate tables. But their efforts at self-effacement did little good, for Olney was at last a step ahead of them: After they fled New York, he'd taken the precaution of sending "wanted" circulars to a spate of Canadian police departments.

"Office of the District Attorney, City and County of New York," the circulars read:

Fugitives from justice—Arrest Frederica [sic] Mandelbaum, known as "Mother Mandelbaum"; Julius Mandelbaum, son of Frederica Mandelbaum; Herman [sic] Stoude.

The above named parties were arrested on July 22, 1884, and charged with grand larceny and receiving stolen goods, and held in bail to appear for trial before the court of Oyer and

Terminer, of the city and county of New York, on Dec. 4, 1884.
Upon the case being called the defendants failed to appear,
and their bonds were declared forfeited and bench warrants
have been issued for their apprehension.

Frederica Mandelbaum, about 55 years of age . . . stout
build . . . is unusually richly dressed and wears a profusion of
diamond jewelry. Is a German Jewess.

Julius Mandelbaum, about 24 years of age . . . dresses fash-
ionably. Is a German Jew.

Herman Stoude, about 45 years of age . . . dresses moder-
ately. The locket attached to his watch chain bears a cameo of
Helen of Troy. He is a German.

A suitable remuneration will be paid for any information
leading to the apprehension of [any] of the above described
parties.

Send information to Peter B. Olney, district attorney, city
and county of New York; or to Pinkerton's national detective
agency.

On Monday, December 8, Chief Alexander Stewart of the Hamilton police, armed with the circular and accompanied by one of his
detectives, entered the ladies' parlor of Allerton House. Encounter-
ing Fredericka and Julius there, he addressed them by their real
names. "Mrs. Mandelbaum was thunderstruck," a newspaper account said the next day. "Her countenance betrayed much emotion.
Her breath became rapid and her bosom heaved tumultuously."

Chief Stewart smiled at her. "It's all right," he is reported to have
said. "You had better come along quietly now and save any trouble."

"I am an American citizen," Fredericka retorted. "Where is an
American consul? You have no right to touch me." But Chief Stewart confiscated the ten-pound package and arrested her and Julius
on suspicion of bringing stolen goods over the border. Stoude, who'd
been out on an errand, was arrested on returning to the tavern.

The arrest was trumpeted in the Hamilton press, which found it
especially gratifying that the suspects had slipped through the

clutches of the law in big-town Toronto. "The Toronto police were aware that they were in the city," the *Hamilton Spectator* crowed, "but of course could not find them, though they were hunting for them high and low, after their own peculiar and superlatively idiotic fashion. The Toronto idea of hunting for criminals is something that the average mind cannot readily grasp. . . . While the sleepy Toronto peelers are vaguely wondering whether the woman and her pals are in Toronto or Montreal or anywhere else, the shrewd, energetic Hamilton detectives are gathering them in, and showing the Toronto people how these little things are done."

Fredericka, Julius and Stoude were taken to Hamilton's Central Police Station, where their package was found to contain $30,000 to $40,000 worth* of jewelry and precious stones, along with a six-ounce lump of melted gold. The suspects were then searched individually, a procedure to which Fredericka, attired in "a rich black silk dress, a long sealskin sacque, and . . . profusely decorated with diamonds," objected vehemently, and no wonder: When she finally relented, a further $30,000 worth of jewels—"diamonds, pearls, rubies, loose and set in rings, lockets, pins, and brooches"—was discovered secreted in her clothing. Also found on the prisoners was several hundred dollars in cash.

Marm insisted that all the jewels were her own, a transparently absurd claim. "A plea that it is their personal effects is not good," the *Boston Globe* would note. "There are too many rings, lockets, etc., [even] for three persons to wear, especially 'fences' and fugitives from justice." When her argument failed to persuade the police, she tried another, perennial gambit: "She and Julius asked the chief to see them alone in the room, as they wanted to speak with him," the *Detroit Free Press* reported. "Speaking to him meant bribing him to release them. They had 'spoken' to many New York officers, they said, and were astonished to find that this easy way of escaping the law did not prevail here."

---

*   Thirty to forty thousand U.S. dollars in 1884 is the equivalent of more than $900,000 to more than $1.2 million in today's money.

The jewels were impounded by Canadian Customs for nonpayment of duty; Marm, Julius and Stoude were removed to the county jail, where they would await arraignment on charges of vagrancy and bringing stolen goods into Canada. "The arrest has caused considerable excitement here and apparently has excited a great deal of interest elsewhere, for Chief Stewart has received scores of messages of inquiry and congratulation from every part of the country, and they are still pouring in," the *New-York Tribune* reported from Hamilton the next day.

The vagrancy charge, as newspaper accounts made clear, was never intended to stick: It was simply a pretext for holding the fugitives until additional evidence could be gathered and jurisdictional issues resolved. "The great question now is what shall be done with them?" the *St. Louis Post-Dispatch* reported. The crown attorney who oversaw prosecutions in Hamilton believed they couldn't be extradited. Mrs. Mandelbaum (who "has evidently been STUDYING INTERNATIONAL LAW," the *Post-Dispatch* declared in ardent capitals) readily concurred.* "I am sure of that," she told the newspaper's correspondent. "I found that out from the very best lawyers before I left New York. They can't take me back." She added: "And they had better not. It will not be good for some people if I go back." Asked to elaborate, she "contented herself with remarking, 'They'll see,' emphasizing the remark with MANY SAGACIOUS NODS OF THE HEAD."

From New York, Olney vowed to review the question of extradition with officials in Washington; he also planned to send a U.S. prosecutor to Hamilton to advise the crown attorney. But Fredericka proved correct. There was no formal extradition treaty between the United States and Canada then;[†] by convention, suspects could be extradited to the United States only for major crimes such as murder, arson, piracy, forgery and counterfeiting. And thus, despite the

---

* A reporter for the *Cincinnati Enquirer* once wrote, "A New York detective told me . . . that old Mandelbaum knew as much about law as most of the lawyers."

[†] The first extradition treaty between the two nations would not be signed until 1971.

prospect of a night in jail, she was upbeat. "Mrs. Mandelbaum was apparently light hearted and talked of her troubles volubly," a correspondent for the *New-York Tribune* reported. "She expects to be released tomorrow morning after their preliminary examination":

> She is self-possessed and appears to regard her arrest with indifference, excepting for the inconvenience it causes her. . . .
>
> "What can they do with me?" she asked. . . . "All this stuff I have with me is mine. I bought it and paid for it. I was not going to [go] away and leave my personal property behind. I have done nothing against the law here that they can touch me for."
>
> "Then you admit that you have broken the laws across the line?" she was asked.
>
> "I admit nothing," she replied. "I have done nothing. I thought it better to leave than stand all the worry and bother of a trial."
>
> She intimated that she could, if she chose, make things unpleasantly warm for some members of the [New York] detective force. "What kind of man is your chief?" she asked. "Do you think I could fix him to get us off without much bother?" She was answered in the negative. "Ah!" said she. "How different in New-York. There I could fix things as easy as possible. Why, plenty of the detectives there would do anything almost to get me off."
>
> Just here Mr. [Stoude], who had been listening to the conversation, interpolated the remark that she had better not talk so much.
>
> "You be quiet," said the woman. "I am no fool. They can do nothing to us."

Fredericka retained a local lawyer, David Steele, who telegraphed Howe & Hummel for assistance; Hummel promptly set out for Hamilton by train. Though he could not officially represent his clients in a Canadian court, he planned to advise Steele on their de-

fense. He cabled Marm en route: DEAR MRS. MANDELBAUM: CHEER UP.
DONE NOTHING CAN HOLD YOU IN CANADA FOR AND HAVE GOOD LAW-
YERS. GOD WILLING, I'LL BE WITH YOU IN MORNING.

Also en route to Hamilton was Fred Marks, a manager of
E. Marks & Son, a jewelry store in Troy, New York: Some of the diamonds confiscated by the Canadian authorities were believed to
have been stolen in a burglary of that store in February 1884 by two
of Fredericka's regular employees, Michael Kurtz and Billy Porter.
"It was suspected that the Mandelbaum crowd were at the bottom
of it, but it could never be proved against them or, indeed, against
any person else," the *Chicago Tribune* reported. If the stones could
be shown to have come from that heist, which had netted $30,000
in assorted jewels, it would make the prosecution's case.

But as Marm knew, the chances of firm identification were slim
to none: She would have had the stones removed from their settings,
and other characteristic marks effaced, as soon as they were stolen.
And without identification, she also knew, the prosecution had no
case. "The Chief is holding the trio on suspicion of having brought
stolen goods into Canada," the *Chicago Tribune* reported. "If he
cannot prove that the goods were stolen he will release them at
once."

On Tuesday, December 9, Fredericka, Julius and Stoude were
transported by carriage for arraignment at Hamilton Police Court.
This hearing, at which Fredericka had expected to be cut loose, was
now billed as the first of at least two pretrial court dates: Hummel
was still in transit, and the diamonds, locked by Canadian Customs
in a vault in Ottawa, wouldn't be available for Marks to examine
until the next day. Possibly owing to these delays, the prisoners'
carefree mood of the day before had evaporated. "The Mandelbaum
party looked downhearted when they arrived in a hack at the Police
Court from the county jail," the *Boston Globe* reported. Doubtless
adding to their dejection was the fact that the court had added a
third charge—smuggling—for each of them.

The new charge was a savvy move on the prosecution's part, because it closed the loophole that could have let the prisoners go free.

"If the goods were stolen," a newspaper account explained, "they go to the penitentiary sure." But now, because the fugitives had paid no duty when they brought the loot over the border, "if they prove that it was not stolen and say they only smuggled it, then they will go to prison just the same."

After the arraignment ended, the prisoners met with their lawyer, Steele, over beer before being returned to the county jail. "They are much disgusted at being locked up and allowed no newspapers," the *Boston Globe* said. "They have such meals as they choose to pay for sent in, and do not live on prison fare."

Pining for company from outside her prison walls, Fredericka sent for Steele as often as she could. "Oh, don't be long," she would implore him when he departed. "When I see your face it is like angels." (Steele, the *Globe* saw fit to add, "is not much of an angel.") She asked him for novels to while away the time, and after buying a few of Allan Pinkerton's books—and then thinking better of it— he brought her *The Mysteries of Paris,* by Eugène Sue. Whether chosen by accident or advertence, the gift was a strikingly apt fit for its recipient: The novel, originally serialized in French in the 1840s, furnishes a dark tour of an urban demimonde of gangs, prostitutes, murderers and other underworld figures.

On Wednesday, December 10, Abraham Hummel reached Hamilton in time for an afternoon hearing. But when the case was called, Chief Stewart requested an adjournment, to give Olney's representative time to arrive. Hummel, the *New-York Times* reported, laughed out loud: "He said District Attorney Olney . . . knew well enough that Mrs. Mandelbaum could not be held [in Canada] nor extradited." Arguing for the defense, first Steele and then Hummel, "of counsel for Mrs. Mandelbaum by courtesy of the magistrate," maintained that the fugitives should not be detained while awaiting trial. Hummel told the court that "it was quite evident that the authorities in New-York were aware that they could not convict the prisoners or they would ere this have had a man here on the spot." The presiding magistrate declined to release them, but he did adjourn the proceedings until Saturday morning, December 13.

That hearing would never take place. On Friday, December 12, 1884, the case was dismissed outright, for Fredericka's rigorous professional practice had once again paid dividends: Marks, the jeweler, had failed to identify any of the diamonds. Lacking identification, the crown attorney chose not to pursue the case, and she, Julius and Stoude were released. Nor would Canadian authorities seek convictions on the smuggling charges, and Marm was soon able to recoup her jewels by paying $500 duty, plus costs. From New York, Olney responded, "I am much chagrined at the facility with which Mother Mandelbaum and her two accomplices have eluded justice."

In fact, Olney and his federal colleagues weren't quite ready to give up. In early 1885, a newspaper article reported that "the Washington authorities have asked the Governor-General of Canada to exert his prerogatives and hand over Mother Mandelbaum and accomplices . . . without extradition, as a matter of international courtesy." The report continued: "The request was ignored."

Fredericka Mandelbaum was now entirely free—provided she never again ventured south of the border. She could hardly have envisioned the circumstances that would compel her to do so before her first year in Canada was out.

AFTER THEIR RELEASE, the fugitives remained in Hamilton. Their residence in Canada, a nation fast acquiring a reputation as a haven for American malefactors,* was newsworthy enough to be remarked upon in a spate of American publications. "Mother Mandelbaum says she will never again return to New York," one newspaper article declared. "She has found a greater measure of peace under the hospitable Canadian skies. . . . But they will all ultimately tire of Canada, where burglars have nothing to steal and banks are few and far between. It is a land of gorgeous hotels for the accommodation of such Americans as have left their country for their country's good."

* "In Canada," a U.S. newspaper would observe in 1885, "the people appear to take the presence of a certain percentage of American defaulters in their midst as a matter of course."

Mrs. Mandelbaum, safely on the Canadian side of the " 'fence' for American defaulters," depicted in a *Puck* cover from 1885

Fredericka, however, was grimly determined to stay. By the end of 1884, her two younger children, Gustav and Annie, had moved to Hamilton to join her. (Her elder daughter, Sarah, now married, remained in New York.) "Quite a colony of her crook friends grew up about her there," the *New-York World* wrote of Marm's Canadian odyssey. "Of course, her bail was forfeited, but the city never collected it, as it was discovered that the surety was worthless." Marm joined a local synagogue, Anshe Sholom, where she regularly attended services; she also continued her tradition of lavish parties. She would eventually purchase an elegant brownstone in North Hamilton, where the family lived "in splendor." There, the *Boston Globe* reported, they "entertained many visitors of their own kind from New York [with] all the pleasures that money could buy."

But for all the roots she tried to sink in Canadian soil, Marm longed for the genial clamor of Kleindeutschland. "She has told persons who have seen her [in Canada] that she would gladly forfeit every penny of her wealth in order to once more breathe freely the atmosphere of the Thirteenth Ward," the New York police chief George Washington Walling wrote. But a return would mean arrest and imprisonment. She would have to resign herself to a life in exile.

IN THE AUTUMN OF 1885, Annie Mandelbaum, who was not under indictment and could cross into the United States at will, left Hamilton to visit New York. At the home of a family friend there, a Mrs. Marx, of 99 Clinton Street, she caught a cold. The cold turned into pneumonia. From Canada, Marm wrote or telegraphed daily for updates on Annie's condition; in early November, Annie died, at the age of eighteen. "Annie was the sole redeeming feature of the Mandelbaum family and was the acknowledged belle of the east side Hebrew district," the *Detroit Free Press* declared. "From first to last she always refused to aid 'Marm' in the latter's enterprises. 'Marm' sent a wreath of flowers and regrets and telegraphed that owing to the hostility of the New York police she did not dare come on here to the funeral."

In fact, any such message would have been a blind: Fredericka fully intended to see her youngest child one last time, whatever the danger. "The thought of having her favorite child buried without taking a last look at her face touched a tender chord in the heart of the hardened criminal," the *New-York Times* wrote, at full Victorian throttle. "To gratify her wish she took the chance of falling into the hands of the police and passing her remaining days in prison."

On learning of Annie's death, Mrs. Mandelbaum, possibly in disguise, boarded a southbound train with Julius. In some accounts, they traveled to Buffalo, and from there caught a direct train to New York City. In others, they took a deliberately circuitous route through Upstate New York before arriving in Manhattan. From Grand Central Depot, a carriage brought them to Mrs. Marx's house in Kleindeutschland, where Annie's body lay. "So as not to attract suspicion, the mother of the dead girl wore only a walking dress and had nothing on to indicate in any way her mourning," the *Times* reported.

Making certain the house was not watched, Marm and Julius entered. "As soon as she reached the bier," the *Times* said, "she clapped her hands, kissed her dead girl and fell in a faint. When she recovered, she cried and moaned, and her sobs could be heard a block away." Fearing the noise would attract the cop on the beat, a friend persuaded Fredericka to leave the premises and sequester herself in another neighbor's home.

Because Annie's death had been reported in the New York papers, there was a real danger that the police would be watching Jewish burial grounds around the city. Anticipating this surveillance, someone in Marm's circle proposed that Annie be given a Christian burial instead. Fredericka wouldn't hear of it: Annie was to be buried in accordance with their faith—and under Jewish law, the funeral would need to take place as soon as possible. On Marm's orders, Annie's body was removed to the Mandelbaums' home at Clinton and Rivington to be prepared for burial.

The next morning, Fredericka left her neighborhood hiding place and slipped into her old house once more. "She showered kiss after kiss upon the cheeks of the dead girl, and her piteous cries brought tears to the eyes of the persons who witnessed the scene," the *Times* said. "Several times she attempted to leave the room, but she kept returning to the coffin, and finally she had to be almost carried away. This was the last time the mother had the chance to see her dead child."

Word soon swept around Kleindeutschland that Mother Mandelbaum's pretty daughter had died, and before long, the *Times* reported, "large crowds were attracted through curiosity to the house":

Every person who entered the building was scrutinized closely, and a number of persons expected to see the old woman enter the house in defiance of the law. About 1 o'clock the carriages began to arrive for the funeral. As the occupants stepped out, various remarks were passed by the throng on the sidewalk. "I guess she's a shoplifter," was a stereotyped expression whenever a gaudily attired woman entered the house; and "I guess he's a burglar," referring to the male escorts.

At 2 o'clock, the time set for the funeral, about 20 coaches had emptied passengers before the door. The street was crowded with women, young girls, and boys, and it was only through the efforts of a muscular policeman who stood in front of the door that a passageway was cleared. Some of the visitors brought handsome flowers. Among those present well known in police circles ... were "Shang" Draper; ... Mrs. Miller, an old-time shoplifter; ... "Liz" Davis, a 60-year-old shoplifter; ... "Jack" Greenthal, a brother of "Gen." Greenthal; ... "Dutch Adam"; "Irish Mag" Nugent; and a host of others who have established reputations as burglars, receivers of stolen goods, and shoplifters.

The funeral itself was conducted in situ in the Mandelbaums' parlor. Julius, who had shaved his beard and was now barely recognizable, remained there for the service, but Marm dared not stay. Never had her home's secret exits proved more valuable: Slipping from the house undetected, she returned to her hiding place, above a beer hall across the street; Julius joined her there after the service ended. Peering through the shutter slats, mother and son watched as the hearse, with two dozen carriages following, pulled away from Clinton Street, bound for the family plot at Union Field Cemetery in Queens.

Marm and Julius waited an hour before boarding a closed carriage to the station for the trip back to Canada. They had managed to spend two days in New York without being spotted. Their furtive journey to the city was the last time Fredericka would set foot in the United States, her thirty-five years there bracketed by the deaths of two daughters: the infant Bertha and now Annie, who died, Chief Walling wrote, "just as she came to know what her mother really was."

———

MARM ABHORRED LIFE IN CANADA. "The name of the place is enough to sicken me," she once told a reporter. Annie's death, she later said, "made it worse than ever." But over time, her constitutional resilience—and her constitutional penchant for doing business—came to her aid. In the summer of 1886, she dispatched a spate of carefully worded circulars to her old contacts in the States. "My Dear _____," they read:

> I beg to announce to you that I have opened my new empo-rium, in every respect the equal of my late New York establish-ment. I shall be pleased to continue our former pleasant business relations, promising not [only] to pay the best prices for the articles which you may have for sale, but also to care-fully protect all my customers, no matter at what expense. With my present facilities I am able to dispose of all commod-ities forwarded to me with dispatch and security. Trusting to hear from you soon and assuring you that a renewal of past favors will be greatly appreciated, I am yours faithfully,
>
> F. Mandelbaum.
>
> N.B.—Ship goods by any express and notify me by mail.

The fruit of her efforts was the grand opening that summer of "a handsome store" in Hamilton, which bore the sign

"Since then," an American newspaper article said, "it has been well patronized by the residents of Hamilton, who are curious to see what sort of a business woman the notorious American fence is."

Inside, Marm, Julius and three saleswomen offered customers a selection of "handsome garments, a trifle worn, perhaps," priced "at ruinous figures."

"She has a large stock of wares, nearly all of American make, which came from New York through the custom house in due form," the article continued. "Mme. Mandelbaum explains to her customers that she is in a position to sell her wares cheaper than anybody else in Canada because they are job lots, bought cheap in New York."

Much of Marm's stock was fine silk and lace, and a noteworthy feature was that "it does not bear any trade marks or labels, and the cases they come in do not have any other marks on them but her address. A great many purchasers have availed themselves of the opportunity of purchasing some beautiful [silver] plate, which she also sells at very low figures. There are erasures on some of the ware, which leads to the supposition that names which at one time may have been engraved on them have been carefully obliterated."

Given Marm's history with Canadian Customs, her new business venture carried an inherent challenge: how to get her wares across the border. She solved the problem in time-honored fashion, establishing a northern outpost of the Bureau for the Prevention of Conviction. (Its membership appeared to comprise not only Customs officers but also local policemen.) "She is very shrewd and makes no concealment of her business," the *New York Herald* reported in the fall of 1886. "There was . . . a pretty clever scheme put up to get this fence over the line some weeks ago. All apparently went well, but it seemed as if the chief official engaged in the job was more anxious to secure a few precious stones than to capture the fence. She compromised with this official by making him a present of a magnificent diamond. He left quite delighted, and so did Mandelbaum. The latter got on to the job and the former next day discovered that he had been given a paste diamond."

And with that—since the official could scarcely complain to authorities that he'd been swindled in the course of taking a bribe—Fredericka bought herself a sustained dose of protection, at a deep, satisfying discount.

———

THROUGHOUT HER YEARS IN EXILE, Marm remained an object of fascination for the American press. In August 1886, a correspondent from the States came to her grand opening "and entered into a chat with the famous lady."

"It was generally understood," the journalist put to her, "that you had retired from active business?"

"Oh, no, my friend," Marm replied. (The accompanying shake of the head caused "a pair of great solitaire earrings to dance and sparkle.") "I have not retired, as you see. I am in business once more. I'm an old woman now, but, you see, I can't be idle."

"With a wink, the import of which was left to the imagination," the writer continued, "Mme. Mandelbaum suggested that she had some very pretty watches, some a little used, but just as good as new for all that, which she would sell at a bargain."

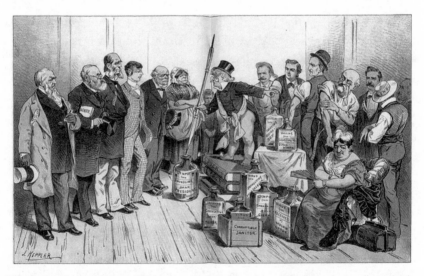

"Scientists Assert That All Diseases Can Be Prevented by Inoculation," reads the caption of a *Puck* cartoon from 1885—although, as the illustration itself makes plain, there is no effective inoculation against the disease of corruption. Depicted at left is an array of bank employees, including "Swindling Bank President," "Embezzling Bank Clerk," "Defaulting Bank Cashier" and "Thieving Office Boy." At right is a lineup of known criminals, including, seated in the foreground, Fredericka Mandelbaum.

"I have agents in New York," she explained. "And we buy those things so cheap—why, you'd be surprised."

In the end, Mrs. Mandelbaum told her inquisitor, what it all came down to was this: "It's fun for me to keep a store, and I'm so used to it." (And here one can imagine her eyes, behind their grandmotherly spectacles, flashing as brightly as the diamonds in her ears.) "Can I sell you anything?"

Epilogue: Kaddish

Though she would live abroad for the rest of her life, Fredericka Mandelbaum remained such a storied figure in the United States that in the spring of 1893 an urban legend arose, flung around the world by American newspapers, that she had died. "Mother Mandelbaum Dead: The Famous Fence Succumbs to Paralysis at Hamilton, Ont.," a headline in the *New York Evening World* cried. "Queen of Crooks: Mother Mandelbaum's Existence Ended by a Stroke of Paralysis," the *Fall River Daily Evening News* announced on its front page. "According to a letter received yesterday at the office of Howe & Hummel she died two weeks ago at the age of 65 from paralysis at her Canadian home," the newspaper reported on March 23. "She had lived like a princess since she escaped from [New York]."

A flurry of corrections ensued. "Mother Mandelbaum: Very Much Alive and Living in Splendor at Hamilton," the *Cincinnati Enquirer* said on page one. " 'Mother' Mandelbaum Not Dead," the *New-York Tribune* reported, adding: "The dispatch announcing the death . . . of Mrs. Mandelbaum, the notorious New-York 'fence' . . . has no foundation. Mrs. Mandelbaum was seen at her home [in Hamilton] and reports herself as in good health. She cannot imagine a reason for circulating a report of her death."

For Fredericka, who had so cherished her life in the United States that she flew the Stars and Stripes from her Clinton Street rooftop on holidays, expatriation had proved to be a kind of living death. "She has few friends," the *St. Louis Post-Dispatch* had reported, after a correspondent visited her there in 1887. In 1889, a writer for the *Cincinnati Enquirer* called on Marm. Her shop in Hamilton, the article reported, was "under the surveillance of the detectives."

"Frequently a well-dressed man gets off one of the trains and goes to her house," the story quotes a Hamilton police official as saying. "We watch them, however. They do not remain long, and when we see them . . . go away we are satisfied."

Inside the store, the journalist wrote, "at any hour of the day, will be found a neat-looking, rather stoutly built though not fleshy woman, whose features, though strong, are pleasant and complexion good. It is the notorious Madam Mandelbaum. . . . The old woman dresses neatly and wears a pair of steel-rimmed spectacles. She would be the last person to be taken for a criminal."

The writer asked her if business was good. "No, indeed," Marm said. "What would it be in a place like Hamilton? The trouble is that I am in the wrong business. No person here wants to buy children's underwear.* They make it themselves. I am not kept busy enough, either, and fret and worry so that sometimes I think I'll go crazy. I have tried to sell out here, but can't do it. It is either that no one wants to buy or they haven't got the money. Then my daughter's death."

"You went on there to the funeral, didn't you?" the reporter inquired.

"That is foolish," she replied. "It is the talk of detectives and some of those New York newspaper men. Why, I am too well known there to risk such a thing, unless I wanted to be arrested." She added: "I wish I had gone, though. I had my mind made up at one time to

---

*   The sale of ladies' and children's underwear was clearly Marm's "front"—the one legitimate strand of her business in Hamilton.

go. If I had, then this trouble would all be over by this time. It would be settled one way or the other."

Fredericka would continue to ply her trade in Hamilton until the early 1890s. But it was clear, from the moment she set foot on Canadian soil, that her days as a baroness of organized crime were over. "The army of enemies of society must have its general," her reformed protégée Sophie Lyons wrote in 1913. "The greatest of them all was 'Mother' Mandelbaum."

WHAT HAD LET MRS. MANDELBAUM assume that generalship in the first place? The times, of course, were on her side: She made her underworld ascent in a congenial climate of mass production, middle-class desire, rampant political graft, endemic police corruption, ubiquitous banks and portable paper money.

But those things augured success for *every* would-be crime baron, the overwhelming majority of them men. What was it that allowed a woman—*this* woman—to attain the summit of a profession famously inhospitable to her sex? Two answers present themselves. The first centers on Mrs. Mandelbaum's ethnic background. The second illuminates a particular moment in the history of American crime.

The fact that Marm was not only a woman but also a Jewish woman turned out to have enormous implications for her professional prospects. Unlike many immigrant women of the mid-nineteenth century, Jewish women were expected to be employed outside the home, and even to work as entrepreneurs: Such work sustained their families while freeing their husbands for Torah study. As the historian Hasia R. Diner and the journalist Beryl Lieff Benderly have written: "America's Jewish women emigrated or descended from places where women routinely ran their own businesses and earned incomes distinct from men's. Both homemaking and earning formed part of the sacred work of Jewish womanhood, which is seeing to the physical, economic, and spiritual welfare of her family. They brought the strategy of separate earning, devised in places where Jewish life was precarious, across the sea to a land of plenty."

In the Old Country, women's work had been limited mainly to domestic jobs of various kinds:

> A small-town Jewish woman . . . brought a very particular set of expectations molded by the life she had known in Europe. First, she had worked hard helping her mother with the time-honored tasks of Jewish womanhood. Beyond household duties, a good daughter did what she could to contribute to the family's income. She might work in the family's shop—often its front room—or mind younger children while her mother did the accounts. She might also bake or sew items to sell and might also start a small business of her own. And if worse came to worst, she would hire herself out to clean another family's house or cook or serve another family's meals, or tend another mother's children.

But on coming to America, many Jewish women discovered that the sex-based segregation they had known in Europe need not apply. "More than in any other liberal, industrial, modern society—more than in England, France, Germany, Canada—American Jewish women have asserted their sense of entitlement to power, influence, and equality in the Jewish world," the authors write. "In nearly all [of] the many countries where Jews have lived and built the institutions that sustained their religious lives, women accepted the notion of separate Judaic spheres for men and women. In the United States, however, Jewish women responded differently. The first of their sisters to claim the synagogue as their space too, they pioneered institutions and practices that brought them down from the balcony, out from behind the curtain, and into the main arena of Jewish communal, political, and ritual life."

And even, they might well have added, into the main arena of criminal life.

In that arena, Fredericka learned to thrive by intertwining her activities with those of powerful upper-world men. "She was *part* of the process rather than *'under'* it," Rona Holub told me recently. The arena she carved out for herself was not some "shifty underworld that was separated from the political economy of the mainstream," but rather a haven for a capitalist enterprise that had been carefully calibrated to mesh *with* the mainstream—an unofficial Ladies' Auxiliary of Tammany Hall.

Crucially, too, Fredericka was the product of a tradition in which her intelligence and drive could largely be given free rein. As Diner and Benderly write:

> Every week for thousands of years, the Jewish people have welcomed the Sabbath into their homes. . . . As ordinary time recedes and sacred time begins, every Jewish husband traditionally recites verses from Proverbs 31 to his wife, the bride and queen whose cooking, cleaning, shopping, fretting, and candle lighting has brought the Sabbath's pleasures into their home. Whether in Spain or Lithuania, in Turkey or Poland or Morocco, in Iraq or America, whether in the tenth century or the twenty-first, he declares her an *ashet hayil*, a woman of valor, and enumerates the qualities that make a woman admirable.
>
> She need not be beautiful, for "grace is deceitful and beauty is vain." Rather, she serves her family, and her husband "doth safely trust in her." Motherhood matters, and "her children rise up and call her blessed." She has charge of the domestic, and "she looketh well to the ways of her household." . . . "She worketh willingly." Indeed, "she is like the merchant ships [that] bringeth her food from afar." Above all, "she eateth not the bread of idleness."
>
> Nor does the woman of valor fit any mold of delicate femininity. Rather, "strength and dignity are her clothing." She has a mind of her own, and the confidence to act in the world. . . .

She also "considereth a field and buyeth it; with the fruit of her hands she planteth a vineyard." . . . She is neither meek nor passive, but an activist, a doer, an accomplisher of deeds.

Many immigrant women from other backgrounds were smart, hardworking and ambitious, of course. But in mid-nineteenth-century America, few other traditions so overtly prescribed a woman's role as embodying personal confidence, bold activism and singlemindedness of purpose. And those attributes, so vital to Jewish family life down the ages, turn out to be sublime preparation for running a crime family. "Along with piety, thrift and good management marked the worthy wife," the authors write:

> If she married an impecunious middling scholar, she might have to bear the entire burden of supporting the family. If she married a man who worked hard but earned little, she might join him in a combined business venture or go into business on her own. Unlike nineteenth-century American or English wives, who lost control of their assets at marriage, a wife under Jewish law could own property and make contracts in her own right.

Fredericka's Germanic background also served her well in this regard. "The German culture and community . . . had its own attitudes about gender that had an influence on how women operated within that milieu," Rona Holub writes. "German working class women in general, like German Jewish women in particular . . . were expected to work and be part of the family economy. German people strove to advance and take care of their families, and German men often expected the women in their lives to give their all in this endeavor."

THE SECOND THING THAT MADE Marm's ascent possible was that she embarked on it as early as she did. The late 1850s, when she began her rise, was the barest cusp of the first Golden Age of American crime. At the time, the field, like upper-world callings such as medicine and law, was just starting to organize and professionalize. Only after the Civil War did American enterprise—both in the upper world and the underworld—begin to implement rigorous professional standards. "By the late [eighteen-]seventies, the theory within which men would maneuver for the balance of the century was already more or less complete," a historian has written. "A few [had] discovered more effective ways to combine land, labor, and capital, and drew society upward as the rest reorganized behind their leaders."

Professional reorganizations like these were a way for the dominant culture to restrict membership, consolidate power and control markets in a given enterprise. Doctors drove out the quacks. Lawyers marginalized those who had not been to law school. And a spate of upper-world occupations could already capitalize on an age-old tradition in which "laboring women were confined within a patriarchal economy," as the historian Christine Stansell has written. She continues:

> Sex segregation and its associated forms of exploitation were consequences, not causes, of women's inferior position in the labor market. Sex segregation grew out of a deeper political economy of gender, founded in the sexual division of labor in the household. It resulted from the incorporation of patterns of female subordination within the family into those of capitalist exploitation.

And so it would be in the newly professionalized underworld, where the more profit there came to be in organized crime, the more patriarchal and exclusionary it became. By the Prohibition-era heyday of syndicated crime, women have disappeared entirely from its upper ranks, and almost completely from the field as a whole.* Had Fredericka Mandelbaum attempted her career twenty

---

*   "The Mafia is the surest stronghold of male chauvinism in America," the journalist Nicholas Gage wrote in 1971. "In the Mafia a woman may be a means to a profitable alliance with another Mafia 'family'; a showcase for displaying her husband's wealth,

years later than she did—perhaps even ten—the path to becoming "arguably the most influential criminal in America" would have been closed to her.

IN THE SUMMER OF 1888, Julius Mandelbaum paid a surprise visit to the New York district attorney's office. Surrendering himself, he asked to renew his bail so that his case might be heard at last. Julius, then in his late twenties, explained that he'd been studying medicine in Berlin: He wanted to return to New York to practice but couldn't do so with an indictment hanging over him. Interviewed by the *New York Evening World* that day, Robert Pinkerton said that "he could in a short time produce the required testimony that would make out a strong case against Julius Mandelbaum, which he believed would convict the young man."

Julius, however, remained confident—or at least defiant. "He says that no proof can be offered of his complicity [in] the crime charged against his mother of knowingly receiving the silks stolen from Simpson, Crawford & Simpson," the *New-York Tribune* reported. What he wanted, the *Times* said, was to have all the indictments against him dismissed.

Julius's $5,000 bail was accepted, and he was released on his own recognizance; he would stand trial, most likely in the autumn, in the renewed case against him. But in the end, he got his wish: The New York authorities dropped all charges against him before his case ever came to trial.

Some observers saw Julius's surrender as a litmus test, designed to gauge whether New York's legal climate would let his mother return. But Marm was too savvy to risk going back. However much she pined for the city, she knew that if she ventured there, prison would be a foregone conclusion. There was little of her organization left to go back to in any case: Her beloved George Leslie lay in Cy-

---

status, and power; a valuable piece of property; a loyal helpmate; a good cook; a showy and ego-boosting mistress. But what she must never be is a liberated woman."

press Hills Cemetery. Adam Worth, "Piano Charley" Bullard and
Mark Shinburn had all fled the country for the relative safety of
Europe. (There, Shinburn bought himself a title, Baron Shindell of
Monaco, and lived in splendor between stints behind bars; Bullard
would die in a Belgian jail in 1892.) Michael Kurtz, tried in 1886 for
the Troy jewelry store robbery, was convicted and sentenced to eighteen and a half years in the state prison at Dannemora, New York.
Sophie Lyons, who divorced her husband, Ned, in 1887, was beset
by continued incarcerations before assuming her righteous public
persona as a crusader against crime.

And so Marm remained in Hamilton with her younger son, Gustav, who ran a billiard parlor there. Julius, who rejoined his family
in Canada, appears not to have practiced medicine after all.* Over
the years, Marm's married daughter, Sarah, would move—
strategically—back and forth between Hamilton and New York.†

FREDERICKA MANDELBAUM'S LAST YEARS are painful to contemplate.
The newspapers that had mistakenly reported her death were right
about one thing: She was by then living with partial paralysis. She
also suffered from Bright's disease, as nephritis, an inflammation of
the kidneys, was then known. In 1892, Canadian authorities again
brought her up on smuggling charges; indomitable to the end, she
tried the stratagem that had served her so well in the past. "A few
weeks ago, Mother Mandelbaum's daughter visited New York and

---

* Julius may have returned to the United States in the early twentieth century to
work in an allied field: 1908 records list a Julius Mandelbaum as a founder of the
Maltzone Company, a maker or distributor of medicines in New York. The company
went out of business the next year. Hamilton, Ontario, city directories of the late
1880s and early 1890s list Julius's occupation as "salesman," Gustav's as "tobacconist"
and Marm's as "fancy goods."

† Sarah Mandelbaum would marry twice, first to a New York City alderman named
Weill and later, after her divorce from Weill, to a crook named Samuel Koller (also
spelled Kohler). When Sarah's daughter, Dorothy Blower (née Weill), jumped her bail
in 1915 after being arrested and charged with passing a bad check—and again, later
that year, when she was sent to the Tombs for stealing a fur muff—the newspapers
made much of her connection to her notorious grandmother.

brought back with her what purported to be a quantity of her household goods," a newspaper report from that January read:

> They were stored in a warehouse and billed in Mother Man-
> delbaum's name. On Friday last the goods were all seized in
> Her Majesty's name, and among them were found a very
> valuable quantity of lace, embroideries, silks, jewelry and
> other goods.
>
> Mother Mandelbaum and her pretty daughter were
> brought upon the carpet to Collector Kelvert's office. The old
> woman begged the Collector not to expose her before her
> friends in this city, and promised to make everything right if
> he would only keep the matter quiet.

In the end, Marm got off with a $250 fine, but the episode, to-
gether with her declining health, appears to have forced her into
retirement: For the last two years of her life, she transacted no business whatsoever.

ON THE MORNING OF FEBRUARY 26, 1894, Fredericka Mandelbaum
died of Bright's disease at her home in Hamilton, at the age of
sixty-eight. "Mrs. Mandelbaum had been ailing for the past four or
five years," a Canadian newspaper reported, "and from time to time
during this period she was prostrated by severe attacks of the disease that preyed upon her frame; but her remarkably vigorous constitution enabled her to rally from all these repeated attacks except
the last, fatal one. For six weeks she was confined to her bed, and
suffered so intensely that death was looked forward to by her as a
happy release."

Her death made headlines around the world: "Queen of Fences:
Mother Mandelbaum Is Dead in Hamilton," said the *Boston Globe*.
"End of a Wicked Life," cried the *San Francisco Chronicle*. "Old
'Mother' Mandelbaum Is Dead: She Was a Famous 'Fence' Well
Known to the Police of This City," the *Times* wrote. And, from the

New-York World, spanning eight lines and leaving nothing to chance: "Queen of the 'Crooks': Mother Mandelbaum, the Famous 'Fence,' Is Dead, After Ten Years of Exile in Canada. Twenty Years in 'Queer' Street. Burglars, Highwaymen, Shoplifters, Sneak-Thieves, All Brought Their Plunder to Her."

But Marm's reputation succeeded her: Soon after the spate of obituaries came a flurry of printed reports that Fredericka Mandelbaum, crafty as ever, had faked her own demise. "A story is published . . . to the effect that Mother Mandelbaum, the notorious 'fence,' . . . is not dead," the *Brooklyn Standard Union* said. "The reported death was for the purpose of concealing her further movements. A coffin filled with stone was said to have been shipped to New York as her remains." In an interview with the *New York Evening World,* an unnamed city police official said, "It would not be a scheme too wild for Mother Mandelbaum to undertake to pull the wool over the eyes of the police and the people, for the purpose of at last coming to the city that she loved better than all other abiding places."

The reports were pure rumor, nothing more. This time, as one newspaper declaimed, Mrs. Mandelbaum had truly been "arrested on a warrant which cannot be disobeyed. It was issued from the Court of Death, and to it the wicked old woman bowed."

Even in death, however, Marm had the last laugh. Of the masses of silk seized in the Pinkertons' raid of 1884, some 3,000 yards remained unclaimed. They had languished for a decade in a vault of the American Safe Deposit Company in Manhattan. Now, the sitting district attorney, John R. Fellows, ordered that the silk be turned over to the police department property clerk. "If it is not claimed," the *New York Sun* reported, "it will be sold for the benefit of the pension fund of the Police Department." And thus, from the ill-gotten gains of the late Mother Mandelbaum, the police of New York City were able to pull one last sweet plum.

ON FEBRUARY 28, 1894, the train carrying Fredericka Mandelbaum's coffin from Canada was met by a hearse at Weehawken, New Jersey.

Ferried across the Hudson, the hearse was joined on the New York side by eight carriages filled with family and friends. No services were held: The coffin was conveyed directly to Union Field Cemetery in Queens, where Fredericka was buried in the family plot near Wolf and Annie.

At the interment, it was reported afterward, some mourners deftly picked the pockets of others. Whether they did so in tribute to their fallen leader or simply from occupational reflex is unrecorded.

Acknowledgments

DURING THE YEARS I SPENT PANNING THE PAST FOR GLIMMERS OF Mrs. Mandelbaum's life, a bevy of friends and colleagues lent sustained support to the enterprise. Foremost among them are my agent, Katinka Matson, and my editor, Hilary Redmon. Katinka's associates at Brockman, Inc., among them Michael Healey, Russell Weinberger, Stephen Dimaio and Matthew Perez, and Hilary's at Random House, including Miriam Khanukaev, Nancy Delia, Ted Allen, Rachel Parker, Ayelet Durantt and Alison Rich, also gave professional aid and comfort. Likewise my screen agent, Joe Veltre, and his assistant, Hayley Nusbaum, and my lecture agent, Anya Backlund, and her colleagues Shannon Hearn, Rebecca Rhodes, Ana Paula Simões, Miyako Hannan-Scarponi, Alice Yang and Cale Zepernick. As he has for nearly all my books, Jonathan Corum created the impeccable maps. The stellar copyeditor was Emily DeHuff; Charlee Trantino prepared the index. The documentarian Vanessa Gould and the photographer Ivan Farkas contributed enduring brilliance, as did the web designer Mary K. Elkins Birch.

Three historians of nineteenth-century America have vetted the manuscript of *The Talented Mrs. Mandelbaum* with the rigor and savvy of a master fence going over a load of swag: Robert W. Snyder, emeritus professor at Rutgers University and the official historian of the Borough of Manhattan; Timothy J. Haggerty, of Carnegie

Mellon University; and Rona L. Holub, the only scholar to have devoted sustained attention to Fredericka Mandelbaum's life. To all three, who have collectively saved me from the interloper's idiocies that are an occupational hazard of popular-nonfiction writing, I owe an indelible debt of thanks. The historian Hasia R. Diner provided invaluable information on the German and Yiddish dialects spoken in mid-nineteenth-century New York. The mathematician Christopher Baltus handily confirmed—purely as a theoretical abstraction, it should be stressed—the number of permutations required to crack safe combinations of three and four digits.

This book could not have been written without the assistance of a shining constellation of archivists and library personnel throughout North America. I am indebted above all to Kenneth Cobb, assistant commissioner of the New York City Department of Records and Information Services, who repeatedly scoured the city's Municipal Archives for the faintest traces of Mrs. Mandelbaum. Aidan Flax-Clark and Tal Nadan, of the New York Public Library; Ruby Landau-Pincus and Stefanie Halpern, of YIVO; and Jeff Roth, of the *New York Times,* also gave vital assistance, as did the reference staffs of the New-York Historical Society, the Center for Jewish History, and the Local History and Archives division of the Hamilton, Ontario, Public Library.

In my fledgling reincarnation as an executive producer, it has been a privilege and a joy to begin working with David Brooks, of Gold Circle Films, and with Basil Iwanyk, Esther Hornstein and Charlie Morrison, of Thunder Road Films.

Closer to home, my thanks, love and admiration to Robin, Duncan, Ricki, Josh, Leah and Ben for being menschen of valor. And to George Robinson, my perennial first reader and boon companion of forty years, more love and gratitude than I can ever fully express.

A Note on Sources

Reanimating Frederica Mandelbaum from a diverse array of printed sources—newspapers, magazines, memoirs, court records—has been a deeply pleasurable act of bricolage. There are, however, two published volumes invoked by earlier writers on Marm that I deliberately do not cite in this book. The first, *Cell 202, Sing Sing*, by Lewis E. Lawes (New York: Farrar & Rinehart, 1935), is "fiction . . . based on fact," as an advance notice describes it. Lawes (1883–1947), the longtime warden of Sing Sing, organized his book as a series of case studies, "embellished with imaginative conversations and descriptions intended to fill out the picture," of successive occupants of a single cell there. In one section, the tale of a convicted murderer he calls Stephen Yerkes, Lawes devotes several pages to describing a meeting between Yerkes and Mrs. Mandelbaum. But that vignette, like everything in the book, has in all likelihood been "reconstructed . . . with high imagination," in the words of a 1935 reviewer, and thus poses a deep danger for nonfiction chroniclers.

The second volume is even more problematic. It is *Nell Kimball: Her Life as an American Madam*, by Herself, edited and with an introduction by Stephen Longstreet (New York: Macmillan, 1970). The book is "the alleged confession of a woman who began her career as a prostitute in St. Louis in 1867 and who retired in 1917 as the madam of her own swank brothel in New Orleans." Longstreet (1907–2002) was an American writer of popular fiction and nonfiction. He wrote that Kimball had given him her manuscript in 1932, two years before her death, in the hope that he could find a publisher; only in the more tolerant climate of circa-1970 America was he able to do so.

The published book, which includes Kimball's account of her time in New York and her acquaintance with Mother Mandelbaum, garnered acclaim in the popular press. The *New York Times Book Review* said that "in many respects it is a remarkable book by a remarkable woman" and commended Longstreet for "rescuing it from oblivion and somewhat reworking it."

The trouble is, Longstreet did far more than "rework" the memoir: He made it, and Nell Kimball, up out of whole cloth. As an incisive scholarly review of 1972 points out, many of Kimball's "accounts" of underworld life, including her descriptions of Fredericka Mandelbaum, were lifted, with only a little tweaking, straight from *The Gangs of New York*, Herbert Asbury's 1927 book. (Asbury, the reviewer points out, never mentions anyone by the name of Nell Kimball.)

"It is clear that portions of Nell Kimball's memoir are fake," the reviewer wrote. "But was there really such a woman? Unfortunately there appears to be no evidence other than Longstreet's word and we are therefore forced to assume that she is the product of his imagination."

More recently, Yale University, the repository of Stephen Longstreet's papers, confirmed this assessment, writing in its online finding aid to those papers:

> Longstreet wrote both novels and non-fiction works. Most of the latter were not reviewed kindly, with reviewers questioning his accuracy of content and reliability of sources. Perhaps his most notable hoax was *Nell Kimball: Her Life as an American Madam*. . . . Kimball's autobiography received positive

notices in newspapers and mass-market periodicals, but academics found too many close parallels in narrative and language to the works of Herbert Asbury (1889–1963), and shortly, both the text and the madam were found to be Longstreet's fabrications.

References

"Abe Hummel Left Million to Sisters: On Their Death the Estate Will Revert to Paris Nephew—Lawyer's Body Due Tonight." *New York Times*, Feb. 3, 1926, 1.

Abelson, Elaine S. *When Ladies Go A-Thieving: Middle-Class Shoplifters in the Victorian Department Store*. New York: Oxford University Press, 1992; originally published 1989.

Ackerman, Kenneth D. *The Gold Ring: Jim Fisk, Jay Gould, and Black Friday, 1869*. New York: Dodd, Mead, 1988.

An Act for Encourageing the Apprehending of Highway Men. Statutes of the Realm: Volume 6, 1685–94. british-history.ac.uk/statutes-realm/vol6/pp390-391.

Adams, James Truslow. *The Epic of America*. Boston: Little, Brown & Company, 1931.

Alger, Horatio. *Ragged Dick: Or, Street Life in New York with the Boot-Blacks*. Boston: James Loring, Publisher, 1868.

"Allan Pinkerton." *Brooklyn Daily Eagle*, July 2, 1884, 2.

"Allan Pinkerton." *Encyclopaedia Britannica*. britannica.com/biography/Allan-Pinkerton.

"Allan Pinkerton Dead: The Great Detective's Life Ended at the Age of 64." *Boston Globe*, July 2, 1884, 5.

"Allan Pinkerton's Death: The Career of the Great Detective Ended." *New-York Times*, July 2, 1884, 1.

Allen, Irving Lewis. *The City in Slang: New York Life and Popular Speech*. New York: Oxford University Press, 1993.

"Amusements: Union Square Theatre." Advertisement. *New-York Times*, Dec. 18, 1874, 7.

Anbinder, Tyler. *Five Points: The 19th-Century New York City Neighborhood That Invented Tap Dance, Stole Elections, and Became the World's Most Notorious Slum*. New York: Free Press, 2001.

"Another Great Bank Robbery." *Maine Farmer*, July 10, 1869, 3.

"Another Wholesale Bank Robbery in New York—The Ocean National Bank Broken Open and Plundered." Baltimore *Sun*, June 29, 1869, 1.

Article, no title. *Allentown (Pa.) Morning Call*, Dec. 18, 1884, 2.

Article, no title. *Atlanta Constitution*, July 31, 1884, 4.

Article, no title. *Brooklyn Daily Eagle*, Dec. 9, 1884, 2.

Article, no title. *Brooklyn Union*, Dec. 9, 1884, 2.

Article, no title. *Corvallis (Ore.) Gazette*, Jan. 2, 1885, 7.

Article, no title. *Neenah (Wis.) Daily Times*, Jan. 9, 1885, 1.

Article, no title. *New York Daily Herald*, March 24, 1872, 10.

Asbury, Herbert. *The Gangs of New York: An Informal History of the Underworld.* New York: Vintage Books, 2008; originally published 1927.

"At the Polls: A Big Blow to Boss Kelly and Tammany." *New York Herald,* Nov. 3, 1875, 5.

"Attack and Defence in Burglary." *Daily News* (London), Nov. 2, 1897, 5.

Avery, Ron. "America's First Bank Robbery." Carpenters' Hall, carpentershall.org/americas -first-bank-robbery.

"Bank Robber Who Exposed Secrets in Book Is Dead: George White Regarded Burglary as a Respectable Profession." New York *Evening World,* Feb. 13, 1909, 10.

"Bank Treasurer Murdered." *New-York Times,* Feb. 24, 1878, 7.

"Banking Act of 1933 (Glass-Steagall)." Federal Reserve History. federalreservehistory.org /essays/glass-steagall-act.

"Barron Proved No Hero: Shown to Be a Defaulter and a Suicide. Result of the Investigation of the Supposed Murder of the Cashier of the Dexter Savings Bank—A Defaulter to the Amount of $3,600—Taking Poison After Arranging the Appearance of Outrage." *New-York Times,* Feb. 1, 1879, 1.

Beecher, Catharine Esther, and Harriet Beecher Stowe. *The American Woman's Home: Or, Principles of Domestic Science, Being a Guide to the Formation and Maintenance of Economical, Healthful, Beautiful, and Christian Homes.* New York : J. B. Ford & Company, 1869.

Berkvist, Robert. "In Brief: *Nell Kimball: Her Life as an American Madam,*" *New York Times Book Review,* July 5, 1970, 10.

"Bernard Shaw Resents Action of Librarian: Calls 'American Comstockery' World's Standing Joke." *New York Times,* Sept. 26, 1905, 1.

Betts, John Rickards. "Sporting Journalism in Nineteenth-Century America." *American Quarterly* 5:1 (Spring 1953), 39–56.

"Between Two Fires: The Unhappy Condition of Marm Mandelbaum and Confederates." *Detroit Free Press,* Dec. 10, 1884, 2.

"A Big 'Fence': 'Marm' Mandelbaum, a Noted Receiver of Stolen Goods. History of the Ruler of All the City Thieves and Shoplifters—Her Immense Wealth." *San Francisco Examiner,* Aug. 3, 1884, 8, via *New York World.*

"A Big Haul." *Chicago Tribune,* July 25, 1884, 3.

"A Bill to Authorize the Issue of United States Notes and for the Redemption or Funding Thereof, and for the Funding of the Floating Debt of the United States," H.R. 240, Thirty-seventh Congress, Second Session, Jan. 28, 1862, congress.gov/bill/37th-congress /house-bill/240.

" 'Billy' Porter: Eventful Life of the King of Cracksmen." *Boston Daily Globe,* Jan. 23, 1886, 1.

"Blackwell's Island (Roosevelt Island), New York City." National Park Service. nps.gov/places /blackwell-s-island-new-york-city.htm.

"A Bold Bank Robbery: The Ocean National Bank Burglariously Entered." *New York Herald,* June 29, 1869, 3.

"Boss Tweed." *Encyclopaedia Britannica.* britannica.com/biography/Boss-Tweed.

"The Boston Bank Robbery: Full Particulars of the Burglarious Operations at the Boylston National Bank." *New York Herald,* Nov. 24, 1869, 8, via *Boston Post.*

"The Boycott." *Wichita Citizen,* Jan. 8, 1887, 1.

Brands, H[enry] W[illiam]. *Greenback Planet: How the Dollar Conquered the World and Threatened Civilization as We Know It.* Austin: University of Texas Press, 2011.

"A Brave Cashier's Death: Further Particulars of the Attempted Bank Robbery in Dexter, Me.—How the Cashier Was Found." *Boston Globe,* Feb. 24, 1878, 1.

Breger, Sarah. "New York's First Female Crime Boss," *Forward,* Nov. 4, 2014. forward.com /life/208460/new-yorks-first-female-crime-boss/.

"Brieflets." *Boston Evening Transcript,* Jan. 16, 1877, 8.

"Broadbrim's New York Letter." *Newberry (S.C.) Weekly Herald,* Aug. 14, 1884, 1.

Bronner, Simon J. "Reading Consumer Culture" [hereafter Bronner (1989a)]. In Bronner (1989b), 13–53.

———, ed. *Consuming Visions: Accumulation and Display of Goods in America, 1880–1920*. New York: W. W. Norton, 1989 [hereafter Bronner (1989b)].

Browning, Frank, and John Gerassi. *The American Way of Crime*. New York: G. P. Putnam's Sons, 1980.

"Bulldozing the Court: Mrs. Mandelbaum's Lawyer Rebuked by Judge Murray." *New-York Times*, July 31, 1884, 5.

Bunson, Matthew E. *Encyclopedia Sherlockiana: An A-to-Z Guide to the World of the Great Detective*. New York: Macmillan, 1994.

"Burglary as an Art: Personal Habits of the Fraternity." *New-York Times*, March 7, 1875, 10.

Burrows, Edwin G., and Mike Wallace. *Gotham: A History of New York City to 1898*. New York: Oxford University Press, 1999.

Byrne, Richard. *Safecracking*. Golden, Colo.: ReAnimus Press, 2016; originally published 1991.

Byrnes, Thomas. *Professional Criminals of America*. Introductions by Arthur M. Schlesinger, Jr., and S. J. Perelman. New York: Chelsea House, 1969; originally published 1886.

———. *Professional Criminals of America: New and Revised Edition*. New York: G. W. Dillingham, 1895.

Callow, Alexander B., Jr. *The Tweed Ring*. Oxford: Oxford University Press, 1969; originally published 1965.

"Canada: Hard Lines for 'Marm' Mandelbaum." *Detroit Free Press*, Dec. 11, 1884, 2.

"The Case of Mrs. Mandelbaum," *New-York Times*, Dec. 3, 1884, 8.

Cassidy, Tom. "Sadism at Ossining." *New York Daily News*, Oct. 13, 1935, 84.

Chan, Sewell. "Disgraced and Penalized, Kerik Finds His Name Stripped Off Jail." *New York Times*, July 3, 2006, B1.

"Chartism." *Encyclopaedia Britannica*. britannica.com/event/Chartism-British-history.

"The Chartist Movement." UK Parliament. parliament.uk/about/living-heritage/transforming society/electionsvoting/chartists/overview/chartistmovement/.

"The Christmas Holidays: What There Is to Purchase and Where It May Be Found." *New-York Times*, Dec. 21, 1865, 8.

City of Hamilton: Alphabetical, General, Street, Miscellaneous and Subscribers' Classified Business Directory. Hamilton, Ont.: W. H. Irwin & Company, 1887–88; 1892–93; 1893–94.

Clark, Jerry, and Ed Palattella. *A History of Heists: Bank Robbery in America*. Lanham, Md.: Rowman & Littlefield, 2015.

"A Clever Capture." *St. Louis Post-Dispatch*, July 23, 1.

Cohen, Patricia Cline, Timothy J. Gilfoyle, and Helen Lefkowitz Horowitz, in association with the American Antiquarian Society. *The Flash Press: Sporting Male Weeklies in 1840s New York*. Chicago: University of Chicago Press, 2008.

Cohen, Rich. *Tough Jews*. New York: Simon & Schuster, 1998.

Cohn, Henry S. "Abraham Lincoln at the Bar." *Federal Lawyer* (May 2012), 52–55.

"Col. John R. Fellows Is Dead: The District Attorney Passed Away Yesterday. His Older Son Reached Home Too Late to See His Father in Life." *New York Times*, Dec. 8, 1896, 8.

"Comstock and Horse Ponds." *Lucifer—the Light-Bearer* (Valley Falls, Kan.), April 26, 1889, 2, via *Philadelphia Record*, April 9, 1889.

Conan Doyle, Sir Arthur. "The Red-Headed League." In *The Complete Sherlock Holmes*, Volume 1, 176–90. Garden City, N.Y.: Doubleday & Company, 1930.

"Condensed Telegrams." *Fall River (Mass.) Daily Evening News*, Sept. 16, 1884, 3.

"Congregation Rodeph Sholom." rodephsholom.org/about-us/our-history.

Conway, J. North. *King of Heists: The Sensational Bank Robbery of 1878 That Shocked America*. Guilford, Conn.: Lyons Press, 2009.

———. *Queen of Thieves: The True Story of "Marm" Mandelbaum and Her Gangs of New York*. New York: Skyhorse, 2014.

"The Court of General Sessions." Historical Society of the New York Courts. history.nycourts
.gov/court/court-general-sessions.

"Court of Oyer and Terminer," Historical Society of the New York Courts, history.nycourts
.gov/court/court-oyer-terminer/.

Crapsey, Edward. *The Nether Side of New York: Or, The Vice, Crime and Poverty of the Great
Metropolis.* New York: Sheldon & Company, 1872.

"Crime: The Ocean Bank Robbery. Railroad Bonds, Bank Checks, and Other Securities to the
Amount of $268,021.29 Returned." *New-York Tribune,* July 1, 1869, 2.

"Crime and the Police." *New-York Times,* July 24, 1884, 4.

"Croton Water Filtration Plant Activated." New York City Department of Environmental
Protection press release, May 8, 2015. nyc.gov/html/dep/html/press_releases/15-034pr
.shtml.

"Cypress Hills Cemetery: Famous & Notable Burials." cypresshillscemetery.org/timeline-2
/notable-burials.

"Cypress Hills Cemetery: Map of Cemetery." cypresshillscemetery.org/map.

Czitrom, Daniel. *New York Exposed: The Gilded Age Police Scandal That Launched the Progressive Era.* New York: Oxford University Press, 2016.

Dapson, Leon A. "The Loomis Gang." *New York History* 19:3 (July 1938), 269–79.

Davidson, Shayne. *Queen of the Burglars: The Scandalous Life of Sophie Lyons.* Jefferson, N.C.:
Exposit Books, 2020.

"David Stain." National Registry of Exonerations. law.umich.edu/special/exoneration/Pages
/casedetailpre1989.aspx?caseid=309.

"A Dead Detective: Allan Pinkerton, the Expert Ferret, Dies at His Home in Chicago—Notes
of His Life and Works." *Kansas City Daily Times,* July 2, 1884, 1.

"Death Closes Spectacular Career of America's Most Notorious Divorce Lawyer." *Buffalo Courier* via Associated Press, Jan. 25, 1926, 2.

"Death Ends Her Troubles: Mrs. Frederika [*sic*] Mandelbaum Died This Morning." *Hamilton
Spectator,* Feb. 26, 1894, n.p.

"Death of James Fisk: Closing Scenes in the Life of the Great Speculator." *New-York Times,*
Jan. 8, 1872, 1.

"Death of Wm. M. Tweed: The Ex-Tammany Chief's Last Hours in Jail. A Peaceful Death-
Bed Scene in the Ludlow-Street Prison." *New-York Times,* April 13, 1878, 1–2.

"Defaulters' Paradise: Criminals From the United States Who Now Reside in Canada."
St. Louis Post-Dispatch, Jan. 12, 1885, 1.

Defoe, Daniel. *The Great Law of Subordination Consider'd; Or, The Insolence and Unsufferable
Behaviour of SERVANTS in England Duly Enquired Into.* London: S. Harding, 1724.

———— [attributed]. *The True and Genuine Account of the Life and Actions of the Late Jonathan Wild: Not Made Up of Fiction and Fable, but Taken from His Own Mouth, and Collected from Papers of His Own Writing.* London: John Applebee, 1725.

"Device Makes Heart Beats More Audible to Doctor." *Buffalo Evening News* via Associated
Press, Oct. 21, 1944, 6.

Dickens, Charles. *American Notes for General Circulation.* Volume 1. London: Chapman &
Hall, 1842.

"Did Business With Crooks: 'Mother Mandelbaum, Gotham's Noted 'Fence,' Is Dead." Erroneous report, *Fall River (Mass.) Daily Evening News,* March 23, 1893, 3.

DiFabio, Anne. "Thomas Nast Takes Down Tammany: A Cartoonist's Crusade Against a Political Boss." Museum of the City of New York, Sept. 24, 2013, mcny.org/story/thomas
-nast-takes-down-tammany-cartoonists-crusade-against-political-boss.

Diner, Hasia R. *Hungering for America: Italian, Irish, and Jewish Foodways in the Age of Migration.* Cambridge, Mass.: Harvard University Press, 2001.

Diner, Hasia R., and Beryl Lieff Benderly. *Her Works Praise Her: A History of Jewish Women
in America from Colonial Times to the Present.* New York: Basic Books, 2002.

" 'Dodger's' Expositions." *National Police Gazette*, March 30, 1867, 2.

"Doom of the Old Tombs. Soon to Be Removed to Make Way for New Prison: Something About the Grim Structure in Centre Street Where Many Notorious Criminals Have Been Confined and Numbers of Executions Have Taken Place—The Structure to Be Substituted Will Have More Room." *New York Times*, July 4, 1896, 1.

"Dorothy Blower's Bond Forfeited: Warrant Issued for the Arrest of Mother Mandelbaum's Granddaughter." *Brooklyn Daily Eagle*, Jan. 11, 1915, 2.

"Doubt Mandelbaum's Death: Police Sceptics Believe She Is Alive and in This City. Her Legacy of Silk May Cause Some Litigation." *New York Evening World*, March 29, 1894, 5.

"Dr. Howard Crosby Dead: His Noble Struggle Against Pneumonia Was in Vain. He Passed Away Late Yesterday Afternoon, Fully Conscious That His Work on Earth Was Done—A Long Life of Well-Doing." *New-York Times*, March 30, 1891, 1.

Drummond, James O., and Kate Lauber. "Horses." In Jackson (2010), 612–13.

Editors, *Law Review*. "Private Police Forces: Legal Powers and Limitations," *University of Chicago Law Review* 38:3, Spring 1971, 555–82.

Eldridge, Benj. P., and William B. Watts. *Our Rival, the Rascal: A Faithful Portrayal of the Conflict Between the Criminals of This Age and the Defenders of Society—the Police.* Boston: Pemberton Publishing Company, 1897.

"The Elections Next Tuesday: Public Officers to Be Chosen in Twenty States." *New York Herald*, Oct. 30, 1875, 4.

Ellis, Edward Robb. *The Epic of New York City.* New York: Old Town Books, 1966.

Elwell, Craig K. "Brief History of the Gold Standard in the United States." Congressional Research Service, Report R41887, June 23, 2011. crsreports.congress.gov/product/details?prodcode=R41887.

"End of a Criminal Career: Old Abe Greenthal Dies of Old Age—His Life Story." *New-York Times*, Nov. 20, 1889, 8.

"The End of a Notorious Career: Mother Mandelbaum, the Famous 'Fence.' " *Cincinnati Enquirer*, Feb. 27, 1894, 1.

"End of a Wicked Life: Old Mother Mandelbaum Is Dead." *San Francisco Chronicle*, Feb. 27, 1894, 1.

Ernst, Robert. *Immigrant Life in New York City.* Port Washington, N.Y.: Ira J. Friedman, 1965; originally published 1949.

———. "The One and Only Mike Walsh." *New-York Historical Society Quarterly* 36:1 (January 1952), 43–65.

"Even Unto the Third Generation." Baltimore *Sun*, April 11, 1915, Section II, 4.

"Ex-Chief Byrnes Dies of Cancer: Best Known of All the City's Police Officials Had Been Ill Since August." *New York Times*, May 8, 1910, 1, 6.

"Ex-Justice Barrett Dies in Saratoga." *New York Times*, June 8, 1906, 9.

"Ex-Justice Charles Donohue." *New-York Daily Tribune*, April 19, 1910, 7.

"Fahreda Mahzar: Thrilled the Public with Exotic Dancing." Coney Island History Project. coneyislandhistory.org/hall-of-fame/fahreda-mahzar.

"Famed Lawyer Dies in London: Abraham H. Hummel Closes Spectacular Life. New York Law Office Haven for Miscreants." *Los Angeles Times* via Associated Press, Jan. 25, 1926, 6.

"The Female Fence's Work: 'Marm' Mandelbaum Is Much Frightened and Worried." *New York World*, July 29, 1884, n.p., from District Attorney Scrapbooks, Municipal Archives, City of New York.

Fielding, Henry. *The Life of Mr. Jonathan Wild, the Great.* New York: New American Library/Signet Classic, 1961; originally published 1743.

"Fiskiana: 'Menelaus' Fisk, 'Belle Helene' Mansfield, 'Achilles' Stokes and 'Ulysses' Pittman in an Infernal Quadrille. How Fisk and Stokes Quarreled, Fought and Did Not Bleed About a Lady Fair with Jet Black Hair." *New York Herald*, Jan. 18, 1871, 5.

"$500 Reward and No Questions Asked." *New York Herald,* June 30, 1869, 7.

Foner, Eric. "The Education of Abraham Lincoln." *New York Times Book Review,* Feb. 10, 2002, 11.

Ford, James L. *Forty-odd Years in the Literary Shop.* New York: E. P. Dutton & Company, 1921.

"Foreign News: The Mandelbaums Arrested at Hamilton, Ont." *Detroit Free Press,* Dec. 9, 1884, 2.

Fried, Albert. *The Rise and Fall of the Jewish Gangster in America.* New York: Columbia University Press, 1993; originally published 1980.

Gage, Nicholas. *The Mafia Is Not an Equal Opportunity Employer.* New York: McGraw-Hill, 1971.

"A Gay Bird Captured: Mother Mandelbaum in Canada. She Waves the Star Spangled Banner and Telegraphs for Her Lawyer." *Lancaster (Pa.) Examiner,* Dec. 17, 1884, 1.

"General Telegraph News: Barron's Book-Keeping. A Statement by the Trustees of Dexter Savings Bank—The Charges of False Entries Again Made." *New-York Times,* March 15, 1879, 2.

"Geo. Howard, Burglar: An Extraordinary Career—College Graduate, Linguist and Scholar—Partner in Robberies to the Amount of $4,000,000—Shot Dead and His Body Left in the Woods." *Kansas Reporter,* April 10, 1879, 6, via New York *Sun.*

"George Washington's Birthday." National Archives, Center for Legislative Archives, archives. gov/legislative/features/Washington.

Gerety, Rowan Moore. "Street Vendors." In Jackson (2010), 1254.

Gilfoyle, Timothy J. "Comstock, Anthony." In Jackson (2010), 298.

———. *A Pickpocket's Tale: The Underworld of Nineteenth-Century New York.* New York: W. W. Norton, 2006.

Gillen, J. L., "Book Review: Cell 202, Sing Sing," *Journal of Criminal Law and Criminology* 26:5 (January–February 1936), 798–99.

Glanz, Rudolf. *The Jewish Woman in America: Two Female Immigrant Generations, 1820–1929.* Volume 2: *The German Jewish Woman.* Brooklyn: Ktav Publishing House/National Council of Jewish Women, 1976.

Glass, Andrew. "This Day in Politics: Congress Passes Legal Tender Act, Feb. 25, 1862." *Politico,* Feb. 25, 2019. politico.com/story/2019/02/25/this-day-in-politics-february-25 -1180225.

"Got Mother Mandelbaum." New-York *Sun,* July 23, 1884, 1.

Grannan's Pocket Gallery of Noted Criminals of the Present Day: Containing Portraits of Noted and Dangerous Criminals, Pickpockets, Burglars, Bank Sneaks, Safe Blowers, Confidence Men and All-Around Thieves. Cincinnati: Grannan Detective Bureau, third edition, 1890; fourth edition, 1892.

Gray, Christopher. "Streetscapes: The A. T. Stewart Department Store; A City Plan to Revitalize the 1846 'Marble Palace.'" *New York Times,* March 20, 1994; Section 7:10.

"The Great American Fence: Mother Mandelbaum, the Notorious, Arrested Across the Border." *Lebanon (Pa.) Daily News,* Dec. 9, 1884, 1.

"A Great Bank Robbery: The Manhattan Savings Institution Robbed. The Janitor Handcuffed and Compelled to Give Up the Safe Keys and Tell the Combination." *New-York Times,* Oct. 28, 1878, 1.

"The Great Post Office Robbery at Chicago." *Daily Union* (Washington, D.C.), July 8, 1855, 3, via *Chicago Daily Press.*

Green, Nancy L. *Ready-to-Wear and Ready-to-Work: A Century of Industry and Immigrants in Paris and New York.* Durham, N.C.: Duke University Press, 1997.

Grimes, William. *Appetite City: A Culinary History of New York.* New York: North Point Press, 2009.

Hagen, Carrie. *We Is Got Him: The Kidnapping That Changed America.* New York: Overlook Press, 2011.

Halttunen, Karen. "From Parlor to Living Room: Domestic Space, Interior Decoration, and the Culture of Personality." In Bronner (1989b), 157–89.

Hamilton Police Historical Society & Museum. "Annual Report, 2018/2019." hpa.on.ca/wp-content/uploads/2020/11/HistoricalSociety-AnnualReport-2018-19-Nov.20-2020.pdf

Hammack, David C. "Consolidation." In Jackson (2010), 305–306.

Hammer, Carl. *Expedient B&E: Tactics and Techniques for Bypassing Alarms and Defeating Locks.* Boulder, Colo.: Paladin Press, 1992.

Hammer, Richard. *The Illustrated History of Organized Crime.* Philadelphia: Courage Books, 1989; originally published 1975.

Hapgood, Hutchins, ed. *The Autobiography of a Thief.* New York: Fox, Duffield & Company, 1903.

Henry, Stuart. "On the Fence." *British Journal of Law and Society* 4:1 (Summer 1977), 124–33.

Herman, Michele. "Five Points." In Jackson (2010), 456.

Hershkowitz, Leo. *Tweed's New York: Another Look.* Garden City, N.Y.: Anchor Press/Doubleday, 1978.

"Her Son Julius Bailed: Mrs. Mandelbaum Refused as Surety by The Justice." *New-York Times,* July 26, 1884, 5.

"He Wanted to Be a Knuck: Patrolman's Son Attempts to Apprentice Himself to a Pickpocket." *Cincinnati Enquirer,* Feb. 25, 1884, 2; originally published in the *New York Star.*

Heywood, Herbert. "Richard Olney's Boyhood: The Early Life of the Secretary of State at His Home in Oxford, Mass." *Los Angeles Times,* July 14, 1895, 21.

Hill, Harry. "'Old Mother Mandelbaum': A Character Dickens Would Have Been Delighted to Portray—History of a Remarkable Woman." *Boston Globe* via *New York Mercury,* Nov. 11, 1883, 16.

Hill, Mrs. Margaret. "Revelations by the Queen of the Underworld." Chapter XIV. *Pittsburgh Press,* July 2, 1922, 96–97.

Hirtl, Leo. "City Needs Press Agent; Publicity's Not So Good." *Cincinnati Post,* July 24, 1947, 1.

"A History of American Currency." American Numismatic Society. numismatics.org/a-history-of-american-currency/.

"The History of [the] New York City Police Department." National Criminal Justice Reference Service document no. 145539, 1993. ojp.gov/ncjrs/virtual-library/abstracts/history-new-york-city-police-department.

"The History of U.S. Currency." U.S. Currency Education Program. uscurrency.gov/history.

"Holding Mrs. Mandelbaum: Silk Buyers Swearing to the Stolen Goods Bought of Her." *New-York Sun,* July 29, 1884, 3.

Holub, Rona. "Fredericka Mandelbaum." *Immigrant Entrepreneurship.* Online article, 2013. immigrantentrepreneurship.org/entries/fredericka-mandelbaum/.

Holub, Rona L. "Fredericka 'Marm' Mandelbaum, 'Queen of Fences': The Rise and Fall of a Female Immigrant Criminal Entrepreneur in Nineteenth-Century New York City." Doctoral dissertation, Columbia University, 2007.

———. "The Rise of Fredericka 'Marm' Mandelbaum: Criminal Enterprise and the 'American Dream' in New York City, 1850–1884." Master's thesis, Sarah Lawrence College, 1998.

Homans, I[saac] Smith, Jr. *The Merchants and Bankers' Almanac.* New York: Banker's Magazine and Statistical Register, 1868.

Homer, Frederic D. *Guns and Garlic: Myths and Realities of Organized Crime.* West Lafayette, Ind.: Purdue University Studies, 1974.

Horan, James D., and Howard Swiggett. *The Pinkerton Story.* New York: G. P. Putnam's Sons, 1951.

Howe, William F., and Abraham H. Hummel. *Danger! A True History of a Great City's Wiles and Temptations: The Veil Lifted, and Light Thrown on Crime and Its Causes, and Criminals and Their Haunts.* Gloucester, U.K.: Dodo Press, 2009; originally published 1886.

Howson, Gerald. *Thief-Taker General: The Rise and Fall of Jonathan Wild.* London: Hutchinson, 1970.

"Huge Crowds Attend Sophie Lyons Funeral." *Detroit Free Press,* May 10, 1924, 13.

"An Impudent Demand." *New-York Times,* Feb. 17, 1880, 8.

"In and About the City: Is Detective Frank on Trial? Mother Mandelbaum's Counsel Trying to Prove Him a Forger." *New-York Times,* Sept. 16, 1884, 8.

Inciardi, James A. *Careers in Crime.* Chicago: Rand McNally College Publishing Company, 1975.

"In Denial: What Draper, Porter and Irving Have to Say. They Deny the Accusation That They Had Any Complicity in George Howard's Death—The Shute Mystery Cleared Up. Who It Was That Robbed Morton's Safe. A History of George Howard's Wife. Who She Is and What She Was." *Brooklyn Daily Eagle,* March 12, 1879, 4.

"In the Toils: Arrest of a Notorious Receiver of Stolen Property." *Detroit Free Press,* July 24, 1884, 2.

"Is She Dead? Mother Mandelbaum, the Notorious Fence, Said to Be Alive." *Brooklyn Standard Union,* Aug. 27, 1894, 3.

Jackson, Kenneth T., ed. *The Encyclopedia of New York City.* Second edition. New Haven and New York: Yale University Press/New-York Historical Society, 2010.

Jackson, N. Hart. *The Two Orphans: A Romantic Play (and Dramatic Composition) in Four Acts and Seven Tableaux.* Adapted from the French of Ad. D'Ennery and Eugene Cormon, expressly for dramatic representation at the Union Square Theatre of New York City, 1875. Hathi Trust Digital Library. babel.hathitrust.org/cgi/pt?id=hvd.32044024345399.

Jaffe, Steven H., and Jessica Lautin. *Capital of Capital: Money, Banking + Power in New York City, 1784–2012.* New York: Museum of the City of New York/Columbia University Press, 2014.

"James L. Madara, MD, on AMA's Continuing Commitment to Doctors 175 Years Later." American Medical Association podcast, May 10, 2022. ama-assn.org/about/leadership/james-l-madara-md-amas-continuing-commitment-doctors-175-years-later.

"James Scott against Frederika [*sic*] Mendlebaum [*sic*]." "Supreme Court: Trial Desired in New York County." New York: C. G. Burgoyne, Law Printer, n.d.

"John K. Hackett's Death: The Peaceful Ending of a Busy Life. A Sketch of the Recorder's Career and an Estimate of His Character—The Aldermen to Appoint His Successor." *New-York Times,* Dec. 27, 1879, 1–2.

"'Johnny' Hope Released: The Bank Burglar's Son Receives His Liberty From Gov. Hill." *New-York Times,* Oct. 23, 1890, 8.

Johnson, David R. *Policing the Urban Underworld: The Impact of Crime on the Development of the American Police, 1800–1887.* Philadelphia: Temple University Press, 1979.

Joselit, Jenna Weissman. *Our Gang: Jewish Crime and the New York Jewish Community, 1900–1940.* Bloomington: Indiana University Press, 1983.

"Jourdan Dead: Decease of the Police Superintendent Yesterday Morning." *New-York Times,* Oct. 11, 1870, 8.

"Journal of the Assembly of the State of New York: At Their One Hundred and Ninth Session. Begun and Held at the Capitol, in the City of Albany, on the Fifth Day of January, 1886." Volume 2. Albany: Weed, Parsons & Company, Legislative Printers, 1886.

"Julius Mandelbaum Surrenders." *New-York Times,* June 23, 1888, 9.

"Justice at Last: W. M. Tweed Convicted. Guilty on Two Hundred and Four Counts of the Indictment—Sentence Postponed—Scenes in the Court of Oyer and Terminer—Now the People Received the Verdict." *New-York Times,* Nov. 20, 1873, 1.

Kanigel, Robert. *The One Best Way: Frederick Winslow Taylor and the Enigma of Efficiency.* New York: Viking, 1997.

"Das Kapital." *Encyclopaedia Britannica.* britannica.com/topic/Das-Kapital.

"Kashmir Shawls." *Victoriana Magazine.* victoriana.com/Shawls/kashmir-shawl.html.

Kaufman, Andrew L. *Cardozo*. Cambridge, Mass.: Harvard University Press, 1998.

"Kelly's Candidates." *New-York Times*, Oct. 12, 1875, 1.

Kessler-Harris, Alice. *Out to Work: A History of Wage-Earning Women in the United States*. Oxford: Oxford University Press, 2003; originally published 1982.

Kirchner, L[arry] R. *Robbing Banks: An American History, 1831–1999*. Edison, N.J.: Castle Books, 2003; originally published 2001.

Kirshenblatt-Gimblett, Barbara. "Street Life." In Jackson (2010), 1251–52.

Klockars, Carl B. *The Professional Fence*. New York: Free Press/Macmillan, 1974.

Koeppel, Gerard. "Croton Aqueduct." In Jackson (2010), 332–33.

"Labor in New-York: Its Circumstances, Conditions and Rewards. No. XI: General Condition of the Shoe-Makers—the Ladies' Branch." *New-York Daily Tribune*, Sept. 9, 1845, 1.

Lardner, James, and Thomas Reppetto. *NYPD: A City and Its Police*. New York: A John Macrae Book/Henry Holt, 2000.

"Lawes Is Retiring as Sing Sing Head: Foe of Capital Penalty Put 303 to Death—Found Some Prisoners 'Very Fine Men.'" *New York Times*, July 7, 1941, 1.

Leach, William. "Strategists of Display and the Production of Desire." In Bronner (1989b), 99–132.

Leverton, Garrett H., ed. *The Great Diamond Robbery and Other Recent Melodramas by Edward M. Alfriend & A. C. Wheeler, Clarence Bennett [and Others]*. Princeton, N.J.: Princeton University Press, 1940.

"Life in New York City: Personal, Political and Dramatic Gossip From Across the River." *Brooklyn Daily Eagle*, July 27, 1884, 3.

"Light on the Barron Tragedy: Detectives Think That the Dead Cashier Committed Suicide—Further Investigation to Be Made—History of the Case." *New-York Times*, Jan. 31, 1879, 1.

"Lillie Safe Co." *Friends of Albany History*, April 5, 2019. friendsofalbanyhistory.wordpress .com/tag/lillie-safe-co.

"A Line on Books." *Buffalo Evening News*, Jan. 12, 1935, 3.

Luskey, Brian P., and Wendy A. Woloson, eds. *Capitalism by Gaslight: Illuminating the Economy of Nineteenth-Century America* (Philadelphia: University of Pennsylvania Press, 2015).

Lyon, Patrick. *The Narrative of Patrick Lyon: Who Suffered Three Months Severe Imprisonment in Philadelphia Gaol, on Merely a Vague Suspicion of Being Concerned in the Robbery of the Bank of Pennsylvania, With His Remarks Thereon*. Philadelphia: Francis and Robert Bailey, 1799.

Lyons, Sophie. *Why Crime Does Not Pay*. Fairford, U.K.: Echo Library, 2019; originally published 1913.

Macintyre, Ben. *The Napoleon of Crime: The Life and Times of Adam Worth, the Real Moriarty*. London: HarperPress, 2012; originally published 1997.

MacQueen, Hector L., ed. *Money Laundering*. Hume Papers on Public Policy. Volume 1, No. 2. Edinburgh: Edinburgh University Press, 1993.

Mahdavi, Pardis. "New York's Hyphenated History." *Paris Review*, May 27, 2021. www.the parisreview.org/blog/2021/05/27/new-yorks-hyphenated-history.

Mahon, Elizabeth Kerri. *Pretty Evil New York: True Stories of Mobster Molls, Violent Vixens, and Murderous Matriarchs*. Guilford, Conn.: Globe Pequot, 2021.

Manaugh, Geoff. *A Burglar's Guide to the City*. New York: Farrar, Straus & Giroux, 2016.

"The Mandelbaum Cases: Transferred to the Court of Oyer and Terminer for Trial." *New-York Times*, Nov. 20, 1884, 3.

"The Mandelbaum Charges: Not Accepted as Bail for Her Son. The Police Indignant at the District-Attorney for Putting Pinkerton's Men on the Case." *New-York Tribune*, July 26, 1884, 10.

"Mandelbaum Discharged: The Notorious Madame Receives the Benefit of Canadian Clemency." *Boston Globe*, Dec. 13, 1884, 1.

"Mandelbaum Goes Free." *Journal-Times* (Racine, Wis.), Dec. 12, 1884, 2.

"The Mandelbaum Mizzle: Skips for Canada, Leaving $21,000 in Bail to Shift for Itself." *Detroit Free Press*, Dec. 5, 1884, 1.

"The Mandelbaums Arrested in Canada." *Daily New Era* (Lancaster, Pa.), Dec. 9, 1884, 1.

"Mandelbaum's Den: Canadians Buying New York Goods Remarkably Cheap." *Bridgewater (N.J.) Courier-News*, Aug. 14, 1886, 3.

"The Mandelbaums in Town: They Had Some Lively Doings in Canada a Few Days Ago." *New York Evening World*, July 6, 1894, 2.

"Manhattan Savings Institution." history.hsbc.com/collections/global-archives/manhattan-savings-institution.

"Mary Hoey Pardoned: Her Reward for Betraying Mother Mandelbaum to Justice." *New-York Times*, Jan. 6, 1885, 3.

Matsell, George W. *Vocabulum: Or, the Rogue's Lexicon, Compiled from the Most Authentic Sources*. New York: George W. Matsell & Company, 1859.

Maurer, David W. *Whiz Mob: A Correlation of the Technical Argot of Pickpockets with Their Behavior Pattern*. New Haven, Conn.: College & University Press, 1964.

Mayhew, Henry. *London Labour and the London Poor*. Volume 4: *Those That Will Not Work, Comprising Prostitutes, Thieves, Swindlers, Beggars*. London: Griffin, Bohn & Company, 1862.

McCabe, James D., Jr. *Lights and Shadows of New York Life: Or, the Sights and Sensations of the Great City. A Work Descriptive of the City of New York in All Its Various Phases; with Full and Graphic Accounts of Its Splendors and Wretchedness; Its High and Low Life; Its Marble Palaces and Dark Dens; Its Attractions and Dangers; Its Rings and Frauds; Its Leading Men and Politicians; Its Adventurers; Its Charities; Its Mysteries, and Its Crimes*. Philadelphia et al.: National Publishing Company, 1872.

"Meeting of the Society for the Prevention of Crime." *New-York Times*, April 17, 1877, 5.

Morris, Charles R. *The Tycoons: How Andrew Carnegie, John D. Rockefeller, Jay Gould, and J. P. Morgan Invented the American Supereconomy*. New York: Owl Books/Henry Holt, 2006; originally published 2005.

"Most Extensive Robbery." *National Gazette and Literary Register* (Philadelphia), March 22, 1831, 2.

"Mother Baum: The Party Charged With Vagrancy and Bringing Stolen Goods Into Canada." *Boston Globe*, Dec. 10, 1884, 4.

"Mother Baum Runs Away: Off to Canada With Son Julius and Salesman Herman." *New York Sun*, Dec. 5, 1884, 1.

"Mother Baum's Customer: Detective Frank Begins the Story of His Silk Buying." *New York Sun*, July 26, 1884, 3.

"Mother Mandelbaum." *Belfast News-Letter*, Aug. 13, 1884, 6.

"Mother Mandelbaum." *Chicago Tribune*, Dec. 10, 1884, 3.

"Mother Mandelbaum." *New-York Times*, Dec. 5, 1884, 4.

"Mother Mandelbaum." *San Francisco Call*, March 7, 1894, 6.

"Mother Mandelbaum: A Belief That Her Diamonds Are Stolen Property." *New-York Times*, Dec. 10, 1884, 1.

"Mother Mandelbaum Again." *Middletown (N.Y.) Times-Press*, Jan. 19, 1892, 5.

"Mother Mandelbaum Away," *New York Herald*, Dec. 16, 1884, n.p., from District Attorney Scrapbooks, Municipal Archives, City of New York.

"Mother Mandelbaum at Bay: Detective Frank Tells How He Tricked the Famous Patron of Thieves. Her Diamond Studded Lawyer," *New York Herald*, July 26, 1884, n.p., from District Attorney Scrapbooks, Municipal Archives, City of New York.

"Mother Mandelbaum Busy: The Noted 'Fence' Plays a Neat Trick on a Customs Officer." *Rochester (N.Y.) Democrat and Chronicle*, Oct. 20, 1886, 8, via *New York Herald*.

"The Mother Mandelbaum Case." *St. Louis Globe-Democrat*, Dec. 17, 1884, 6.

"Mother Mandelbaum Dead." Erroneous obituary. *New York Evening World*, March 23, 1893, 1.

"'Mother' Mandelbaum Disappears." *Harrisburg (Pa.) Telegraph*, Dec. 5, 1884, 1.

"Mother Mandelbaum: Her Son Endeavors to Become a Detective at Hamilton." *Cincinnati Enquirer*, May 19, 1889, 9.

"Mother Mandelbaum in New York." *Sacramento Weekly Bee*, Nov. 13, 1885, 8, via *New-York Times*.

"'Mother' Mandelbaum Not Dead." *New-York Tribune*, March 24, 1893, 1.

"Mother Mandelbaum: The Notorious Fence, Arrested Here." *Hamilton Spectator*, Dec. 9, 1884, n.p.

"Mother Mandelbaum: The Notorious Fence Jumps Her Bail and Flies to Canada." *Chicago Tribune*, Dec. 5, 1884, 3.

"Mother Mandelbaum: The Notorious New York Fence Caged in a Canadian Jail." *St. Louis Post-Dispatch*, Dec. 9, 1884, 1.

"'Mother' Mandelbaum: The Notorious New York Fence Keeping a Store in Hamilton, Ontario." *St. Louis Post-Dispatch*, Oct. 12, 1887, 4.

"Mother Mandelbaum Out." *New York Sun*, July 24, 1884, 1.

"Mother Mandelbaum: Trouble That She and Some of Her Gang Are Having." *New-York Times*, Dec. 11, 1884, 1.

"Mother Mandelbaum: Very Much Alive and Living in Splendor at Hamilton," *Cincinnati Enquirer*, March 25, 1893, 1.

"Mother Mandelbaum's Booty." *Buffalo Courier*, March 15, 1894, 10.

"Mother Mandelbaum's Burial." *New York Sun*, March 2, 1894, 9.

"Mother Mandelbaum's Case." *New-York Times*, Sept. 9, 1884, 8.

"Mother Mandelbaum's Den: Canadians Buying New York Goods Remarkably Cheap." *National Police Gazette*, Sept. 4, 1886, 7.

"'Mother' Mandelbaum's Departure: What Mr. Pinkerton Says About It—Not Ordered to Watch Her Till She Was Gone." *New-York Tribune*, Dec. 6, 1884, 7.

"Mother Mandelbaum's Silk: An Order Issued That It Be Sold by the Property Clerk." *New York Evening World*, March 20, 1894, 2.

"Mother Mandelbaum's Son: Julius Has Tired of Canada and Is in a Fair Way for Sing Sing." *New York Evening World*, June 23, 1888, 1.

"'Mother' Mandelbaum's Son Returns: He Had Studied Medicine in Berlin and Wants to Practice It Here." *New-York Tribune*, June 23, 1888, 4.

"Mother Mandelbaum's Struggles." *New-York Times*, Sept. 20, 1884, 8.

"Mother Mandlebaum [*sic*] Trapped." *New-York Times*, July 23, 1884, 5.

"Mr. Abraham Hummel." *Daily Telegraph*, London, Jan. 25, 1926, 11.

"Mrs. Leslie Carter." Internet Broadway Database. ibdb.com/broadway-cast-staff/mrs-leslie-carter-23300.

"Mrs. Leslie Carter Dies in California: Actress Starred for Thirty Years Here and Abroad in Wide Variety of Plays. Got Start With Belasco." *New York Times* via Associated Press, Nov. 14, 1937, 11.

"Mrs. Mandelbaum Fights Hard: Despite Her Diamond Studded Lawyer She and Her Accomplices Are Held for Trial." *New York Herald*, July 29, 1884, n.p., from District Attorney Scrapbooks, Municipal Archives of the City of New York.

"Mrs. Mandelbaum and Gustave Frank." *New-York Tribune*, Sept. 16, 1884, 5.

"Mrs. Mandelbaum in Jail: The Fugitives Arrested in Canada." *New-York Tribune*, Dec. 9, 1884, 1.

"Mrs. Mandelbaum Missing: The Notorious Receiver Flies From the City." *New-York Times*, Dec. 5, 1884, 1.

"Mrs. Mandelbaum Nabbed: The Old Lady Indignant That the Law Should Lay Its Hands on Her." *Savannah Morning News*, Dec. 9, 1884, 1.

"Mrs. Mandelbaum's Flight." *Brooklyn Daily Eagle*, Dec. 5 1884, 4.

"Mrs. Mandelbaum's Query: She Desires to Know Who Drew Her Picture for 'The World.'" *New York World*, Dec. 9, 1884, n.p., from District Attorney Scrapbooks, Municipal Archives of New York.

"Mrs. Mandelbaum's Riches." *New-York Sun*, July 25, 1884, 1.

"Mrs. Mandelbaum's Statement." *New-York Tribune*, July 31, 1884, 8.

"Mrs. Mandelbaum's Visit: Her Favorite Daughter's Death Brings Her Here. Visiting the Body at Night With Her Son Julius. Tired of Canada, But on Her Way Back There." *New-York Times*, Nov. 12, 1885, 2.

"Mrs. Mandlebaum's [*sic*] Bonanza: How She Has Coined Money by Harboring and Assisting Thieves." *Boston Globe*, Jan. 25, 1884, 2.

"Murdered: A Bank-Officer Suffers Death Rather Than Be False to His Trust." *Buffalo Commercial*, Feb. 25, 1878, 2, via New-York *Sun*.

Murphy, Cait. *Scoundrels in Law: The Trials of Howe & Hummel, Lawyers to the Gangsters, Cops, Starlets, and Rakes Who Made the Gilded Age*. New York: Smithsonian Books/HarperCollins, 2010.

Nadel, Stanley. *Little Germany: Ethnicity, Religion, and Class in New York City, 1845–80*. Urbana: University of Illinois Press, 1990.

"Necrological." *American Register* (London, U.K.), March 17, 1894, 6.

"The New District Attorney." *New-York Times*, Dec. 12, 1883, 3.

"A New District-Attorney: Mr. Peckham's Sudden Resignation. Ill-Health Stated as the Cause—Peter B. Olney Appointed." *New-York Daily Tribune*, Dec. 11, 1883, 5.

"New York City." *New York Herald*, March 24, 1872, 10.

"New York Notes: Fresh Developments in the Police Scandals." *Detroit Free Press*, Aug. 5, 1884, 2.

"New York Nubbins." *St. Joseph (Mo.) Gazette*, July 29, 1884, 1.

"New York Society for the Suppression of Vice Records." Library of Congress. loc.gov/item /mm78034587.

Nightingale, Adam. *Masters of Crime: Fiction's Finest Villains and Their Real-Life Inspirations*. Stroud, U.K.: History Press, 2011.

Nilsson, Jeff. "America's (Not Quite) First Bank Robbery." *Saturday Evening Post*, March 16, 2013. saturdayeveningpost.com/2013/03/first-bank-robbery-in-united-states.

"19th Amendment to the U.S. Constitution: Women's Right to Vote (1920)." National Archives. archives.gov/milestone-documents/19th-amendment.

"No Commission in the Mandelbaum Case." *Brooklyn Union*, Sept. 16, 1884, 1.

"No Redeeming Feature Left: Death of Mrs. Mandelbaum's Well-Behaved Daughter." *Detroit Free Press*, Nov. 12, 1885, 1.

"The Northampton Bank Robbery—List of the Stolen Deposits—Conduct of the Thieves." *Boston Globe*, Jan. 28, 1876, 2.

"The Northampton National Bank Heist, the Biggest in U.S. History." New England Historical Society. newenglandhistoricalsociety.com/northampton-national-bank-heist.

"The Northampton Robbers: Only Three out of the Seven in Confinement—Some Facts About Shang Draper." *New York Sun*, July 16, 1878, 4, via *Boston Herald*.

"Notorious 'Crooks' Dead: Stealers of Fortunes. End of 'Sheeny Mike' and the 'Prince of Cross Roaders.'" *New-York Daily Tribune*, May 26, 1905, 11.

"Nugent Dismissed From the Force." *New-York Times*, Jan. 25, 1880, 10.

"Obituary: George Washington Matsell." *Philadelphia Inquirer*, July 26, 1877, 4.

"Ocean Bank Robbery: Recovery of $268,021 of the Stolen Securities." *New-York Times*, July 1, 1869, 8.

"The Ocean Bank Robbery: Three Hundred Thousand Dollars Graciously Returned—A Trunk Full of Securities Not Negotiable Sent to the Police." *Cincinnati Daily Enquirer* via *New York World*, July 3, 1869, 3.

"The Ocean Bank Robbery—The Total Loss Over Half a Million of Dollars." Unattributed wire-service article published, e.g., in Baltimore *Sun*, July 1, 1869, 1.

O'Hara, S. Paul. *Inventing the Pinkertons. Or, Spies, Sleuths, Mercenaries, and Thugs: Being a Story of the Nation's Most Famous (and Infamous) Detective Agency.* Baltimore: Johns Hopkins University Press, 2016.

O'Kane, James M. *The Crooked Ladder: Gangsters, Ethnicity, and the American Dream.* New Brunswick, N.J.: Transaction Publishers, 1992.

"Old Mother Mandelbaum: Charges Against Byrnes' Detectives Are to Be Investigated." *New York Star*, July 27, 1884, n.p., from District Attorney Scrapbooks, Municipal Archives, City of New York.

"Old 'Mother' Mandelbaum Is Dead: She Was a Famous 'Fence' Well Known to the Police of This City." *New-York Times*, Feb. 27, 1894, 9.

"Oliver Cromwell." National Registry of Exonerations. law.umich.edu/special/exoneration /pages/casedetailpre1989.aspx?caseid=71.

Oller, John. *Rogues' Gallery: The Birth of Modern Policing and Organized Crime in Gilded Age New York.* New York: Dutton, 2021.

"Olney Dies: Veteran Statesman," *New York Times*, April 10, 1917, 13.

O'Malley, Brendan P. "Lickspittles and Land Sharks: The Immigrant Exploitation Business in Antebellum New York." In Luskey & Wolloson (2015a), 93–108.

"On a Murderer's Track." *New-York Times*, June 8, 1878, 5.

"One Woman's Career: How Mother Mandelbaum Gained Her Notoriety as a Fence." *New York Evening World*, March 10, 1894, 6.

Opdycke, Sandra. "Sewers." In Jackson (2010), 1173–74.

Paoli, Letizia, ed. *The Oxford Handbook of Organized Crime.* Oxford: Oxford University Press, 2014 [hereafter Paoli (2014a)].

———. Introduction to Paoli (2014a), 1–10 [hereafter Paoli (2014b)].

Paoli, Letizia, and Tom Vander Beken. "Organized Crime: A Contested Concept." In Paoli (2014a), 13–31.

Papke, David Ray. *Framing the Criminal: Crime, Cultural Work and the Loss of Critical Perspective, 1830–1900.* Hamden, Conn.: Archon Books, 1987.

Pelham, Camden, ed. *The Chronicles of Crime: Or, the New Newgate Calendar. Being a Series of Memoirs and Anecdotes of Notorious Characters Who Have Outraged the Laws of Great Britain from the Earliest Period to 1841.* London: T. Miles & Company, 1887.

"Perturbed Police." *Detroit Free Press*, July 26, 1884, 2.

"Peter B. Olney, Lawyer, Dead of Pneumonia." *Brooklyn Times Union*, Feb. 9, 1922, 10.

"Peter Butler Olney, Noted Lawyer, Dead." *New York Evening World*, Feb. 9, 1922, 2.

"Philharmonic Society." *Evening Post* (New York), Dec. 5, 1842, 2.

Pike, Luke Owen. *A History of Crime in England: Illustrating the Changes of the Laws in the Progress of Civilisation.* Volume 1: *From the Roman Invasion to the Accession of Henry VII.* London: Smith, Elder & Company, 1873.

"Pinkerton & Co., North-Western Police Agency." Advertisement. *Chicago Tribune*, May 5, 1856, 1.

"Plain Talk About Byrnes: Dr. Parkhurst Discusses the Superintendent." *New-York Daily Tribune*, Sept. 21, 1894, 5.

Pleasants, Samuel Augustus. *Fernando Wood of New York.* New York: Columbia University Press, 1948.

"Points About the Cabinet." *Twin-City Daily Sentinel* (Winston-Salem, N.C.), Feb. 24, 1893, 1.

"The Police: Report of the Board of Metropolitan Police for 1864." Reprinted in the *New-York Times*, Jan. 5, 1865, 8.

"Policing in London: How Suspects Were Apprehended." Proceedings of the Old Bailey. oldbaileyonline.org/static/Policing.jsp.

Pollak, Michael. "F.Y.I.: Two-Track Soap Opera." *New York Times*, Aug. 20, 2006, 14:2.

"A Queen Among Thieves." *New-York Times,* July 24, 1884, 5.

"Queen of Crooks: Mother Mandelbaum's Existence Ended by a Stroke of Paralysis." Erroneous obituary. *Fall River (Mass.) Daily Evening News,* March 23, 1893, 1.

"Queen of the 'Crooks': Mother Mandelbaum, the Famous 'Fence,' Is Dead, After Ten Years
of Exile in Canada. Twenty Years in 'Queer' Street. Burglars, Highwaymen, Shoplifters,
Sneak-Thieves, All Brought Their Plunder to Her." *New-York World,* Feb. 27, 1894, 14.

"Queen of Fences: Mother Mandelbaum Is Dead in Hamilton. She Made a Million Out of
Stolen Goods Received. She Employed Thieves and Often Betrayed Them. Blackmailed
and Abetted by New York Police. Forced to Flee After 30 Years of Unchecked Trade."
Boston Globe, Feb. 26, 1894, 8.

"Queen of 'Fences': The Trial of a Woman Whose Name Is a Proverb in New York. Inquiries
as to the Placing of Certain Silks and Shawls by Sheeny Mike After a Robbery in Boston—
Matters Odd to Think Of." *Buffalo Evening News,* Jan. 26, 1884, 7.

"Queer Mrs. Mandelbaum." *New-York Sun,* Jan. 24, 1884, 4.

"Raided a Big Fence: Mother Mandelbaum, a Well-Known Smuggler, on the Carpet." *Pittsburgh Dispatch,* Jan. 20, 1892, 11.

"Real and Bogus Detectives." *Philadelphia Times,* July 30, 1884, 2.

"Receiving Stolen Goods: A Verdict Against Mrs. Mandelbaum for $6,666." *New-York Tri-
bune,* Jan. 24, 1884, 3.

"Recent Incorporations." *American Druggist and Pharmaceutical Record: A Semi-monthly Illustrated Journal of Practical Pharmacy,* April 13, 1908, 212.

"Record of Infamy: Career of Some of New York's Worst Criminals." *St. Johnsbury (Vt.) Index*
via *New York Herald,* Nov. 1, 1883, 2.

*Report of the Special Committee of the Board of Aldermen Appointed to Investigate the "Ring"
Frauds: Together With the Testimony Elicited During the Investigation.* New York: Martin
B. Brown, Printer and Stationer, 1878.

"Richard Olney Dies: Veteran Statesman." *New York Times,* April 10, 1917, 13.

Richardson, James F. *The New York Police: Colonial Times to 1901.* New York: Oxford University Press, 1970.

————. "Wards." In Jackson (2010), 1376–77.

Riis, Jacob A. *The Making of an American: New Edition With Numerous Illustrations and an
Introduction by Theodore Roosevelt.* New York: Macmillan Company, 1919; originally published 1901.

"The Ring and the City Armories." *New-York Times,* July 8, 1871, 4.

Riordon, William L. *Plunkitt of Tammany Hall: A Series of Very Plain Talks on Very Practical
Politics, Delivered by Ex-Senator George Washington Plunkitt, the Tammany Philosopher,
from His Rostrum—the New York County Court House Bootblack Stand.* New York:
E. P. Dutton, 1963; originally published 1905.

"A Robbed Merchant's Suit: Verdict Against a Receiver of Stolen Goods. Growing Out of a
Robbery in Boston in Which 'Sheeny Mike' Was the Actor—Where the Goods Went."
New-York Times, Jan. 24, 1884, 8.

Robinson, Solon. *Hot Corn: Life Scenes in New York Illustrated, Including the Story of Little
Katy, Madalina, the Rag-Picker's Daughter, Wild Maggie, &c.* New York: De Witt & Davenport, 1854.

Roth, Andrew, and Jonathan Roth. *Devil's Advocates: The Unnatural History of Lawyers.*
Berkeley, Calif.: Nolo Press, 1989.

Rovere, Richard H. *Howe & Hummel: Their True and Scandalous History.* London: Arlington
Books, 1986; originally published 1947.

Safire, William. "On Language: Hyphenating Americans." *New York Times Magazine,*
Dec. 23, 1979, 2.

Salvo, Joseph J., and Arun Peter Lobo. "Population." In Jackson (2010), 1018–20.

Samuel, Lawrence R. *The American Dream: A Cultural History.* Syracuse: Syracuse University Press, 2012.

Sanger, William W., M.D. *The History of Prostitution: Its Extent, Causes, and Effects Throughout the World.* New York: Harper & Brothers, 1858.

"Second Protocol Amending Extradition Treaty With Canada: Senate Consideration of Treaty Document 107-11." congress.gov/treaty-document/107th-congress/11.

"The Secret Accounts: Proofs of Undoubted Frauds Brought to Light." *New-York Times,* July22, 1871, 1.

"'Shang' Draper's Fight for Liberty." *New-York Times,* Oct. 31, 1878, 2.

"Shang Draper: To Be Tried for the Northampton Bank Robbery." *Brooklyn Daily Eagle,* July 10, 1879, 4.

Share, Allen J. "Tweed, William M(agear) 'Boss.'" In Jackson (2010), 1431.

"She Dies in Canada: End of Mother Mandelbaum, the Once Notorious 'Fence.'" *New York Evening World,* Feb. 26, 1894, 1.

"'Sheeney Mike,' Burglar: Suit of James Scott of Boston to Recover for Silks Stolen by Him— 'Mike's' Checkered Career—A Thief and Bank Breaker of National Repute." *Boston Globe,* Jan. 17, 1884, 2.

"'Sheeny' Mike as a Witness: In Boston Man's Suit Against a 'Fence' to Recover Stolen Silks and Shawls." *Boston Globe,* Jan. 24, 1884, 5.

"'Sheeny' Mike's Career: The Latest Effort of Our Best Burglar—A Singular Criminal Record." *New-York Times,* April 29, 1876, 8.

Sifakis, Carl. *The Encyclopedia of American Crime.* New York: Smithmark, 1992; originally published 1982.

"The Situation: The Excitement Everywhere." New York *Herald,* Oct. 9, 1862, 4.

Sloat, Warren. "Society for the Prevention of Crime." In Jackson (2010), 1201.

Smith, Alexander. *A Compleat History of the Lives and Robberies of the Most Notorious Highway-Men, Foot-Pads, Shop-Lifts and Cheats of Both Sexes, in and around London and Westminster, and All Parts of Britain, for about a Hundred Years Past, Continu'd to the Present Time.* London: Sam. Briscoe, 1719.

Spann, Edward K. *Gotham at War: New York City, 1860–1865.* Wilmington, Del.: SR Books, 2002.

———. *The New Metropolis: New York City, 1840–1857.* New York: Columbia University Press, 1981.

Spaulding, E[lbridge] G[erry]. *A Resource of War: The Credit of the Government Made Immediately Available. History of the Legal Tender Paper Money Issued During the Great Rebellion. Being a Loan Without Interest and a National Currency.* Buffalo, N.Y.: Express Printing Company, 1869.

Spofford, Harriet Elizabeth Prescott. *Art Decoration Applied to Furniture.* New York: Harper & Brothers, 1877.

Stansell, Christine. *City of Women: Sex and Class in New York, 1789–1860.* Urbana: University of Illinois Press, 1987; originally published 1986.

Steffensmeier, Darrell J. *The Fence: In the Shadow of Two Worlds.* Lanham, Md.: Rowman & Littlefield, 1986.

"Stephen Longstreet (1907–2002)." Finding Aid, Stephen Longstreet Papers, Yale University Archives. archives.yale.edu/repositories/11/resources/1485.

"A Story of a Famous Bank Robbery Retold." *Banker's Magazine and Statistical Register* 44:1, July 1889, 64–65.

"A Story of Recorder Smyth." *New York Times,* Oct. 6, 1901, 6.

"Street Talk." *Cincinnati Enquirer,* Dec. 14, 1884, 12.

"Suit for the Recovery of Stolen Property." *Boston Evening Transcript,* Jan. 18, 1884, 3.

Swierczynski, Duane. *This Here's a Stick-Up: The Big Bad Book of American Bank Robbery.* Indianapolis: Alpha Books, 2002.

"Talk, But No Business: The Police Still Hunting the Bank Burglars Without Success." *New-York Times,* Nov. 1, 1878, 8.

"The Temperance Crusade: Mass Meeting at Indianapolis." *National Republican,* March 4, 1874, 1.

"A Terrible Accident: Mr. David Steele Probably Fatally Injured." *St. John's (Newfoundland) Evening Telegram,* Dec. 27, 1886, 7, via *Hamilton (Ont.) Evening Times.*

"The Thieves' Route to Canada." *San Francisco Chronicle,* Dec. 6, 1884, 3.

"Thomas F. Byrnes Dead After 2 Years' Illness: Famous Police Superintendent a Victim of Chronic Indigestion. He Was a Terror to Crooks. Broke Up Band of Burglars That Took $3,000,000 From Manhattan Savings Bank." *Brooklyn Daily Eagle,* May 8, 1910, 7.

"3,000 Yards of Unclaimed Stolen Silk." *New York Sun,* March 21, 1894, 4.

"Today in History—August 25: The Pinkertons." Library of Congress Digital Collections. loc.gov/item/today-in-history/august-25.

"Today in History—March 4: Inauguration Day." Library of Congress Digital Collections. loc.gov/item/today-in-history/march-04.

"To-Night's Meeting of the Bar Association." *New-York Times,* Jan. 4, 1872, 4.

Torrey, E. Fuller. *Frontier Justice: The Rise and Fall of the Loomis Gang.* Utica, N.Y.: North Country Books, 1992.

The Trow (Formerly Wilson's) Copartnership and Corporation Directory of the Boroughs of Manhattan and the Bronx, City of New York. New York: Trow Directory, Printing & Bookbinding Company, March 1909.

Twain, Mark, and Charles Dudley Warner. *The Gilded Age: A Tale of Today.* Hartford, Conn.: American Publishing Company, 1873.

"Tweed in Prison: Twelve Years in Prison and Fined $12,500." *New-York Times,* Nov. 23, 1873, 1.

"Twenty-first Annual Report of the Executive Committee of the Prison Association of New York. Part I: Transmitted to the Legislature January 22, 1866." Albany: C. Wendell, Legislative Printer, 1866.

"Two Murders: Two Terrible Chapters of Crime Among the Hills of New England. A Brave Cashier at Dexter, Maine, Who Died Rather Than Surrender. Murder in Western Massachusetts for the Sake of a Little Money." *Boston Post,* Feb. 25, 1878, 2.

Van Every, Edward. *Sins of New York: As "Exposed" by the Police Gazette.* New York: Frederick A. Stokes Company, 1930.

"Verdict in Favor of Mr. James Scott." *Boston Evening Transcript,* Jan. 24, 1884, 2.

Vos, Frank. "Tammany Hall." In Jackson (2010), 1277–78 [hereafter Vos (2010a)].

———. "Plunkitt, George Washington." In Jackson (2010), 1004 [hereafter Vos (2010b)].

Walling, George W. *Recollections of a New York Chief of Police.* New York: Caxton Book Concern, 1887.

"Wheeler H. Peckham Resigns." *New-York Times,* Dec. 11, 1883, 1.

White, George M., alias George Bliss. *From Boniface to Bank Burglar: Or, the Price of Persecution. How a Successful Business Man, Through the Miscarriage of Justice, Became a Notorious Bank Looter.* Bellows Falls, Vt.: Truax Printing Company, 1905.

"Wide-Awake Retailing: A Bolt of Silk's Story." *Dry Goods Economist,* March 2, 1918, 41.

Wiebe, Robert H. *The Search for Order: 1877–1920.* New York: Hill & Wang, 1967.

"William Howe." Digital Panopticon. digitalpanopticon.org/life?id=obpdef1-997-18540918.

"William Howe, William Thompson, Gavin Rickards, Miscellaneous: Conspiracy, 18th September 1854." Proceedings of the Old Bailey, Reference Number t18540918-997 .oldbaileyonline.org/browse.jsp?div=t18540918-997.

"William Kelley's Trial: The Purse the Burglars Raised—An Envelope Full of Money." *New-York Times,* Dec. 19, 1879, 8.

Williams, David Ricardo. *Call in Pinkerton's: American Detectives at Work for Canada.* Toronto: Dundurn Press, 1998.

"Wm. F. Howe, Old-Time Lawyer: Reminiscences of the Man Who Once Dominated the Criminal Courts of New York." *Law Student's Helper: A Monthly Magazine for the Student In and Out of Law School* 11:1, January 1903, 7–10.

Wunsch, James L. "Book Review: *Nell Kimball: Her Life as an American Madam.*" *Journal of Social History* 6:1 (Autumn 1972), 121–26.

Yoder, Robert M. "The Best Friend a Thief Ever Had." *Saturday Evening Post,* Dec. 25, 1954, 18–19, 72–73.

"The Yonkers Mystery." *New-York Times,* June 9, 1878, 2.

Zapata, Janet. "Tiffany and Company." In Jackson (2010), 1315.

Zuckerman, Michael. "The Nursery Tales of Horatio Alger." *American Quarterly* 24:2, May 1972, 191–209.

Notes

PROLOGUE: A GLITTERING HOARD

xiii **They were detectives:** For accounts of the Pinkertons' raid on Marm Mandelbaum's premises, see, e.g., Rona L. Holub, "Fredericka 'Marm' Mandelbaum, 'Queen of Fences': The Rise and Fall of a Female Immigrant Criminal Entrepreneur in Nineteenth-Century New York City" (doctoral dissertation, Columbia University, 2007), 139ff.; J. North Conway, *Queen of Thieves: The True Story of "Marm" Mandelbaum and Her Gangs of New York* (New York: Skyhorse Publishing, 2014), 123ff.; and, *cum grano salis,* a work commissioned by the Pinkerton Agency, James D. Horan and Howard Swiggett, *The Pinkerton Story* (New York: G. P. Putnam's Sons, 1951), 314ff. Newspaper accounts of the raid and its immediate aftermath include "Got Mother Mandelbaum," *New-York Sun,* July 23, 1884, 1; "Mother Mandlebaum [*sic*] Trapped," *New-York Times,* July 23, 1884, 5; "A Queen Among Thieves," *New-York Times,* July 24, 1884, 5; "A Big Haul," *Chicago Tribune,* July 25, 1884, 3; and "Perturbed Police," *Detroit Free Press,* July 26, 1884, 2.

xiii **diamond cluster earrings and a lace-trimmed gown:** "Got Mother Mandelbaum."

xiii **"No," she declared:** "A Big Haul."

xiii **her heavy Germanic English:** Several period newspaper accounts refer to Mrs. Mandelbaum's German accent, among them "Queer Mrs. Mandelbaum," *New-York Sun,* Jan. 24, 1884, 4.

xiii **They summoned a blacksmith:** "A Big Haul."

xiii **a pretty teenage girl:** Anna Mandelbaum, familiarly known as Annie, was born in 1867, per Holub (2007), 42. A week after the raid, a newspaper article, "Holding Mrs. Mandelbaum: Silk Buyers Swearing to the Stolen Goods Bought of Her," *New-York Sun,* July 29, 1884, 3, described Annie as looking "like a rosebud."

xiii **"Stop!" Annie cried:** "A Big Haul."

xiii **An Aladdin's Cave:** e.g., Holub (2007), 150ff.; Horan and Swiggett (1951), 315; "Got Mother Mandelbaum"; and "Mrs. Mandelbaum's Riches," *New-York Sun,* July 25, 1884, 1.

xiii **"almost every ornament":** "Mrs. Mandelbaum's Riches," quoting Robert A. Pinkerton.

xiv **"heaps of gold watches":** Ibid., quoting Robert A. Pinkerton.

xiv **the size of peas:** Ibid., quoting Robert A. Pinkerton.

xiv   **worth thousands of dollars alone:** Ibid., quoting Robert A. Pinkerton.

xiv   **Concealed under newspapers:** Ibid., quoting Robert A. Pinkerton.

xiv   **melting pots and scales:** Ibid., quoting Robert A. Pinkerton.

xiv   **FN would not be known as the New York City Police Department:** "The History of
      [the] New York City Police Department," National Criminal Justice Reference
      Service document no. 145539 (1993), n.p., ojp.gov/ncjrs/virtual-library/abstracts
      /history-new-york-city-police-department.

xiv   **"You are caught this time":** "Got Mother Mandelbaum."

xiv   **punched him in the face:** Ibid.

xiv   **across the country and beyond:** Holub (2007), 8–9.

xv   **"the nucleus and centre":** "Crime and the Police," *New-York Times,* July 24, 1884, 4.

xv   **FN "New-York" was often hyphenated:** Pardis Mahdavi, "New York's Hyphenated
      History," *Paris Review,* May 27, 2021, theparisreview.org/blog/2021/05/27/new
      -yorks-hyphenated-history.

xv   **FN on December 1, 1896:** William Safire, "On Language: Hyphenating Americans,"
      New York Times Magazine, Dec. 23, 1979, 2.

xv   **FN "without a word":** Ibid.

xvi   **scarcely a day behind bars:** Mrs. Mandelbaum does not appear to have passed even
      slight time in jail until her arrest in 1884, the prelude to her downfall. See, e.g.,
      Holub (2007), 303 ff.

xvi   **"Without question":** Carl B. Klockars, *The Professional Fence* (New York: Free Press/
      Macmillan, 1974), 176.

xvi   **Her network of thieves:** Holub (2007), 8–9.

xvi   **her death, in 1894:** Holub (2007), 235–36.

xvi   **amassed a personal fortune:** Holub (2007), 1.

xvi   **"The ramifications":** George W. Walling, *Recollections of a New York Chief of Police*
      (New York: Caxton Book Concern, 1887), 281–82.

xvi   **FN *The Two Orphans:*** N. Hart Jackson, *The Two Orphans: A Romantic Play (and
      Dramatic Composition) in Four Acts and Seven Tableaux,* adapted from the French of
      Ad. D'Ennery and Eugene Cormon, expressly for dramatic representation at the
      Union Square Theatre of New York City, 1875. Hathi Trust Digital Library, babel.
      hathitrust.org/cgi/pt?id=hvd.32044024345399.

xvi   **FN *The Great Diamond Robbery:*** Edward M. Alfriend and A. C. Wheeler, *The Great
      Diamond Robbery* (1895); anthologized in Garrett H. Leverton, ed., *The Great Dia-
      mond Robbery and Other Recent Melodramas by Edward M. Alfriend & A. C.
      Wheeler, Clarence Bennett [and Others]* (Princeton, N.J.: Princeton University Press,
      1940).

xvii **FN as far away as London:** "Necrological," *American Register* (London, U.K.),
      March 17, 1894, 6.

xvii **in a spate of books:** See, e.g., Herbert Asbury, *The Gangs of New York: An Informal
      History of the Underworld* (New York: Vintage Books, 2008; originally published
      1927); Hutchins Hapgood, ed., *The Autobiography of a Thief* (New York: Fox, Duf-
      field & Company, 1903); Jenna Weissman Joselit, *Our Gang: Jewish Crime and the
      New York Jewish Community, 1900–1940* (Bloomington: Indiana University Press,
      1983); Stanley Nadel, *Little Germany: Ethnicity, Religion, and Class in New York
      City, 1845–80* (Urbana: University of Illinois Press, 1990); John Oller, *Rogues' Gal-
      lery: The Birth of Modern Policing and Organized Crime in Gilded Age New York*
      (New York: Dutton, 2021); and David Ray Papke, *Framing the Criminal: Crime, Cul-
      tural Work and the Loss of Critical Perspective, 1830–1900* (Hamden, Conn.: Archon
      Books, 1987).

xvii **few in-depth studies:** The only serious scholarly study of Mrs. Mandelbaum has been
      carried out in two works by the historian Rona L. Holub: "The Rise of Fredericka

'Marm' Mandelbaum: Criminal Enterprise and the 'American Dream' in New York City, 1850–1884." (master's thesis, Sarah Lawrence College, 1998) and Holub (2007). To date, the only book-length treatment of Marm Mandelbaum for a general readership has been Conway (2014).

xvii **"She was shrewd":** Walling (1887), 283.

xvii **"the Flash Age":** James L. Ford, *Forty-odd Years in the Literary Shop* (New York: E. P. Dutton & Company, 1921), 44. Ford, an American journalist, writes, "My boyhood was passed during what a local chronicler has aptly termed the 'Flash Age of New York,' a period of crime, reckless extravagance, political corruption and false prosperity engendered by the Civil War, the inflation of currency and the rapid rise of contractors and others from poverty to wealth. Its annals are punctuated with murders, bank robberies, spectacular Wall Street gambling and the doings of many bizarre characters."

xvii **"I seen my opportunities":** William L. Riordon, *Plunkitt of Tammany Hall: A Series of Very Plain Talks on Very Practical Politics, Delivered by Ex-Senator George Washington Plunkitt, the Tammany Philosopher, from His Rostrum—the New York County Court House Bootblack Stand* (New York: E. P. Dutton & Company, 1963; originally published 1905), 3.

xvii **"guns-and-garlic":** Frederic D. Homer, *Guns and Garlic: Myths and Realities of Organized Crime.* (West Lafayette, Ind.: Purdue University Studies, 1974).

xvii **first attested in the United States:** Letizia Paoli and Tom Vander Beken, "Organized Crime: A Contested Concept," in Letizia Paoli, ed., *The Oxford Handbook of Organized Crime.* (Oxford: Oxford University Press, 2014) [hereafter Paoli (2014a)], 15. The *Oxford English Dictionary* records an earlier citation of the phrase, from 1867, in a slightly different sense.

xvii **FN "a fuzzy and contested":** Letizia Paoli, Introduction to Paoli (2014a) [hereafter Paoli (2014b)], 2.

xvii **FN to entities as distinct:** Ibid.

xviii **FN when it comes to a precise definition:** See, e.g., Homer (1974), 6ff., 94 and passim; Paoli (2014b), 2ff.

xviii **"a mogul of illegitimate capitalism":** Holub (2007), 24.

xviii **"Crime cannot be carried on":** Sophie Lyons., *Why Crime Does Not Pay.* Fairford, U.K.: Echo Library, 2019; originally published 1913, 113.

xviii **a flock of stolen sheep:** J. North Conway, *King of Heists: The Sensational Bank Robbery of 1878 That Shocked America* (Guilford, Conn.: Lyons Press, 2009), 50.

xviii **as much as $10 million:** Holub (2007), 30.

xviii **"the undisputed financier":** Lyons, (2019), 118.

xix **FN "several cameo appearances":** Asbury (2008), 193, 195, 199–200.

xix **Some modern observers:** See, e.g., Holub (2007), 58; Edwin G. Burrows and Mike Wallace, *Gotham: A History of New York City to 1898* (New York: Oxford University Press, 1999), 1,000.

xix **simultaneously embodied and upended:** Holub (2007), 27, also makes this point.

xix **"is not an equal-opportunity employer":** Nicholas Gage, *The Mafia Is Not an Equal Opportunity Employer* (New York: McGraw-Hill, 1971).

xix **"New York's First Female Crime Boss":** Sarah Breger, "New York's First Female Crime Boss," *Forward,* Nov. 4, 2014, forward.com/life/208460/new-yorks-first-female -crime-boss/.

xix **she stole little to nothing herself:** Lyons (2019), 114.

xx **"What plannings of great robberies":** Quoted in Hapgood (1903), 250.

xx **her "chicks":** Conway (2014), 65.

xx **"There is still standing":** Ford (1921), 48.

xx **The front part of the ground floor:** Ford (1921), 48–49.

xxi **the textbook definition of an organized-crime boss:** While I am constructing "organized crime" as denoting an urban corporate entity that draws its foot soldiers from the underworld community as a whole, some modern observers also describe the family-based criminal cohorts that dotted the landscape of nineteenth-century rural America as crime syndicates. Among the best known of these cohorts were the Loomises, a mid-nineteenth-century gang of horse thieves, robbers and counterfeiters consisting primarily of family members and operating out of Central New York. See, e.g., Leon A. Dapson, "The Loomis Gang," *New York History* 19:3 (July 1938), 269–79, and E. Fuller Torrey, *Frontier Justice: The Rise and Fall of the Loomis Gang* (Utica, N.Y.: North Country Books, 1992).

xxi **About six feet tall:** E.g., Holub (2007), 62; "Queen of the 'Crooks': Mother Mandelbaum, the Famous 'Fence,' Is Dead, After Ten Years of Exile in Canada. Twenty Years in 'Queer' Street. Burglars, Highwaymen, Shoplifters, Sneak-Thieves, All Brought Their Plunder to Her," *New-York World*, Feb. 27, 1894, 14.

xxi **between 250 and 300 pounds:** Holub (2007), 62; Conway (2014), xiv.

xxi **soberly but expensively:** See, e.g., "The End of a Notorious Career: Mother Mandelbaum, the Famous 'Fence,'" *Cincinnati Enquirer*, Feb. 27, 1894, 1; Asbury (2008), 195; Conway (2014), 50; Holub (2007), 62.

xxii **"Her attire was at once":** "End of a Notorious Career."

xxii **her clapboard building:** Holub (2007), 42.

xxii **one of her famous dinner parties:** For accounts of Marm's parties, see, e.g., Conway (2009), 51ff; Conway (2014), 52ff.; Holub (2007), 53, 76.

xxii **"perhaps the most notorious":** Asbury (2008), 196.

xxii **said to have fallen in love:** Holub (2007), 76.

xxii **"would have been rated":** Walling (1887), 283.

xxiii **"would have attracted the cupidity":** Ibid.

xxiii **rare old paintings:** "Old Mother Mandelbaum: Charges Against Byrnes' Detectives Are to Be Investigated," *New York Star*, July 27, 1884, n.p., from District Attorney Scrapbooks, Municipal Archives, City of New York.

xxiii **"Scattered about the room":** Ibid.

xxiii **"Servants of wealthy New York families":** Lyons (2019), 116.

xxiii **"conducted with as much attention":** Walling (1887), 291.

xxiv **she hadn't spent so much:** Holub (2007), 303 ff.

xxiv **"The police of New York":** "Life in New York City: Personal, Political and Dramatic Gossip From Across the River," *Brooklyn Daily Eagle*, July 27, 1884, 3.

xxiv **kept on permanent retainer:** See, e.g., Holub (2007), 10; Walling (1887), 281.

CHAPTER ONE: "THE MERE PRIVILEGE OF BREATH"

3 **One of seven children:** For Fredericka Mandelbaum's birthplace, family structure and parents' names, see Rona Holub, "Fredericka Mandelbaum," *Immigrant Entrepreneurship* (2013), an online article at immigrantentrepreneurship.org/entries/fredericka-mandelbaum/; for her full name at birth, see Holub (2007), 28.

3 **Samuel Abraham Weisner:** The family name appears as "Wiesener" in some sources.

3 **Fredericka Henriette Auguste Weisner:** Holub (2007), 28n. Mrs. Mandelbaum's first name has been spelled variously in news articles and other documents over the years. In keeping with Holub, the only historian to have given her serious attention, I use "Fredericka," the spelling most common in English-language sources.

3 **March 28, 1825:** The literature records various birth dates for Fredericka Mandelbaum, sometimes within a single document. Holub (1998), 6, for instance, gives February 17, 1827, as does Holub (2007), 28. Cf. Holub (2013), n.p., which at different

points gives March 25, 1825, and March 28, 1825. The date adopted in this book, March 28, 1825, is the one inscribed on Mrs. Mandelbaum's tombstone, in Union Field Cemetery, Ridgewood, New York. Photograph at findagrave.com/memorial /130475634.

3   FN **"a variety of local rulers":** Hasia R. Diner and Beryl Lieff Benderly, *Her Works Praise Her: A History of Jewish Women in America from Colonial Times to the Present* (New York: Basic Books, 2002), 69.

3   **itinerant peddlers:** Holub (2013), n.p.

3   **numbering fourteen to fifteen thousand:** Ibid.

3   **Restrictive laws:** See, e.g., Holub (2007), 29–30; Holub (2013), n.p.

3   **which by extension restricted:** Diner and Benderly (2002), 73.

3   **Jews sometimes paid:** Holub (2007), n.p.

3   **"Jews occupied":** Diner and Benderly (2002), 69–70.

4   **at a local Jewish elementary school:** Holub (2013), n.p.

4   **sewing, spinning, knitting:** Rudolf Glanz, *The Jewish Woman in America: Two Female Immigrant Generations, 1820–1929*, Volume 2: *The German Jewish Woman* (Brooklyn: Ktav Publishing House/National Council of Jewish Women, 1976), 12.

4   **"Whatever the precise circumstances":** Holub (2013), n.p.

4   **In 1848, Fredericka married:** Ibid.

4   **a few years her senior:** Ibid.

4   **possibly with Fredericka helping him:** Holub (2007), 28; Holub (2013), n.p.

4   **The birth, in 1849:** Holub (2007), 29; Holub (2013), n.p.

4   **in the midst of an economic depression:** Holub (2007), 30.

4   **a potato blight:** Ibid.

4   **the thousands of European Jews:** Diner and Benderly (2002), 68.

4   **FN "In 1820 the Jewish population":** Ibid.

4   **"Das Dollarland":** Lawrence R. Samuel, *The American Dream: A Cultural History* (Syracuse: Syracuse University Press, 2012), 16.

4   **Wolf left first:** Holub (2007), 31.

5   **After traveling to Bremen:** Holub (2007), 31–32.

5   **six weeks or longer:** Diner and Benderly (2002), 68. Robert Ernst, *Immigrant Life in New York City* (Port Washington, N.Y.: Ira J. Friedman, 1965; originally published 1949), 14, puts the duration of a transatlantic sailing-ship voyage in this period at "about two months."

5   **roughly $140 U.S.:** Holub (2007), 32.

5   **paying twenty dollars:** Ibid.

5   **low-ceilinged, badly ventilated:** Holub (2007), 32–33.

5   **spectacularly good business:** Brendan P. O'Malley, "Lickspittles and Land Sharks: The Immigrant Exploitation Business in Antebellum New York," in Brian P. Luskey and Wendy A. Woloson, eds., *Capitalism by Gaslight: Illuminating the Economy of Nineteenth-Century America* (Philadelphia: University of Pennsylvania Press, 2015), 97ff.

5   **"three tiers":** From Melville's novel *Redburn*, quoted in O'Malley (2015), 98.

5   **In September 1850:** Holub (2007), 31.

5   **It comprised only Manhattan:** David C. Hammack, "Consolidation," in Kenneth T. Jackson, ed., *The Encyclopedia of New York City*, second edition (New Haven and New York: Yale University Press/New-York Historical Society, 2010), 305.

5   **a population of just over half a million:** Joseph J. Salvo and Arun Peter Lobo, "Population," in Jackson (2010), 1019.

5   **FN Portions of what is now the Bronx:** Hammack (2010), 305–306.

5   **FN January 1, 1898:** Hammack (2010), 305.

5   **lived below Fourteenth Street:** See, e.g., Edward K. Spann, *The New Metropolis: New York City, 1840–1857* (New York: Columbia University Press, 1981), 307, and Edward Robb Ellis, *The Epic of New York City* (New York: Old Town Books, 1966), 251.

5   **the city teemed:** Holub (2007), 34.ff., and Conway (2014), 5, e.g., make a similar point.

6   **factories, foundries and slaughterhouses:** Holub (2007), 45–46.

6   **few immigrants, if any, believed:** Hasia R. Diner, *Hungering for America: Italian, Irish, and Jewish Foodways in the Age of Migration* (Cambridge, Mass.: Harvard University Press, 2001), xvii.

6   **streets filled with ordure:** See, e.g., Holub (2007), 46–47; James O. Drummond and Kate Lauber, "Horses," in Jackson (2010), 612–13; Sandra Opdycke, "Sewers," in Jackson (2010), 1173–74; Charles Dickens, *American Notes for General Circulation*, Volume 1 (London: Chapman & Hall, 1842), 205 ff.

6   **"by no means so clean":** Dickens (1842), 191.

6   **FN So named because the neighborhood:** Michele Herman, "Five Points," in Jackson (2010), 456.

6   **"the world's most notorious":** Tyler Anbinder, *Five Points: The 19th-Century New York City Neighborhood That Invented Tap Dance, Stole Elections, and Became the World's Most Notorious Slum* (New York: Free Press, 2001).

6   **he felt it necessary to make:** Dickens (1842), 211.

6   **the voyeuristic tours:** Anbinder (2001), 33.

6   **myriad houses of prostitution:** Anbinder (2001), 19.

6   **and by the lively social mixing:** Robert W. Snyder, personal communication; Anbinder (2001), 199.

6   **This is the place:** Dickens (1842), 211–16.

7   **about a square mile:** Holub (2007), 39.

7   **Tenth, Eleventh, Thirteenth and Seventeenth wards:** Nadel (1990), 29.

7   **FN The ward was for more than 250 years:** James F. Richardson, "Wards," in Jackson (2010), 1376–77.

7   **383 East Eighth Street:** Holub (2007), 39.

7   **settling permanently in the Thirteenth Ward:** Holub (2007), 42.

8   **twenty families or more:** Holub (2007), 39.

8   **no running water:** Holub (2007), 37.

8   **"The most modern":** Anbinder (2001), 85–86.

8   **diseases like consumption:** Ibid.

9   **FN sixty-five children of immigrants:** Holub (2007), 41.

9   **little Bertha Mandelbaum's name:** Holub (2007), 41.

9   **FN It is even possible:** Holub (2007), 41n.

9   **the first of the country's large foreign-language settlements:** Nadel (1990), 2.

9   **"German New York":** Nadel (1990), 1.

9   **attending German-language theater performances:** Holub (2007), 47.

9   **FN "that has been denoted as Western Yiddish":** Hasia R. Diner, personal communication.

9   **"Unser Haus":** Nadel (1990), 46.

10 **with deep reluctance:** According to George Washington Walling, New York City's chief of police from 1874 to 1885, the exiled Mrs. Mandelbaum "would gladly forfeit every penny of her wealth in order to once more breathe freely the atmosphere of the Thirteenth Ward" [Walling (1887), 289].

10 **often menial, exploitative:** See, e.g., Anbinder (2001), 120.

10 **fell from construction sites or were crushed:** Ibid.

10 **when cold or wet weather:** Ibid.

10 **butchers, bakers, brewers:** Nadel (1990), 63; Timothy J. Haggerty, personal communication.

11 **There is no class of mechanics:** "Labor in New-York: Its Circumstances, Conditions and Rewards. No. XI: General Condition of the Shoe-Makers—the Ladies' Branch," *New-York Daily Tribune*, Sept. 9, 1845, 1.

12 **expected to do likewise:** Holub (2007), 121; Glanz (1976), 12.

12 **FN So, too, was a woman's ability:** Holub (2007). 14.

12 **up to sixteen hours:** Alice Kessler-Harris, *Out to Work: A History of Wage-Earning Women in the United States* (Oxford: Oxford University Press, 2003; originally published 1982), 55.

12 **room, board and a dollar:** Kessler-Harris (2003), 55.

12 **"tailoresses":** A common term in accounts of the period. See, e.g., Nadel (1990), 75.

12 **stooped posture and impaired eyesight:** Christine Stansell, *City of Women: Sex and Class in New York, 1789–1860* (Urbana: University of Illinois Press, 1987; originally published 1986), 113–14.

12 **the average yearly income:** Nadel (1990), 75.

13 **The condition of women:** Nadel (1990), 76.

13 **"crooked ladder":** James M. O'Kane, *The Crooked Ladder: Gangsters, Ethnicity, and the American Dream* (New Brunswick, N.J.: Transaction Publishers, 1992).

13 **these activities might include:** See, e.g., O'Kane (1992), passim.

14 **"upper world":** See, e.g., Paoli and Vander Beken (2014), 16.

14 **in bold economic self-determination:** See, e.g., Kessler-Harris (2003), 104–105, and Stansell (1987), 175–76, for historical discussions of prostitution as a reasoned choice by some nineteenth-century women for the earning power it afforded.

14 **Among immigrant German women:** Nadel (1990), 89.

14 **An 1858 study:** William W. Sanger, M.D., *The History of Prostitution: Its Extent, Causes, and Effects Throughout the World* (New York: Harper & Brothers, 1858). Cited in Kessler-Harris, 58.

14 **the average life expectancy:** Kessler-Harris (2003), 58.

14 **"While lower-class women":** Timothy J. Haggerty, personal communication; italics added.

14 **FN beginning in 1867 and continuing:** "Das Kapital." *Encyclopaedia Britannica*, britannica.com/topic/Das-Kapital.

14 **proffering their wares:** See, e.g., Anbinder (2001), 119; Barbara Kirshenblatt-Gimblett, "Street Life," in Jackson (2010), 1251; Rowan Moore Gerety, "Street Vendors," in Jackson (2010), 1254; William Grimes, *Appetite City: A Culinary History of New York* (New York: North Point Press, 2009), 19; Irving Lewis Allen, *The City in Slang: New York Life and Popular Speech* (New York: Oxford University Press, 1993), 203ff.; Solon Robinson, *Hot Corn: Life Scenes in New York Illustrated, Including the Story of Little Katy, Madalina, the Rag-Picker's Daughter, Wild Maggie, &c* (New York: De Witt & Davenport, 1854), 18, 249–54.

15 **FN The particular goods and services:** See, e.g., Anbinder (2001), 119; Grimes (2009), 19; Allen (1993), 203ff.

15 **"Rags—rags—any rags?":** Allen (1993), 204.

15 **"Fresh sha-a-d!":** Anbinder (2001), 119.

15 **"Oysters":** Grimes (2009), 19.

15 **"Pots and pans":** Allen (1993), 204.

15 **"Here's clams":** Grimes (2009), 19.

15 **"Glass put'een!":** Allen (1993), 204.

15 **"Hot corn! Hot corn!":** Ibid.

15 **"Sweepho!":** Ibid.

15 **"Strawberries":** Ibid.

15 **"Umbrellas to mend":** Ibid.

15 **FN "the bottom level":** Nadel (1990), 81.

15 **appears to have become a protégée:** "A Queen Among Thieves."

15 **"one of the oldest and shrewdest":** "End of a Criminal Career: Old Abe Greenthal Dies of Old Age—His Life Story," *New-York Times,* Nov. 20, 1889, 8.

15 **the Sheeny Mob:** Richard H. Rovere, *Howe & Hummel: Their True and Scandalous History* (London: Arlington Books, 1986; originally published 1947), 6. The group was also known as the "Sheeny Gang," e.g., Albert Fried, *The Rise and Fall of the Jewish Gangster in America* (New York: Columbia University Press, 1993; originally published 1980), 25.

15 **"a gang of clever pickpockets":** "End of a Criminal Career."

15 **"when he was not actually engaged":** Ibid.

16 **Mose Ehrich:** Holub (2007), 78; Nadel (1990), 88. Ehrich's surname is also rendered Erich, Ehrlich and Ehrick in accounts of the period.

16 **Mrs. Mandelbaum became expert:** Holub (2007), 74.

16 **"The woman took the lead":** Walling (1887), 280–81.

CHAPTER TWO: NO QUESTIONS ASKED

17 **as far back as the fourteenth century:** Luke Owen Pike, *A History of Crime in England: Illustrating the Changes of the Laws in the Progress of Civilisation,* Volume 1: *From the Roman Invasion to the Accession of Henry VII* (London: Smith, Elder & Company, 1873), 282ff.

17 **"The Common Receiver":** Pike (1873), 285–86.

17 **few consider themselves criminals:** James A. Inciardi, *Careers in Crime* (Chicago: Rand McNally College Publishing Company, 1975), 33.

18 **a quasi-legitimate business:** Darrell J. Steffensmeier, *The Fence: In the Shadow of Two Worlds* (Lanham, Md.: Rowman & Littlefield, 1986), 4.

18 **FN The city experienced major financial panics:** Timothy J. Gilfoyle, *A Pickpocket's Tale: The Underworld of Nineteenth-Century New York* (New York: W. W. Norton, 2006), 186.

18 **FN The more euphemistic term:** Timothy J. Haggerty, personal communication.

19 **"Her success, in part":** Holub (2013), n.p.

19 **Many of these scavengers:** Ibid.; Holub (2007), 43.

19 **bits of coal and wood:** Holub (2013), n.p.; Stansell (1987), 50, 204–205.

19 **rags, rope and scrap metal:** Holub (2013), n.p.; Nadel (1990), 80.

19 **FN might realize two cents a pound:** Anbinder (2001), 376.

19 **FN "By midcentury":** Stansell (1987), 206.

19 **at least some of her wares came:** Holub (2007), 77.

19 **getting the lion's share:** Per, e.g., Oller (2021), 68, and Lyons (2019), 113–14, in the heyday of her fencing operations, Mrs. Mandelbaum typically paid the thieves who worked for her 10 to 25 percent of an item's wholesale price. This enabled her to sell the item onward for less than its wholesale value, resulting in a bargain for the buyer while still ensuring a tidy profit for herself.

20 **asking no questions:** Holub (2007), 95.

20 **FN *The Gilded Age:*** Mark Twain and Charles Dudley Warner, *The Gilded Age: A Tale of Today* (Hartford, Conn.: American Publishing Company, 1873).

20 **FN historians locate the start:** See, e.g., William Leach, "Strategists of Display and the Production of Desire," in Simon J. Bronner, ed., *Consuming Visions: Accumulation and Display of Goods in America, 1880–1920* (New York: W. W. Norton & Company, 1989) [hereafter Bronner (1989b)], 101.

20 **first Golden Age of robbery:** Oller (2021), 86.

20 **A corresponding vocabulary:** Gilfoyle (2006), 61; David R. Johnson, *Policing the Urban Underworld: The Impact of Crime on the Development of the American Police,*

1800–1887 (Philadelphia: Temple University Press, 1979), 54; George W[ashington] Matsell, *Vocabulum: Or, the Rogue's Lexicon, Compiled from the Most Authentic Sources* (New York: George W. Matsell & Company, 1859), passim; and David W. Maurer, *Whiz Mob: A Correlation of the Technical Argot of Pickpockets with Their Behavior Pattern* (New Haven, Conn.: College & University Press, 1964), passim.

21 **Amid an economic downturn:** Robert H. Wiebe, *The Search for Order: 1877–1920* (New York: Hill & Wang, 1967), 41.

21 **a seventy-room summer home:** Ibid.

21 **thirty-three servants and thirteen grooms:** Ibid.

21 **a cost of $5 million:** Ibid.

21 **costing a mere $2 million:** Ibid.

21 **boasted $9 million worth:** Ibid.

21 **they were now *consumers:*** See, e.g., Simon J. Bronner, "Reading Consumer Culture" [hereafter Bronner (1989a)], in Bronner (1989b), 25.

21 **wealth was typically measured:** Byrne, Richard, *Safecracking* (Golden, Colo.: ReAnimus Press, 2016; originally published 1991), 19.

21 **FN The phrase "American Dream":** Samuel (2012), 2.

21 **FN it is clear that the vision:** Samuel (2012), 3.

21 **FN "a better, deeper, richer life":** James Truslow Adams, *The Epic of America* (Boston: Little, Brown & Company, 1931). Quoted in Samuel (2012), 13.

22 **manuals of domestic advice:** See, e.g., *The American Woman's Home: Or, Principles of Domestic Science, Being a Guide to the Formation and Maintenance of Economical, Healthful, Beautiful, and Christian Homes,* by the sisters Catharine Esther Beecher and Harriet Beecher Stowe (New York: J. B. Ford & Company, 1869).

22 **glutted with settees:** See, e.g., Karen Halttunen, "From Parlor to Living Room: Domestic Space, Interior Decoration, and the Culture of Personality," in Bronner (1989b), 162–64.

22 **"Provided there is space":** Harriet Elizabeth Prescott Spofford, *Art Decoration Applied to Furniture* (New York: Harper & Brothers, 1877), quoted in Halttunen (1989), 164.

22 **"Everything is elaborately arranged":** Quoted in Joselit (1983), 36.

22 **the *National Police Gazette:*** policegazette.us.

23 **FN the "Flash Press":** Patricia Cline Cohen, Timothy J. Gilfoyle, and Helen Lefkowitz Horowitz, in association with the American Antiquarian Society, *The Flash Press: Sporting Male Weeklies in 1840s New York* (Chicago: University of Chicago Press, 2008).

23 **Mike Weaver unquestionably:** "'Dodger's' Expositions," *National Police Gazette,* March 30, 1867, 2.

23 **FN "an old New York safe burglar":** Thomas Byrnes, *Professional Criminals of America: New and Revised Edition* (New York: G. W. Dillingham, 1895), 188.

24 **"rampant quackery":** "James L. Madara, MD, on AMA's Continuing Commitment to Doctors 175 Years Later," American Medical Association podcast, May 10, 2022, ama-assn.org/about/leadership/james-l-madara-md-amas-continuing-commitment-doctors-175-years-later.

24 **FN only 25 percent of American lawyers:** Cait Murphy, *Scoundrels in Law: The Trials of Howe & Hummel, Lawyers to the Gangsters, Cops, Starlets, and Rakes Who Made the Gilded Age* (New York: Smithsonian Books / HarperCollins, 2010), 9.

24 **Abraham Lincoln:** See, e.g., Henry S. Cohn, "Abraham Lincoln at the Bar," *Federal Lawyer* (May 2012), 52–55.

24 **whose formal education:** See, e.g., Eric Foner, "The Education of Abraham Lincoln," *New York Times Book Review,* Feb. 10, 2002, 11.

24 **So had Mrs. Mandelbaum's longtime attorneys:** Murphy (2010), xvi.

24 **So, too, had William M. Tweed:** Leo Hershkowitz, *Tweed's New York: Another Look* (Garden City, N.Y.: Anchor/Doubleday, 1978), 85.

24 **FN it was actually Magear:** Hershkowitz (1978), 5.

24 **"In the course of the century":** Papke (1987), 151.

24 **While there had been some professional theft:** Inciardi (1975), 47.

24 **it was only with the rise:** Ibid.

24 **By the 1840s:** O'Kane (1992), 55.

24 **violence from nativist Anglo-Saxon Americans:** Ibid.; Holub (2007), 94.

24 **FN "a usually careful":** Anbinder (2001), 68.

24 **the Plug Uglies:** Asbury (2008), 20.

25 **FN By 1860, as a modern historian notes:** Stansell (1987), xi.

25 **FN "both the nation's premier port":** Ibid.

25 **remained largely "disorganized":** A similar point is made by Richard Hammer, *The Illustrated History of Organized Crime* (Philadelphia: Courage Books, 1989; originally published 1975), 3.

25 **not especially remunerative:** Hammer (1989), 8.

25 **FN considered the city's most violent gang:** Frank Browning and John Gerassi, *The American Way of Crime* (New York: G. P. Putnam's Sons, 1980), 298.

25 **FN first to pursue crime:** Gilfoyle (2006), 190.

25 **FN did not come to power:** Gilfoyle (2006), 181.

25 **"Eye-gougers and mayhem artists":** Asbury (2008), 21.

25 **FN "had few German counterparts":** Nadel (1990), 87.

25 **"Among the ladies":** Alexander B. Callow, Jr., *The Tweed Ring* (Oxford: Oxford University Press, 1969; originally published 1965), 58–59.

25 **Gallus Mag, who supported:** Callow (1969), 59.

26 **The robber barons had won:** See, e.g., Browning-Gerassi (1980), 201 ff.; Callow (1969), 218–19; Charles R. Morris, *The Tycoons: How Andrew Carnegie, John D. Rockefeller, Jay Gould, and J. P. Morgan Invented the American Supereconomy* (New York: Owl Books / Henry Holt, 2006; originally published 2005), passim; S. Paul O'Hara, *Inventing the Pinkertons. Or, Spies, Sleuths, Mercenaries, and Thugs: Being a Story of the Nation's Most Famous (and Infamous) Detective Agency* (Baltimore: Johns Hopkins University Press, 2016), 2, 11, 72–73; O'Kane (1992), 48; Wiebe (1967), 37–39.

26 **"I can hire":** Quoted in Browning-Gerassi (1980), 201.

26 **FN "Honesty Is the Best Policy":** Browning-Gerassi (1980), 211.

26 **"Law!":** Quoted in ibid.

26 **"While workers starved":** Browning-Gerassi (1980), 213–14.

27 **"The larger society":** O'Kane (1992), 48; italics added.

27 **thirteenth-century Sicily:** Gage (1971), 30.

27 **at the end of the nineteenth century:** Ibid.

27 **FN the first recorded Mafia murder:** Gage (1971), 30–31.

27 **in the early twentieth:** Gage (1971), 31.

27 **Jewish gangsters:** See, e.g., Rich Cohen, *Tough Jews* (New York: Simon & Schuster, 1998).

27 **A survey of the State:** Twenty-first Annual Report of the Executive Committee of the Prison Association of New York. Part I: Transmitted to the Legislature January 22, 1866. (Albany: C. Wendell, Legislative Printer, 1866), 144–45.

28 **A son, Julius, was born:** Holub (2007), 42.

28 **Sarah:** Spelled "Sara" in some accounts.

28 **In 1864, she rented:** Holub (2007), 50.

29 **"the most celebrated fence":** Inciardi (1975), 34.

29 **considered one of the most dominant criminals:** Steffensmeier (1986), 7.

29 **the father of modern professional fencing:** Klockars (1974), 3.

29 **imaginatively embellished works:** Klockars (1974), 3.

29 **a satirical novel by Henry Fielding:** *The Life of Mr. Jonathan Wild, the Great* (New York: New American Library / Signet Classic, 1961; originally published 1743).

29 **a pamphlet attributed to Daniel Defoe:** *The True and Genuine Account of the Life and Actions of the Late Jonathan Wild: Not Made Up of Fiction and Fable, but Taken from His Own Mouth, and Collected from Papers of His Own Writing* (London: John Applebee, 1725).

29 **born in Wolverhampton:** Gerald Howson, *Thief-Taker General: The Rise and Fall of Jonathan Wild.* (London: Hutchinson, 1970), 2.

29 **circa 1682:** As Howson (1970), 10, points out, Wild "was baptized . . . 6 May 1683, though we do not know when he was born."

29 **eldest of five children:** Howson (1970), 10.

29 **His father was a joiner:** Ibid.

29 **his mother a fruit seller:** Ibid.

29 **apprenticed to a buckle maker:** Howson (1970), 11.

29 **married and became the father of a son:** Ibid.

29 **his résumé included:** Howson (1970), 12–13.

30 **Wild moved into a brothel:** Howson (1970), 20.

30 **Mary Milliner:** Her surname, per ibid., sometimes appears as Molyneux.

30 **The *Buttock and Twang* by Night:** Alexander Smith, *A Compleat History of the Lives and Robberies of the Most Notorious Highway-Men, Foot-Pads, Shop-Lifts and Cheats of Both Sexes, in and around London and Westminster, and All Parts of Britain, for about a Hundred Years Past, Continu'd to the Present Time* (London: Sam. Briscoe, 1719), 126–27.

30 **established only in 1829:** "Policing in London: How Suspects Were Apprehended," Proceedings of the Old Bailey, oldbaileyonline.org/static/Policing.jsp.

30 **Thieves often sold:** Howson (1970), 47.

31 **the parlor of a London tavern:** Howson (1970), 75.

31 **"Office for the Recovery":** Howson (1970), 77.

31 **"had an idea where":** Howson (1970), 67.

31 **"If the person questioned":** Howson (1970), 68. The interpolated quotation is from Defoe (1725), 12.

31 **Lady Henrietta Godolphin:** Howson (1970), 76.

32 **"of no use to anyone":** Quoted in Howson (1970), 66.

32 **"Whoever will bring":** Quoted in ibid.

32 **"No Questions asked":** Quoted in ibid.

32 **"highwaymen, pick-pockets, housebreakers":** Warrant of detainer for Jonathan Wild, Feb. 26, 1725. Reproduced in Camden Pelham, ed., *The Chronicles of Crime: Or, the New Newgate Calendar. Being a Series of Memoirs and Anecdotes of Notorious Characters Who Have Outraged the Laws of Great Britain from the Earliest Period to 1841* (London: T. Miles & Company, 1887), 59.

32 **"several artists to make alterations":** Warrant of detainer. In Pelham (1887), 60.

32 **He also owned a constellation:** Ibid.

32 **FN "From about 1605":** Howson (1970), 36.

32 **Fencing was then a misdemeanor:** Ibid.

33 **"An Act for Encourageing":** *An Act for Encourageing the Apprehending of Highway Men*, Statutes of the Realm: Volume 6, 1685–94. Full text at british-history.ac.uk /statutes-realm/vol6/pp390-391.

33 **a reward of £40:** *An Act for Encourageing.*

33 **enough to buy seven horses:** nationalarchives.gov.uk/currency-converter.

33 **avidly informing on their fellow citizens:** Howson (1970), 37.

33 "THIEF-TAKER GENERAL": Howson (1970), 111; capitals in original.

34 "He . . . was oblig'd": Defoe (1725), 46; italics in original.

35 Defoe estimated that Wild employed: Daniel Defoe, *The Great Law of Subordination Consider'd; Or, The Insolence and Unsufferable Behaviour of SERVANTS in England Duly Enquired Into* (London: S. Harding, 1724), 210.

35 In February 1725: Howson (1970), 6.

35 "Further disclosures revealed": Ibid.

35 in May 1725: Ibid.

35 On May 24: Howson (1970), 274.

35 a large, enthusiastic crowd: Ibid.

CHAPTER THREE: BREAKFAST AT TIFFANY'S

36 FN Frederick Winslow Taylor: See, e.g., Robert Kanigel, *The One Best Way: Frederick Winslow Taylor and the Enigma of Efficiency* (New York: Viking, 1997).

36 "In the public imagination": Holub (2007), 9–10; italics in original.

37 FN "Unlike other retail businesses": Timothy J. Haggerty, personal communication.

37 a mentor to underworld women: Holub (2007), 58, 115.

37 Many joined her earliest broods: Holub (2013), n.p.

37 Besides Sophie Lyons, they included: See, e.g., Asbury (2008), 196; O'Kane (1992), 52; Oller (2021), 67–68.

37 a German-born jewel thief nicknamed for her olive complexion: Thomas Byrnes, *Professional Criminals of America*; introductions by Arthur M. Schlesinger, Jr., and S. J. Perelman (New York: Chelsea House Publishers, 1969; originally published 1886), 198.

37 "satchel work": Byrnes (1969), photo 117, following p. 94.

37 four feet eleven inches tall: Byrnes (1969), 197–98.

38 "Mother Mandelbaum": " 'Billy' Porter: Eventful Life of the King of Cracksmen," *Boston Daily Globe*, Jan. 23, 1886, 1.

38 an urban legend sprang up: Holub (2007), 54, describes this story as mere rumor.

38 it persists to this day: Twentieth- and twenty-first-century sources that recapitulate the legend unquestioned include Asbury (2008), 199; Conway (2009), 49–50; and Conway (2014), 55.

38 FN "During the fifteenth and sixteenth centuries": Inciardi (1975), 61.

38 FN "Many . . . ragged urchins": Henry Mayhew, *London Labour and the London Poor,* Volume 4: *Those That Will Not Work, Comprising Prostitutes, Thieves, Swindlers, Beggars* (London: Griffin, Bohn & Company, 1862), 304.

38 a tantalizing newspaper article: "He Wanted to Be a Knuck: Patrolman's Son Attempts to Apprentice Himself to a Pickpocket," *Cincinnati Enquirer*, Feb. 25, 1884, 2; originally published in the *New York Star*.

40 "Since the parties": Steffensmeier (1986), 129.

40 Americans had resisted the idea: Johnson (1979), 13.

40 In 1844, the New York State legislature: "The History of [the] New York City Police Department" (1993), n.p.

40 established the next year: Ibid.

40 constables, marshals and night watchmen: Holub (2007), 86.

40 had been unsalaried: Ibid.

40 "These men were objects": Holub (2007), 90.

40 often working in concert: Oller (2021), 25.

41 one-year terms: Richardson (1970), 54.

41 with the appointments controlled: Johnson (1979), 26.

41 In 1848: Johnson (1979), 100.

41 **"it was received":** Ibid.

41 **was instituted, in 1853:** "The History of [the] New York City Police Department" (1993), n.p.

41 **little more than military drills:** Ibid.

41 **that the applicant read the name:** James F. Richardson, *The New York Police: Colonial Times to 1901* (New York: Oxford University Press, 1970), 98.

41 **some eighteen hundred civil-service posts:** Richardson (1970), 61.

41 **"inspectors of hacks and stages":** Ibid.

41 **"were also used":** Ibid.

41 **policemen had little idea:** Holub (2007), 83.

41 **neither physical nor age requirements:** Oller (2021), 25.

41 **eight hundred men in 1845:** "The History of [the] New York City Police Department" (1993), n.p.

41 **just under twelve hundred:** Richardson (1970), 51.

41 **The city's population:** Holub (2007), 87.

41 **FN London had more than twice as many:** Oller (2021), 25.

41 **chiefly vagrancy and public drunkenness:** Holub (2007), 85.

41 **"'Assault, Battery,' 'Petit Larceny'":** Ibid.

42 **They also enjoyed:** Anbinder (2001), 147.

42 **continued the tradition:** Holub (2007), 88.

42 **before a robbery was committed:** Richardson (1970), 31.

42 **"The Republicans believed":** Nadel (1990), 132.

42 **In April 1857:** Samuel Augustus Pleasants, *Fernando Wood of New York* (New York: Columbia University Press, 1948), 77.

42 **Mayor Wood refused to acknowledge:** Oller (2021), 26.

42 **"battle of the bulls":** Nadel (1990), 132.

42 **duking it out:** Papke (1987), 122.

42 **At times, suspects arrested:** Richardson (1970), 104.

42 **in July 1857:** Nadel (1990), 132.

42 **FN In 1870:** "The History of [the] New York City Police Department" (1993), n.p.

42 **the Metropolitans wielded little influence:** Nadel (1990), 133.

42 **"a state of war is a school":** "The Police: Report of the Board of Metropolitan Police for 1864," reprinted in the *New-York Times*, Jan. 5, 1865, 8.

42 **both the upper world and underworld:** Holub (2013), n.p.

43 **"triggered a wild scramble":** Charles (2005), 60.

43 **FN During a single week:** Edward K. Spann, *Gotham at War: New York City, 1860–1865* (Wilmington, Del.: SR Books, 2002), 45.

43 **"shoddy aristocracy":** See, e.g., Richardson (1970), 130.

43 **founded in the city in 1818:** brooksbrothers.com.

43 **In the spring of 1861:** Spann (2002), 46.

43 **FN The Brooks Brothers contract:** Spann (2002), 49–50.

44 **FN "a price that by one estimate":** Spann (2002), 49.

44 **in favor of cloth woven from "shoddy":** Spann (2002), 46.

44 **ushering "shoddy":** From the *Oxford English Dictionary*: "In the U.S. the word seems to have been first used [as an adjective] with reference to those who made fortunes by army contracts at the time of the Civil War, it being alleged that the clothing supplied by the contractors consisted largely of shoddy."

44 **and for fences to deal:** Holub (2007), 97.

44 **"Robbery, burglary and larceny":** "The Police: Report of the Board of Metropolitan Police for 1864"; italics added.

44 **"from silks to securities":** Holub (2007), 45.

44 **fifty thousand stolen cigars:** "Mother Mandelbaum Away," *New York Herald*, Dec. 16,

1884, n.p., from District Attorney Scrapbooks, Municipal Archives, City of New York.

44 **except the man who cut them:** Inciardi (1975), 99–100.

45 **in particular diamond stickpins:** Lyons (2019), 114.

45 **knew exactly what they were getting:** See, e.g., Holub (2007), 48, 70–71.

45 **Marm typically paid the thief:** Oller (2021), 68.

45 **She then charged the buyer:** Ibid.

45 **"While pickpockets are 'pickers'":** Lyons (2019), 114.

45 **resolving to expand her trade:** Ibid.

45 **Fredericka Mandelbaum paid several visits:** Ibid.

46 **FN the store occupied various addresses:** Janet Zapata, "Tiffany and Company," in Jackson (2010), 1315.

46 **in the secret back rooms:** Lyons (2019), 115.

46 **"Swell" Robinson:** Ibid.

46 **Mary Wallenstein:** Ibid.

46 **Robinson entered Tiffany's alone:** An account of the robbery is given in ibid.

46 **"There was no objection made":** Ibid.

46 **a single large diamond, worth $8,000:** Ibid.

46 **a discreet wad of chewing gum:** Ibid. As the story was recalled by the New York crook Margaret Hill in a 1922 newspaper serial, it was Wallenstein, chewing gum, who entered the store first and Robinson who retrieved the diamond: Mrs. Margaret Hill, "Revelations by the Queen of the Underworld," chapter XIV, *Pittsburgh Press*, July 2, 1922, 96–97.

47 **"was so delightfully successful":** Lyons (2019), 115.

47 **The next morning:** Ibid.

47 **alerted the jewelers' association:** Ibid.

47 **a remarkable instruction manual:** William F. Howe and Abraham H. Hummel, *Danger! A True History of a Great City's Wiles and Temptations: The Veil Lifted, and Light Thrown on Crime and Its Causes, and Criminals and Their Haunts* (Gloucester, U.K.: Dodo Press, 2009; originally published 1886).

47 **"The revelations of the newspapers":** Howe and Hummel (2009), i.

47 **"By hoisting the Danger signal":** Howe and Hummel (2009), ii.

48 **"moralistic and titillating":** Daniel Czitrom, *New York Exposed: The Gilded Age Police Scandal That Launched the Progressive Era.* (New York: Oxford University Press, 2016), 6.

48 ***The Nether Side of New York:*** Edward Crapsey, *The Nether Side of New York: Or, The Vice, Crime and Poverty of the Great Metropolis* (New York: Sheldon & Company, 1872).

48 ***Lights and Shadows of New York Life:*** James D. McCabe, Jr., *Lights and Shadows of New York Life: Or, The Sights and Sensations of the Great City. A Work Descriptive of the City of New York in All Its Various Phases; With Full and Graphic Accounts of Its Splendors and Wretchedness; Its High and Low Life; Its Marble Palaces and Dark Dens; Its Attractions and Dangers; Its Rings and Frauds; Its Leading Men and Politicians; Its Adventurers; Its Charities; Its Mysteries, and Its Crimes* (Philadelphia: National Publishing Company, 1872).

48 **"a kind of Real Estate Board brochure":** Rovere (1986), 116.

48 **New York, from being:** Howe and Hummel (2009), 5.

48 **Ships are unloading cargoes:** Howe and Hummel (2009), 21–22.

49 **FN would not be coined until 1876:** Morris (2006), 161.

49 **FN "A converted Pennsylvania Railroad station":** Ibid.

49 **the stores would not come:** See, e.g., Elaine S. Abelson, *When Ladies Go A-Thieving:*

Middle-Class Shoplifters in the Victorian Department Store (New York: Oxford University Press, 1992; originally published 1989), passim; Leach (1989), 106.

50 **"marble palace":** Christopher Gray, "Streetscapes: The A. T. Stewart Department Store; A City Plan to Revitalize the 1846 'Marble Palace,'" *New York Times,* March 20, 1994; Section 7: 10.

50 **Opened in 1846 and spanning four stories:** Ibid.

50 **five stories and an entire city block:** Ibid.

50 **"Traditional dry-goods store interiors":** Abelson (1992), 75.

50 **The aim of the department store:** Abelson (1992), 6.

51 **would not begin the transition to glass:** Abelson (1992), 76.

51 **the shoplifter should attire herself:** Howe and Hummel (2009), 47ff.

51 **"with broad, strong bands":** Howe and Hummel (2009), 47.

51 **"Upon selecting a store":** Howe and Hummel (2009), 48.

51 **Asking the saleswoman:** Ibid.

52 **the retrofitted muff:** Howe and Hummel (2009), 47–48.

52 **"In the bottom of the muff":** Howe and Hummel (2009), 48.

52 **At police headquarters:** Howe and Hummel (2009), 49.

53 **an impeccable leather valise:** Howe and Hummel (2009), 50–51.

53 **a confederate—and a discreet piece of string:** Howe and Hummel (2009), 44–45.

53 **"While pretending to examine them":** Howe and Hummel (2009), 45.

CHAPTER FOUR: HOME IMPROVEMENTS

57 **"She would buy":** "A Queen Among Thieves."

57 **"She was scheming":** Quoted in Carl Sifakis, *The Encyclopedia of American Crime* (New York: Smithmark, 1992; originally published 1982), 470.

57 **actor and musician turned robber:** Lyons (2019), 95.

57 **For a sealskin bag:** Holub (2007), 69.

57 **FN the soft, fine-spun undercoat:** victoriana.com/Shawls/kashmir-shawl.html.

57 **FN "at Messrs. A. T. Stewart & Co.'s":** "The Christmas Holidays: What There Is to Purchase and Where It May Be Found." *New-York Times,* Dec. 21, 1865, 8.

58 **"Mandelbaum gained respect":** Holub (2007), 131.

58 **When she first rented:** Holub (2007), 50.

58 **lived next door:** Holub (2007), 48,

58 **buy the whole building:** Holub (2007), 81.

58 **also own warehouses:** Holub (2007), 48.

58 **FN "She also held property":** Ibid.

58 **paid the monthly rental:** Murphy (2010), 135.

58 **were doing a stretch:** Ibid.

58 **"Mrs. Mandelbaum invariably refused":** "A Queen Among Thieves."

58 **purchase her entire building:** Holub (2007), 81.

58 **actually conjoined buildings:** Holub (2007), 50–51.

58 **79 Clinton and 163 Rivington:** Holub (2007), 50.

58 **net worth was $5,000:** Ibid.

58 **increase at least a hundredfold:** Per Holub (2007), 1, Mrs. Mandelbaum had amassed a personal fortune of at least half a million dollars (in some estimates as much as $1 million) by the time of her death in 1894.

59 **"Mrs. Mandelbaum was very suspicious":** "A Queen Among Thieves."

59 **"No one could stand":** Ibid.

59 **"the most notorious depot":** "Old 'Mother' Mandelbaum Is Dead: She Was a Famous 'Fence' Well Known to the Police of This City," *New York Times,* Feb. 27, 1894, 9.

59   **"Every member of the underworld":** Lyons (2019), 116.

59   **a heavy oak door:** Ibid.

59   **heavy steel bars:** Ibid.

59   **"'Mother' Mandelbaum was never seen":** Lyons (2019), 112.

59   **"But, realizing that thieves":** Lyons (2019), 116.

60   **a trick chimney:** Lyons (2019), 116–17.

60   **a hidden lever:** Conway (2014), 51.

60   **more secret chambers:** Lyons (2019), 116–17.

60   **a bulk storage area:** Lyons (2019), 117.

60   **until "the heat was off":** Cf. Holub (2007), 51.

60   **the shipping department:** Lyons (2019), 117.

60   **A third room:** Ibid.

60   **"At the end of the passageway":** Lyons (2019), 117.

61   **a combination boardroom:** Lyons (2019), 115.

61   **"Many able and successful":** Ibid.

61   **immigrant German artisans:** Holub (2007), 50–51.

61   **"Suppose you are a burglar":** Lyons (2019), 113–14.

61   **FN "Some merchandise I would alter":** Steffensmeier and Ulmer (2005), 119–20.

62   **80 percent of U.S. textile imports:** Holub (2007), 66.

62   **FN Ready-to-wear skirts and shirtwaists:** Nancy L. Green, *Ready-to-Wear and Ready-to-Work: A Century of Industry and Immigrants in Paris and New York* (Durham, N.C.: Duke University Press, 1997), 23.

62   **comprising 40 or more yards:** See, e.g., "Wide-Awake Retailing: A Bolt of Silk's Story," *Dry Goods Economist* (March 2, 1918), 41, which describes a 60-yard bolt of silk crêpe de Chine.

63   **inhabited by pickpockets:** Lyons (2019), 117.

63   **Just above the pickpockets:** Oller (2021), 38.

63   **"shakedown workers":** Steffensmeier and Ulmer (2005), 216.

63   **muggers, stickup men:** Ibid.; Oller (2021), 38.

63   **house burglars, or "sneak thieves":** Oller (2021), 38.

63   **forgers and counterfeiters:** Steffensmeier and Ulmer (2005), 216.

63   **FN "Already within the Elizabethan":** Steffensmeier and Ulmer (2005), 215.

63   **"the aristocrats of the underworld":** Lyons (2019), 117.

63   **"the High Mob":** "Attack and Defence in Burglary," *Daily News* (London), Nov. 2, 1897, 5.

64   **a safe-company employee:** Johnson (1979), 57.

64   **"the champion burglar":** Walling (1887), 286.

64   **"'Marm' Mandelbaum's methods":** Walling (1887), 285–86.

65   **"Her custom to rent":** "Old Mother Mandelbaum," *New York Star.*

65   **In 1876, for instance:** Ibid.

65   **Johnny Irving and Billy Valte:** Ibid.

65   **$50,000 worth of silk:** Ibid.

65   **a Lower Manhattan stable:** Ibid.

65   **in the Hackensack Meadowlands:** Ibid.

65   **"was carted piecemeal":** Ibid.

65   **"With silk":** "A Queen Among Thieves."

66   **sixty-five cents a yard:** Holub (2007), 69.

66   **thousands of dollars' worth of silk:** "Mrs. Mandelbaum's Riches."

66   **as in 1875:** Holub (2007), 55–56.

66   **"None of the merchandise":** Holub (2007), 56.

66   **"The bulls toss stocks":** "The Situation: The Excitement Everywhere," New York *Herald,* Oct. 9, 1862, 4.

66 **a military expedition to Canada:** "A History of American Currency," American Numismatic Society, numismatics.org/a-history-of-american-currency/.

66 **believed to be the first issue:** Ibid.

66 **Other American colonies:** "The History of U.S. Currency," U.S. Currency Education Program, uscurrency.gov/history.

66 **all thirteen colonies were issuing:** "A History of American Currency."

67 **widely distrusted:** Ibid.

67 **before long was devalued:** Ibid.

67 **FN "not worth a Continental":** "The History of U.S. Currency."

67 **Mindful of this history:** H[enry] W[illiam] Brands, *Greenback Planet: How the Dollar Conquered the World and Threatened Civilization as We Know It* (Austin: University of Texas Press, 2011), 1.

67 **"Demand Notes":** "A History of American Currency."

67 **seven designated banks:** Ibid.

67 **less readily redeemable:** Ibid.

67 **"United States Notes":** "The History of U.S. Currency."

67 **FN "the Confederate government printed":** Brands (2011), 9.

67 **FN import duties or interest on federal bonds:** Brands (2011), 12.

67 **"The dollar had been":** Brands (2011), 1.

68 **on February 25, 1862:** Andrew Glass, "This Day in Politics: Congress passes Legal Tender Act, Feb. 25, 1862," *Politico*, Feb. 25, 2019, politico.com/story/2019/02/25/this-day-in-politics-february-25-1180225. See also "A Bill to Authorize the Issue of United States Notes and for the Redemption or Funding Thereof, and for the Funding of the Floating Debt of the United States," H.R. 240, Thirty-seventh Congress, Second Session, Jan. 28, 1862, congress.gov/bill/37th-congress/house-bill/240. Full text of the debate over H.R. 240 is reproduced in E[lbridge] G[erry] Spaulding, *A Resource of War: The Credit of the Government Made Immediately Available. History of the Legal Tender Paper Money Issued During the Great Rebellion. Being a Loan Without Interest and a National Currency* (Buffalo, N.Y.: Express Printing Company, 1869).

68 **FN only in 1933:** Craig K. Elwell, "Brief History of the Gold Standard in the United States," Congressional Research Service, Report R41887, June 23, 2011, crsreports.congress.gov/product/details?prodcode=R41887.

68 **a constellation of national banks:** Steven H. Jaffe and Jessica Lautin, *Capital of Capital: Money, Banking + Power in New York City, 1784–2012* (New York: Museum of the City of New York/Columbia University Press, 2014), 78–79.

68 **intended to make the new money:** Jaffe and Lautin (2014), 78.

68 **$150 million:** Brands (2011), 12.

68 **nearly $500 million:** Glass (2019).

68 **"Fully recognizable professional crime":** Papke (1987), 14.

68 **had been relatively rare:** Inciardi (1975), 13.

CHAPTER FIVE: OCEAN'S FOUR

70 **Monday, June 28, 1869:** "A Bold Bank Robbery: The Ocean National Bank Burglariously Entered," *New York Herald*, June 29, 1869, 3.

70 **Edward Dunn:** Walling (1887), 247.

70 **from the bank president's private office:** Ibid.

70 **It was gunpowder:** "A Bold Bank Robbery."

70 **triple-locked vault:** Walling (1887), 247.

70 **granite blocks and lined with iron:** Walling (1887), 248.

70 **outer door was standing open:** Walling (1887), 247.

70 **books, papers, discarded clothing:** Ibid.

70 **nickels in still-smoldering cloth bags:** Ibid.

70 **a dark lantern, half-eaten sandwiches:** Walling (1887), 249.

70 **tin safe-deposit boxes:** Ibid.; "A Bold Bank Robbery."

70 **The lock on the vault's outer door:** Walling (1887), 247–48.

70 **likewise, that of the middle door:** Walling (1887), 247.

70 **an inch and a quarter thick:** Walling (1887), 248.

70 **"the force exerted":** "A Bold Bank Robbery."

71 **here the smell of powder:** Walling (1887), 249.

71 **The floor was another riot:** Ibid.; "A Bold Bank Robbery."

71 **vaunted as burglarproof:** Walling (1887), 248.

71 **painstakingly drilled open:** George M. White, alias George Bliss, *From Boniface to Bank Burglar: Or, the Price of Persecution. How a Successful Business Man, Through the Miscarriage of Justice, Became a Notorious Bank Looter* (Bellows Falls, Vt.: Truax Printing Company, 1905), 331.

71 **blasted clean off its hinges:** White (1905), 333–34.

71 **"a most audacious burglary":** "A Bold Bank Robbery."

71 **a crowd of panicked depositors:** Ibid.

71 **tried to rush the front door:** Ibid.

71 **FN Glass-Steagall Act:** "Banking Act of 1933 (Glass-Steagall)," Federal Reserve History, federalreservehistory.org/essays/glass-steagall-act.

71 **nearly $800,000:** Walling (1887), 250, says that the bank put the figure at $768,879.74.

71 **well over $1 million:** "Another Wholesale Bank Robbery in New York—The Ocean National Bank Broken Open and Plundered" (Baltimore *Sun*, June 29, 1869, 1), estimates the loss to have been "two millions of dollars." White (1905), 344, puts the gross haul at $2.75 million—nearly $60 million in today's money.

71 **then the largest bank burglary:** White (1905), 336.

71 **"There is no clue":** "Another Wholesale Bank Robbery in New York."

71 **expensive jewelry:** "A Bold Bank Robbery."

71 **some $50,000 in gold coins:** Ibid.

71 **the welter of tools and equipment:** See, e.g., ibid.; Walling (1887), 249ff.

71 **"Every thing that could suggest":** "Another Great Bank Robbery," *Maine Farmer*, July 10, 1869, 3.

72 **all 125 pounds of it:** White (1905), 330.

72 **more than a hundred different sizes:** "The Ocean Bank Robbery—The Total Loss Over Half a Million of Dollars," unattributed wire-service article published, e.g., in Baltimore *Sun*, July 1, 1869, 1.

72 **"six or seven overcoats":** "A Bold Bank Robbery."

72 **"three pairs of elegant rubber shoes":** Ibid.

72 **"various kinds of liquor":** "Another Great Bank Robbery."

72 **"The entire kit":** "A Bold Bank Robbery."

72 **"It is more than a business":** "The Ocean Bank Robbery."

72 **"Most of the articles":** Quoted in ibid.

72 **more than $5,000:** Conway (2009), 80–81, says that Mrs. Mandelbaum backed the enterprise with an initial contribution of $3,000, followed by a second contribution of $1,000.

74 **"Cracksmen of this class":** Byrnes (1969), 2.

74 **It requires rare qualities:** Ibid.

74 **many months of planning:** White (1905), 204ff., 236, 320ff.

74 **featured four principals:** See, e.g., Byrnes (1969), 139–40; Shayne Davidson, *Queen of the Burglars: The Scandalous Life of Sophie Lyons.* (Jefferson, N.C.: Exposit Books, 2020), 32; and White (1905), 243ff., 319ff., 341ff. While the first-person account of the

robbery in White's memoir features Shinburn prominently, it does not mention Hope or Lyons by name, referring instead (319) to "two men"—almost certainly Hope and Lyons—who helped him and Shinburn keep watch on the bank from accommodations across the street. The omission doubtless owed to White's unwillingness to compromise associates who were still living: Ned Lyons died in 1907; Hope, who died in June 1905, may still have been alive when White's book was first published. (By that time, Shinburn, who lived until 1916, was comfortably ensconced in a European castle, well out of reach of American law enforcement.) Both Byrnes and Davidson identify all four men—White (aka George Bliss), Shinburn, Hope and Lyons—as the prime movers of the Ocean National Bank robbery. White died in 1909.

74 FN **Myriad modern-day sources:** See, e.g., Conway (2009), 75ff.; Conway (2014), 62, 82–83; Jerry Clark and Ed Palattella, *A History of Heists: Bank Robbery in America* (Lanham, Md.: Rowman & Littlefield, 2015), 53; Davidson (2020), 32ff.; L[arry] R. Kirchner, *Robbing Banks: An American History, 1831–1999* (Edison, N.J.: Castle Books, 2003; originally published 2001), 24; Geoff Manaugh, *A Burglar's Guide to the City* (New York: Farrar, Straus & Giroux, 2016), 10; Sifakis (1992), 421; Duane Swierczynski, *This Here's a Stick-Up: The Big Bad Book of American Bank Robbery* (Indianapolis: Alpha Books, 2002), 25.

74 FN **"probably had nothing to do":** Oller (2021), 58.

74 **alias George Bliss:** White (1905), iii.

74 **a Massachusetts hotelkeeper:** "Bank Robber Who Exposed Secrets in Book Is Dead: George White Regarded Burglary as a Respectable Profession," New York *Evening World,* Feb. 13, 1909, 10.

74 **who in 1864:** White (1905), 9.

75 **Maximilian Schenbein:** Johnson (1979), 57; also spelled Schoenbein, per Ben Macintyre, *The Napoleon of Crime: The Life and Times of Adam Worth, the Real Moriarty* (London: HarperPress, 2012), 29; originally published 1997. Shinburn's other aliases, per ibid., included M. H. Baker, M. H. Zimmerman and The Dutchman.

75 **Prussian-born burglar:** Nadel (1990), 88.

75 **aristocratic yearnings:** Ibid.

75 **"a daring and skillful":** Byrnes (1969), 82.

75 **English-born husband:** Byrnes (1969), 139.

75 **a former protégé of Hope's:** Byrnes (1969), 139–40.

75 **sundry supporting players:** Byrnes (1969), 140.

75 **The first recorded bank burglary:** Clark and Palattella (2015), 14.

75 **took place in 1831:** Jeff Nilsson, "America's (Not Quite) First Bank Robbery," *Saturday Evening Post,* March 16, 2013, saturdayeveningpost.com/2013/03/first-bank-robbery-in-united-states.

75 **homemade duplicate keys:** Nilsson (2013).

75 FN **taken place in Philadelphia in 1798:** Ron Avery, "America's First Bank Robbery," Carpenters' Hall (n.d.), carpentershall.org/americas-first-bank-robbery. For a first-person account by a man wrongly imprisoned for the crime, see Patrick Lyon, *The Narrative of Patrick Lyon: Who Suffered Three Months Severe Imprisonment in Philadelphia Gaol, on Merely a Vague Suspicion of Being Concerned in the Robbery of the Bank of Pennsylvania, With His Remarks Thereon* (Philadelphia: Francis and Robert Bailey, 1799).

75 FN **$162,821:** Avery (n.d.).

75 **52 Wall Street:** Clark and Palattella (2015), 14.

75 **$245,00:** Nilsson (2013).

75 **"138,911 dollars":** "Most Extensive Robbery," *National Gazette and Literary Register,* Philadelphia, March 22, 1831, 2.

75 **"200 doubloons":** Byrnes (1969),

75 **surreptitious wax impressions:** Nilsson (2013).

75 **metal-plated wooden chests:** Byrne (2016), 18–19.

75 **picked up, carried off:** Swierczynski (2002), 220.

75 **"The essential design":** Byrne (2016), 22.

75 **FN James Honeyman and William J. Murray:** Nilsson (2013).

75 **FN five years in Sing Sing:** Nilsson (2013).

75 **Partly in response:** Clark and Palattella (2015), 15.

75 **The escalating war:** Byrne (2016), 6, 29; Oller (2021), 41–42.

76 **Combination locks were not widely adopted:** Oller (2021), 41.

76 **Lillie Safe Company of Troy, New York:** "Lillie Safe Co.," *Friends of Albany History,* April 5, 2019, friendsofalbanyhistory.wordpress.com/tag/lillie-safe-co.

76 **in 1860:** Oller (2021), 41.

76 **only three numbers:** Ibid.

76 **numbered from 0 to 100:** Ibid.

76 **nearly a million:** Carl Hammer, *Expedient B&E: Tactics and Techniques for Bypassing Alarms and Defeating Locks* (Boulder, Colo.: Paladin Press, 1992), 49; Christopher Baltus, personal communication.

76 **nearly 100 million:** Ibid.

76 **telltale clicks:** Oller (2021), 41.

76 **Electronic stethoscopes:** Hammer (1992), 50.

76 **until the mid-twentieth century:** "Device Makes Heart Beats More Audible to Doctor," *Buffalo Evening News* via Associated Press, Oct. 21, 1944, 6.

76 **gunpowder, dynamite:** Oller (1941).

76 **"Gunpowder first appeared":** Johnson (1979), 56.

77 **the Little Joker:** White (1905), 185.

77 **FN White himself takes credit:** White (1905), 204ff.

77 **FN Other accounts:** See, e.g., Clark and Palattella (2015), 54; Conway (2014), 81; Kirchner (2003), 25; and Swierczynski (2002), 25. But as Oller (2021), 57, writes, "Despite many claims to the contrary, there is no evidence that Leslie ever used, much less invented, the little joker, which had become obsolete around the time Leslie's career was taking off."

77 **Connecticut, Vermont and Maryland:** Oller (2021), 41.

77 **a bank burglary in New Jersey:** Ibid.

77 **"After that":** Ibid.

77 **Founded after the Civil War:** I[saac] Smith Homans, Jr., *The Merchants and Bankers' Almanac* (New York: Bankers' Magazine and Statistical Register, 1868), 77–78.

77 **a brownstone building:** Davidson (2020), 32.

77 **southeast corner of Fulton and Greenwich streets:** White (1905), 43.

77 **late in 1868:** White (1905), 216, 223.

77 **John Taylor:** White (1905), 217.

78 **Taylor had a gambling problem:** White (1905), 217ff.

78 **Taylor supplied White:** White (1905), 246.

78 **"The lock on the vault":** White (1905), 234.

78 **"I had seen from the first":** White (1905), 236.

78 **couldn't get close enough:** Ibid.

78 **in the guise of an out-of-town banker:** White (1905), 237–39.

78 **The company was only too happy:** White (1905), 238–39.

78 **he schooled the young clerk:** White (1905), 240.

78 **"We kept at it":** Ibid.

78 **In January 1869:** White (1905), 319.

79 **Consulting with Shinburn:** White (1905), 320.

79 **"We discussed the advisability":** Ibid.

79 In March, a man called Kohler: White (1905), 321.

79 FN In one later account: Conway (2009), 81.

79 Mark Shinburn's brother-in-law: White (1905), 321.

79 directly under the office: White (1905), 322.

79 FN The burglars' modus operandi anticipates: Sir Arthur Conan Doyle, "The Red-Headed League," in *The Complete Sherlock Holmes*, Volume 1 (Garden City, N.Y.: Doubleday & Company, 1930), 176–90.

79 FN a Sherlock Holmes story of 1891: Matthew E. Bunson, *Encyclopedia Sherlockiana: An A-to-Z Guide to the World of the Great Detective* (New York: Macmillan, 1994), xv.

79 bespoke burglar's tools: White (1905), 323.

79 in May: Ibid.

79 together with explosives: Ibid.

79 with blankets hung: White (1905), 322.

79 "When the plastering": White (1905), 324.

79 Their tools had been designed: Ibid.

80 "We used up": White (1905), 324.

80 on Canal Street: White (1905), 325.

80 place to store their tools: Ibid.

80 Just after eleven o'clock:White (1905), 328–29.

80 Stripped to their underclothes: White (1905), 328.

80 Three hours later: White (1905), 329.

80 not to damage the carpet: White (1905), 329–30.

80 The shutters on the windows: White (1905), 330.

80 the almost imperceptible light of a cigar: Ibid.

80 hanging up just inside the first: White (1905), 329.

80 only cash and negotiable securities: White (1905), 331.

80 "That was not our graft": Ibid.

81 "The cutting, or drilling": Ibid.

81 much sterner stuff: Ibid.

81 The space inside the vault: Ibid.

81 they withdrew: White (1905), 332.

81 bracing it underneath: Ibid.

81 The next afternoon: White (1905), 333.

82 They realized: Ibid.

82 White gave instructions: Ibid.

82 "Shinburn and I at once": White (1905), 333–34.

82 "rumble and gongs": White (1905), 334.

82 "Shinburn turned the switch": Ibid.

82 FN "a division of the Hell's Kitchen gangs": Inciardi (1975), 13.

82 into a small trunk: White (1905), 334.

82 two feet long and a foot high: "Ocean Bank Robbery: Recovery of $268,021 of the Stolen Securities," *New-York Times*, July 1, 1869, 8.

82 boarded a waiting carriage: White (1905), 335.

82 a time-honored way: Hector L. MacQueen, ed., *Money Laundering*, Hume Papers on Public Policy, Volume 1, No. 2 (Edinburgh: Edinburgh University Press, 1993), 13.

82 "Nearly all of the $800,000": Conway (2009), 94. This observation is reprised in Conway (2014), 65.

83 as much as 50 percent: Conway (2014), 65.

83 On Wednesday, June 30: "$500 Reward and No Questions Asked," *New York Herald*, June 30, 1869, 7.

83 $3,500 in bonds: Ibid.

83 "NO QUESTIONS ASKED": Ibid.

83 **were widely suspected:** Oller (2021), 43.

83 **no one was charged:** Ibid.; Davidson (2020), 33.

83 **the afternoon of June 30:** "Crime: The Ocean Bank Robbery. Railroad Bonds, Bank Checks, and Other Securities to the Amount of $268,021.29 Returned," *New-York Tribune*, July 1, 1869, 2.

83 **"known to the police":** Ibid.

83 **FN "an alternative to the barroom":** Timothy J. Haggerty, personal communication.

83 **attached to the cord was a note:** Ibid.

83 **summoned a passing policeman:** Ibid.

83 **the Franklin Street station house:** Ibid.

83 **a dead infant:** "Crime: The Ocean Bank Robbery."

83 **"infernal machine":** "The Ocean Bank Robbery: Three Hundred Thousand Dollars Graciously Returned."

83 **Captain John Jourdan:** White (1905), 289.

83 **$268,000 in railroad bonds:** "Crime: The Ocean Bank Robbery."

84 **in the same trunk:** Ibid.

84 **"filled the hearts":** "Ocean Bank Robbery: Recovery of $268,021 of the Stolen Securities."

84 **"The police seemed to have":** "Crime: The Ocean Bank Robbery."

84 **a negotiated settlement:** Walling (1887), 252.

84 **"having a safe outlet":** Walling (1887), 291.

84 **"The policy of the bank":** Walling (1887), 250.

CHAPTER SIX: BUREAU FOR THE PREVENTION OF CONVICTION

85 **one of the best known—and richest:** Holub (2007), 52.

85 **"It takes money":** Walling (1887), 279.

86 **She was said, for instance:** Macintyre (2012), 194.

86 **at least $150,000:** Macintyre (2012), 35.

86 **in some estimates:** Macintyre (2012), 36.

86 **Boylston National Bank:** Macintyre (2012), 34ff.

86 **in November 1869:** Macintyre (2012), 35.

86 **Adam Worth, "Piano Charley" Bullard and Ike Marsh:** Macintyre (2012), 34.

86 **the previous spring:** Macintyre (2012), 31–32.

86 **"almost certainly Marm Mandelbaum":** Macintyre (2012), 32.

86 **for train robbery:** Macintyre (2012), 32.

86 **an empty office building next door:** Conway (2014), 69–70.

86 **a partner, Mark Shinburn:** Macintyre (2012), 32.

86 **tunnel covertly through:** Ibid.

86 **FN "was the first and only time":** Ibid.

86 **makers of patent medicine:** Lyons (2019), 30.

86 **erected a partition:** Ibid.

86 **"Gray's Oriental Tonic":** "The Boston Bank Robbery: Full Particulars of the Burglarious Operations at the Boylston National Bank," *New York Herald*, Nov. 24, 1869, 8, via *Boston Post*.

86 **had specially brewed:** "The Boston Bank Robbery."

86 **"Quite what was in":** Macintyre (2012), 34.

86 **FN "The partition was to hide":** Lyons (2019), 30.

87 **a week of nocturnal tunneling:** Ibid.

87 **shipped by train:** Swierczynski (2002), 49.

87 **laundered by Marm:** Macintyre (2012), 37–38.

87 *Ragged Dick:* Horatio Alger, *Ragged Dick: Or, Street Life in New York with the Boot-Blacks* (Boston: James Loring, Publisher), 1868.

87 five sequels: Michael Zuckerman, "The Nursery Tales of Horatio Alger," *American Quarterly* 24:2 (May 1972), 191.

87 "The Honorable and Mrs.": Holub (1998), 33.

87 FN sometimes called Frances: See, e.g., Walling (1887), 280.

87 "thieves knew": Holub (2007), 76.

87 jewel thief and blackmailer: Holub (2007), 114.

87 Hackensack, New Jersey, mansion: Ibid.

88 flaunting an emerald ring: Macintyre (1997), 27.

88 the guest was a judge: Conway (2009), 78.

88 "It just goes to prove": Holub (2007), 114–15.

88 FN In one account: Conway (2009), 77–78.

88 newspaper articles described: See, e.g., "Burglary as an Art: Personal Habits of the Fraternity," *New-York Times,* March 7, 1875, 10.

89 Once a bright reporter: Hapgood (1903), 251–52.

89 FN The English translation: Jackson (1875).

89 FN on December 21, 1874: "Amusements: Union Square Theatre," Advertisement, *New-York Times,* Dec. 18, 1874, 7.

89 FN "old hag": Jackson (1875), 51.

89 FN Marie Wilkins: Internet Broadway Database, ibdb.com/broadway-cast-staff/marie-wilkins-64960.

89 FN "sat in a box one night": "One Woman's Career: How Mother Mandelbaum Gained Her Notoriety as a Fence," *New York Evening World,* March 10, 1894, 6.

89 FN The play was filmed: Internet Movie Database, imdb.com/title/tt0012532/.

89 Congregation Temple Rodeph Sholom: Holub (2007), 101.

89 FN established in Lower Manhattan in 1842: "Congregation Rodeph Sholom," rodephsholom.org/about-us/our-history.

89 Her neighbors adored her: Holub (2007), 59.

90 "All of her children": Holub (2007), 60.

90 "as a woman and a mother": Walling (1887), 289.

91 hosted elegant dances: Asbury (2008), 195.

91 "company picnics": Holub (2007), 48.

91 reported in 1884: "Between Two Fires: The Unhappy Condition of Marm Mandelbaum and Confederates," *Detroit Free Press,* Dec. 10, 1884, 2.

91 "'Marm' Mandelbaum was": Walling (1887), 281.

91 She attained a reputation: Walling (1887), 281, 286.

91 a fence confronts two threats: Steffensmeier (1986), 3.

92 "criminals lack the institutional supports": Steffensmeier (1986), 3.

92 William Mosher and Joe Douglas: Asbury (2008), 195–96.

92 the most notorious kidnapping: Ibid. See also Carrie Hagen, *We Is Got Him: The Kidnapping That Changed America* (New York: Overlook Press, 2011).

92 The child was never found: Asbury (2008), 196.

92 FN Mosher and Douglas were shot: Hagen (2011), 172ff.

92 a bank heist, underwritten by Marm: This is the burglary, in 1878, of the Dexter Savings Bank, discussed in Chapter Seven.

92 "captain of crime": Holub (2007), 52.

92 "There are thieves and receivers": "Crime and the Police."

92 "She changed character": Walling (1887), 281.

93 Founded in 1788: Frank Vos, "Tammany Hall," in Jackson (2010), 1277 [hereafter Vos (2010a)].

93 **a fraternal organization of craftsmen:** Ibid.

93 **"By the end of the Civil War":** Anbinder (2001), 147.

93 **diamond-decked, mansion-dwelling, kickback-grubbing:** See, e.g., Allen J. Share, "Tweed, William M(agear) 'Boss,'" in Jackson (2010), 1431.

93 **FN from 1863 to 1871:** Share (2010).

93 **FN a range of elective offices:** Ibid.

93 **between $30 million and $200 million:** "Boss Tweed," *Encyclopaedia Britannica*, britannica.com/biography/Boss-Tweed.

93 **"an empire of patronage":** Callow (1969), 8.

93 **an 1878 investigation found:** *Report of the Special Committee of the Board of Aldermen Appointed to Investigate the "Ring" Frauds: Together With the Testimony Elicited During the Investigation* (New York: Martin B. Brown, Printer and Stationer, 1878), 13–14.

93 **This surplus was split:** Ibid.

93 **It is not known:** Holub (2007), 176.

94 **"Whether or not Mandelbaum":** Holub (2007), 176–77; italics in original.

94 **In an era before:** Czitrom (2016), xiii, 70–71, and Anbinder (2001), 328, also make this point.

94 **"The ward captain":** Callow (1969), 104.

94 **an alderman, state senator:** Frank Vos, "Plunkitt, George Washington," in Jackson (2010), 1004 [hereafter Vos (2010b)]. See also Mann (1963).

94 **"I seen my opportunities":** Riordon (1963), 3.

94 **more than $1 million:** Mann (1963), x.

94 **"honest graft":** Riordon (1963), 3.

94 **Everybody is talkin':** Riordon (1963), 3–5.

95 **another rung on the "crooked ladder":** O'Kane (1992), 28.

95 **until 1920:** "19th Amendment to the U.S. Constitution: Women's Right to Vote (1920)," National Archives, archives.gov/milestone-documents/19th-amendment.

95 **Nor did they have access:** I am indebted to Timothy J. Haggerty for this observation.

96 **"In this way":** Holub (2007), 57.

96 **"crime organizes successfully":** Holub (2007), 91–92.

97 **"Machine rule":** Callow (1969), 146; italics added.

97 **the 300-pound form:** Browning and Gerassi (1980), 150.

97 **"probably the most corrupt":** Ibid.

97 **a bookseller and publisher:** "Obituary: George Washington Matsell," *Philadelphia Inquirer*, July 26, 1877, 4.

97 **he would one day own:** John Rickards Betts, "Sporting Journalism in Nineteenth-Century America," *American Quarterly* 5:1 (Spring 1953), 42. Matsell bought the publication in 1856.

97 **Before his tenure was out:** Richardson (1970), 69–70.

97 **"Beastly Bloated Booby":** Quoted in Robert Ernst, "The One and Only Mike Walsh," *New-York Historical Society Quarterly* 36:1 (January 1952), 51.

97 **a twenty-room summer home:** Browning-Gerassi (1980), 151; Richardson (1970), 69–70.

97 **where he entertained visitors:** Richardson (1970), 70.

98 **"politically protected vice":** Czitrom (2016), ix.

98 **nearly seven hundred witnesses:** Czitrom (2016), x.

98 **FN convened in February 1894:** Czitrom (2016), 135.

98 **FN in early 1885:** Czitrom (2016), x–xi.

98 **FN "to a powerful national movement":** Czitrom (2016), xi.

98 **"A veritable parade":** Ibid.

98 **"the unholy wolf police":** "Plain Talk About Byrnes: Dr. Parkhurst Discusses the Superintendent," *New-York Daily Tribune*, Sept. 21, 1894, 5. The quotation is from

the Reverend Dr. John A. B. Wilson, pastor of New York's Eighteenth Street Methodist Episcopal Church.

98 **"Tribute from harlots":** *New York Morning Journal*, June 6, 1895, n.p. Quoted in Czitrom (2016), 196–97.

98 **"Bureau for the Prevention":** Walling (1887), 281.

98 **"With the capital":** Holub (2007), 57. The interpolated quotation is from the *New-York Tribune*, July 23, 1884, n.p.

98 **time-honored components:** Steffensmeier (1986), 180; Stuart Henry, "On the Fence," *British Journal of Law and Society* 4:1 (Summer 1977), 132; Robert M. Yoder, "The Best Friend a Thief Ever Had," *Saturday Evening Post* (Dec. 25, 1954), 72.

99 **cash payments:** Holub (2007), 57, 196, 204.

99 **Line items include these:** White (1905), 348.

100 **"Bank Ring":** White (1905), 301.

100 **"to John Jourdan":** White (1905), 348.

100 **FN In April 1870:** "Jourdan Dead: Decease of the Police Superintendent Yesterday Morning," *New-York Times*, Oct. 11, 1870, 8.

100 **FN six months later, after an illness:** "Jourdan Dead."

100 **FN "inflexible integrity":** Quoted in ibid.

101 **Mrs. Mandelbaum included:** Gilfoyle (2006), 152.

101 **"Like Fagin":** "Record of Infamy: Career of Some of New York's Worst Criminals," *St. Johnsbury (Vt.) Index* via *New York Herald*, Nov. 1, 1883, 2.

101 **the 1875 raid:** "Burglary as an Art"; Holub (2007), 55–56.

101 **"some costly shawls":** "Burglary as an Art."

101 **"There was not the slightest":** Ibid.

101 **On another occasion:** "New York City," *New York Herald*, March 24, 1872, 10.

101 **Essex Market Courthouse:** Ibid.

101 **In March 1875:** Holub (2007), 50, note 84.

101 **at fifty-one:** Ibid.

101 **"wasting away disease":** Holub (2007), 49; 50, note 84.

101 **the family plot:** Holub (2007), 49–50.

101 **Union Field Cemetery:** Holub (2007), 28.

102 **from eight to fifteen:** Holub (2007), 27.

102 **her favorite thief:** Lyons (2019), 117, says that Mrs. Mandelbaum considered Leslie "her one pet and star."

102 **Broadway and Bleecker streets:** Oller (2021), 36.

102 **three years of planning:** Clark and Palattella (2015), 53; Oller (2021), 58.

CHAPTER SEVEN: WHERE THE MONEY WAS

103 **"King of the Bank Robbers":** See, e.g., Clark and Palattella (2015), 50; Oller (2021), 87; Swierczynski (2002), 24.

103 **some $7 million:** Walling (1887), 278.

103 **laundered by Marm:** Conway (2009), 80.

103 **"alias Western George":** Walling (1887), 269.

103 **born in the early 1840s:** Oller (2021), 58.

103 **moved to Cincinnati:** Ibid.

103 **prospered as a brewer:** Byrne (2016), 149.

103 **"His parents were well to do":** "The Yonkers Mystery," *New-York Times*, June 9, 1878, 2.

104 **FN The claim is reprised:** See, e.g., Asbury (2008), 185; Conway (2009), x; Conway (2014), 80; Kirchner (2003), 23; Swierczynski (2002), 24; Walling (1887), 269–70.

104 **There is no record:** Leo Hirtl, "City Needs Press Agent; Publicity's Not So Good," *Cincinnati Post,* July 24, 1947, 1.

104 **nor did the university grant:** Ibid.

104 **Entranced throughout his life:** Clark and Palattella (2015), 53.

104 **bestowed fondly by Marm:** Clark and Palattella (2015), 54.

104 **he disdained:** Clark and Palattella (2015), 53.

104 **he could often obtain bank blueprints:** Manaugh (2016), 6.

104 **re-create blueprints accurately:** Manaugh (2016), 7.

104 **starting in the 1860s:** Murphy (2010), 115.

104 **"consulting" burglar:** Asbury (2008), 191.

104 **"George Leslie's special gift":** Oller (2021), 57.

104 **Like a film director:** Ibid.

105 **Leslie moved to New York:** Manaugh (2016), 2.

105 **able to wangle an invitation:** Conway (2009), 28–29.

105 **She was quickly taken:** See, e.g., Harry Hill, " 'Old Mother Mandelbaum': A Character Dickens Would Have Been Delighted to Portray—History of a Remarkable Woman," *Boston Globe* via *New York Mercury,* Nov. 11, 1883, 16.

105 **"the chief of her clique":** Walling (1887), 269.

105 **"Outside of bank robberies":** "Geo. Howard, Burglar: An Extraordinary Career— College Graduate, Linguist and Scholar—Partner in Robberies to the Amount of $4,000,000—Shot Dead and His Body Left in the Woods," *Kansas Reporter,* April 10, 1879, 6, via New York *Sun.*

105 **she was urging him:** Conway (2009), 118.

105 **avoiding a storm of notoriety:** Ibid.

105 **swirling in the press:** See, e.g., "Fiskiana: 'Menelaus' Fisk, 'Belle Helene' Mansfield, 'Achilles' Stokes and 'Ulysses' Pittman in an Infernal Quadrille. How Fisk and Stokes Quarreled, Fought and Did Not Bleed About a Lady Fair with Jet Black Hair," *New York Herald,* Jan. 18, 1871, 5.

106 **FN With the financier Jay Gould:** Kenneth D. Ackerman, *The Gold Ring: Jim Fisk, Jay Gould, and Black Friday, 1869* (New York: Dodd, Mead, 1988).

106 **FN he was shot and killed:** "Death of James Fisk: Closing Scenes in the Life of the Great Speculator," *New-York Times,* Jan. 8, 1872, 1.

106 **also included George Leonidas Leslie:** Conway (2009), 76.

106 **would focus unwanted attention:** Conway (2009), 118.

106 **Mary Henrietta Coath:** Ibid.

106 **known as Mollie:** Also spelled "Molly."

106 **"resort for thieves":** "In Denial: What Draper, Porter and Irving Have to Say. They Deny the Accusation That They Had Any Complicity in George Howard's Death— The Shute Mystery Cleared Up. Who It Was That Robbed Morton's Safe. A History of George Howard's Wife. Who She Is and What She Was," *Brooklyn Daily Eagle,* March 12, 1879, 4.

106 **she was just fifteen:** Conway (2009), 118.

106 **a fellow boarder:** Ibid.

106 **"Pretty Tom" Parnell:** Ibid. His surname also appears as "Parrell," per "In Denial."

106 **she hired Parnell:** Conway (2009), 118–19.

106 **a jewelry store in Norristown, Pennsylvania:** Conway (2009), 118.

106 **Parnell was arrested:** Conway (2009), 119.

106 **Leslie settled in Brooklyn:** "In Denial."

106 **"Leslie was given":** Manaugh (2016), 7.

107 **Here Leslie's spatial skills:** Manaugh (2016), 7–8.

107 **Founded in 1851:** "Manhattan Savings Institution," history.hsbc.com/collections /global-archives/manhattan-savings-institution.

107 FN **The bank is today HSBC:** Ibid.

107 **deposits of $397,000:** Ibid.

107 **jewels, securities:** Conway (2009), ix.

107 **"composed of men":** Walling (1887), 278.

107 **a "pudding":** Walling (1887), 262.

107 **"The bank was wealthy":** Walling (1887), 262–63.

108 **In February 1878:** "Bank Treasurer Murdered," *New-York Times*, Feb. 24, 1878, 7.

108 **arrived separately:** Conway (2009), 170.

108 **totaling nearly $800,000:** Conway (2009), 169.

108 **James W. Barron:** Conway (2009), 172.

108 **many thousands of dollars:** Conway (2014), 86, puts her contribution at $30,000—more than $800,000 in today's money.

108 **getaway horse and sleigh:** Conway (2009), 170.

109 **stout railway trunks:** Conway (2009), 171.

109 **Leslie had planned and rehearsed:** Conway (2009), 169.

109 **this job was also intended:** Ibid.

109 **Johnny Irving, Billy Porter:** Conway (2009), 171.

109 **separate boardinghouses:** Ibid.

109 **Friday, February 22:** Ibid. gives the date as February 23, but it is clear from myriad newspaper accounts that the botched robbery took place on the evening of Friday, February 22, 1878, the night Barron failed to return home from work. See, e.g., "A Brave Cashier's Death: Further Particulars of the Attempted Bank Robbery in Dexter, Me.—How the Cashier Was Found," *Boston Globe*, Feb. 24, 1878, 1; "Bank Treasurer Murdered"; "Murdered: A Bank-Officer Suffers Death Rather Than Be False to His Trust," *Buffalo Commercial*, Feb. 25, 1878, 2, via New-York *Sun;* and elsewhere.

109 **an assortment of wigs:** Conway (2009), 171.

109 **stolen from New York's Grand Opera House:** Manaugh (2016), 10.

109 FN **The Opera House:** Michael Pollak, "F.Y.I.: Two-Track Soap Opera," *New York Times*, Aug. 20, 2006, 14:2.

109 FN **did not become a federal holiday:** "George Washington's Birthday," National Archives, Center for Legislative Archives, archives.gov/legislative/features/Washington.

109 **let them into the building:** Conway (2009), 170.

109 **skilled at defeating locks:** Lyons (2019), 89–90; Oller (2021), 62.

109 **planned to open the safe himself:** Conway (2009), 170.

110 **they got no answer:** Conway (2009), 171.

110 **They broke it down:** Ibid.

110 **reconsidered his involvement:** Conway (2009), 171–72.

110 **pistol-whipped and beat Barron:** Conway (2009), 172.

110 **"slashed him with knives":** Walling (1887), 245.

110 **Leslie tried to intervene:** Conway (2009), 172.

110 **the gang locked Barron:** "Bank Treasurer Murdered."

110 **gagged, handcuffed:** "A Brave Cashier's Death."

110 **$100 nabbed:** Conway (2009), 172.

110 **a $500 United States bond:** "Barron Proved No Hero: Shown to Be a Defaulter and a Suicide. Result of the Investigation of the Supposed Murder of the Cashier of the Dexter Savings Bank—A Defaulter to the Amount of $3,600—Taking Poison After Arranging the Appearance of Outrage." *New-York Times*, Feb. 1, 1879, 1.

110 **Discovered late that night:** "A Brave Cashier's Death."

110 **he died the next morning:** Ibid.

110 FN **None of Leslie's gang:** Walling (1887), 247.

110 FN **Much of the initial press coverage:** See, e.g., "A Brave Cashier's Death"; "Two

Murders: Two Terrible Chapters of Crime Among the Hills of New England. A Brave Cashier at Dexter, Maine, Who Died Rather Than Surrender. Murder in Western Massachusetts for the Sake of a Little Money," *Boston Post,* Feb. 25, 1878, 2. The scenario of Barron's non-involvement is reprised in Walling (1887), 244–47.

110   FN **several newspaper articles propounded:** See, e.g., "Light on the Barron Tragedy: Detectives Think That the Dead Cashier Committed Suicide—Further Investigation to Be Made—History of the Case," *New-York Times,* Jan. 31, 1879, 1; "Barron Proved No Hero"; "General Telegraph News: Barron's Book-Keeping. A Statement by the Trustees of Dexter Savings Bank—The Charges of False Entries Again Made," *New-York Times,* March 15, 1879, 2.

111   FN **convicted in 1888:** "David Stain," National Registry of Exonerations, law.umich .edu/special/exoneration/Pages/casedetailpre1989.aspx?caseid=309; "Oliver Cromwell," National Registry of Exonerations, law.umich.edu/special/exoneration/pages /casedetailpre1989.aspx?caseid=71.

111   FN **"He explained that he was angry":** Ibid.

111   **said to have been so shaken:** Walling (1887), 274.

111   **what was to be his magnum opus:** Oller (2021), 58.

111   **October 27, 1878:** Walling (1887), 261.

111   **his hands cuffed:** "A Great Bank Robbery: The Manhattan Savings Institution Robbed. The Janitor Handcuffed and Compelled to Give Up the Safe Keys and Tell the Combination," *New-York Times,* Oct. 28, 1878, 1.

111   **"he danced up and down":** Lyons (2019), 97.

111   **Louis Werkle:** Lyons (2019), 92.

111   **"The bank's been robbed!":** Walling (1887), 261.

111   **Just after six o'clock that morning:** Lyons (2019), 94.

111   **black muslin masks:** "A Great Bank Robbery."

111   **brandishing pistols:** Lyons (2019), 94.

111   **on the second floor:** "A Great Bank Robbery."

111   **"a little old man":** Ibid.

111   **less than three hours later:** Walling (1887), 266.

111   **nearly $3 million:** Lyons (2019), 86.

111   **"one of the most daring":** "A Great Bank Robbery."

111   **"Traveling Mike" Grady:** Conway (2009), 106; Walling (1887), 262.

111   **"the number-two fence":** Conway (2009), 181.

111   **he erected a stage set:** Conway (2009), 169.

112   **He obtained a lock:** Lyons (2019), 90.

112   **"undoubtedly was the greatest":** Ibid.

112   **Patrick Shevlin:** Walling (1887), 264; also spelled "Shevelin," per Lyons (2019), 87ff.

112   **substitute night watchman:** Lyons (2019), 92.

112   **Shevlin let Leslie:** Conway (2009), 177.

112   **varies with the telling:** Cf., e.g., Lyons (2019), 86ff.; Walling (1887), 261ff; Conway (2014), 89ff.; Oller (2021), 36ff.; James Lardner and Thomas Reppetto, *NYPD: A City and Its Police* (A John Macrae Book/Henry Holt, 2000), 72ff.; and "A Story of a Famous Bank Robbery Retold," *Banker's Magazine and Statistical Register* 44:1, July 1889, 64–65.

112   **the principal actors:** Walling (1887), 264: Oller (2021), 77; Conway (2014); Lardner and Reppetto (2000), 78.

112   **Billy Kelly:** Also spelled Kelley, per "William Kelley's Trial: The Purse the Burglars Raised—An Envelope Full of Money," *New-York Times,* Dec. 19, 1879, 8.

113   **on Saturday, October 26:** Lyons (2019), 93.

113   **in a storeroom:** Ibid.

113   **rubber-soled shoes:** Lyons (2019), 94.

113 **as he was dressing:** "A Great Bank Robbery."

113 **Shevlin had learned:** Lyons (2019), 93.

113 **employee of twenty years:** "A Great Bank Robbery."

113 **Pressing a gun:** Ibid.

113 **Werkle demurred at first:** Ibid.

113 **The gang bound:** Lyons (2019), 94.

113 **Johnny Hope and John Nugent:** Lyons (2019), 95.

113 **They left "Banjo Pete":** Lyons (2019), 95.

113 **armed with a feather duster:** Ibid.

113 **with false whiskers:** Ibid.

113 **bade him a cheery good morning:** Ibid.

113 **"the finest kit of tools":** Walling (1887), 266.

113 **paid for by Marm Mandelbaum:** "A Story of a Famous Bank Robbery Retold."

113 **several smaller compartments:** "A Great Bank Robbery."

113 **"The gang [was] growing":** Lyons (2019), 96.

113 **"ten extra minutes":** Lyons (2019), 94.

113 **$2,758,700:** Lyons (2019), 99.

113 **helped carry the bags:** Walling (1887), 266.

114 **"Though any number of clues":** "Talk, But No Business: The Police Still Hunting the Bank Burglars Without Success," *New-York Times*, Nov. 1, 1878, 8.

114 **Alcoholic, garrulous:** Lyons (2019), 97ff.

114 **initially promised $250,000:** Lyons (2019), 97.

114 **got just $600:** Lyons (2019), 98.

114 **he began airing his discontent:** Ibid.

114 **FN that would soon be known:** The *Oxford English Dictionary*'s first citation of "third degree" in this sense is from the *Harvard Lampoon* in 1880, though the practice itself demonstrably predates the phrase.

114 **FN "Perhaps he was a tyrant":** Jacob A. Riis, *The Making of an American: New Edition With Numerous Illustrations and an Introduction by Theodore Roosevelt* (New York: The Macmillan Company, 1919; originally published 1901), 341.

114 **chief of detectives:** "Thomas F. Byrnes Dead After 2 Years' Illness: Famous Police Superintendent a Victim of Chronic Indigestion. He Was a Terror to Crooks. Broke Up Band of Burglars That Took $3,000,000 From Manhattan Savings Bank," *Brooklyn Daily Eagle*, May 8, 1910, 7.

115 **named superintendent of police:** "Ex-Chief Byrnes Dies of Cancer: Best Known of All the City's Police Officials Had Been Ill Since August," *New-York Times*, May 8, 1910, 6.

115 **Johnny Hope and Billy Kelly:** Walling (1887), 268.

115 **FN Johnny Hope's conviction was overturned:** " 'Johnny' Hope Released: The Bank Burglar's Son Receives His Liberty From Gov. Hill," *New-York Times*, Oct. 23, 1890, 8.

115 **$90,000:** Murphy (2010), 116–17.

115 **John Nugent, was acquitted:** "An Impudent Demand," *New-York Times*, Feb. 17, 1880, 8.

115 **Eighteenth Precinct:** "Nugent Dismissed From the Force," *New-York Times*, Jan. 25, 1880, 10.

115 **June 4, 1878:** Conway (2009), 184.

115 **Tramp's Rock:** Ibid.

115 **expensive diamond pin:** "On a Murderer's Track," *New-York Times*, June 8, 1878, 5.

115 **shot in the chest:** Conway (2009), 184.

115 **a pearl-handled pistol:** Ibid.

115 **through the victim's head:** Ibid.

115 She was aware: Walling (1887), 269.
115 But traveling to Yonkers: Walling (1887), 269.
115 Hermann Stoude: Ibid.; Holub (2007), 51, for correct spelling.
115 he identified the dead man: Walling (1887), 269.
115 the clothes on his body: "On a Murderer's Track."
116 "[Leslie] had a wife": Ibid.
116 Babe Draper: Conway (2009), 151ff.
116 no one was ever charged: Conway (2009), 186.
116 at Draper's home in Brooklyn: Conway (2009), 185–86.
116 Mrs. Mandelbaum notified: Walling (1887), 278.
116 paid her fare: Ibid.
116 supplied her with money: Ibid.
116 paid the funeral expenses: Ibid.
116 "her one pet and star": Lyons (2019), 117.
116 Cypress Hills Cemetery: Clark and Palattella (2015), 56.
116 straddles Brooklyn and Queens: "Cypress Hills Cemetery: Map of Cemetery," cypresshillscemetery.org/map.
116 FN Other notable people: "Cypress Hill Cemetery: Famous & Notable Burials," cypresshillscemetery.org/timeline-2/notable-burials.
116 brought the young widow: Ford (1921), 50.
116 "this hard-faced": Ibid.
116 "Poor George": Ibid. Ford, writing in 1921 and hewing to the style of his era, rendered the quotation from Mrs. Mandelbaum in "eye dialect" ("Poor Shorge, he vas such a nais man!"), a mannerism that can be hard on modern eyes and discomforting to modern sensibilities. Throughout this book, I have rendered "eye dialect" from period sources in conventional English spelling.
117 $2,506,700 worth: "A Great Bank Robbery."
117 registered in the bank's name: Ibid.
117 most were recovered: Asbury (2008), 190–91.

CHAPTER EIGHT: THIEVES FALL OUT

121 "eight or nine pieces of silk": Article, no title, New York Daily Herald, March 24, 1872, 10.
121 by her regular foot soldiers: "'Sheeny' Mike's Career: The Latest Effort of Our Best Burglar—A Singular Criminal Record," New-York Times, April 29, 1876, 8.
121 since he was in his early teens: Holub (2007), 60.
121 a burly blond widower: Holub (2007), 51.
121 "the only person": Ibid.
121 her life partner: Holub (2007), 51–52.
121 "he was . . . always seen": Holub (2007), 52.
122 January 15, 1877: "Brieflets," Boston Evening Transcript, Jan. 16, 1877, 8.
122 a duplicate key: Ibid.
122 Washington Street: Ibid.
122 FN according to an account: "A Robbed Merchant's Suit: Verdict Against a Receiver of Stolen Goods. Growing Out of a Robbery in Boston in Which 'Sheeny Mike' Was the Actor—Where the Goods Went," New-York Times, Jan. 24, 1884, 8.
122 bored a hole: "'Sheeney Mike,' Burglar: Suit of James Scott of Boston to Recover for Silks Stolen by Him—'Mike's' Checkered Career—A Thief and Bank Breaker of National Repute," Boston Globe, Jan. 17, 1884, 2.
122 James Scott & Co.: "Brieflets."

122 **Michael Kurtz:** " 'Sheeny' Mike as a Witness: In Boston Man's Suit Against a 'Fence' to Recover Stolen Silks and Shawls," *Boston Globe*, Jan. 24, 1884, 5.

122 **twenty-six shawls:** "James Scott against Frederika [*sic*] Mendlebaum [*sic*]."

122 **a combined value of $780:** Ibid.

122 **2,000 yards of fine black silk:** Ibid.

122 **valued at $4,000:** Ibid.

122 **coolly out the front door:** " 'Sheeney Mike,' Burglar."

122 **Taking a waiting carriage:** Ibid.

122 **boarded the night train:** Ibid.

122 **the Lower East Side home:** "A Robbed Merchant's Suit."

122 **Sarah Fox:** Ibid.

122 **Joining him:** Ibid.

123 **accompanied by Hermann Stoude:** "Receiving Stolen Goods: A Verdict Against Mrs. Mandelbaum for $6,666," *New-York Tribune*, Jan. 24, 1884, 3.

123 **paid Kurtz about $1,600:** "A Robbed Merchant's Suit."

123 **she expected to make:** Ibid.

123 **a sensation in Boston:** " 'Sheeney Mike,' Burglar."

123 **Only some months later:** Ibid. gives an erroneous arrest date of March 1876, where March 1877 was seemingly intended.

123 **Wiggin & Wood:** Ibid.

123 **FN had the power of arrest:** Inciardi (1975), 51; Editors, *Law Review*, "Private Police Forces: Legal Powers and Limitations," *University of Chicago Law Review* 38:3, Spring 1971, 555–82.

123 **" 'Sheeny Mike' is one of the cleverest":** " 'Sheeney Mike,' Burglar."

123 **he asked to be permitted:** "A Robbed Merchant's Suit."

123 **appears to have told the detectives:** " 'Sheeney Mike,' Burglar."

123 **On reaching Philadelphia:** "A Robbed Merchant's Suit."

123 **meet the train in Jersey City, New Jersey:** " 'Sheeney Mike,' Burglar."

123 **the Harlem station:** Ibid.

123 **armed with a writ:** "A Robbed Merchant's Suit."

123 **served only on Detective Wiggin:** " 'Sheeney Mike,' Burglar."

123 **out of sight in a compartment:** Ibid.

123 **handcuffed to Detective Wood:** Ibid.

123 **Stepping onto the platform alone:** Ibid.

124 **Kurtz exhorted Marm:** "A Robbed Merchant's Suit."

124 **"What goods?":** Ibid.

124 **"Now what do you think":** Ibid.

124 **in German:** " 'Sheeney Mike,' Burglar."

124 **got off the train at New Rochelle:** "A Robbed Merchant's Suit."

124 **Marm convened a meeting:** Ibid.

124 **the "notorious" burglar Jimmy Hoey:** " 'Sheeney Mike,' Burglar."

124 **Hoey's wife, Mollie:** Spelled "Molly" in some accounts.

124 **an equally notorious:** Byrnes (1969), 195.

124 **Marm gave Jimmy Hoey $500:** "A Robbed Merchant's Suit."

124 **a $1,000 government bond:** Ibid.

124 **Through his attorney, Scott declared:** Ibid.

124 **Marm replied:** Ibid.

124 **held firm on the monetary offer:** Ibid.

125 **He pleaded guilty:** " 'Sheeney Mike,' Burglar."

125 **sentenced to twelve years:** Ibid.

125 **less than four years later:** "Suit for the Recovery of Stolen Property," *Boston Evening Transcript*, Jan. 18, 1884, 3.

125 **a cohort of moneyed Protestant men:** See, e.g., Callow (1969), 95–96.

125 **"Politics as a vocation":** Wiebe (1967), 6.

126 **"saloonkeepers, grocers":** Anbinder (2001), 145.

126 **music halls and boxing matches:** Holub (2007), 186.

126 **founding rarefied institutions:** For founding dates, see nyphil.org/explore/history;
amnh.org/about; and metmuseum.org/about-the-met/history.

126 **FN Philharmonic Society of New York:** nyphil.org/explore/history/phil-facts.

126 **FN December 7, 1842:** Ibid.

126 **FN by subscription only:** "Philharmonic Society," *Evening Post* (New York), Dec. 5,
1842, 2.

126 **"While corruption was no stranger":** Holub (2007), 189–90.

126 **Undergirding their efforts:** Callow (1969), 263.

126 **their agendas largely reactionary:** Callow (1969), 299.

126 **founded in 1873:** "New York Society for the Suppression of Vice Records," Library of
Congress, loc.gov/item/mm78034587.

126 **a devout Congregationalist:** Timothy J. Gilfoyle, "Comstock, Anthony," in Jackson
(2010), 298.

126 **obscenity, prostitution and birth control:** Ibid.

126 **FN One of Comstock's most notorious:** Ibid.

127 **FN as far back as 1889:** "Comstock and Horse Ponds," *Lucifer—the Light-Bearer*
(Valley Falls, Kan.), April 26, 1889, 2, via *Philadelphia Record*, April 9, 1889.

127 **FN "Comstockery is the world's":** "Bernard Shaw Resents Action of Librarian: Calls
'American Comstockery' World's Standing Joke," *New York Times*, Sept. 26, 1905, 1.

127 **founded the next year:** "The Temperance Crusade: Mass Meeting at Indianapolis,"
National Republican, March 4, 1874, 1.

127 **established in 1877:** "Meeting of the Society for the Prevention of Crime," *New-York
Times*, April 17, 1877, 5.

127 **the Presbyterian minister Howard Crosby:** "Dr. Howard Crosby Dead: His Noble
Struggle Against Pneumonia Was in Vain. He Passed Away Late Yesterday After-
noon, Fully Conscious That His Work on Earth Was Done—A Long Life of Well-
Doing," *New-York Times*, March 30, 1891, 1.

127 **curbing gambling, prostitution:** Warren Sloat, "Society for the Prevention of Crime,"
in Jackson (2010), 1201.

127 **in *Harper's Weekly* in 1870–71:** Anne DiFabio, "Thomas Nast Takes Down Tammany:
A Cartoonist's Crusade Against a Political Boss," Museum of the City of New York,
Sept. 24, 2013, mcny.org/story/thomas-nast-takes-down-tammany-cartoonists-crusade
-against-political-boss.

127 **a multipart exposé:** See, e.g., "The Ring and the City Armories," *New-York Times*,
July 8, 1871, 4, and "The Secret Accounts: Proofs of Undoubted Frauds Brought to
Light," *New-York Times*, July 22, 1871, 1.

127 **arrested late that year:** Share (2010).

127 **220 counts of corruption:** Ibid.; Callow (1969), 289; "Justice at Last: W. M. Tweed
Convicted. Guilty on Two Hundred and Four Counts of the Indictment—Sentence
Postponed—Scenes in the Court of Oyer and Terminer—Now the People Received
the Verdict," *New-York Times*, Nov. 20, 1873, 1; "Tweed in Prison: Twelve Years in
Prison and Fined $12,500," *New-York Times*, Nov. 23, 1873, 1.

127 **convicted of 204:** Share (2010); Callow (1969), 289; "Justice at Last."

127 **he wound up being released:** Share (2010).

127 **fleeing the country, living on the lam:** Ibid.

127 **Ludlow Street Jail:** "Death of Wm. M. Tweed: The Ex-Tammany Chief's Last Hours
in Jail. A Peaceful Death-Bed Scene in the Ludlow-Street Prison," *New-York Times*,
April 13, 1878, 1–2.

127 **in 1878, at fifty-five:** Ibid. Per the *Times,* Tweed was born on April 3, 1823.
127 **"It could not have been lost":** Holub (2007), 188.
127 **"that soap, taken internally":** "Notorious 'Crooks' Dead: Stealers of Fortunes. End of 'Sheeny Mike' and the 'Prince of Cross Roaders,' " *New-York Daily Tribune,* May 26, 1905, 11.
128 **granted Kurtz an official pardon:** " 'Sheeney Mike,' Burglar."
128 **"on his plea":** "Verdict in Favor of Mr. James Scott," *Boston Evening Transcript,* Jan. 24, 1884, 2.
128 **FN born c.1850:** Byrnes (1969), 152.
128 **FN would live until 1904:** "Notorious 'Crooks' Dead."
128 **Meeting with Scott's attorney:** Conway (2014), 119–20.
128 **He further swore:** "Receiving Stolen Goods."
128 **she had helped him remove:** "Suit for the Recovery of Stolen Property."
128 **Jimmy and Mollie Hoey:** " 'Sheeney Mike,' Burglar."
128 **as did Kurtz's sister:** Holub (2007), 142.
128 **"The most peculiar thing":** " 'Sheeney Mike,' Burglar."
128 **in early 1881:** Holub (2007), 141.
128 **It sought $6,666:** "A Robbed Merchant's Suit."
128 **"Mrs. Mandelbaum is":** "Mrs. Mandlebaum's [*sic*] Bonanza: How She Has Coined Money by Harboring and Assisting Thieves," *Boston Globe,* Jan. 25, 1884, 2.
129 **"Delay, delay, delay":** Murphy (2010), 141.
129 **denied all allegations:** "James Scott against Frederika [*sic*] Mendlebaum [*sic*]."
129 **demanded the suit be dismissed:** Ibid.
129 **Charles Donohue:** Holub (2007), 141.
129 **New York State Supreme Court:** "Ex-Justice Charles Donohue," *New-York Daily Tribune,* April 19, 1910, 7.
129 **a Mandelbaum crony:** Holub (2007), 176.
129 **"The case was again passed":** "James Scott against Frederika [*sic*] Mendlebaum [*sic*]."
129 **including the dismissal:** Ibid.
129 **ordered that Scott's lawyers:** Holub (2007), 141.
129 **no recorded rationale:** Ibid.
129 **"grossly abused his powers":** Association of the Bar of the City of New York, quoted in "Journal of the Assembly of the State of New York: At Their One Hundred and Ninth Session. Begun and Held at the Capitol, in the City of Albany, on the Fifth Day of January, 1886," Volume 2 (Albany: Weed, Parsons & Company, Legislative Printers, 1886), 1567.
129 **FN "granted to corrupt and powerful classes":** Ibid.
129 **FN In 1886:** Ibid.
129 **FN the committee held:** Association of the Bar of the City of New York, quoted in "Journal of the Assembly of the State of New York," 1567–68.
129 **FN Donohue left the bench in 1889:** Andrew L. Kaufman, *Cardozo* (Cambridge, Mass.: Harvard University Press, 1998), 54.
129 **FN Cardozo, Newcombe & Donohue:** Kaufman (1998), 54.
130 **On January 23, 1884:** Holub (2007), 142.
130 **in the State Supreme Court:** "A Robbed Merchant's Suit."
130 **Hooper C. Van Vorst:** Holub (2007), 142.
130 **Marm entered the courtroom clad:** "A Robbed Merchant's Suit"; "Queen of 'Fences': The Trial of a Woman Whose Name Is a Proverb in New York. Inquiries as to the Placing of Certain Silks and Shawls by Sheeny Mike After a Robbery in Boston— Matters Odd to Think Of," *Buffalo Evening News,* Jan. 26, 1884, 7.
130 **"somber though rich":** "Queen of 'Fences.' "

130 "immense sealskin sacque": Ibid.

130 "with a beautiful bird's wing": Ibid.

130 "set thick with pearls": "A Robbed Merchant's Suit."

130 "a score of New York": "Queen of 'Fences.'"

130 "'Bill' Smith, 'Big Bill'": "A Robbed Merchant's Suit."

130 "as honest as anybody else": Ibid.

130 James Scott described: "Receiving Stolen Goods." As Holub (2007), 142, note 8, points out, while there appears to be no surviving transcript of this trial, the nature of the proceedings can be gleaned from other legal documents and newspaper accounts.

130 Detective Wood recounted: Ibid.

130 Jimmy Hoey testified: Ibid.

130 "She wanted me to go": Ibid.

130 She was just then in jail: Ibid.

130 Her affidavit was read: "Queen of 'Fences.'"

130 nowhere to be found: "A Robbed Merchant's Suit."

130 Nor was his sister: "Queen of 'Fences.'"

130 "sudden resumption of friendship": Ibid.

130 Their affidavits, too: "Queen of 'Fences.'"

131 "had been made the victim": "A Robbed Merchant's Suit."

131 Detective Sergeant Thomas Dusenbury: Ibid.

131 a twenty-five-year veteran: "Queen of 'Fences.'"

131 "would not believe them": "A Robbed Merchant's Suit."

131 Other police officers testified: "Queen of 'Fences.'"

131 a visible stir: Ibid.

131 FN "She is a gross woman": "A Robbed Merchant's Suit."

131 "I am fifty-one years of age": Quoted in "Queen of 'Fences.'"

131 FN born March 28, 1825: Per Fredericka Mandelbaum's tombstone, Union Field Cemetery, Ridgewood, New York. Photograph at www.findagrave.com/memorial /130475634.

131 that Kurtz had telegraphed her: "A Robbed Merchant's Suit."

131 "She had *heard*": Ibid.; italics added.

131 "The counsel for the defense": "Queen of 'Fences.'"

131 "referred to the array": Ibid.

132 trial of a single day: "A Robbed Merchant's Suit," et al., from Jan. 24, 1884.

132 only a short time: "Receiving Stolen Goods."

132 It returned a verdict: "A Robbed Merchant's Suit," et al.

132 the full $6,666: "A Robbed Merchant's Suit."

132 a total of $7,267.75: Holub (2007), 147.

132 On January 25: Ibid.

132 Peter B. Olney: Holub (2007), 148.

132 to mount a watertight criminal case: Holub (2007), 147ff.

CHAPTER NINE: THE THIEF-TAKER GENERAL
OF THE UNITED STATES OF AMERICA

133 One day in 1847: O'Hara (2016), 16.

133 a covert encampment: Ibid.

133 summoned the county sheriff: Ibid.

133 other local businessmen: Ibid.

133 Pinkerton had been born: "Allan Pinkerton," *Encyclopedia Britannica*, britannica .com/biography/Allan-Pinkerton.

133 **the son of a weaver:** "Allan Pinkerton Dead: The Great Detective's Life Ended at the Age of 64," *Boston Globe*, July 2, 1884, 5.

133 **a local police sergeant:** "Allan Pinkerton," *Encyclopaedia Britannica.*

133 **When Allan was nine:** "Allan Pinkerton's Death: The Career of the Great Detective Ended," *New-York Times*, July 2, 1884, 1.

133 **first to a printer:** Ibid.

133 **an impassioned Chartist:** "Allan Pinkerton," *Encyclopaedia Britannica.*

133 **in the late 1850s:** "Chartism," *Encyclopaedia Britannica*, britannica.com/event /Chartism-British-history.

133 **FN At the time, British law:** "The Chartist Movement," UK Parliament, parliament .uk/about/living-heritage/transformingsociety/electionsvoting/chartists/overview /chartistmovement/.

134 **In 1842:** "Allan Pinkerton," *Encyclopaedia Britannica.*

134 **surviving a shipwreck:** "A Dead Detective: Allan Pinkerton, the Expert Ferret, Dies at His Home in Chicago—Notes of His Life and Works," *Kansas City Daily Times*, July 2, 1884, 1.

134 **The following year:** "Allan Pinkerton," *Encyclopaedia Britannica.*

134 **"Private policing grew":** Johnson (1979), 60.

134 **made a sheriff's deputy:** O'Hara (2016), 16.

134 **named a special agent:** Ibid.

134 **"the most important arrest":** "The Great Post Office Robbery at Chicago," *Daily Union* (Washington, D.C.), July 8, 1855, 3, via *Chicago Daily Press*.

134 **on Washington Street:** "Pinkerton & Co., North-Western Police Agency," Advertisement, *Chicago Tribune*, May 5, 1856, 1.

134 **in the early 1850s:** O'Hara (2016), 3.

134 **"the transaction of a general":** "Pinkerton & Co., North-Western Police Agency."

134 **A committed abolitionist:** "Today in History—August 25: The Pinkertons," Library of Congress Digital Collections, loc.gov/item/today-in-history/august-25.

134 **North West Police Agency:** O'Hara (2016), 13.

134 **Pinkerton's National Police Agency:** O'Hara (2016), 14.

134 **in the late 1860s:** David Ricardo Williams, *Call in Pinkerton's: American Detectives at Work for Canada* (Toronto: Dundurn Press, 1998), 20.

134 **"We Never Sleep":** O'Hara (2016), 4.

134 **"without jurisdictional limits":** O'Hara (2016), 14.

134 **New York, Philadelphia and elsewhere:** O'Hara (2016), 23, 72.

135 **full power of arrest:** Inciardi (1975), 51.

135 **forgers and bank burglars:** Ibid.

135 **"the best known":** "Allan Pinkerton," *Brooklyn Daily Eagle*, July 2, 1884, 2.

135 **to supply intelligence:** O'Hara (2016), 13ff.

135 **His duties included:** O'Hara (2016), 13.

135 **furnished private security:** O'Hara (2016), 3.

135 **FN he also claimed:** O'Hara (2016), 19.

135 **FN Some later chroniclers:** O'Hara (2016), 23ff.

135 **FN still others suggest:** O'Hara (2016), 24–25.

136 **seventeen volumes:** O'Hara (2016), 32.

136 **between 1875 and 1884:** Ibid.

136 **FN "novelizations":** O'Hara (2016), 35.

136 **the inability to capture:** O'Hara (2016), 42ff.

136 **left two Pinkerton agents dead:** O'Hara (2016), 42.

136 **frame labor activists and break strikes:** Browning and Gerassi (1980), 223.

136 **"a quasi-official arm":** O'Hara (2016), 55.

136 **"capital's muscle":** O'Hara (2016), 87.

136 **Between 1877 and 1892:** O'Hara (2016), 76.

136 **at least seventy strikes:** Ibid.

136 **on more than one occasion firing:** Ibid.

136 **"Capital is marshaling":** Quoted in "The Boycott," *Wichita Citizen,* Jan. 8, 1887, 1.

136 **FN "Perhaps the most infamous":** O'Hara (2016), 11.

136 **On July 1, 1884:** "Allan Pinkerton Dead."

137 **"[His] name has been a terror":** Ibid.

137 **"His whole record":** "A Dead Detective."

137 **"Very few great crimes":** "Allan Pinkerton's Death."

137 **FN now known simply as Pinkerton:** pinkerton.com.

137 **Pinkerton's son William:** "Allan Pinkerton's Death."

137 **his son Robert:** Ibid.

137 **In late 1883:** "A New District-Attorney: Mr. Peckham's Sudden Resignation. Ill-Health Stated as the Cause—Peter B. Olney Appointed," *New-York Daily Tribune,* Dec. 11, 1883, 5.

137 **"for all intents and purposes":** O'Hara (2016), 2.

138 **banker and textile manufacturer:** "Olney Dies: Veteran Statesman," *New York Times,* April 10, 1917, 13.

138 **Peter Butler Olney:** Herbert Heywood, "Richard Olney's Boyhood: The Early Life of the Secretary of State at His Home in Oxford, Mass.," *Los Angeles Times,* July 14, 1895, 21.

138 **born in Oxford, Massachusetts, in 1843:** "Peter B. Olney, Lawyer, Dead of Pneumonia," *Brooklyn Times Union,* Feb. 9, 1922, 10.

138 **an old and distinguished:** "Points About the Cabinet," *Twin-City Daily Sentinel* (Winston-Salem, N.C.), Feb. 24, 1893, 1.

138 **His elder brother:** Richard Olney was born in 1835; see, e.g., "Richard Olney Dies: Veteran Statesman."

138 **Phillips Andover:** "Peter B. Olney, Lawyer, Dead of Pneumonia."

138 **bachelor's and law degrees:** Ibid.

138 **He spent two years:** Ibid.

138 **Evarts, Southmayd & Choate:** "Peter Butler Olney, Noted Lawyer, Dead," *New York Evening World,* Feb. 9, 1922, 2.

138 **partnership with Francis C. Barlow:** "Peter B. Olney, Lawyer, Dead of Pneumonia."

138 **in 1869:** Ibid.

138 **in 1872:** "To-Night's Meeting of the Bar Association," *New-York Times,* Jan. 4, 1872, 4.

138 **a reformist Democrat:** "Peter B. Olney, Lawyer, Dead of Pneumonia."

138 **investigate and prosecute:** Ibid.; *Report of the Special Committee of the Board of Aldermen,* 78off.

138 **In 1875:** "The Elections Next Tuesday: Public Officers to Be Chosen in Twenty States," *New York Herald,* Oct. 30, 1875, 4.

138 **post-Tweed Tammany candidate:** "Kelly's Candidates," *New-York Times,* Oct. 12, 1875, 1.

138 **Benjamin K. Phelps:** "At the Polls: A Big Blow to Boss Kelly and Tammany," *New York Herald,* Nov. 3, 1875, 5.

138 **In December 1883:** "Wheeler H. Peckham Resigns," *New-York Times,* Dec. 11, 1883, 1.

138 **Wheeler H. Peckham, resigned:** Ibid.

138 **little more than a week:** "A New District-Attorney."

138 **FN moved from March 4 to January 20:** "Today in History—March 4: Inauguration Day," Library of Congress Digital Collections, loc.gov/item/today-in-history/march-04.

138 **"This office was not"**: "The New District Attorney." *New-York Times*, Dec. 12, 1883, 3.
138 **"If [Olney's] private utterances"**: Walling (1887), 287.
139 **"Her intimacy"**: "Crime and the Police."
139 **They had already helped**: "Shang Draper: To Be Tried for the Northampton Bank Robbery," *Brooklyn Daily Eagle*, July 10, 1879, 4; "The Northampton Robbers: Only Three out of the Seven in Confinement—Some Facts About Shang Draper," *New York Sun*, July 16, 1878, 4, via *Boston Herald*.
139 **an 1876 bank burglary**: "The Northampton Bank Robbery—List of the Stolen Deposits—Conduct of the Thieves," *Boston Globe*, Jan. 28, 1876, 2.
139 **FN appears to have had no involvement**: Mrs. Mandelbaum's name is not mentioned, for instance, in the account of the burglary—planned by George Leonidas Leslie—in Conway (2014), 85ff. Nor is the Northampton burglary mentioned at all in Rona L. Holub's rigorously researched master's thesis and doctoral dissertation, Holub (1998) and Holub (2007).
139 **FN of the Northampton National Bank**: "The Northampton Bank Robbery."
139 **FN on January 26, 1876**: "The Northampton National Bank Heist, the Biggest in U.S. History," New England Historical Society, newenglandhistoricalsociety.com /northampton-national-bank-heist.
139 **FN Robert Pinkerton would arrest**: "'Shang' Draper's Fight for Liberty," *New-York Times*, Oct. 31, 1878, 2.
139 **in early 1884**: Holub (2007), 149.
139 **Pinkerton agents spent weeks**: "Got Mother Mandelbaum."
139 **from rented rooms**: "A Queen Among Thieves."
140 **"They say that among"**: "Got Mother Mandelbaum."
140 **would alert her**: Holub (2007), 59.
140 **FN also happened on the frontier**: O'Hara (2016), 36.
140 **"We shadowed the place"**: "Mrs. Mandelbaum's Riches."
140 **It was difficult work**: Ibid.
140 **Pinkerton and Olney determined**: Holub (2007), 148.
141 **entrapment**: Holub (2007), 148–49.
141 **Gustave Frank**: Holub (2007), 14. His first name is spelled "Gustav" in some accounts.
141 **since 1865**: "Holding Mrs. Mandelbaum."
141 **from Cologne**: "In and About the City: Is Detective Frank on Trial? Mother Mandelbaum's Counsel Trying to Prove Him a Forger," *New-York Times*, Sept. 16, 1884, 8.
141 **in the spring of 1884**: Holub (2007), 149.
141 **Frank shaved**: Ibid.
141 **memorized the latest silk prices**: "A Queen Among Thieves."
141 **Olney had already written**: "Got Mother Mandelbaum."
141 **Armed with $1,000**: "A Queen Among Thieves."
141 **a shady silk jobber named Stein**: Holub (2007), 149.
141 **had grown even more so**: "Holding Mrs. Mandelbaum."
141 **She turned Frank down**: "A Queen Among Thieves."
141 **"Burned children"**: "The Female Fence's Work: 'Marm' Mandelbaum Is Much Frightened and Worried," *New York World*, July 29, 1884, n.p., from District Attorney Scrapbooks, Municipal Archives, City of New York.
141 **not before she tested**: "A Queen Among Thieves."
141 **not to resell it in New York**: "A Queen Among Thieves."
141 **"As fast as the silks"**: Ibid.
141 **Not every silk merchant**: Ibid.
141 **"disappeared in other"**: "Mother Mandlebaum [*sic*] Trapped."
142 **Julius diligently examined**: "Got Mother Mandelbaum."

142   **"that he shut out":** "A Queen Among Thieves."

142   **On June 22:** "Mother Baum's Customer: Detective Frank Begins the Story of His Silk Buying," *New York Sun*, July 26, 1884, 3.

142   **a speckled gray piece:** "Her Son Julius Bailed; Mrs. Mandelbaum Refused as Surety by The Justice," *New-York Times*, July 26, 1884, 5.

142   **"Hold on, Mother":** Ibid.

142   **The letters LL:** Ibid.

142   **the knife proved too dull:** Ibid.

142   **It left him holding:** Ibid.

142   **when Fredericka sheared through it:** Ibid.

142   **She ordered him:** Ibid.

142   **he carried the strip:** Ibid.

142   **announced that he had thrown:** "Mother Baum's Customer."

142   **"You mustn't be":** Ibid.

142   **he should burn it:** "Her Son Julius Bailed."

142   **Frank had pocketed:** "Mother Baum's Customer."

142   **Simpson, Crawford & Simpson:** "Her Son Julius Bailed."

142   **from which the silk had been stolen:** "Mother Mandlebaum [*sic*] Trapped."

142   **12,000 yards of silk:** "A Noted 'Fence.'"

142   **only 160:** Oller (2021), 123.

142   **"a bit":** Ibid.

142   **On July 18, 1884:** Holub (2007), 150.

142   **obtained a search warrant:** "Got Mother Mandelbaum."

143   **along with arrest warrants:** Ibid.

143   **Tuesday, July 22, 1884:** Ibid.

143   **three fellow agents:** "Mother Mandlebaum [*sic*] Trapped."

143   **"So you are the one":** Quoted in Holub (2007), 139.

143   **"I can't believe":** "Mrs. Mandelbaum's Riches."

143   **who was not in the shop:** "Got Mother Mandelbaum."

143   **as far away as Ireland:** "Mother Mandelbaum," *Belfast News-Letter*, Aug. 13, 1884, 6.

143   **"Got Mother Mandelbaum":** Op. cit.

143   **"A Clever Capture":** *St. Louis Post-Dispatch*, July 23, 1.

143   **"She will doubtless go":** "Real and Bogus Detectives," *Philadelphia Times*, July 30, 1884, 2.

143   **many Americans had looked upon:** Holub (2007), 185–86.

143   **"These were the perpetrators":** Ibid.; italics in original.

143   **"to deflect attention":** Holub (2007), 186.

144   **FN "Alas! I knew her well":** Lyons (2019), 109.

144   **FN In later years:** Davidson (2020), 147ff.

144   **FN She died in 1924:** Davidson (2020), 168.

144   **FN at seventy-six:** "Huge Crowds Attend Sophie Lyons Funeral," *Detroit Free Press*, May 10, 1924, 13.

144   **perennial, no-holds-barred blackmail:** "In the Toils: Arrest of a Notorious Receiver of Stolen Property," *Detroit Free Press*, July 24, 1884, 2; "Perturbed Police"; "Mother Mandelbaum's Booty," *Buffalo Courier*, March 15, 1894, 10.

144   **"She claimed that":** Holub (2007), 169–70.

145   **"to the end":** "In the Toils."

CHAPTER TEN: THE MAYPOLE AND THE EGG

146   **"crime, reckless extravagance":** Ford (1921), 44.

146   **intended as professional advertising:** Rovere (1986), 118–19.

146 **"what we may be pardoned":** Howe and Hummel (2009), i.

146 **Established in 1869:** Rovere (1986), 5.

146 **"the unofficial bar":** Andrew Roth and Jonathan Roth, *Devil's Advocates: The Un-natural History of Lawyers* (Berkeley, Calif.: Nolo Press, 1989), 107.

146 **89 Centre Street:** Rovere (1986), 5.

147 **across the street from the Tombs:** Rovere (1986), 14.

147 **FN The prison's nickname stems:** Sewell Chan, "Disgraced and Penalized, Kerik Finds His Name Stripped Off Jail," *New York Times*, July 3, 2006, B1.

147 **FN The building occupied a lot:** "Doom of the Old Tombs. Soon to Be Removed to Make Way for New Prison: Something About the Grim Structure in Centre Street Where Many Notorious Criminals Have Been Confined and Numbers of Executions Have Taken Place—The Structure to Be Substituted Will Have More Room," *New York Times*, July 4, 1896, 1.

147 **an on-site saloon:** Murphy (2010), 125.

147 **professional advertising by lawyers:** Rovere (1986), 14.

147 **25 feet long and illuminated at night:** Ibid.; Murphy (2010), 1.

147 **in great capital letters:** Rovere (1986), 14.

147 **when ethical elasticity:** Rovere (1986), 41–42.

147 **They bribed, they blackmailed:** Murphy (2010), passim; Rovere (1986), passim.

147 **FN "There are no recorded instances":** Rovere (1986), 73.

147 **FN "More likely than not":** Ibid.

147 **a temporary disbarment:** Murphy (2010), 5.

147 **FN "for a bit of careless bribery":** Ibid.

147 **FN he would be disbarred permanently:** Murphy (2010), 7, 247–48.

147 **FN He spent a year:** Murphy (2010), xiii–xiv.

147 **FN the city penitentiary on Blackwell's Island:** "Blackwell's Island (Roosevelt Island), New York City," National Park Service, nps.gov/places/blackwell-s-island-new-york-city.htm.

147 **personal bankruptcy:** Murphy (2010), 5.

147 **"Here's how!":** Rovere (1986), 8.

147 **the year after Howe died:** Murphy (2010), 105.

148 **Another story is told:** "Wm. F. Howe, Old-Time Lawyer: Reminiscences of the Man Who Once Dominated the Criminal Courts of New York," *Law Student's Helper: A Monthly Magazine for the Student In and Out of Law School* 11:1, January 1903, 7.

148 **FN John Keteltas Hackett:** "John K. Hackett's Death: The Peaceful Ending of a Busy Life. A Sketch of the Recorder's Career and an Estimate of His Character—The Aldermen to Appoint His Successor," *New York Times*, Dec. 27, 1879, 1–2.

148 **FN from 1866 to 1879:** "John K. Hackett's Death."

148 **kept them on an annual retainer:** See, e.g., Burrows and Wallace (1999), 1,000; Holub (2007), 10.

148 **"The timing was simply right":** Murphy (2010), 4.

148 **clients over the years:** Rovere (1986), 6.

149 **"an organization of thugs and killers":** Ibid.

149 **"When seventy-four madams":** Ibid.

149 **would not take personal checks:** Rovere (1986), 27.

149 **born circa 1828:** Like most details of his early life, Howe's birth date is unclear. The Library of Congress, in its catalog entry for an 1888 edition of *In Danger!* (New York: J. S. Ogilvie & Company), lists the date as 1828.

149 **FN Howe states that he was born:** Howe and Hummel (2009), vii.

149 **FN "However much the inclination":** Ibid.

149 **he appears to have been a clerk:** "William Howe, William Thompson, Gavin Rick-

ards, Miscellaneous: Conspiracy, 18th September 1854, the Proceedings of the Old Bailey, Reference Number t18540918-997," oldbaileyonline.org.

149 **In 1854, Howe was convicted:** Ibid.
149 **whether he actually served:** "William Howe," Digital Panopticon, digitalpanopticon.org/life?id=obpdef1-997-18540918.
149 **By the late 1850s:** Rovere (1986), 21.
149 **"washed up in New York":** Murphy (2010), 3.
149 **"The evolution from criminal":** Rovere (1986), 41–42.
150 **William Frederick Howe:** For Howe's middle name, see "Wm. F. Howe, Old-Time Lawyer," 7.
150 **his suit coat:** Rovere (1986), 18.
150 **When Mr. Howe made his appearance:** "Bulldozing the Court: Mrs. Mandelbaum's Lawyer Rebuked by Judge Murray," *New-York Times,* July 31, 1884, 5.
151 **Then there was the jewelry:** See, e.g., Rovere (1986), 17–18; Murphy (2010), 136.
151 **"When the notorious":** Article, no title, *Atlanta Constitution,* July 31, 1884, 4.
151 **"He had the voice":** Rovere (1986), 86.
152 **"Howe's defenses":** Rovere (1986), 125.
152 **FN employees of that playhouse:** "The Ocean Bank Robbery: Three Hundred Thousand Dollars Graciously Returned—A Trunk Full of Securities Not Negotiable Sent to the Police." *Cincinnati Daily Enquirer,* via *New York World,* July 3, 1869, 3.
152 **an arsonist-for-hire named Owen Reilly:** Rovere (1986), 52.
152 **plead guilty to *attempted* arson:** Rovere (1986), 52–53.
152 **the sentence for an attempted:** Rovere (1986), 53.
152 **"Scripture tells us":** Ibid.
152 **"The court agreed":** Ibid.
152 **"I guess that most":** Quoted in Rovere (1986), 20.
152 **"probably to highlight":** Rovere (1986), 19.
152 **elevator shoes:** Rovere (1986), 20.
152 **"called 'toothpick shoes'":** Rovere (1986), 19.
153 **"'Before I took anti-fat'":** "Her Son Julius Bailed."
153 **born in Boston:** Rovere (1986), 87.
153 **brought up in Kleindeutschland:** Ibid.
153 **"cold, clear water":** Quoted in ibid.
153 **FN In 1852, a cholera epidemic:** Gerard Koeppel, "Croton Aqueduct," in Jackson (2010), 332–33.
153 **FN "'Croton,'" a historian writes:** Koeppel (2010), 333.
153 **FN as much as 30 percent:** "Croton Water Filtration Plant Activated," New York City Department of Environmental Protection press release, May 8, 2015, nyc.gov/html/dep/html/press_releases/15-034pr.shtml.
153 **joined Howe's practice in 1863:** Rovere (1986), 45.
154 **"evolved a division of labor":** Rovere (1986), 89.
154 **luminaries like P. T. Barnum:** Rovere (1986), 9.
154 **"scandalized Victorian New York":** "Fahreda Mahzar: Thrilled the Public with Exotic Dancing," Coney Island History Project, coneyislandhistory.org/hall-of-fame/fahreda-mahzar.
154 **"The firm's theatrical practice":** Rovere (1986), 10.
154 **FN "When Barnum, a prohibitionist":** Rovere (1986), 9.
154 **oversaw the merger of circuses:** Rovere (1986), 107.
154 **"repulsive and apelike killers":** Rovere (1986), 57.
155 **between $5,000 and $10,000:** Rovere (1986), 13.
155 **in the iron brazier:** Rovere (1986), 24.

155 split fifty-fifty: Rovere (1986), 13.

155 "was said to have enriched": Rovere (1986), 77.

155 FN After being stung twice: Rovere (1986), 95.

155 FN attempts to extort John Barrymore: Ibid.

155 FN retained him as his civil attorney: Ibid.

155 suing the producer David Belasco: Rovere (1986), 108–109.

155 FN (c.1862–1937): Sources cannot agree on the precise year of Mrs. Leslie Carter's birth. The 1862 date is from the obituary news article "Mrs. Leslie Carter Dies in California: Actress Starred for Thirty Years Here and Abroad in Wide Variety of Plays. Got Start With Belasco," *New York Times* via Associated Press, Nov. 14, 1937, 11.

155 FN born Caroline Louise Dudley: "Mrs. Leslie Carter," Internet Broadway Database, ibdb.com/broadway-cast-staff/mrs-leslie-carter-23300.

155 FN *Rocky Mountain Mystery* (1935): Internet Movie Database.

155 "the American Sarah Bernhardt": "Mrs. Leslie Carter."

156 purchased a front-row seat: Rovere (1986), 109.

156 "Mrs. Carter met the applause": Ibid.

156 convicted, in 1905: Murphy (2010), 244ff.

156 In 1907: Murphy (2010), 262.

156 a lavish going-away party: Rovere (1986), 163; Murphy (2010), 262.

156 his one-year term: Murphy (2010), 262ff.

156 died in his flat there: "Death Closes Spectacular Career of America's Most Notorious Divorce Lawyer," *Buffalo Courier* via Associated Press, Jan. 25, 1926, 2.

156 in Baker Street: "Mr. Abraham Hummel," *Daily Telegraph* (London), Jan. 25, 1926, 11.

156 more than $1 million: "Abe Hummel Left Million to Sisters: On Their Death the Estate Will Revert to Paris Nephew—Lawyer's Body Due Tonight," *New York Times*, Feb. 3, 1926, 1.

156 "also marks the passing": "Famed Lawyer Dies in London: Abraham H. Hummel Closes Spectacular Life. New York Law Office Haven for Miscreants," *Los Angeles Times* via Associated Press, Jan. 25, 1926, 6.

CHAPTER ELEVEN: A STRIP OF SILK

157 onto the elevated train: "Holding Mrs. Mandelbaum."

157 Harlem Police Court: "Got Mother Mandelbaum."

157 it was conjectured afterward: Elizabeth Kerri Mahon, *Pretty Evil New York: True Stories of Mobster Molls, Violent Vixens, and Murderous Matriarchs* (Guilford, Conn.: Globe Pequot, 2021), 56.

157 Justice Henry Murray: "Got Mother Mandelbaum."

157 a reputation as an honest jurist: Mahon (2021), 56.

157 it was he who had issued: "Got Mother Mandelbaum."

157 five counts of grand larceny: Ibid.; "Mother Mandelbaum [sic] Trapped."

157 also arraigned on five counts: "Got Mother Mandelbaum."

157 pleaded not guilty: "Mother Mandelbaum [sic] Trapped."

157 "I am going to be": "Mother Mandelbaum Out," *New York Sun*, July 24, 1884, 1.

157 held for the night: "Got Mother Mandelbaum."

157 "It is all unjust": Ibid.

158 the next morning: "Mother Mandelbaum Out."

158 "looking as meek": Ibid.

158 a row of young women: Ibid.

158 who fluttered their fans: Ibid.

158 **looked daggers at a group:** Ibid.

158 **away on vacation:** "A Queen Among Thieves."

158 **Leroy Gove:** Conway (2014), 142.

158 **"The chances":** "'Mother' Mandelbaum's Departure: What Mr. Pinkerton Says About It—Not Ordered to Watch Her Till She Was Gone," *New-York Tribune*, Dec. 6, 1884, 7.

158 **"because the Justice of his choice":** "Mother Mandelbaum Out."

158 **"because it was cool":** Ibid.

158 **demanded a pretrial hearing:** "Got Mother Mandelbaum."

158 **set for Friday:** "The Mandelbaum Charges: Not Accepted as Bail for Her Son. The Police Indignant at the District-Attorney for Putting Pinkerton's Men on the Case," *New-York Tribune*, July 26, 1884, 10.

158 **Kleindeutschland neighbors:** "Mother Mandelbaum Out"; "A Big Haul."

158 **Manassah Goldman:** "Mother Mandelbaum Out."

158 **Goldman had already pledged:** Ibid.

158 **He turned down another:** Ibid.

158 **a retired wine importer named Shatler:** Ibid.

158 **Susan Chambetta:** Holub (2007), 155.

158 **a wine importer's wife:** Holub (2007), 156.

158 **worth $100,000:** "Mother Mandelbaum Out."

159 **"I consider her":** "A Big 'Fence': 'Marm' Mandelbaum, a Noted Receiver of Stolen Goods. History of the Ruler of All the City Thieves and Shoplifters—Her Immense Wealth," *San Francisco Examiner*, Aug. 3, 1884, 8, via *New York World*.

159 **accompanied by Robert Pinkerton:** "Mother Mandelbaum Out."

159 **A second textile merchant:** "Got Mother Mandelbaum."

159 **James A. Hearn & Son:** Ibid.

159 **two more charges:** "Mother Mandelbaum Out."

159 **only specific, marked pieces:** "A Big Haul."

159 **"Silks worth thousands":** Ibid.

159 **At $2,000 per count:** "Got Mother Mandelbaum."

159 **"A good deal has been said":** "Mother Mandelbaum Out."

159 **She has never been indicted:** Ibid.

159 **Howe then moved:** Ibid.

160 **"I don't believe":** Ibid.

160 **"Yes," A.D.A. Gove concurred:** Ibid.

160 **stepped forward and kissed her:** Ibid.

160 **by executing a mortgage:** "A Big Haul."

160 **FN According to some sources:** See, e.g., Holub (2007), 155; "Mrs. Mandelbaum Missing: The Notorious Receiver Flies From the City," *New-York Times*, Dec. 5, 1884, 1.

160 **FN George Speckhardt:** Holub (2007), 155.

160 **FN a Lower East Side baker:** Ibid.

160 **"Just to think":** "Mother Mandelbaum Out."

160 **drawing her arm:** Ibid.

160 **showered her with kisses:** Ibid.

160 **"was a picture worthy":** "Mother Mandelbaum at Bay: Detective Frank Tells How He Tricked the Famous Patron of Thieves. Her Diamond Studded Lawyer," *New York Herald*, July 26, 1884, n.p., from District Attorney Scrapbooks, Municipal Archives, City of New York.

160 **a gown of glossy black satin:** "Her Son Julius Bailed"; "Mother Baum's Customer."

160 **beaded stars and much lace:** "Mother Mandelbaum at Bay."

160   diamond earrings, long black gloves: "Her Son Julius Bailed"; "Mother Baum's Customer."

160   "which stood up erect": "Her Son Julius Bailed."

161   mobbed by sketch artists: Ibid.

161   next to Julius: Ibid.

161   buried her face: "Mother Baum's Customer."

161   "sulking like a caged tigress": "Mother Mandelbaum at Bay."

161   "a placid heap": "Old Mother Mandelbaum," *New York Star.*

161   Seated behind his mother: "Mother Baum's Customer."

161   Gustav Mandelbaum was joined: Ibid.

161   "[Howe] wore a big white vest": "Mother Mandelbaum at Bay."

161   "whose countenance wore": "Her Son Julius Bailed."

161   Henry B. Porter: Ibid.

161   speckled gray silk: Ibid.

161   "Did you ever see": "Mother Baum's Customer."

162   "Is there any part": Ibid.

162   withdrew a blue envelope: "Her Son Julius Bailed."

162   "Have you ever seen": Ibid.

162   "Yes, Sir": Ibid.

162   "Our private mark": "Mother Baum's Customer."

162   "Are you able to swear": Ibid.

162   "I can swear": Ibid.

162   "in other than the usual": "Mother Mandlebaum [*sic*] Trapped."

162   "What's your name": "Mother Baum's Customer."

162   Howe barked: Ibid.

162   to laughter in the court: Ibid.

162   Frank went on to testify: Ibid.

162   "Upon all this evidence": "Her Son Julius Bailed."

162   He likewise moved: Ibid.

162   "It is refreshing to see": Ibid.

163   "As long as I live": Ibid.

163   Both motions to dismiss: Ibid.

163   set at $5,000: Ibid.

163   real estate worth $50,000: Ibid.

163   "I don't think it is proper": Ibid.

163   "Your Honor will be committing": "Mother Baum's Customer."

163   "The question is whether": Quoted in Holub (2007), 184–85.

163   an elderly man: "Her Son Julius Bailed."

163   John Briggs: Ibid.

163   "I do it from impulse": Ibid.

163   Bail was accepted: "The Mandelbaum Charges."

163   FN Briggs was evidently: Ibid.; "Mother Baum's Customer."

164   "A purple ostrich feather": "Holding Mrs. Mandelbaum."

164   "she grasped her green silk umbrella": "Mrs. Mandelbaum Fights Hard: Despite Her Diamond Studded Lawyer She and Her Accomplices Are Held for Trial." *New York Herald,* July 29, 1884, n.p., from District Attorney Scrapbooks, Municipal Archives, City of New York.

164   Stoude joined her: "Holding Mrs. Mandelbaum."

164   who had waived examination: Ibid.

164   followed by dry-goods dealers: Ibid.

164   the row of young women: Ibid.

164 "like a rosebud": Ibid.

164 "turned their faces away": Ibid.

164 "the glare of diamonds": "Mrs. Mandelbaum Fights Hard."

164 "I'm going to test": Ibid.

164 then moved again: Ibid.

164 Judge Murray denied: Ibid.

164 Stoude kissed the Bible: Ibid.

164 "I have been": Ibid.

164 Howe again moved: Ibid.

164 It could not be proved: Ibid.

164 "You're making": Ibid.

165 a series of dry-goods men: Ibid.

165 One after another: Ibid.

165 moved for the dismissal: Ibid.

165 though he did reduce: Ibid.

165 the afternoon of Wednesday, July 30: "Bulldozing the Court."

165 At three o'clock: Ibid.

165 "My name is Fredericka Mandelbaum": "Mrs. Mandelbaum's Statement," *New-York Tribune*, July 31, 1884, 8; "Bulldozing the Court."

165 I am fifty-two years old: "Bulldozing the Court."

165 FN March 28, 1825: Per Fredericka Mandelbaum's tombstone, Union Field Cemetery, Ridgewood, New York. Photograph at www.findagrave.com/memorial /130475634.

165 *"There was a world of pathos":* "Bulldozing the Court."

166 *"There were tears":* Ibid.

166 *Here the lawyer paused:* Ibid.

166 "Well," he said: Ibid.

166 "She shall make her defense": Ibid.

167 "I don't think": Ibid.

167 "Bring in the criminal code," Howe roared: Ibid.

167 Motion denied: Ibid.

167 "I refuse to let her": Ibid.

167 "You must not speak": Ibid.

167 now bright crimson: Ibid.

167 "the only missing color": Ibid.

167 He added, bellowing: Ibid.

167 He threatened to have Murray: Ibid.

167 Howe then demanded: Ibid.

167 pencil behind his ear: Ibid.

167 "she must confine herself": Ibid.

167 "Strike it out": Ibid.

167 Stoude posted his bail of $5,000: "Mrs. Mandelbaum's Statement."

167 ruled that the evidence: "Bulldozing the Court"; Holub (2007), 165.

167 In mid-August: Holub (2007), 165.

167 FN in existence from 1683 to 1962: "The Court of General Sessions," Historical Society of the New York Courts, history.nycourts.gov/court/court-general-sessions.

167 FN not punishable by death or life imprisonment: "The Court of General Sessions."

167 September 22, 1884: Holub (2007), 165.

167 Recorder Frederick Smyth: "Mother Mandelbaum's Case," *New-York Times*, Sept. 9, 1884, 8; "A Story of Recorder Smyth," *New York Times*, Oct. 6, 1901, 6.

167 widely respected New York jurist: "A Story of Recorder Smyth."

167 "the terror of evildoers": Ibid.

168 **"Should justice fail":** "Broadbrim's New York Letter," *Newberry (S.C.) Weekly Herald,* Aug. 14, 1884, 1.

168 **On Monday, September 8:** "Mother Mandelbaum's Case."

168 **Howe asked Recorder Smyth:** Ibid.

168 **He declared that Frank:** Ibid.

168 **forgery and fraudulent bankruptcy:** "Mrs. Mandelbaum and Gustave Frank," *New-
York Tribune,* Sept. 16, 1884, 5.

168 **FN In an affidavit:** Ibid.

168 **Howe then moved:** Ibid.

168 **would travel to Germany:** "Condensed Telegrams," *Fall River (Mass.) Daily Evening
News,* Sept. 16, 1884, 3.

168 **to question officials there:** "In and About the City."

169 **"Is Detective Frank on Trial?":** Ibid.

169 **On September 15:** "No Commission in the Mandelbaum Case," *Brooklyn Union,*
Sept. 16, 1884, 1; New York District Attorney Indictments, 1884, Municipal Archives,
City of New York.

169 **Recorder Smyth turned it down:** Ibid.

169 **The trial was to start:** Ibid.

169 **"the war on the police":** "Bulldozing the Court."

169 **"The detective force":** "Perturbed Police."

169 **The greatest scandal:** Ibid.

169 **"She was protected":** "A Big 'Fence' "; italics added.

169 **an unnamed law-enforcement official:** Ibid.

170 **In the affidavits:** Ibid.

170 **In late July:** "New York Nubbins," *St. Joseph (Mo.) Gazette,* July 29, 1884, 1.

170 **As they also knew:** Mollie Hoey's help to the prosecution was widely discussed in the
newspapers. See, e.g., "New York Notes: Fresh Developments in the Police Scandals,"
Detroit Free Press, Aug. 5, 1884, 2, and "A Queen Among Thieves."

170 **"a complete history":** "New York Notes."

170 **"Mollie . . . came under a threat":** "A Queen Among Thieves."

171 **she was rewarded:** Hoey was pardoned on Jan. 5, 1885. "Mary Hoey Pardoned: Her
Reward for Betraying Mother Mandelbaum to Justice," *New-York Times,* Jan. 6,
1885, 3.

171 **at Olney's request:** Ibid.

171 **an ardent anti-Tammany Democrat:** Czitrom (2016), 94.

171 **On Friday, September 19:** "Mother Mandelbaum's Struggles," *New-York Times,*
Sept. 20, 1884, 8.

171 **Howe and Hummel:** Ibid.

171 **"Delay, delay, delay":** Murphy (2010), 141.

172 **Judge Charles Donohue:** "Mother Mandelbaum's Struggles."

172 **"intricate, novel, and perplexing":** Ibid.

172 **FN from 1788 to 1895:** "Court of Oyer and Terminer," Historical Society of the New
York Courts, history.nycourts.gov/court/court-oyer-terminer/.

172 **FN its bench comprised:** Ibid.

172 **FN "all felony cases":** Ibid.

172 **D.A. Olney opposed:** "Mother Mandelbaum's Struggles."

172 **on November 19:** "The Mandelbaum Cases: Transferred to the Court of Oyer and
Terminer for Trial," *New-York Times,* Nov. 20, 1884, 3.

172 **the change of venue was granted:** Ibid.

172 **for December 2, 1884:** "The Case of Mrs. Mandelbaum," *New-York Times,* Dec. 3,
1884, 8.

172 **the morning of Tuesday, December 2:** Ibid.

172   *The People vs. Frederica Mandelbaum:* Holub (2007), 74, note 25.

172   **Justice George C. Barrett:** "Ex-Justice Barrett Dies in Saratoga," *New York Times,*
      June 8, 1906, 9.

172   **wielding opera glasses:** "Mother Mandelbaum: The Notorious Fence Jumps Her
      Bail and Flies to Canada," *Chicago Tribune,* Dec. 5, 1884, 3.

172   **"all anxious to see":** Ibid.

172   **"Detective Pinkerton leaned":** Ibid.

172   **three assistant district attorneys:** "Mrs. Mandelbaum Missing."

172   **fourteen witnesses:** "The Case of Mrs. Mandelbaum."

172   **Howe and Hummel arrived:** "Mother Baum Runs Away: Off to Canada With Son
      Julius and Salesman Herman," *New York Sun,* Dec. 5, 1884, 1.

172   **Howe immediately asked:** "The Case of Mrs. Mandelbaum."

172   **"that the indictments charged":** Ibid.; italics added.

172   **Olney protested vehemently:** Ibid.

172   **difficult to keep:** Ibid.

172   **keep them on ice:** Ibid.

172   **ruled against Howe:** "Mrs. Mandelbaum Missing."

173   **until Thursday, December 4:** Ibid.

173   **"sternly imposing":** Ibid.

173   **"plumply serene":** Ibid.

173   **The clock struck eleven:** Ibid.

173   **"Hear ye! Hear ye!":** Ibid.

173   **"Fredericka Mandelbaum!" he called again:** Ibid.

173   **"Hermann Stoude!":** Ibid.

173   **As before:** Ibid.

CHAPTER TWELVE: NORTH BY NORTHWEST

174   **The court waited an hour:** " 'Mother' Mandelbaum Disappears," *Harrisburg (Pa.)
      Telegraph,* Dec. 5, 1884, 1.

174   **"had, in the parlance":** "Mrs. Mandelbaum's Flight," *Brooklyn Daily Eagle,* Dec. 5,
      1884, 4.

174   **"The defendants are not here":** "Mrs. Mandelbaum Missing."

174   **"In the words of Shakespeare":** "Mother Baum Runs Away."

174   **"seemed proud of his quotation":** "Mrs. Mandelbaum Missing."

174   **issued bench warrants:** Ibid.

174   **"I suspected it":** Ibid.

174   **"scour the United States":** Ibid.

175   **One real estate transfer after another:** Ibid.; "The Mandelbaum Mizzle: Skips for
      Canada, Leaving $21,000 in Bail to Shift for Itself," *Detroit Free Press,* Dec. 5,
      1884, 1; Holub (2007), 80.

175   **pieces of real estate, worth some $50,000:** Holub (2007), 80.

175   **"Of course the claim":** "Mrs. Mandelbaum Missing."

175   **"profound tranquillity":** Ibid.

175   **"In the course of being interviewed":** Rovere (1986), 29.

175   **Howe replied:** Ibid.

176   **watching her house round the clock:** "Mrs. Mandelbaum Missing."

176   **One morning:** Holub (2007), 206–207; "Mother Mandelbaum Dead," erroneous
      obituary, *New York Evening World,* March 23, 1893, 1.

176   **clad in a capacious black shawl:** Holub (2007), 206.

176   **FN In most accounts:** Ibid.

176   **FN Rona Holub speculates:** Ibid.

176 FN **In some accounts Grand Central Depot:** See, e.g., "Mother Mandelbaum Dead."

176 FN **in others New Rochelle:** See, e.g., "Queen of the 'Crooks.'"

176 **Julius and Stoude joined her:** Holub (2007), 207.

177 **on or about December 5, 1884:** Ibid.

177 **a ten-pound package:** Article, no title, *Brooklyn Union,* Dec. 9, 1884, 2.

177 **"How did we let her":** "'Mother' Mandelbaum's Departure."

177 **"I had no right":** "Mrs. Mandelbaum Missing."

177 **"I'm sick and tired":** "Mrs. Mandelbaum's Visit: Her Favorite Daughter's Death Brings Her Here. Visiting the Body at Night With Her Son Julius. Tired of Canada, But on Her Way Back There," *New-York Times,* Nov. 12, 1885, 2.

177 **"The police have been":** "Mother Mandelbaum," *New-York Times,* Dec. 5, 1884, 4.

177 **That, at least:** Ibid.

178 **Rossin House:** "The Thieves' Route to Canada," *San Francisco Chronicle,* Dec. 6, 1884, 3.

178 **"C. Newman and mother":** Ibid.

178 **"J. Pink":** "The Great American Fence: Mother Mandelbaum, the Notorious, Arrested Across the Border," *Lebanon (Pa.) Daily News,* Dec. 9, 1884, 1. The alias appears as "J. Puck" in some accounts, e.g., "The Thieves' Route to Canada."

178 **made the Toronto papers:** "The Great American Fence."

178 **growing nervous:** Ibid.

178 **an elegant part of town:** Ibid.

178 **descriptions of Marm's singular appearance:** Ibid.

178 **took the evening train:** Ibid.

178 **Allerton House:** "Mrs. Mandelbaum Nabbed: The Old Lady Indignant That the Law Should Lay Its Hands on Her," *Savannah Morning News,* Dec. 9, 1884, 1. The name is given as "Allison House" in some accounts, e.g., "Mother Mandelbaum: The Notorious Fence, Arrested Here," *Hamilton Spectator,* Dec. 9, 1884, n.p.

178 **a seedy tavern near the railway depot:** "The Great American Fence."

178 **"H. and L. Harris and sister":** "Mother Mandelbaum: The Notorious New York Fence Caged in a Canadian Jail," *St. Louis Post-Dispatch,* Dec. 9, 1884, 1.

178 **artfully smearing the ink:** "Foreign News: The Mandelbaums Arrested at Hamilton, Ont," *Detroit Free Press,* Dec. 9, 1884, 2.

178 **took her meals in her room:** "The Great American Fence."

178 **at separate tables:** Ibid.

178 **sending "wanted" circulars:** Article, no title, *Brooklyn Daily Eagle,* Dec. 9, 1884, 2.

178 **"Office of the District Attorney":** Quoted in "Mother Mandelbaum: The Notorious New York Fence Caged in a Canadian Jail."

178 **Fugitives from justice:** Ibid.

179 **On Monday, December 8:** Holub (2007), 211.

179 **Chief Alexander Stewart:** Hamilton Police Historical Society & Museum. "Annual Report, 2018/2019," hpa.on.ca/wp-content/uploads/2020/11/HistoricalSociety-Annual Report-2018-19-Nov.20-2020.pdf.

179 **accompanied by one of his detectives:** Sources give the detective's surname variously as Cassel [Holub (2007), 211]; Cassells ["The Mandelbaums Arrested in Canada," *Daily New Era* (Lancaster, Pa.), Dec. 9, 1884, 1]; and Castell ["The Great American Fence"].

179 **ladies' parlor:** Ibid.

179 **by their real names:** Ibid.

179 **"Mrs. Mandelbaum was thunderstruck":** "Mother Mandelbaum: The Notorious New York Fence Caged in a Canadian Jail."

179 **Chief Stewart smiled:** "Mother Mandelbaum: The Notorious Fence, Arrested Here."

179 **"It's all right":** Ibid.

179   **"I am an American citizen"**: "A Gay Bird Captured: Mother Mandelbaum in Canada. She Waves the Star Spangled Banner and Telegraphs for Her Lawyer." *Lancaster (Pa.) Examiner,* Dec. 17, 1884, 1. The "eye dialect" has been rendered in conventional English.

179   **confiscated the ten-pound package**: Article, no title, *Brooklyn Union,* Dec. 9, 1884.

179   **suspicion of bringing stolen goods**: Ibid.

179   **was arrested on returning**: "The Great American Fence."

180   **"The Toronto police"**: "Mother Mandelbaum: The Notorious Fence, Arrested Here."

180   **Central Police Station**: "Foreign News: The Mandelbaums Arrested at Hamilton, Ont."

180   **$30,000 to $40,000 worth**: "Mother Mandelbaum: The Notorious New York Fence Caged in a Canadian Jail."

180   **a six-ounce lump**: "Mother Baum: The Party Charged With Vagrancy and Bringing Stolen Goods Into Canada," *Boston Globe,* Dec. 10, 1884, 4; "Canada: Hard Lines for 'Marm' Mandelbaum," *Detroit Free Press,* Dec. 11, 1884, 2.

180   **"a rich black silk dress"**: "Mrs. Mandelbaum in Jail: The Fugitives Arrested in Canada," *New-York Tribune,* Dec. 9, 1884, 1.

180   **objected vehemently**: Ibid.

180   **a further $30,000 worth**: "A Gay Bird Captured."

180   **"diamonds, pearls, rubies"**: "Foreign News: The Mandelbaums Arrested at Hamilton, Ont."

180   **Also found on the prisoners**: "A Gay Bird Captured."

180   **"A plea that it is"**: "Mother Baum."

180   **"She and Julius asked"**: "Foreign News: The Mandelbaums Arrested at Hamilton, Ont."

181   **The jewels were impounded**: "Mother Mandelbaum: The Notorious New York Fence Caged in a Canadian Jail."

181   **the county jail**: "Mrs. Mandelbaum in Jail."

181   **vagrancy and bringing stolen goods**: Article, no title, *Brooklyn Daily Eagle.*

181   **"The arrest has caused"**: "Mrs. Mandelbaum in Jail."

181   **as newspaper accounts made clear**: See, e.g., "The Mother Mandelbaum Case," *St. Louis Globe-Democrat,* Dec. 17, 1884, 6.

181   **"The great question now"**: "Mother Mandelbaum: The Notorious New York Fence Caged in a Canadian Jail."

181   **The crown attorney**: Ibid.

181   **"has evidently been STUDYING INTERNATIONAL LAW"**: Ibid.

181   **FN "A New York detective told me"**: "Street Talk." *Cincinnati Enquirer,* Dec. 14, 1884, 12.

181   **"I am sure of that"**: "Mother Mandelbaum: The Notorious New York Fence Caged in a Canadian Jail."

181   **"And they had better not"**: Ibid.

181   **"contented herself with remarking"**: Ibid.

181   **Olney vowed to review**: "Mrs. Mandelbaum in Jail."

181   **he also planned to send**: Ibid.

181   **FN would not be signed until 1971**: "Second Protocol Amending Extradition Treaty With Canada: Senate Consideration of Treaty Document 107-11," congress.gov /treaty-document/107th-congress/11.

181   **such as murder, arson**: Mother Mandelbaum: The Notorious New York Fence Caged in a Canadian Jail."

182   **"Mrs. Mandelbaum was apparently"**: "Mrs. Mandelbaum in Jail."

182   **She is self-possessed**: Ibid. (The direct quotations from Fredericka Mandelbaum are written in "eye dialect" in the original article.)

182. **David Steele:** Ibid.; "A Terrible Accident: Mr. David Steele Probably Fatally Injured." *St. John's (Newfoundland) Evening Telegram*, Dec. 27, 1886, 7, via *Hamilton (Ont.) Evening Times.*

182 **Hummel promptly set out:** "Mother Baum."

183 DEAR MRS. MANDELBAUM: Ibid.

183 **Fred Marks:** "Mother Mandelbaum: Trouble That She and Some of Her Gang Are Having," *New-York Times*, Dec. 11, 1884, 1.

183 **E. Marks & Son:** "Mother Mandelbaum," *Chicago Tribune*, Dec. 10, 1884, 3.

183 **in February 1884:** Ibid.

183 **Michael Kurtz and Billy Porter:** "Mother Mandelbaum: A Belief That Her Diamonds Are Stolen Property," *New-York Times*, Dec. 10, 1884, 1.

183 **"It was suspected":** "Mother Mandelbaum," *Chicago Tribune.*

183 **which had netted $30,000:** Ibid.

183 **"The Chief is holding":** Ibid.

183 **in a vault in Ottawa:** "Mother Baum."

183 **wouldn't be available:** Ibid.

183 **"The Mandelbaum party":** Ibid.

183 **added a third charge:** Ibid.

184 **"If the goods were stolen":** Ibid.

184 **"if they prove":** "Between Two Fires."

184 **over beer:** "Mother Baum."

184 **"They are much disgusted":** Ibid.

184 **Pining for company:** Ibid.

184 **"Oh, don't be long":** Ibid.

184 **"is not much of an angel":** Ibid.

184 **buying a few of Allan Pinkerton's books:** "Mrs. Mandelbaum's Query: She Desires to Know Who Drew Her Picture for 'The World,'" *New York World*, Dec. 9, 1884, n.p., from District Attorney Scrapbooks, Municipal Archives, City of New York.

184 *The Mysteries of Paris:* "Mother Baum."

184 **On Wednesday, December 10:** "Mother Mandelbaum: Trouble That She and Some of Her Gang Are Having."

184 **an afternoon hearing:** Ibid.

184 **Chief Stewart requested:** Ibid.

184 **laughed out loud:** Ibid.

184 **"He said District Attorney Olney":** Ibid.

184 **"of counsel for Mrs. Mandelbaum":** Ibid.

184 **"it was quite evident":** Ibid.

184 **declined to release them:** Ibid.

184 **Saturday morning, December 13:** Ibid.

185 **On Friday, December 12:** "Mandelbaum Goes Free," *Journal-Times* (Racine, Wis.), Dec. 12, 1884, 2; "Mandelbaum Discharged: The Notorious Madame Receives the Benefit of Canadian Clemency," *Boston Globe*, Dec. 13, 1884, 1.

185 **had failed to identify:** "Mother Mandelbaum: Trouble That She and Some of Her Gang Are Having."

185 **the crown attorney chose:** "Mandelbaum Discharged."

185 **$500 duty, plus costs:** Article, no title, *Neenah (Wis.) Daily Times*, Jan. 9, 1885, 1.

185 **"I am much chagrined":** "Mandelbaum Discharged."

185 **"the Washington authorities":** Article, no title, *Corvallis (Ore.) Gazette*, Jan. 2, 1885, 7.

185 FN **"In Canada":** "Defaulters' Paradise: Criminals From the United States Who Now Reside in Canada," *St. Louis Post-Dispatch*, Jan. 12, 1885, 1.

185 **"Mother Mandelbaum says":** Article, no title, *Allentown (Pa.) Morning Call*, Dec. 18, 1884, 2.

186 **By the end of 1884:** Holub (2007), 169.

186 **now married:** Holub (2007), 215; "Even Unto the Third Generation," Baltimore *Sun*, April 11, 1915, Section II, 4.

186 **"Quite a colony":** "Queen of the 'Crooks.'"

186 **Anshe Sholom:** Holub (2007), 223; anshesholom.ca.

186 **she regularly attended services:** "Death Ends Her Troubles: Mrs. Frederika [*sic*] Mandelbaum Died This Morning," *Hamilton Spectator*, Feb. 26, 1894, n.p.

186 **an elegant brownstone in North Hamilton:** "Queen of Fences: Mother Mandelbaum Is Dead in Hamilton. She Made a Million Out of Stolen Goods Received. She Employed Thieves and Often Betrayed Them. Blackmailed and Abetted by New York Police. Forced to Flee After 30 Years of Unchecked Trade," *Boston Globe*, Feb. 26, 1894, 8.

186 **"in splendor":** "Mother Mandelbaum: Very Much Alive and Living in Splendor at Hamilton," *Cincinnati Enquirer*, March 25, 1893, 1.

186 **"entertained many visitors":** "Queen of Fences: Mother Mandelbaum Is Dead in Hamilton."

186 **"She has told persons":** Walling (1887), 289.

187 **In the autumn of 1885:** "Mother Mandelbaum in New York," *Sacramento Weekly Bee*, Nov. 13, 1885, 8, via *New-York Times*.

187 **Mrs. Marx, of 99 Clinton Street:** "Mrs. Mandelbaum's Visit."

187 **Marm wrote or telegraphed:** Ibid.

187 **in early November:** Sources vary on the precise date of Annie's death. "No Redeeming Feature Left: Death of Mrs. Mandelbaum's Well-Behaved Daughter," *Detroit Free Press*, Nov. 12, 1885, 1, gives a date of Nov. 10, 1885; findagrave.com/memorial/130475633/anna-mandelbaum lists Nov. 8.

187 **"Annie was the sole":** "No Redeeming Feature Left."

187 **"The thought of having":** "Mrs. Mandelbaum's Visit."

187 **possibly in disguise:** Walling (1887), 289.

187 **In some accounts:** Holub (2007), 216.

187 **In others:** Walling (1887), 289.

187 **From Grand Central Depot:** Holub (2007), 216.

187 **"So as not to attract":** "Mrs. Mandelbaum's Visit."

188 **Making certain the house:** "Mother Mandelbaum in New York."

188 **"As soon as she reached":** "Mrs. Mandelbaum's Visit."

188 **a friend persuaded:** Ibid.

188 **Anticipating this surveillance:** Holub (2007), 217.

188 **proposed that Annie be given:** "Mrs. Mandelbaum's Visit."

188 **Fredericka wouldn't hear of it:** Ibid.

188 **On Marm's orders:** Ibid.

188 **"She showered kiss after kiss":** Ibid.

188 **"large crowds were attracted":** Ibid.

188 **Every person who entered:** Ibid.

189 **The funeral itself:** Ibid.

189 **in the Mandelbaums' parlor:** "No Redeeming Feature Left."

189 **now barely recognizable:** "Mrs. Mandelbaum's Visit."

189 **remained there for the service:** Ibid.

189 **above a beer hall:** Ibid.

189 **Julius joined her there:** Ibid.

189 **Peering through the shutter slats:** Ibid.

189 **two dozen carriages:** Ibid.

189 **Marm and Julius waited:** Ibid.

189 **boarding a closed carriage:** Ibid.

189 **two days in New York:** Ibid.

189 **"just as she came":** Walling (1887), 289.

190 **"the name of the place":** "Mrs. Mandelbaum's Visit."

190 **"made it worse than ever":** "Mother Mandelbaum: Her Son Endeavors to Become a Detective at Hamilton," *Cincinnati Enquirer,* May 19, 1889, 9.

190 **In the summer of 1886:** "Mandelbaum's Den: Canadians Buying New York Goods Remarkably Cheap," *Bridgewater (N.J.) Courier-News,* Aug. 14, 1886, 3. The same article appears as "Mother Mandelbaum's Den: Canadians Buying New York Goods Remarkably Cheap," *National Police Gazette,* Sept. 4, 1886, 7.

190 **"My Dear _____":** "Mandelbaum's Den."

190 **grand opening that summer:** Ibid.

190 **"a handsome store":** Ibid.

190 **which bore the sign:** Sign illustration from "Mother Mandelbaum: Her Son Endeavors to Become a Detective at Hamilton."

190 **"Since then":** "Mandelbaum's Den."

191 **three saleswomen:** Ibid.

191 **"handsome garments":** Ibid.

191 **"at ruinous figures":** Ibid.

191 **"She has a large stock":** Ibid.

191 **"it does not bear":** Ibid.

191 **"She is very shrewd":** "Mother Mandelbaum Busy: The Noted 'Fence' Plays a Neat Trick on a Customs Officer," *Rochester (N.Y.) Democrat and Chronicle,* Oct. 20, 1886, 8, via *New York Herald.*

192 **"and entered into a chat":** "Mandelbaum's Den."

192 **"It was generally understood":** Ibid.

192 **"a pair of great solitaire earrings":** Ibid.

192 **"With a wink":** Ibid.

193 **"I have agents":** Ibid.

193 **"It's fun for me":** Ibid.

193 **behind their grandmotherly spectacles:** An illustration in Lyons (2019), 110, depicts Mrs. Mandelbaum wearing glasses. "Mother Mandelbaum: Her Son Endeavors to Become a Detective at Hamilton" says, "The old woman dresses neatly and wears a pair of steel-rimmed spectacles. She would be the last person to be taken for a criminal."

EPILOGUE: KADDISH

195 **"Mother Mandelbaum Dead":** "Mother Mandelbaum Dead," erroneous obituary, *New York Evening World.*

195 **"Queen of Crooks":** "Queen of Crooks: Mother Mandelbaum's Existence Ended by a Stroke of Paralysis," erroneous obituary, *Fall River (Mass.) Daily Evening News,* March 23, 1893, 1.

195 **"According to a letter":** "Did Business With Crooks: 'Mother Mandelbaum, Gotham's Noted 'Fence,' Is Dead," erroneous report, *Fall River (Mass.) Daily Evening News,* March 23, 1893, 3.

195 **"Mother Mandelbaum: Very Much Alive":** "Mother Mandelbaum: Very Much Alive and Living in Splendor at Hamilton."

195 **"'Mother' Mandelbaum Not Dead":** "'Mother' Mandelbaum Not Dead," *New-York Tribune,* March 24, 1893, 1.

195 **"The dispatch announcing":** Ibid.

196 **flew the Stars and Stripes:** "Got Mother Mandelbaum."

196 **"She has few friends":** "'Mother' Mandelbaum: The Notorious New York Fence Keeping a Store in Hamilton, Ontario," *St. Louis Post-Dispatch,* Oct. 12, 1887, 4.

196 **In 1889, a writer:** "Mother Mandelbaum: Her Son Endeavors to Become a Detective at Hamilton."

196 **"under the surveillance":** Ibid.

196 **"Frequently a well-dressed man":** Ibid.

196 **"at any hour of the day":** Ibid.

196 **"No, indeed":** Ibid.

196 **"You went on there":** Ibid.

196 **"That is foolish":** Ibid.

197 **until the early 1890s:** Mrs. Mandelbaum, who died in 1894, was said to have been retired for about two years before her death, per "End of a Wicked Life: Old Mother Mandelbaum Is Dead," *San Francisco Chronicle*, Feb. 27, 1894, 1.

197 **"The army of enemies":** Lyons (2019), 114.

197 **"America's Jewish women":** Diner and Benderly (2002), xvi.

198 **A small-town Jewish woman:** Diner and Benderly (2002), 76.

198 **"More than in any":** Diner and Benderly (2002), xvi.

198 **"In nearly all":** Diner and Benderly (2002), xv–xvi.

198 **"She was *part* of the process":** Rona L. Holub, personal communication; italics added.

199 **not some "shifty underworld":** Ibid.

199 **Every week for thousands of years:** Diner and Benderly (2002), xiii–xiv.

200 **"Along with piety":** Diner and Benderly (2002), 77–78.

200 **"The German culture":** Holub (2007), 121.

201 **"By the late [eighteen-]seventies":** Wiebe (1967), 134–35.

201 **and control markets:** Papke (1987), 9.

201 **"laboring women were confined":** Stansell (1987), 8.

201 **Sex segregation:** Stansell (1987), 106.

201 **FN "The Mafia is the surest:** Gage (1971), 95.

202 **"arguably the most influential":** Macintyre (2012), 27.

202 **In the summer of 1888:** "Mother Mandelbaum's Son: Julius Has Tired of Canada and Is in a Fair Way for Sing Sing," *New York Evening World*, June 23, 1888, 1; "'Mother' Mandelbaum's Son Returns: He Had Studied Medicine in Berlin and Wants to Practice It Here," *New-York Tribune*, June 23, 1888, 4; "Julius Mandelbaum Surrenders," *New-York Times*, June 23, 1888, 9.

202 **to the New York district attorney's office:** "'Mother' Mandelbaum's Son Returns."

202 **explained that he'd been studying medicine:** Ibid.

202 **He wanted to return:** Ibid.

202 **"he could in a short time":** Ibid.

202 **"He says that no proof":** Ibid.

202 **What he wanted:** "Julius Mandelbaum Surrenders."

202 **$5,000 bail was accepted:** Ibid.

202 **most likely in the autumn:** "Mother Mandelbaum's Son."

202 **dropped all charges against him:** "Queen of the 'Crooks.'"

202 **as a litmus test:** "Mother Mandelbaum's Son."

203 **had all fled the country:** Macintyre (1998), 160ff.

203 **Baron Shindell of Monaco:** Asbury (2008), 196.

203 **Bullard would die:** Adam Nightingale, *Masters of Crime: Fiction's Finest Villains and Their Real-Life Inspirations* (Stroud, U.K.: History Press, 2011), 137.

203 **tried in 1886:** Byrne (1969), 154.

203 **eighteen and a half years:** Ibid.

203 **who divorced her husband:** Davidson (2020), 100.

203 **continued incarcerations:** Davidson (2020), 81–82, 95.

203 **who ran a billiard parlor:** "Mother Mandelbaum Dead."

203 **who rejoined his family:** Holub (2007), 227.

203 FN **1908 records list:** "Recent Incorporations," *American Druggist and Pharmaceutical Record: A Semi-monthly Illustrated Journal of Practical Pharmacy*, April 13, 1908, 212.

203 FN **The company went out of business:** *The Trow (Formerly Wilson's) Copartnership and Corporation Directory of the Boroughs of Manhattan and the Bronx, City of New York* (New York: Trow Directory, Printing & Bookbinding Company, March 1909).

203 FN **Hamilton, Ontario, city directories:** See, e.g., *City of Hamilton: Alphabetical, General, Street, Miscellaneous and Subscribers' Classified Business Directory* (Hamilton, Ont.: W. H. Irwin & Company, 1887–88; 1892–93; 1893–94).

203 FN **Sarah Mandelbaum would marry:** Holub (2007), 77.

203 FN **after her divorce:** "The Mandelbaums in Town: They Had Some Lively Doings in Canada a Few Days Ago," *New York Evening World*, July 6, 1894, 2.

203 FN **Sarah's daughter:** "Dorothy Blower's Bond Forfeited: Warrant Issued for the Arrest of Mother Mandelbaum's Granddaughter," *Brooklyn Daily Eagle*, Jan. 11, 1915, 2.

203 FN **sent to the Tombs:** "Even Unto the Third Generation."

203 **living with partial paralysis:** "Queen of Fences."

203 **Bright's disease:** "She Dies in Canada: End of Mother Mandelbaum, the Once Notorious 'Fence,' " *New York Evening World*, Feb. 26, 1894, 1.

203 **In 1892:** "Mother Mandelbaum Again," *Middletown (N.Y.) Times-Press*, Jan. 19, 1892, 5.

203 **"A few weeks ago":** "Raided a Big Fence: Mother Mandelbaum, a Well-Known Smuggler, on the Carpet," *Pittsburgh Dispatch*, Jan. 20, 1892, 11.

204 **They were stored:** Ibid.

204 **a $250 fine:** Ibid.

204 **she transacted no business:** "End of a Wicked Life."

204 **On the morning of February 26, 1894:** "She Dies in Canada."

204 **"Mrs. Mandelbaum had been ailing":** "Death Ends Her Troubles."

204 **"Queen of Fences":** Op. cit.

204 **"End of a Wicked Life":** Op. cit.

205 **"Old 'Mother' Mandelbaum Is Dead":** Op. cit.

205 **"Queen of the 'Crooks' ":** Op. cit.

205 **"A story is published":** "Is She Dead? Mother Mandelbaum, the Notorious Fence, Said to Be Alive," *Brooklyn Standard Union*, Aug. 27, 1894, 3.

205 **"It would not be a scheme":** "Doubt Mandelbaum's Death: Police Sceptics Believe She Is Alive and in This City. Her Legacy of Silk May Cause Some Litigation," *New York Evening World*, March 29, 1894, 5.

205 **"arrested on a warrant":** "Mother Mandelbaum," *San Francisco Call*, March 7, 1894, 6.

205 **some 3,000 yards:** "Mother Mandelbaum's Silk: An Order Issued That It Be Sold by the Property Clerk," *New York Evening World*, March 20, 1894, 2.

205 **the American Safe Deposit Company:** Ibid.

205 **John R. Fellows:** "Col. John R. Fellows Is Dead: The District Attorney Passed Away Yesterday. His Older Son Reached Home Too Late to See His Father in Life," *New York Times*, Dec. 8, 1896, 8.

205 **"If it is not claimed":** "3,000 Yards of Unclaimed Stolen Silk," *New York Sun*, March 21, 1894, 4.

205 **On February 28, 1894:** "Mother Mandelbaum's Burial," *New York Sun*, March 2, 1894, 9.

205 **at Weehawken, New Jersey:** Ibid.

206 **eight carriages:** Ibid.

206 **No services were held:** Ibid.

206 **conveyed directly to Union Field Cemetery:** findagrave.com/memorial/130475634.

206 **At the interment:** Macintyre (2012), 195.

A NOTE ON SOURCES

209 **invoked by earlier writers:** See, e.g., Holub (1998), 31–32, 51; Holub (2007), 269; Conway (2014), 226.

209 **"fiction . . . based on fact":** "A Line on Books," *Buffalo Evening News,* Jan. 12, 1935, 3.

209 **the longtime warden:** "Lawes Is Retiring as Sing Sing Head: Foe of Capital Penalty Put 303 to Death—Found Some Prisoners 'Very Fine Men,'" *New York Times,* July 7, 1941, 1.

209 **"embellished with imaginative conversations":** J. L. Gillen, "Book Review: Cell 202, Sing Sing," *Journal of Criminal Law and Criminology* 26:5 (January–February 1936), 798–99.

209 **"reconstructed . . . with high imagination," in the words:** Tom Cassidy, "Sadism at Ossining," *New York Daily News,* Oct. 13, 1935, 84.

209 **"the alleged confession":** James L. Wunsch, "Book Review: *Nell Kimball: Her Life as an American Madam,*" *Journal of Social History* 6:1 (Autumn 1972), 121–26.

210 **given him her manuscript in 1932:** Wunsch (1972), 121.

210 **"in many respects":** Robert Berkvist, "In Brief: *Nell Kimball: Her Life as an American Madam,*" *New York Times Book Review,* July 5, 1970, 10.

210 **"rescuing it from oblivion":** Berkvist (1970).

210 **lifted, with only a little tweaking:** Wunsch (1972), 122ff.

210 **Asbury, the reviewer points out:** Wunsch (1972), 124.

210 **"It is clear":** Wunsch (1972), 125.

210 **Longstreet wrote both novels:** "Stephen Longstreet (1907–2002)," Finding Aid, Stephen Longstreet Papers, Yale University Archives, archives.yale.edu/repositories /11/resources/1485.

Illustration Credits

Page 96: From the New York Public Library

Page 97: Van Every, *Sins of New York* (1930)

Page 99: Walling, *Recollections of a New York Chief of Police* (1887)

Page 100: Walling, Recollections of a New York Chief of Police (1887)

Page 108: Walling, *Recollections of a New York Chief of Police* (1887)

Page 109: Walling, *Recollections of a New York Chief of Police* (1887)

Page 110: Lyons, *Why Crime Does Not Pay* (1913)

Page 112. Both images: Byrnes, *Professional Criminals of America* (1886)

Page 114: Lyons, *Why Crime Does Not Pay* (1913)

Page 122: Byrnes, *Professional Criminals of America* (1886)

Page 125: Byrnes, *Professional Criminals of America* (1886)

Page 135: Horan and Swiggett, *The Pinkerton Story* (1951)

Page 137: Horan and Swiggett, *The Pinkerton Story* (1951)

Page 139: *Harper's Weekly*

Page 144: Lyons, *Why Crime Does Not Pay* (1913)

Page 150: Howe and Hummel, *Danger!* (1886)

Page 153: Howe and Hummel, *Danger!* (1886)

Page 168: New York District Attorney Indictments, 1884, Municipal Archives, City of New York

Page 171: *Puck* magazine (1884)

Page 186: *Puck* magazine (1885)

Page 190: "Mother Mandelbaum: Her Son Endeavors to Become a Detective at Hamilton." *Cincinnati Enquirer*, May 19, 1889, 9.

Page 192: *Puck* magazine (1885)

Index

Atlanta Constitution, on Mrs.
    Mandelbaum's appearance, 151

bank burglary, 68, 71n
    bank robbery vs., 73
    Boylston National Bank, 86, 87
    City Bank of New York, 75, 75n
    Dexter Savings Bank, 108–11,
        109n, *110*, 110–11n, 121
    first in New York, 75, 249n75
    first in the United States, 75n
    "Little Joker," 76–77, 77n,
        250n77
    Manhattan Savings Institution,
        102, 107n, *108*, 111–15, 121
    Mrs. Mandelbaum and, xiv,
        63–64, 68, 70–84, 86, 87, 102,
        108–17, 257n108
    Northampton National Bank,
        139, 139n, 267n139
    Ocean National Bank, 70–72,
        74–75, 74n, 77–83
    tools for, 70, 70n, 72, *73*
    vaults and safes, 70, 73–77
Banking Act (Glass-Steagall Act),
    71n
Barnum, P. T., 154, 154n
Barrett, George C., 172
Barrymore, John, 155n
Battle Annie, 25, 26
Belasco, David, 155, 155n
Benderly, Beryl Lieff, 4n, 197, 199
Boston Globe, 38
    on Alan Pinkerton's death, 137
    on Mrs. Mandelbaum, 180, 183,
        186, 204

on Scott's lawsuit, 128
on "Sheeny Mike" Kurtz, 123
Boylston National Bank burglary,
    86–87, 86n, *88*
Brooklyn [Daily] Eagle
    on Alan Pinkerton, 135
    on Mrs. Mandelbaum, xxiv, 174
Brooklyn Standard Union, 205
Brooks Brothers, Union Army
    uniform contract, 43–44,
    43–44n, 243n44
Brown, Margaret, aka "Old
    Mother Hubbard," *37*, 37
Bullard, "Piano Charley," xxii, 64,
    86, *87*, 203
burglary
    of cashmere shawls, 57, 57n
    of diamonds and jewelry, xiv,
        xix, xxii, 44, 46–47, 57, 121,
        121n, 183, 185
    Mrs. Mandelbaum and, 44, 57,
        63, 64–66, 85, 121
    need for a financial backer,
        85–86
    planning and surveillance
        for, 85
    of silk, 61–66, 101, 121–23, 121n,
        128, 128n, 141–42, 159, 170,
        191, 202, 204, 205
    See also bank burglary;
        "fence"
Burns, Euchre Kate, 25
Byrnes, Thomas, 23, 74, 74n,
    114–15, 114n, 170
    the "third degree" and, 114n,
        259n114

New York's police force (*cont'd*):
  Mrs. Mandelbaum's escape and,
    177–78
  Municipal Police Force and,
    40–42, 42n
  offenses pursued by, 41
  predatory police captains
    of, 97
  rare prosecution of fences, 18
  replaces civil-service posts, 41
  requirements for the job
    absent, 41
  rivalry of Municipals and
    Metropolitans (Battle of the
    Bulls), 40, 42, 42n, *43*
  size of in 1845 and 1855, 41
  Tammany Hall and, 42
  term of appointments to, 41
  three forms of graft or bribery,
    99–101
  Walling as chief, xvi, xvin, 16
  White's "Bank Ring," 100
New York Star, on Mrs.
    Mandelbaum, 65, 160–61n
New York Sun, on Mrs.
    Mandelbaum, 143, 164
New-York Times, xvn
  on attorney Howe, 150–51
  exposé of Boss Tweed, 127
  on Julius Mandelbaum's return
    to New York, 202
  on the Manhattan Savings
    burglary, 111, 114
  on Mrs. Mandelbaum, xv, 59,
    92, 131, 131n, 139, 160,
    160–61n, 169, 174, 187–89

  on Mrs. Mandelbaum's death,
    204
  on the Ocean National Bank
    burglary, 84
  Olney interview, 138
  on the Pinkertons and Mrs.
    Mandelbaum, 57, 141
  on Pinkerton's death, 137
New-York Tribune
  on Julius Mandelbaum's return
    to New York, 202
  on Mrs. Mandelbaum, 182, 195
  on the Ocean National Bank
    burglary, 84
New-York World, on Mrs.
    Mandelbaum, 186, 205
Northampton National Bank
    burglary, 139, 139n,
    267n139
Nugent, "Irish Mag," 189
Nugent, John, 113, 115

Ocean National Bank burglary,
    70–72, 74–75, 74n, 77–83,
    82n, 84
  amount stolen, 7, 71, 71n, 82,
    248n71
  laundering of the money, 82
  money paid to law enforcement,
    99–100
  Mrs. Mandelbaum and, 72, 75,
    79, 79n, 82–83, 248n72
  plot of a Sherlock Holmes story
    and, 79n
  principals involved in, 74–75,
    74n

Pinkerton Agency (*cont'd*):
  Olney hires, 137, 139
  power of arrest and, 135
  run by Pinkerton's sons, *137*, 137
  strike breaking by, 26, 136, 136n
Plunkitt, George Washington,
  94–95, *96*
Pool Sellers Association, 148–49,
  149n
Porter, Billy, *109*, 109, 121, 183
property crime, xviii, xix, 124
  bourgeois elite's reform
    campaign against (1870s),
    125–27, 143
  criminals at court appearance of
    Mrs. Mandelbaum, 130
  Olney's pursuit of Mrs.
    Mandelbaum and, 138–39

Ragged Dick (Alger), 87
Reles, Abraham "Kid Twist," 27
Robinson, "Swell," 46–47, 244n46
Rosey, Kid Glove, 37
Rothstein, Arnold, 27
Rovere, Richard H., 147n, 148–52,
  154n

Sadie the Goat, 25
San Francisco Chronicle, report on
  Mrs. Mandelbaum's death,
  204
Scott, James, 122–24, 124n
  lawsuit against Mrs.
    Mandelbaum, 128–32, 128n,
    264n130
Shaw, George Bernard, 127n

Shevlin, Patrick, 112, 114–15
Shinburn, Mark (né Maximillan
  Schenbein), *64*, 64, 75–77,
  77n, 79–82, 112, 248–49n74,
  249n75
  flees to Europe, buys a title, 203
  jail break of Bullard and, 86,
    86n
shoplifting, 37, 52, 53, *53*, 63, 63n
  Danger! instruction on, 48, 49,
    51–53
  women working for Mrs.
    Mandelbaum, 36–37, *37*, 45
Smyth, Frederick, 167–68, 169
Stansell, Christine, 201
Steele, David, 182–83, 184
St. Louis Post-Dispatch, on Mrs.
  Mandelbaum, 143, 181, 196
Stokes, Edward, 106n
Stoude, Hermann, 121, 123, 140,
  141, 143
  arrest and case against, 157, 160,
    162, 164–65, 164n, 167, *168*
  escape to Canada, 173, 174,
    176–85

Tammany Hall, 14, 24, 25, 42,
  92–97, *96*, 98n, 126, 127, 138,
  146, 199
  as "an empire of patronage," 92
  "honest graft" and, 94–95
  immigrant men and, 95
  Mrs. Mandelbaum and, 93–96
  profitability of, 92, 94
Taylor, Frederick Winslow, 36n
Temple Rodeph Sholom, 89, 89n

ABOUT THE AUTHOR

MARGALIT FOX trained as a cellist and a linguist before pursuing journalism. As a senior writer in *The New York Times*'s celebrated Obituary News Department, she wrote the front-page sendoffs of some of the leading cultural figures of our age. Winner of the William Saroyan Prize for Literature and author of four previous books, *The Confidence Men, Conan Doyle for the Defense, The Riddle of the Labyrinth*, and *Talking Hands*, Fox lives in Manhattan with her husband, the writer and critic George Robinson.

margalitfox.com

facebook.com/margalitfox

instagram.com/margalit_books

ABOUT THE TYPE

This book was set in Walbaum, a typeface designed in 1810 by German punch cutter J. E. (Justus Erich) Walbaum (1768–1839). Walbaum's type is more French than German in appearance. Like Bodoni, it is a classical typeface, yet its openness and slight irregularities give it a human, romantic quality.